Urban Poetics and Politics in Contemporary South Asia and the Middle East

Moussa Pourya Asl
Universiti Sains Malaysia, Malaysia

A volume in the Advances in Religious and Cultural Studies (ARCS) Book Series

Published in the United States of America by
    IGI Global
    Information Science Reference (an imprint of IGI Global)
    701 E. Chocolate Avenue
    Hershey PA, USA 17033
    Tel: 717-533-8845
    Fax: 717-533-8661
    E-mail: cust@igi-global.com
    Web site: http://www.igi-global.com

Copyright © 2023 by IGI Global. All rights reserved. No part of this publication may be reproduced, stored or distributed in any form or by any means, electronic or mechanical, including photocopying, without written permission from the publisher.
Product or company names used in this set are for identification purposes only. Inclusion of the names of the products or companies does not indicate a claim of ownership by IGI Global of the trademark or registered trademark.

    Library of Congress Cataloging-in-Publication Data

Names: Pourya Asl, Moussa, 1986- editor.
Title: Urban poetics and politics in contemporary South Asia and the Middle
   East / editor, Moussa Pourya Asl.
Description: Hershey PA : Information Science Reference, [2023] | Includes
   bibliographical references and index. | Summary: "Urban Poetics and
   Politics in Contemporary South Asia and the Middle East examines the
   poetics and politics of city and urban spaces in contemporary South Asia
   and the Middle East and seeks to shed light on how individuals
   constitute, experience, and navigate urban spaces in everyday life. This
   book aims to initiate a multidisciplinary approach to the study of city
   life by engaging disciplines such as urban geography, gender studies,
   feminism, literary criticism, and human geography. Covering key topics
   such as racism, urban spaces, social inequality, and gender roles, this
   reference work is ideal for government officials, policymakers,
   researchers, scholars, practitioners, academicians, instructors, and
   students"-- Provided by publisher.
Identifiers: LCCN 2022043278 (print) | LCCN 2022043279 (ebook) | ISBN
   9781668466506 (hardcover) | ISBN 9781668466513 (paperback) | ISBN
   9781668466520 (ebook)
Subjects: LCSH: Indic fiction (English)--History and criticism. | City and
   town life in literature. | Literature and society--India. | Literature
   and society--South Asia. | Literature and society--Middle East. |
   India--In literature. | South Asia--In literature. | Middle East--In
   literature. | LCGFT: Literary criticism. | Essays.
Classification: LCC PR9485.5.C57 U73 2023 (print) | LCC PR9485.5.C57
   (ebook) | DDC 820.9/954--dc23/eng/20221103
LC record available at https://lccn.loc.gov/2022043278
LC ebook record available at https://lccn.loc.gov/2022043279

This book is published in the IGI Global book series Advances in Religious and Cultural Studies (ARCS) (ISSN: 2475-675X; eISSN: 2475-6768)

British Cataloguing in Publication Data
A Cataloguing in Publication record for this book is available from the British Library.

All work contributed to this book is new, previously-unpublished material.
The views expressed in this book are those of the authors, but not necessarily of the publisher.

For electronic access to this publication, please contact: eresources@igi-global.com.

Advances in Religious and Cultural Studies (ARCS) Book Series

ISSN:2475-675X
EISSN:2475-6768

Editor-in-Chief: Nancy Erbe California State University-Dominguez Hills, USA

MISSION

In the era of globalization, the diversity of the world and various cultures becomes apparent as cross-cultural interactions turn into a daily occurrence for individuals in all professions. Understanding these differences is necessary in order to promote effective partnerships and interactions between those from different religious and cultural backgrounds.

The **Advances in Religious and Cultural Studies (ARCS)** book series brings together a collection of scholarly publications on topics pertaining to religious beliefs, culture, population studies, and sociology. Books published within this series are ideal for professionals, theorists, researchers, and students seeking the latest research on collective human behavior in terms of religion, social structure, and cultural identity and practice.

COVERAGE

- Social Stratification and Classes
- Impact of Religion on Society
- Human Rights and Ethics
- Cross-Cultural Interaction
- Politics and Religion
- Cultural Identity
- Sociology
- Globalization and Culture
- Group Behavior
- Gender

IGI Global is currently accepting manuscripts for publication within this series. To submit a proposal for a volume in this series, please contact our Acquisition Editors at Acquisitions@igi-global.com or visit: http://www.igi-global.com/publish/.

The Advances in Religious and Cultural Studies (ARCS) Book Series (ISSN 2475-675X) is published by IGI Global, 701 E. Chocolate Avenue, Hershey, PA 17033-1240, USA, www.igi-global.com. This series is composed of titles available for purchase individually; each title is edited to be contextually exclusive from any other title within the series. For pricing and ordering information please visit http://www.igi-global.com/book-series/advances-religious-cultural-studies/84269. Postmaster: Send all address changes to above address. Copyright © 2023 IGI Global. All rights, including translation in other languages reserved by the publisher. No part of this series may be reproduced or used in any form or by any means – graphics, electronic, or mechanical, including photocopying, recording, taping, or information and retrieval systems – without written permission from the publisher, except for non commercial, educational use, including classroom teaching purposes. The views expressed in this series are those of the authors, but not necessarily of IGI Global.

Titles in this Series

For a list of additional titles in this series, please visit:
www.igi-global.com/book-series/advances-religious-cultural-studies/84269

Strategies for Cultural Assimilation of Immigrants and Their Children Social, Economic, and Political Considerations
Harish Chandra Chandan (Independent Researcher, USA) and Bryan Christiansen (Independent Researcher, USA)
Information Science Reference • © 2023 • 300pp • H/C (ISBN: 9781668448397) • US $215.00

Preservation and Restoration Techniques for Ancient Egyptian Textiles
Harby E. Ahmed (Faculty of Archaeology, Cairo University, Egypt) and Abdulnaser Abdulrahman Al-Zahrani (King Saud University, Saudi Arabia)
Information Science Reference • © 2023 • 272pp • H/C (ISBN: 9781799848110) • US $215.00

Implications of Marginalization and Critical Race Theory on Social Justice
Harish C. Chandan (Independent Researcher, USA) and Bryan Christiansen (Independent Researcher, USA)
Information Science Reference • © 2023 • 300pp • H/C (ISBN: 9781668436158) • US $215.00

Global LGBTQ+ Concerns in a Contemporary World Politics, Prejudice, and Community
Namita Rajput (Sri Aurobindo College, University of Delhi, India) Aishwarya Katyal (Shri Venkateshwara University, India) and Radhhika Katyal (Jagannath University, India)
Information Science Reference • © 2023 • 349pp • H/C (ISBN: 9781668455685) • US $240.00

Fighting for Empowerment in an Age of Violence
Milica Boskovic (Faculty for Diplomacy and Security, University Union Nikola Tesla, Serbia) Gordana Misev (Ministry of Mining and Energy Republic of Serbia, Serbia) and Nenad Putnik (Faculty of Security Studies, University of Belgrade, Serbia)
Information Science Reference • © 2022 • 391pp • H/C (ISBN: 9781668449646) • US $215.00

IGI Global
PUBLISHER of TIMELY KNOWLEDGE

701 East Chocolate Avenue, Hershey, PA 17033, USA
Tel: 717-533-8845 x100 • Fax: 717-533-8661
E-Mail: cust@igi-global.com • www.igi-global.com

Table of Contents

Preface xv

Acknowledgment xxiii

Section 1
Literary Representations of City Life and the Fictional Geographic Constructs

Chapter 1
Postcolonial Metropolitan Cities Go Feral: A Critical Study of Middle
Eastern and South Asian Cities in Selected Anglophone Fiction 1
    Abida Younas, University of Glasgow, UK
    Kawthar Yasser Al Othman, University of Glasgow, UK

Chapter 2
Dystopia and Heterotopia: Poetics and Politics of Space in Khaled Hosseini's
A Thousand Splendid Suns 18
    Jason Tan Jian Wei, Universiti Sains Malaysia, Malaysia
    Moussa Pourya Asl, Universiti Sains Malaysia, Malaysia

Chapter 3
Gender, Caste, and Class in Transnational Urban Spaces: A Reading of
Bharati Mukherjee's Novels 37
    Shilpi Gupta, Vellore Institute of Technology, India

Chapter 4
City, Wall, and (Feminist) Dystopia: Urban Poetics and Narrative in Prayaag
Akbar's *Leila* 59
    Moulina Bhattacharya, Christ University, India

Chapter 5
"Where Do Old Birds Go to Die?": Queer Environmental Geographies and
Liminal Spaces in Arundhati Roy's *The Ministry of Utmost Happiness* 82
    Meghna Prabir, Christ University, India

Chapter 6
A Step Forward, Two Steps Backward: Urbanization as Not a Gender Gap
Equalizer in Indu Sundaresan's Short Story Collection 101
    Anjum Khan M., Avinashilingam Institute for Home Science and Higher
        Education for Women, India

Section 2
Self-Representation and the Re-Mapping of the Urban Geography

Chapter 7
Reshaping Existing Discourses on Urban Spaces: Women's Socio-Spatial
Activism in Indian Autobiographical Narratives 126
    Kiron Susan Joseph Sebastine, School of Arts, Humanities, and
        Commerce, Amrita Vishwa Vidyapeetham, Kochi, India

Chapter 8
Inside and Outside the Hijab: An Urban Utopian Study of Samra Habib's *We
Have Always Been Here: A Queer Muslim Memoir* 148
    Sandhya Devi N. K., Presidency University, India
    Kirankumar Nittali, Presidency University, India

Chapter 9
Reconstructing Urban Spaces in Sushmita Banerjee's *Kabuliwalar Bangali
Bou*: The Memoir as a Narrative of Marital Migration in the South Asian
Context 176
    Monali Chatterjee, Gujarat Arts and Science College, India

Section 3
Ethnographic Representations of Gendered Geographies and
Geographies of Gender

Chapter 10
Transnational Urban Solidarities: A Political-Geographical Study of
Contemporary Iranian Feminists' Activism 199
    Maryam Lashkari, York University, Canada

Chapter 11
Re-Making the City for Women: A Case of New Kolkata 216
    Srestha Chatterjee, St.Xavier's College, India
    Anushyama Mukherjee, St. Xavier's College, India

Chapter 12
A Conceptual Study of Urban Spaces in Bangladesh: Exploring Patriarchy
From a Feminist Perspective 240
    Nasrin Pervin, Universiti Teknologi Malaysia, Malaysia
    Mahani Mokhtar, Universiti Teknologi Malaysia, Malaysia
    Nishat Zarin Haque, Pabna University of Science and Technology,
        Bangladesh

Chapter 13
Engendering the City: A Participatory Approach to Gender-Responsive
Planning and Urban Design in Cairo 269
    Jiayi Jin, Northumbria University, UK
    Kexin Huang, Northumbria University, UK
    Mingyu Zhu, Newcastle University, UK

Compilation of References 291

About the Contributors 322

Index 327

Detailed Table of Contents

Preface xv

Acknowledgment xxiii

Section 1
Literary Representations of City Life and the Fictional Geographic Constructs

This section explores fictional representation of cities in South Asian and Middle Eastern literature in English. It focuses on stories that depict urban life in countries such as Pakistan, Afghanistan, India, Egypt, and Syria through a meaningful exploration of the geographies of discrimination and empowerment, the changing face of sex and gender politics, and national and transnational constructs of space.

Chapter 1
Postcolonial Metropolitan Cities Go Feral: A Critical Study of Middle Eastern and South Asian Cities in Selected Anglophone Fiction 1
    Abida Younas, University of Glasgow, UK
    Kawthar Yasser Al Othman, University of Glasgow, UK

Some postcolonial cities in South Asia and the Middle East have started going feral due to the recent explosion of megacity projects. Even though a feral city encompasses all the unpleasant qualities of corruption, disease, violence, terrorism, crime, and pollution, it plays a significant role in world affairs. Drawing on the notion of the feral cities by Norton and Rafiq, this chapter examines the elements that contribute to the construction of feral cities in Bilal Tanweer's The Scatter Here Is Too Great, Yasmine El Rashidi's The Chronicles of Last Summer, Diana Darke's My House in Damascus, and Christy Lefteri's The Beekeeper of Aleppo. By demonstrating how Karachi, Cairo, Damascus, and Aleppo are depicted at risk of becoming feral cities within the global landscape, the study sheds light on the dangers that contribute to feral conditioning and underlines the multi-dimensional spatial aspects of the represented cities in the selected texts.

Chapter 2
Dystopia and Heterotopia: Poetics and Politics of Space in Khaled Hosseini's
A Thousand Splendid Suns 18
    Jason Tan Jian Wei, Universiti Sains Malaysia, Malaysia
    Moussa Pourya Asl, Universiti Sains Malaysia, Malaysia

The traditional classification of city spaces in Afghan literature in English as either utopian or dystopian overlooks the possibility of other spaces existing within the same spatial structure. This chapter argues that although Khaled Hosseini's A Thousand Splendid Suns is widely known to be teeming with exclusively dystopian elements, the novel depicts the functioning of alternative spaces within the same spatial realities. The authors use Foucault's notion of heterotopia to examine how the actuality of such different spaces throughout the novel allows the reimagining of alternate ways of life for the female characters. Drawing upon Foucault's six principles of heterotopia, the analysis underlines that despite the predominantly dystopian portrayal of the country in the novel, multiple physical and imaginary heterotopias are shown as operating whereby the characters, especially the female ones, are able to reimagine themselves away from the dreads of the chaotic reality.

Chapter 3
Gender, Caste, and Class in Transnational Urban Spaces: A Reading of
Bharati Mukherjee's Novels 37
    Shilpi Gupta, Vellore Institute of Technology, India

Bharati Mukherjee's novels The Tiger's Daughter (1971), Jasmine (1989), and Desirable Daughters (2002) depict transnational urban spaces by situating their characters in multiple geographies from Calcutta in India to major cities in America where the female protagonists are generally shown to have multiple identities based on caste, class, race, nationality, etc. By analyzing the characters' socio-economic positions, this chapter aims to explore how women are marginalized in transnational urban spaces based on their gender, class, and caste. It also seeks to examine how the women of caste and lower class are represented in transnational urban spaces. To achieve these objectives, the chapter employs Susan Friedman's the new geography of identities, Gayatri Spivak's notion of subalternity, Tabish Khair's distinction between Babu and Coolie, and Uma Chakravarti's discussion of caste as parallel to gender and class in order to examine the silences, gaps, and obstacles as present in the selected novels.

Chapter 4
City, Wall, and (Feminist) Dystopia: Urban Poetics and Narrative in Prayaag
Akbar's *Leila* 59
    Moulina Bhattacharya, Christ University, India

Prayaag Akbar's debut novel Leila (2017) is a compendium of dystopian feminism, misogyny, religious and casteist devaluation, and a post-apocalyptic portrayal of a futuristic urban India that is subjugated by a totalitarian government. This chapter aims to examine the narrative ambiguity and the unresolved problem of narrative reliability in the novel by exploring the cognitive process of the female protagonist Shalini in the context of the art of her storytelling. It is argued that the narrative pattern in this dystopian novel is mainly non-linear in spatial terms which creates a fragmented and patchy experience of reading. Using a spatial-psychoanalytical approach, the study reveals that the narrative is defied by the mental projection of the city-space and city as a gendered space.

Chapter 5
"Where Do Old Birds Go to Die?": Queer Environmental Geographies and Liminal Spaces in Arundhati Roy's *The Ministry of Utmost Happiness* 82
Meghna Prabir, Christ University, India

Arundhati Roy's The Ministry of Utmost Happiness (2017) addresses the question of gendered identity through the spaces that its protagonist Anjum inhabits. Applying ideas from intersectional queer ecologies, this study examines liminal spaces in the novel where the dispossessed are shown to be able to find a sense of home. It is widely believed that the novel encompasses the space of two graveyards: Anjum's graveyard, which becomes a paradise, and Kashmir, the paradise that has become a graveyard. It is argued that Roy examines contemporary India's multi-layered spaces, providing incisive observations that are deeply unsettling for the fundamentalist mind to contemplate. The non-normative geography of her literary landscape seems to posit that the liminal, in-between spaces inhabited by those with identities that transcend homogenous definitions are the spaces in which those persecuted for not conforming to acceptable norms of identity can truly find refuge and security.

Chapter 6
A Step Forward, Two Steps Backward: Urbanization as Not a Gender Gap Equalizer in Indu Sundaresan's Short Story Collection 101
Anjum Khan M., Avinashilingam Institute for Home Science and Higher Education for Women, India

Despite the revolutionary changes in the Indian nation's culture and lifestyle over the past few decades, the dominant attitude towards gender has not experienced a significant change. Although gender inequality and violence incited by gender identity prevail mostly in the villages, but the urban spaces are no exception to these phenomena. This chapter focuses on how Indu Sundaresan's short story collection In the Convent of Little Flowers explores and excavates the half-dead truths of gender inequality in the country concealed under pseudo modernity and social progress. It is argued that the collection includes narratives that present counter-histories of urban spaces where women confront challenges and exploitation. In pursuing this argument, the chapter uses a socio-spatial approach to demonstrate how urbanization is not a gender gap equalizer and to show how the line between rural and urban spaces is overlapping and crisscrossing.

Section 2
Self-Representation and the Re-Mapping of the Urban Geography

This section is concerned with autobiographical stories of women's daily experiences of city and city spaces in South Asia. The section explores the processes of reimagining urban spaces and redefining identity constructs and studies the significance of women's activism and resistance practices in everyday life as documented in selected eyewitness accounts by women writers from the region.

Chapter 7
Reshaping Existing Discourses on Urban Spaces: Women's Socio-Spatial Activism in Indian Autobiographical Narratives 126
    Kiron Susan Joseph Sebastine, School of Arts, Humanities, and Commerce, Amrita Vishwa Vidyapeetham, Kochi, India

Activism can occur in urban spaces independent of their spatial proportions. This chapter analyses the representations of women's activism as observed in their autobiographical works. The study focusses on women's activism documented in life writings by Nalini Jameela titled The Autobiography of a Sex Worker (2007) and Kiran Bedi's Dare to Do! For the New Generation (2012). The chapter draws upon the sociologist Mario Diani's deliberations on the different types of grassroot activism and social movements that can be understood as a manifestation of the right to the city struggle. Through a comparative analysis of the texts, the chapter examines how city spaces can become arenas of transformation, and the myriad ways people can come together to propose a common agenda and conjointly act to accomplish their goals.

Chapter 8
Inside and Outside the Hijab: An Urban Utopian Study of Samra Habib's *We Have Always Been Here: A Queer Muslim Memoir* 148
    Sandhya Devi N. K., Presidency University, India
    Kirankumar Nittali, Presidency University, India

The plight of Pakistani women has been normalized under the hegemonic patriarchal rule. As public and urban spaces are gendered, women are normally confined to domestic and private spaces. This chapter explores Samra Habib's autobiographical narrative We Have Always Been Here: A Queer Muslim Memoir (2019) to examine the ways in which the spaces and spatialities in South Asian and Western urban spaces are portrayed. Drawing upon the theoretical perspectives of feminist and queer geography, the chapter argues that the Western urban spaces function as a space of utopia that overcomes the exclusionary practices of Pakistani society. Feminist geography attempts to include women as the primary subjects in the public space, and queer geographies delineate how queer individuals have been ostracized by Pakistani society in public and private spaces. Further, the study reveals that Western urban spaces liberate and provide a normative non-discriminatory environment that empowers women and queer individuals to celebrate femininity and sexuality as it did in the case of Samra.

Chapter 9
Reconstructing Urban Spaces in Sushmita Banerjee's *Kabuliwalar Bangali Bou*: The Memoir as a Narrative of Marital Migration in the South Asian Context 176
  Monali Chatterjee, Gujarat Arts and Science College, India

This chapter explores Sushmita Banerjee's memoir titled Kabuliwalar Bangali Bou (1997) that portrays the horrors of displacement and city life in the South Asian context. The memoir poignantly chronicles the experiences of an urban Bengali woman who marries an Afghan businessman for love and migrates to Afghanistan during the rule of the Taliban. The objectives of the study are four-fold: 1) to establish the relationship between the vitality of urban space and the nature of social conventions that migrants are expected to follow; 2) to observe how such social and urban conventions and geopolitics affect migration, migrants, and diasporic communities; 3) to examine the reconstruction of urban spaces by women within the Taliban-governed nation of Afghanistan; and 4) to examine their narratives of urban space in the light of Foucault's dichotomy between private and public space as well as Heterotopia, Soja's notion of the third space, and Lefebvre's maxim about social space.

Section 3
Ethnographic Representations of Gendered Geographies and Geographies of Gender

The subject matter of essays in this section is women's active participation and agency in reclaiming their right to the city in countries like Iran, India, Bangladesh, and Egypt. Issues that are discussed in the four ethnographic studies in this section include women's alliance and solidarity across borders, women's agency in resisting against spatial injustice and gender inequality, women's active opposition to patriarchy, and women's active participation in re-designing urban spaces with the aim of reasserting their identities and subjectivities.

Chapter 10
Transnational Urban Solidarities: A Political-Geographical Study of
Contemporary Iranian Feminists' Activism 199
    Maryam Lashkari, York University, Canada

In theorizing solidarity among women, feminist scholars often ask what is it that can unite women in their fight against misogynistic social, cultural, and political structures, without reinforcing a victimized discourse and subjectivity. This chapter addresses the question by examining solidarities among Iranian feminist and women's activists in light of the existing dynamics between urban and virtual spaces. To this end, the study examines eye-witness accounts obtained from semi-structured interviews with activists, scholars, and policymakers, and conducts a content analysis of organizations' websites, journals, and documents. The findings indicate that feminist solidarities are moving across geographical scales ranging from the body, neighborhoods, cities, and beyond nation-state borders. Furthermore, although virtual spaces have provided significant tools for shaping feminist solidarities for Iranians, platform biases and authoritarian interventions have posed challenges against feminist activities and agendas.

Chapter 11
Re-Making the City for Women: A Case of New Kolkata 216
    Srestha Chatterjee, St.Xavier's College, India
    Anushyama Mukherjee, St. Xavier's College, India

A city is a place that consists of several diverse categories of individuals surviving together. In such a setting, the creation of cooperation and equal opportunity of competence is expected in order to excel or progress towards a level of sustenance and development. However, if the level of equal access to spaces and resources are not validly applied to all individuals, then that city requires a change of lens and perspective. Building an inclusive city involving all its inhabitants is a crucial starting point. Re-imagining a city from the lens of the silenced requires an active step towards remaking the manifesto of constructing spaces. Through the perspective of a feminist lens and the theory of "Right to the City," this chapter seeks to explore an attempt to re-make the city of New Kolkata.

Chapter 12
A Conceptual Study of Urban Spaces in Bangladesh: Exploring Patriarchy
From a Feminist Perspective 240
    Nasrin Pervin, Universiti Teknologi Malaysia, Malaysia
    Mahani Mokhtar, Universiti Teknologi Malaysia, Malaysia
    Nishat Zarin Haque, Pabna University of Science and Technology,
      Bangladesh

Patriarchy has been commonly referred to as autocratic rule by the male mastery both in public and private spheres. It has become a social framework in which men hold essentials to control and prevail in parts of political administration, ethical specialists, social benefit, and control of property. In Bangladesh, men have historically dominated, oppressed, and exploited women. When women grow up, the tradition in which they are raised emphasizes the need for modesty and virginity, particularly for women. This is unassumingly visible not only in the countryside but also in urban spaces. This research examines the notion of patriarchy and its precise relationship to contemporary urban culture in the country. In addition, it investigates patriarchy as a concept from the perspective of feminists to address the fundamental feminist concerns about women's work and lives in the context of the urban spaces in Bangladesh.

Chapter 13
Engendering the City: A Participatory Approach to Gender-Responsive
Planning and Urban Design in Cairo 269
    Jiayi Jin, Northumbria University, UK
    Kexin Huang, Northumbria University, UK
    Mingyu Zhu, Newcastle University, UK

The city of Cairo has witnessed a considerable increase in crimes against women, compelling women to avoid or minimise their use of public spaces in recent years. The absence of consideration for women in city planning has made Egyptian women feel further excluded and threatened by the public space, in addition to the patriarchal social relations and religious conservatism. As part of the 'gender-inclusive cities' research project, this study adopts a participatory approach as a tool for women's empowerment with the goal of promoting bottom-up models of planning, dissolving gendered norms, and improving women's status in a patriarchal society. The chapter provides an example of localised gender-inclusive design addressing women's spatial sensibilities and connecting them to the broader objectives of participation and emancipation. The findings of this study can help planners and policy makers co-create safer public spaces for local women, reduce spatial inequality, and facilitate their right to the city.

Compilation of References 291

About the Contributors 322

Index 327

Preface

In their *New Companion to the City* (2011), Gary Bridge and Sophie Watson explain the present century as the era in which urban processes affect the whole world as most of humanity now live in cities. In South Asia and the Middle East, rapid urbanization and urban transformations have altered the social landscape of cities and towns over the past few decades. The diversity of populations and the complexity of their daily lives and practices have produced both progressive and regressive changes in both regions. The fast rate of economic growth, urban-societal developments, civil conflicts, wars, rise of dictatorial political figures, religious fundamentalism, and natural disasters are among the major radical transformations that have not only changed urban conditions and city life experiences but also drawn attention to the spatiality of social life (Bose & Jalal, 2017; Fischer-Tiné & Framke, 2022; Jacobsen, 2016; Pourya Asl, 2022; Riaz & Rahman, 2016; Sadiki, 2020; Soja, 1989, 2010). Since the beginning of the millennium, the success of the city in providing a focal point for political demonstrations, radical aspirations, and revolutions (for example: the 2011 revolution in Tahrir Square in Cairo, Egypt; the 2011 Syrian revolution in Damascus and Aleppo, Syria; the 2016 general strike in India; and more recently, women's rights activists' protests in cities across Iran since September 2022) has led to the rise of the city as an intriguing cultural, political, and literary topos in South Asian and Middle Eastern studies.

As a disciplinary field of study, according to Tally Jr. (2017), literature "has a long history of examining such geographically based questions as the relation of an author or a text to its city" (p. 4). Clearly, sub-disciplines such as South Asian studies and Middle East studies are established upon such geographic demarcations. Based on topographical features, as well as on what Rieker and Ali (2008) argue as "the shared history of the colonial encounter, modernity, nationalism, and urbanity" (p. 2), numerous comparative studies have been conducted to examine the urban life and the experiences of men and women in the two regions. For instance, drawing upon critics such as Edward Said's emphasis on the "geographical inquiry into historical experience," postcolonial scholars have given particular attention to city life and the spatiality of socio-political experiences in the larger global south. In like manner, the increased emphasis that feminist geographers (e.g., Hanson, 1992; Massey, 1994, 2005; McDowell, 1993, 1999; Rose, 1993) have placed on the relationship between gendered identities and constructed space, as well as on women and the city, have led to the emergence of a vast amount of research on women's experiences of urban life (Boehmer, 2009; Channa, 2013; Fernandes, 2014; Patel, 2020; Rajan & Desai, 2013; Raju, 2011).

The growing concentration on the possibilities and problems as well as on the diversity and complexity of urban life in South Asia and the Middle East has stimulated an enormous growth of a vast literature of the city, depicting, examining, and reimagining urban life in its myriad forms (Asl, 2022). The cartography of the city is mapped in creative writings by re-imagining real and unreal spaces, both within the confines of the text and in relation to actual places in the real world. While a vast amount of scholarship is carried out on the conditions of cities and city life in the global south, less progress has been made to examine the portrayals and descriptions of the city in literary and cultural texts in the context of the two regions. Hence, the ways in which cities and city spaces in South Asia and the Middle East are constructed, navigated, experienced, and reconstructed in fictional and cultural narratives are complex and developing areas that deserve particular attention.

This edited volume investigates urban poetics and politics in contemporary South Asia and the Middle East through an interpretive and qualitative approach. Therefore, the aim has not been to present a quantitative and statistical analysis but to carry out critical qualitative examinations of the ways in which cities and city spaces are imagined and reimagined. Some of the questions that are of interest in this volume are: How urban spaces are shaped, navigated, and reshaped by people in South Asia and the Middle East; How identities are forged and forge themselves within urban localities; How individuals relate to others and to themselves within urban geographies; How the city is used to construct new identities; How the city and city spaces are remembered against the master-narratives; How urban spaces are appropriated or re-appropriated to make adjustments at micro- and macro-levels. These questions and similar ones are discussed with regards to what takes place both inside and outside of the text. Contributors to this volume mainly use spatially orientated approaches to explore the poetics and politics of the city that are often neglected from mainstream narratives. Furthermore, the recent expansion of various forms and genres (life writing, memoir, autobiographies, autoethnographies, etc.), by writers in the South Asian and the Middle Eastern literature in English (Suleiman & Muhawi, 2006; Tickell, 2016), has provided the rationale to include essays that explore literary works of various genres with the hope of better surveying, understanding, and showing intricacies and complexities of urban experiences in contemporary South Asia and the Middle East.

Preface

Therefore, this edited volume contains essays that examine urban poetics and politics in contemporary South Asia and the Middle East as represented in contemporary fictional and non-fictional writings from both regions. The first section, 'Literary Representations of City Life and the Fictional Geographic Constructs', explores fictional representations of cities in South Asian and the Middle Eastern literature in English. The six essays included in this section focus on stories that depict urban life in countries such as Pakistan, Afghanistan, India, Egypt, and Syria through a meaningful examination of the geographies of discrimination and empowerment, the changing face of sex and gender politics, and national and transnational constructs of space. The second section, 'Self-Representation and the Re-Mapping of the Urban Geography', is concerned with autobiographical stories of women's daily experiences of city and city spaces in South Asia. The three chapters in this section explore the processes of reimagining urban spaces and redefining identity constructs, and studies the significance of women's activism and resistance practices in everyday life as documented in selected eyewitness accounts by women writers from the region. The third section is titled 'Ethnographic Representations of Gendered Geographies and Geographies of Gender'. The subject matter of the four essays in this section is women's active participation and agency in reclaiming their right to the city in countries like Iran, India, Bangladesh, and Egypt. Issues that are discussed in the four ethnographic studies in this part include, women's alliance and solidarity across borders, women's agency in resisting against spatial injustice and gender inequality, women's active opposition to patriarchy, and women's active participation in re-designing urban spaces with the aim of reasserting their identities and subjectivities.

While the essays in the first two sections explore a wide range of literary forms and genres including novels, short stories, life writings, memoirs, and autobiographies from disciplinary and interdisciplinary perspectives, the chapters in the third section mainly use ethnographic accounts and observations to examine matters related to urban life and experiences. Together, the essays in this volume study the urban life experiences of people living in a range of countries such as India, Pakistan, Bangladesh, Afghanistan, Iran, Syria, Egypt as well as those South Asians and Middle Easterners in diaspora. Taken as a whole, the collection of essays in this book initiates a multidisciplinary approach to the study of city life by engaging disciplines such as urban geography, gender studies, feminism, literary criticism, and human geography with the aim of shedding light on how individuals constitute, experience, and navigate urban spaces in everyday life in contemporary South Asia and the Middle East.

ORGANIZATION OF THE BOOK

The book is organized into 13 chapters. A brief description of each of the chapters follows:

Chapter 1 examines the negative impact of megacity projects in transforming postcolonial metropolitan cities in South Asia and the Middle East into feral cities. Drawing upon Norton and Rafiq's definition of the feral city, this chapter investigates the elements that contribute to the construction of feral cities in Bilal Tanweer's *The Scatter Here is too Great* (2013), Yasmine El Rashidi's *The Chronicles of Last Summer* (2016), Diana Darke's *My House in Damascus* (2014), and Christy Lefteri's *The Beekeeper of Aleppo* (2019). By demonstrating how Karachi, Cairo, Damascus, and Aleppo are depicted on the verge of becoming feral cities, this study sheds light on the dangers that contribute to feral conditioning, and in doing so, it underlines the multi-dimensional spatial aspects of the represented cities in the selected texts.

Chapter 2 discusses the fluid boundaries of gender and spatial relations in contemporary South Asia. The authors of this chapter argue that the binary classification of city spaces in Afghan literature in English as either utopian or dystopian overlooks the possibility of other spaces operating within the same spatial structure. They pursue this argument through an analysis of Khaled Hosseini's *A Thousand Splendid Suns* (2007) in light of Michel Foucault's notion of heterotopia. It is contended that despite the predominantly dystopian depiction of the country in the novel, the actuality of heterotopic spaces throughout the story allows the reimagining of alternate ways of life for the female characters.

Chapter 3 studies the representation of transnational urban spaces in Bharati Mukherjee's novels, *The Tiger's daughter* (1971), *Jasmine* (1989), and *Desirable Daughters* (2002). Focusing on the spatial positioning of the female characters in multiple geographies, extending from Calcutta in India to major cities in America, the chapter examines the processes of identity formation based on distinct categories like caste, class, race, and nationality. In pursuing this goal, the chapter employs Susan Friedman's the new geography of identities, Gayatri Spivak's notion of subalternity, Tabish Khair's distinction between Babu and Coolie, and Uma Chakravarti's discussion of caste as parallel to gender and class to examine the silences, gaps, and obstacles as depicted in the selected novels.

Chapter 4 analyzes urban poetics and narrative in Prayaag Akbar's debut novel *Leila* (2017). The chapter presents the novel as a compendium of dystopian feminism, misogyny, religious and casteist devaluation, and a post-apocalyptic portrayal of a futuristic urban India that is subjugated by a totalitarian government. The author argues that the narrative pattern in this dystopian novel is mainly non-linear in spatial terms which creates a fragmented and patchy experience of reading. Using a spatial-psychoanalytical approach, the study reveals that the narrative is defined by the mental projection of the city-space and city as a gendered space.

Chapter 5 carries out a spatial analysis of Arundhati Roy's *The Ministry of Utmost Happiness* (2017) by looking into the workings of queer environmental geographies and liminal spaces in the formation of gendered identities. Drawing upon the theories of intersectional queer ecologies, this study examines the spaces in which the dispossessed are shown to be able to find a sense of home. The author of this chapter suggests that the novel encompasses the space of two graveyards: the female protagonist Anjum's graveyard, which becomes a paradise, and Kashmir, the paradise that has become a graveyard. It is argued the non-normative geography of Roy's literary landscape posits that the liminal, in-between spaces inhabited by those with identities that transcend homogenous definitions are the spaces in which those persecuted for not conforming to acceptable norms of identity can truly find refuge and security.

Chapter 6 explores Indu Sundaresan's short story collection, *In the Convent of Little Flowers* (2008), to show how urbanization is not presented as a gender gap equalizer. The author of this essay argues that the collection includes narratives that present counter histories of urban spaces where women confront challenges and exploitation. In pursuing this argument, the chapter uses a socio-spatial approach to demonstrate how urbanization has led to spatial injustice and gender inequality, and to show how the line between rural and urban spaces is overlapping and crisscrossing each other.

Chapter 7 presents new insights into Indian women's socio-spatial activism as documented in two autobiographical narratives, Nalini Jameela's *The Autobiography of a Sex Worker* (2007) and Kiran Bedi's *Dare to Do! For the New Generation* (2012). The chapter draws upon the sociologist Mario Diani's deliberations on the different types of grassroot activism and social movements that can be understood as a manifestation of the right to the city struggle. Through a comparative analysis of the texts, the chapter examines how city spaces can become arenas of transformation, and studies the myriad ways in which people come together to propose a common agenda and conjointly act to accomplish their goals.

Chapter 8 offers an urban utopian study of Samra Habib's *We Have Always been Here: A Queer Muslim Memoir* (2019) to show that Pakistani women's confinement to domestic and private spaces is rooted in the gendered state of the public and urban spaces in the country. Drawing upon the theoretical perspectives of feminist and queer geography, the chapter argues that the western urban spaces function as a space of utopia that differs from the exclusionary state of Pakistani society.

Chapter 9 discusses the horrors of displacement and city life in South Asian context as depicted in Sushmita Banerjee's *Kabuliwalar Bangali Bou: The Memoir* (2013). The chapter pursues four main objectives: a) to establish the relationship between the vitality of urban space and the nature of social conventions that migrants are expected to follow, b) to observe how such social and urban conventions and geopolitics affect migration, migrants, and diasporic communities, c) to examine the reconstruction of urban spaces by women within the Taliban-governed nation of Afghanistan, and d) to examine their narratives of urban space in the light of Foucault's dichotomy between private and public space as well as Heterotopia, Soja's notion of the third space, and Lefebvre's maxim about social space.

Chapter 10 conducts a political-geographical study of contemporary Iranian feminists' activism to theorize the developments of transnational urban solidarities among Iranian women activists. The author of this chapter examines eye-witness accounts obtained from semi-structured interviews with activists, scholars, and policymakers, and carries out a content analysis of organizations' websites, journals, and documents. The findings indicate that feminist solidarities are moving across geographical scales ranging from the body, neighborhoods, cities, and beyond nation-state borders. Furthermore, it is argued that although virtual spaces have provided significant tools for shaping feminist solidarities for Iranians, platform biases and authoritarian interventions have posed challenges against feminist activities and agendas.

Chapter 11 uses feminist lens and the theory of "Right to the City" to explore an attempt to re-make the city of New Kolkata for women. The authors of this study assert that for a city to progress towards a level of sustenance and development, the creation of cooperation and equal opportunity of competence is crucial. It is also argued that re-imagining a city from the lens of the silenced requires an active step towards remaking the manifesto of constructing spaces.

Chapter 12 is a conceptual study of urban spaces in Bangladesh. The authors examine the notion of patriarchy and its relationship to contemporary urban culture in the country. The chapter investigates patriarchy as a concept from the perspective of feminists to address the fundamental feminist concerns about women's work and lives in the context of the urban spaces in Bangladesh.

Chapter 13 explores the engendering of the city using a participatory approach to gender-responsive planning and urban design in Cairo. The authors of this chapter argue that besides the patriarchal social relations and religious conservatism, the absence of consideration for women in city planning has made Egyptian women feel excluded from and threatened by the public space. The study adopts a participatory approach as a tool for women's empowerment with the goal of promoting bottom-up models of planning, dissolving gendered norms, and improving women's status in a patriarchal society. In this regard, it provides an example of localized gender-inclusive design addressing women's spatial sensibilities and connecting them to the broader objectives of participation and emancipation.

Preface

Moussa Pourya Asl
Universiti Sains Malaysia, Malaysia

REFERENCES

Asl, M. P. (2022). Truth, space, and resistance: Iranian women's practices of freedom in Ramita Navai's City of Lies. *Women's Studies*, *51*(3), 287–306. doi:10.1080/00497878.2022.2030342

Boehmer, E. (2009). *Stories of women: Gender and narrative in the postcolonial nation*. Manchester University Press.

Bose, S., & Jalal, A. (2017). *Modern South Asia: History, culture, political economy*. Routledge. doi:10.4324/9781315106076

Bridge, G., & Watson, S. (Eds.). (2011). *The new Blackwell companion to the city*. Wiley-Blackwell. doi:10.1002/9781444395105

Channa, S. M. (2013). *Gender in South Asia: Social imagination and constructed realities*. Cambridge University Press. doi:10.1017/CBO9781107338807

Fernandes, L. (Ed.). (2014). *Routledge handbook of gender in South Asia*. Routledge. doi:10.4324/9781315848501

Fischer-Tiné, H., & Framke, M. (Eds.). (2022). *Routledge handbook of the history of colonialism in South Asia*. Routledge.

Hanson, S. (1992). Geography and feminism: Worlds in collision? *Annals of the Association of American Geographers*, *82*(4), 569–586. doi:10.1111/j.1467-8306.1992.tb01718.x

Jacobsen, K. A. (Ed.). (2016). *Routledge handbook of contemporary India*. Routledge.

Massey, D. (1994). *Space, place and gender*. University of Minnesota Press.

Massey, D. (2005). *For space*. Sage Publications.

McDowell, L. (1993). Space, place and gender relations: Part II. Identity, difference, feminist geometries and geographies. *Progress in Human Geography*, *17*(3), 305–318. doi:10.1177/030913259301700301

McDowell, L. (1999). *Gender, identity and place: Understanding feminist geographies*. Polity Press.

Patel, G. (2020). Gender trouble in South Asia. *The Journal of Asian Studies*, *79*(4), 947–967. doi:10.1017/S0021911820002399

Pourya Asl, M. (Ed.). (2022). *Gender, place, and identity of South Asian women*. IGI Global. doi:10.4018/978-1-6684-3626-4

Rajan, G., & Desai, J. (2013). *Transnational feminism and global advocacy in South Asia*. Routledge. doi:10.4324/9780203718469

Raju, S. (Ed.). (2011). *Gendered geographies: Space and place in the South Asia*. Oxford University Press.

Riaz, A., & Rahman, M. S. (Eds.). (2016). *Routledge handbook of contemporary Bangladesh*. Routledge. doi:10.4324/9781315651019

Rieker, M., & Ali, K. (Eds.). (2008). *Gendering urban space in the Middle East, South Asia, and Africa*. Springer. doi:10.1057/9780230612471

Rose, G. (1993). Women and everyday space. In *Feminism and geography: The limits of geographical knowledge*. University of Minnesota Press.

Sadiki, L. (Ed.). (2020). *Routledge handbook of Middle East politics*. Routledge. doi:10.4324/9781315170688

Soja, E. W. (1989). *Postmodern geographies: The reassertion of space in critical social theory*. Verso.

Soja, E. W. (2010). *Seeking spatial justice*. University of Minnesota Press. doi:10.5749/minnesota/9780816666676.001.0001

Suleiman, Y., & Muhawi, I. (Eds.). (2006). *Literature and nation in the Middle East*. Edinburgh University Press. doi:10.3366/edinburgh/9780748620739.001.0001

Tally, R. T. Jr., (Ed.). (2017). *The Routledge handbook of literature and space*. Taylor & Francis. doi:10.4324/9781315745978

Tickell, A. (Ed.). (2016). *South-Asian fiction in English: Contemporary transformations*. Springer. doi:10.1057/978-1-137-40354-4

Acknowledgment

First and foremost, I would like to thank and acknowledge the contributors to this volume for their support and patience, and the reviewers for their insightful comments and constructive suggestions that helped in developing the earlier outline of the book and presentation of the material. I extend my deepest thanks to the team from IGI Global production department for their extensive efforts during the many phases of this project and the timely fashion in which the book was produced.

Section 1
Literary Representations of City Life and the Fictional Geographic Constructs

This section explores fictional representation of cities in South Asian and Middle Eastern literature in English. It focuses on stories that depict urban life in countries such as Pakistan, Afghanistan, India, Egypt, and Syria through a meaningful exploration of the geographies of discrimination and empowerment, the changing face of sex and gender politics, and national and transnational constructs of space.

Chapter 1
Postcolonial Metropolitan Cities Go Feral:
A Critical Study of Middle Eastern and South Asian Cities in Selected Anglophone Fiction

Abida Younas
University of Glasgow, UK

Kawthar Yasser Al Othman
https://orcid.org/0000-0002-8967-7135
University of Glasgow, UK

ABSTRACT

Some postcolonial cities in South Asia and the Middle East have started going feral due to the recent explosion of megacity projects. Even though a feral city encompasses all the unpleasant qualities of corruption, disease, violence, terrorism, crime, and pollution, it plays a significant role in world affairs. Drawing on the notion of the feral cities by Norton and Rafiq, this chapter examines the elements that contribute to the construction of feral cities in Bilal Tanweer's The Scatter Here Is Too Great, Yasmine El Rashidi's The Chronicles of Last Summer, Diana Darke's My House in Damascus, and Christy Lefteri's The Beekeeper of Aleppo. By demonstrating how Karachi, Cairo, Damascus, and Aleppo are depicted at risk of becoming feral cities within the global landscape, the study sheds light on the dangers that contribute to feral conditioning and underlines the multi-dimensional spatial aspects of the represented cities in the selected texts.

DOI: 10.4018/978-1-6684-6650-6.ch001

INTRODUCTION

The world population is increasingly urban due to a rapid process of urbanization that has initiated in the second half of the twentieth century. One-third of the world population has started to move to cities and "90 percent of urban growth [has] concentrated in the Global South" (Macaluso & Briscoe, 2015, p. 4). This expansion of megacities largely materializes in less developed countries. According to a 2008 survey, 44% of the population in third-world countries were living in cities. The UN predicts that 67% of the population in less developed countries will be living in cities by 2050. The rapid growth of urban areas is a great danger to human security. Cities though are hubs of economic activities; they are also a site of violence and conflicting issues. With the expansion of cities, the rise of violence, terrorism, disease, pollution, and corruption are becoming pressing matters for any country and a dilemma for individual security. The rapid extension of megacities led to the growth of poverty, disease, inequality, and "socioeconomic heterogeneity" (Bunker, 2014, p. 2). With the recent uprisings across the Middle East, India, and North Africa, cities have become more central in anglophone literature. For instance, in his novel *Fleeing the Ring Road* (originally in Arabic), Kilani (2019) tackles how the so-called urban development of Cairo city is actually damaging the urban infrastructure of the highly populated city, Cairo. The same idea is illustrated in *Utopia* by Tawfik (2008). Tawfik criticizes Cairo by creating a city in his novel which is divided into two classes, extremely rich and extremely poor. Through the urban planning of his imagined city, he shows the social and economic division between the Cairene people where the rich hunt the poor. Postcolonial cities become the stage for argument, where the present and the future of both these places along with their people are challenged and reimagined in postcolonial novels. The drastic socio-economic conditions of the cities have transformed a city from a serene place of living into "a territory where the rule of law has long been replaced by near anarchy" (Norton, 2003, p. 1). Against this backdrop, this chapter reads anglophone fiction to indicate the major megacities (Karachi, Cairo, Damascus, and Aleppo) of postcolonial nations are at risk of becoming feral. In so doing, the crumbling urban structure of postcolonial states is highlighted.

A great deal of scholarly attention has been paid to the phenomenon of failing states and little attention has been paid to the emergence of potential feral cities. For instance, *Gender, Place, and Identity of South Asian Women* (2022) focuses on contemporary literature on South Asian women. While the book addresses gender identity and equality, spatial and social justice, women empowerment, and marginalization, it lacks a discussion of feral cities. This chapter takes the same issues further by placing them in the emerging feral cities of South Asian and Middle Eastern spaces. The feral city is a common feature of the global landscape that indicates any state's faltering and failed condition. The concept of 'failed states' entered the political lexicon of the USA in the early 1990s, occupying a prominent place in international peace and security (Call, 2008). For instance, international attention is focused on the failure of the Afghan state to prevent the operation of al-Qaeda on its territory after the attacks of 9/11. The case of Afghanistan and "subsequent growing concern about other similar states intensified concern about the role of 'failed states' in harboring or aiding terrorism" (Call, 2008, p. 1491). Call (2008) argues that the concept of a 'failed state' is "largely useless and should be abandoned except in so far as it refers to wholly collapsed states—where no authority is recognisable either internally to a country's inhabitants or externally to the international community" (p. 1492). As Call explores the term 'failed state', analysing the factors behind its emergence and its positive contributions to political analysis and policy prescriptions, this chapter illustrates the health of cities in the Middle East and South Asia, shedding light on the multi-spatial aspects of some exemplary cities which have potentials of going feral.

The field of postcolonial literary studies has been marked by an urban turn. Scholars examine the city "as a complex site of colonial and anticolonial struggle, postcolonial politics, and neo-imperial economies" (Herbert, 2014, p. 200). The city, hence, has been frequently understood as a "representational space," to borrow Henri Lefebvre's term that is both lived and narrated. As a colonial intervention, postcolonial megacities (in the context of this chapter, it is Karachi, Cairo, Damascus, and Aleppo) embody the dynamics of postcolonial movement, class inequality, diasporic populations, and a radical assortment of cultures and ethnicities. While these cities remain a centre of power established during colonial rule, they are also a site of new structures of power and politics of identity that emerged after the colonization (Pourya Asl, 2022). Moreover, these cities also experience a global neoliberal mode of urban development and attract foreign investment. Yet these cities witness pandemic terrorism, anarchy, persistent bombing, corruption, violence, and pollution. Since the 1970s, inequality, poverty, violence, and terrorism are recognized phenomena in the urban life of postcolonial nations. The urban structure of postcolonial nations is increasingly "separated spatially, socially and culturally, from the (lower and upper) middle-class city", this has led to social exclusion, and consequently, "urban crime and violence are on the rise" in the urban areas (Koonings & Kruijt, 2007, p. 7). The ineffective presence of authorities has changed the law and order into its antithesis. Urban tenants face fear and violence because the absence of state authorities has opened the way for "armed actors and violence brokers" to operate and rule different places in cities through coercion (Koonings & Kruijt, 2007, p. 7). Subsequently, this condition has led to the "fragmented, ambivalent and hybrid cityscape with varying manifestations of the complex of poverty, exclusion, coercion, violence. and fear" (Koonings & Kruijt, 2007, pp. 7-8). In his writing "Feral Cities", Norton

(2003) draws the attention of the world towards this fragmentation, declining, and crumbling condition of urban spaces. He calls such condition ferality.

Shedding light on the feral conditions in postcolonial Middle Eastern and South Asian cities in this chapter is significant in the field of spatial studies. Cities like the selected ones in this study suffer from severe political and economic issues. Consequently, the quality of life in these cities is becoming worse over time. Addressing the health of cities shows the quality of life their people have. By studying and understanding the elements that make a city go feral, the chance of saving the city and its people is higher. Hence, this chapter contributes to the field of spatial studies by introducing the concept of a 'feral city' into literary studies.

FERAL CITIES

According to Norton (2003), a Feral city is:

a great metropolis covering hundreds of square miles. Once a vital component in a national economy, this sprawling urban environment is now a vast collection of blighted buildings, an immense petri dish of both ancient and new diseases, a territory where the rule of law has long been replaced by near anarchy in which the only security available is that which is attained through brute power. --- Yet this city would still be globally connected. (Norton, 2003, p. 97)

Norton opines that most of the inhabitants in the feral city have no access to basic security or health services. In a feral city, there is no safety network, yet it does not descend into complete chaos. Some elements like "criminal[ity], an armed resistance group, ---corruption, avarice, and violence" are the hallmark of a feral city yet this city "remains a functioning actor in the greater international system" (Norton, 2003, p. 98). Along with this, the feral city also "experiences the massive level of disease and creates enough pollution to qualify for an international environmental disaster zone" (p. 98). Overcrowding, pollution, overpopulation, and poor sewerage system are thus very common in mega feral cities. Asides from these problems, there are plenty of other problems as well like muggers and pickpockets also prey on the inhabitants of the megacities. These problems in most of the megacities threaten their residents "with war, starvation, and misery" (Jordan, 2008, p. 32). However, even under this worse condition, "these cities continue to grow, and the majority of occupants do not voluntarily leave" (Norton, 2003, p. 98).

The question, however, arises that most metropolia of the world have long been bred with different diseases. Criminality, terrorism, violence, and urban pollution have long been the part and parcel of various megacities. What thus makes the city, a feral city? The most notable difference is that in feral cities police officers and state authorities are not able to enforce law and order rather most of the time, it is state authorities who are involved in the disruption of law. In some countries, even military operation is used to subdue the feral city. Criminality and violence in Karachi, Cairo, Damascus, and Aleppo are shaped by ethnic divisions, geography, and socio-economic tensions, but they are "largely the product of inappropriate security policies, including decades of neglected police reform, and poor governance" (*Asia Report*, 2012, p. 1). For instance, Cairo has been under emergency law for more than thirty years and this law has been used against civilians. Everyday mobility in Cairo has been "surveilled, regulated, and policed" to keep the masses oppressed (Smith, 2015, p. 16). Instead of protecting and serving the nation, the state authorities "put the people in the service of the police" (Brownlee, 2013, p. 3). Norton further claims that "the feral city may be a phenomenon that never takes place, yet its emergence should not be dismissed as impossible" (Norton, 2003, p. 97). For centuries, many cities have undergone numerous alterations and experienced a massive level of change. Some cities survive those challenges and change without going feral; however, others experience ferality. Norton puts forward a model *The Health of Cities* through which cities are assessed in order to determine their ferality level.

THE HEALTH OF CITIES

Norton views cities as a patchwork of colors in which the green level shows no danger of ferality whereas the yellow level indicates a danger which illustrates potential conditioning of ferality, and the red level signifies the ferality. A city in the green category has a stable government where the security forces are "well-regulated [and] well-educated" (Norton, 2003, p. 103). The city government in the green city provides all the basic services including education, health, and employment opportunities to its inhabitants equally (Norton, 2003, p. 103). A city in the yellow category is described "as an urban nightmare" (Norton, 2003, p. 103). A yellow indicates that these cities are divided into two and the services are enjoyed in portions of the city. Norton claims that there are squares of slum areas without proper sewerage systems in them and the air is polluted and "unfit to breathe" in yellow cities (Norton, 2003, p. 103). Law and order have been replaced with disorder and crime rates are increasing in such cities. The judicial system, police department, and all the important departments of yellow cities are highly corrupt. State authorities are not able to govern the red city at all. Cities in this category suffer from high levels of pollution and epidemic diseases (Norton, 2003, p. 104). These cities "would have no governmental tax base" (Norton, 2003, p. 102). Thus, it is argued that green cities are regulated by ethical and professional forces and authorities, yellow cities are often marked by high crime rates and terrorist activities, etc., and red cities are marked as criminal organizations.

Given this context, it is argued that some postcolonial megacities are in danger of becoming feral and others are already feral. The four cities (Karachi, Cairo, Damascus, and Aleppo) that are under consideration here exemplify Norton's feral city – megacities in which the government "has lost the ability to maintain the rule of law within the city's boundaries" yet they play a significant part in the world's international affairs (Norton, 2003, p. 1). According to a survey conducted in 2010, Karachi is on the list of the top 12 feral cities in the world because violence has been an integral part of Karachi's ecosystem since the 1980s. Similarly, violence is an embedded part of Cairo life and thereby shapes the urban landscapes and politics of Cairo. According to Thompson Reuters report, the Egyptian capital Cairo is the most dangerous megacity in the world. Since the 1960s, the population in megacities of third-world countries like Karachi, Cairo, and Delhi has grown exponentially while state services have failed to keep up. As the government in third-world countries opens itself for foreign investment, the middle class found it hard to keep their positions and the poor sank deeper into poverty. As a result, the increase in informal houses is seen in big megacities like Cairo and Karachi (Elyachar, 2003; Sims, 2010). Built without government approval, informal houses have risen throughout Pakistan and Egypt. It is estimated that most of the half population lives in informal houses as these houses are lower cost in comparison to formal houses (Dorman, 2011, p. 272). However, these informal houses have limited resources and thus people living here remain "stuck in poverty and vulnerability" (Kelman & Clark-Ginsberg, 2022, p. 121). Such transformation in megacities has applied pressure on the infrastructure of these megacities and the government is unable to keep them.

The case might be worse in Damascus and Aleppo. Roads in the Syrian capital are blocked by the army, and workers race to reach their homes before darkness. Darkness means the time when kidnappers appear, seeking new victims, and when the clashes "raging on the outskirts creep ever closer to the heart of Damascus" (Solomon, 2012). According to the same report, fighting laid waste to much of the northern city of Aleppo, and parts of its vaulted Old City quarter have been burned to the ground. Most Syrians leave their homes or their neighborhoods only when absolutely necessary because getting back requires planning and good timing and sometimes it costs losing one's life. Moreover, violence is an integral part of people living in these megacities. Corruption, torture, and harassment are the hallmarks of daily state practices in the selected megacities. The political power is concentrated in the hands of a few political elites, and they used state machinery for their purposes. Therefore, one can see the absence of a judicial system, and there is no regulation and discipline for the security services specifically the police (Linz, 2000). In fact, in countries like Pakistan, Egypt, and Syria, state security services are used against their own people and thus the daily lives in these megacities are characterized by abuse and harassment by police forces (Singerman 2002; Amar, 2013). Rafiq (2016) claims that postcolonial megacities' urban challenges are by no means unique: "It has its equivalents in Delhi's water tanker mafias, Mexico city's kidnapping networks, and Mumbai's infamous gangsters" (np). Put together, postcolonial megacities' violent dynamics may be among the world's most complex.

The violent scenario of postcolonial megacities affects its occupants very much. The fierce situation of these cities is even apparent in fiction writings as well and many writers have taken up that stance and present such cities as a web of anti-state militants, sectarian, ethnic groups, and real estate mafias where illicit economic activities happen and where terrorist and insurgent groups, private militias, and other forms of violent nonstate actors (VNSAs) are active. In the following pages, this chapter explores Karachi, Cairo, Damascus, and Aleppo as feral cities with a particular reference to Bilal Tanweer's *The Scatter Here is Too Great (2013),* Yasmine El Rashidi's *The Chronicles of Last Summer (2016),* Diana Darke's *My House in Damascus* (2014) and Christy Lefteri's *The Beekeeper of Aleppo (2019)*. Being a resident of Karachi for so many years, Tanweer has firsthand experience of Karachi. His novel reveals human loss in Karachi because of violence. In the same vein, El Rashidi presents three decades of Cairo's transformation and the shifting realities of the Egyptian people. It is worth noting here that the importance of Karachi and Cairo for the country of Pakistan and Egypt respectively cannot be underrated. Politically, socially, and economically, both countries (Pakistan and Egypt) are tightly wound with what happens in Karachi and Cairo respectively. Yet both cities are victims of poor planning and weak governance that have destroyed the entire structure of these cities and thus signify to yellow level. Alternatively, Damascus and Aleppo suffer from both poor governance and warfare and thus indicate the red level of ferality.

KARACHI AND CAIRO AS YELLOW FERAL CITIES

Tanweer tries to map the brutality and diverse inhabitants of Karachi in his novel. His novel encompasses all bombing, violence, disease, corruption, and Karachi's secular past. He shows us how cities in third-world countries are run by "non-state actors" and undermine "the very definition of state" (Post, 2018, p. 118). The novel starts with Karachi's past. Tanweer refers to Zia's regime and reveals that Zia's regime is responsible for the present condition of Karachi as described: "Zia, that dog of CIA. He ate them all up. --- where else do you think all this Islam and drugs and guns and bombs came into this city? They are a recent invention" (Tanweer, 2013, p. 22). He also claims that since Zia's regime, Karachi is a place of jihadi state groups as Sukhansaz in the novel says that "Americans g[a]ve him [Zia] the money and guns and a carte blanche for drugs to fight the Soviets, and he [Zia] fucked the country and this city for his jihad next door" (Tanweer, 2013, p. 22). Aligning with the same idea, in his essay "Operation Karachi: Pakistan's Military Retakes the City" Rafiq (2016) claims that in the feral city there are always terrorist groups that carry out different terrorist activities. He gives an example of Karachi and says that "Karachi is a city in which Anti-state and transnational jihadist groups conduct mass causality terrorist attacks targeting politicians, state personnel and institutions, religious minorities, and foreigners" (np). The ineffective police forces of Karachi encourage citizens to "turn to alternative providers of law and order" which also challenge the state's authority (Post, 2018, p. 122). The terrorist activities are very evident in the text. The novel refers to the ubiquitous violence and terrorism time and again in Karachi. There are many bombing episodes in the novel at Cantt station and at many other places as described "---cross the Cantt signal, when the blast occurred" (Tanweer, 2013, p. 37). Tanweer's novel is a literary witness to trauma in Pakistan and he successfully knits the collective and individual dimensions through diverse narrative voices.

El Rashid's *Chronicle of Last Summer* details three tumultuous decades in Cairo and is divided into three sections. She skillfully represents the city's progression, mirrors the political history, and shows that violence is inseparable from the city space. She also reveals that the everyday violence that Egyptians confronted is made possible by a security apparatus. In addition to this, she also demonstrates that black marketing, snatching, and pickpocketers are some other significant factors that add to the conditioning of ferality and threatened the security of Cairo. It has been revealed that even state authorities are seemed to be involved in black marketing. For instance, the novel reveals that when the prices of wheat increase in the international market, many bakeries in Cairo start selling some of the state flour in the black market for huge profits. The shortage of Egypt's own subsidized food items and goods encourages many people to sell their items at high prices in the black market and "the catastrophe is the government employees are doing it" (Rashidi, 2016. p. 57). Likewise, in Tanweer's novel, when the chief security services lose his money in "betting on the Pakistan cricket team in the final cup", he does not hesitate to use unfair means to return money to the one with whom he had bet. For this purpose, he steals a car and does "the necessary rebranding of the car" to sell it for cash (Tanweer, 2013, p. 124). The chief knows very well that he is using unfair means, yet he has used it by saying "it is not legal but it is smart: instead of turning the defaulted cars into the bank, you sell them at half the price. The police would treat the car as stolen; the bank could claim its money from the insurance, and nobody is ever going to go looking for the car" (Tanweer, 2013, p. 124). This evidence from both texts divulges that government authorities are involved in black marketing and police forces are shown as incapable of doing their duty. Tanweer's novel also refers to the episode of muggers who snatch everything from the bus riders: "whatever, whatever you have, drop it on the floor in front of you. If I find anything near anyone, I swear to God, I will fire a bullet through his head without a thought" (Tanweer, 2013, p. 14). This evidence of the text signals the yellow cities of ferality in which corruption has extended to almost every level of the city, whereas state authorities and police forces are shown as seriously handicapped in terms of performing their duty as happened in yellow cities.

Norton claims that the government could not enact effective legislation in yellow cities. In contrast to the stable and healthy government of the green cities, the city government in yellow cities exercises its authority "only in a portion of the city, producing what might be called "patchwork" governance, or that it exerted authority only during the day—"diurnal" governance" (Norton, 2003, p. 101). This fact has well illustrated by both novelists. A close reading of *The Chronicle of the Last Summer* reveals that only a small section of the Cairene society, which has a close association with the government, profits from the government's resources, and a large section of the poor is alienated from the government. The citizens "only have provisional connections to sewage and electrical infrastructure" (Smith, 2015, p. 6). For instance, power cut occurs routinely in Cairo except for "some people who never have power cuts" because "their fathers are important and work for the government" (Rashidi, 2016, p. 9). These examples suggest the government's refusal to provide equal sources to its own people. The growing gap between the rich and the poor is also illustrated by the way houses are built in Cairo. "[B]ig houses" (Rashidi, 2016, p.52) are built for affluent people on the side of the river Nile and the poor are shown as living in "a shed of the roof of a building with a single lightbulb and no running water" (Rashidi, 2016, p.106). Like Cairo, Karachi also contains many slum areas and Tanweer highlights this aspect of Karachi and shows the miserable condition of Karachi and Karachiites. The novel reveals the densely populated areas of Karachi as: "lanes become narrower, houses turned into shabbier huts made from an assortment of tattered jackets, old bedsheets, wooden lattices, plastic nets, bamboos tied with plastic bags" (Tanweer, 2013, p. 189). He further says that Karachi has "no official source of water or sewage lines. People dug their own holes and installed hand pumps that drew undrinkable water" (Tanweer, 2013, p. 189). These examples from the text show the decaying and deteriorating condition of Karachi. Tanweer (2013) also refers to hospitals that are insufficient and unsatisfactory as described people "lived and [children] played in garbage heaps and died of common fevers and mosquito bites" (p. 189). This condition of Karachi signals the yellow category of the feral city. According to Norton, yellow-category cities cannot provide all facilities to their public through "trash pickup, ambulance service, and access to hospitals" (2003, p. 102). Although these facilities exist, they "maintain a minimal level of public health and sanitation" (Norton, 2003, p. 102). This is perhaps the reason that both novels are full of the description of bizarre diseases: "the visible of his body and hands seemed like shriveled pieces of desiccated, parched mud --- his palms showed mutilated stumps instead of fingers of different length" (Tanweer, 2013, p. 191). These textual excerpts from both texts support Norton's idea that cities with the yellow category are not able to provide satisfactory levels of public health and sanitation. The above examples illustrate the absence of "state power and public institutions" in some parts of cities that are marginal. In such marginal spaces, "an uncivil logic of coercion and violence takes over" as is witnessed in Karachi, and Cairo (Koonings & Kruijt, 2007, p. 2).

The remarkable aspect of both novels is their portrayal of the urban planning of the represented cities which "are not, and cannot, be gender neutral" (Shah, 2022, np). In their urban narratives, El Rashidi and Tanweer show that gender inclusion is a significant factor in the design, vision, development, and planning of cities. This is perhaps the reason, El Rashidi shows us the chaotic lives of people in Cairo via a female protagonist. In the course of the novel, it is revealed that as a filmmaker, the protagonist of the *Chronicles of the Last Summer* is adamant to find the answers to all unanswered questions that make her city, Cairo, a repressing place. For example, the novel discloses that if people in Cairo are asked about "what they would like to see improved in their city", they either stay silent or say they do not want to get themselves in trouble even though "they are angry, disheartened, frustrated" (Rashidi, 2016, p. 87-88). Some of them even say that they cannot "speak about the city" (Rashidi, 2016, p. 88). El Rashidi, However, compensates for their silences and walks around the city to show the plight of those people who are once spatially off-limit. Not only does she highlight the insufficient and discriminating governmental system, but she also foregrounds people of all strata and this makes her novel inclusive in style. Shah (2022) argues that "women are agents of change in society and are best equipped to initiate social change in their communities" (np). This is perhaps the reason that one can see the increased activism at the end of the novel where the narrator and her mother are seen to be involved in the community association. Female characters in both novels are seen as active agents who foreground the ill practices of the government, hence, identifying the weaknesses in urban policies and planning. This confirms the notion of what David Harvey (2012) calls 'the right to the city'. In this notion, planning and creating a 'healthy' city requires meeting humanitarian needs; it is the human's right to make and remake the city "after his [/her] heart's desire" (p.3). This means that all people living within a given city should provide equal opportunities and space without social, economic, gender or any other discrimination aspects.

DAMASCUS AND ALEPPO AS RED CITIES

Poor governance systems and warfare in Syria have led cities like Damascus and Aleppo to become feral, more precisely "red" feral according to Norton's categories. This phenomenon is manifested in Darke's *My House in Damascus* (2014) and Lefteri's *The Beekeeper of Aleppo* (2019). Darke's *My House in Damascus* starts with a reference to the unarmed revolution with a series of peaceful demonstrations. The first one takes place "in Damascus outside the Umayyad Mosque on Tuesday, 15 March 2011" (Darke, 2014, p. 1). The author sheds light on the general atmosphere in Syria and its people's desire for freedom from Assad's regime. During the full blaze of the Syrian revolution and on a visit to the Chapel of Ananias located in the Christian Quarter in the Old City, the author opens the Visitor's Book to find these lines: "God please we ask you to protect us and let our people live with peace and take action against our president Bashar al-Assad. 19/3/2012" (Darke, 2014, p. 11). This total despair and the current condition of Syria are the results of decades of Assad's policies in ruling the country. Taking Norton's model of measuring the health condition of a city, consisting of four categories: government, economy, services, and security, Darke's biography, written at a pace of a novel, and Lefteri's novel provide textual evidence of both Damascus and Aleppo becoming feral "red" cities.

On her first research trip to Damascus in 2005, Darke highlights the bureaucracy of government through her experience with the Ministry of Tourism to get the necessary permissions to visit some places. She describes how the run-down building of the ministry is "a microcosm of the sort of organised chaos" (Darke, 2014, p. 14). The chaos is reflected in the hierarchy of the employees' sizes of rooms and their furniture which are meant to show their status. Although government employees are proud of their work and consider themselves at the top of their fields, they have at least two other jobs besides their governmental one because their salaries are too low to live off. The low rate of salaries has also promoted bribery. Bureaucratic procedures are designed to be around 15 stages involved to ensure that "there [are] ample opportunities for both employment and bribery" (Darke, 2014, p. 17). One of the ironies of the Syrian crisis is that there has been a plan to introduce 'e-government' at the time the revolution broke out, attempting to reduce the opportunities for face-to-face contact between civil servants and the public. Darke also explains how small employees do not have the authority to issue any permissions. Ministries in Syria are "Bloated and underfunded" and they "are highly centralised, controlling organisations. Without access to the top, the wait could be long" (Darke, 2014, p. 15). The Ba'ath Party being in power since the early 1960s has created a system of "corrupt patronage where only the well-connected can break through bureaucratic barriers" (Darke, 2014, p. 35). These examples show the corrupted government ruling in the country.

Even before the revolution in 2011, Assad's regime practices inhumane policies with people who think of criticising or expressing dissatisfaction with the government, spreading fear and a sense of insecurity. On the pretext that the Syrian government considers itself in a permanent state of war with Israel or 'the Zionist entity' as it always calls it, the Assad regime introduced its 1963 Emergency Law, "giving the police and security services absolute power to arrest and detain anyone indefinitely without trial" (Darke, 2014, p. 16). As a result, thousands of Syrians "dissidents languish in Syrian prisons" and are "often subjected to grotesque torture" to the extent that those who survived it said, "Death is easier than Syrian prison" (Darke, 2014, p. 16). On the level of security, in a "red" city, as Norton argues, "the police force has failed altogether or has become merely another armed group seeking power and wealth" (Norton, 2003, p. 102).

On the day of Kofi Annan's ceasefire, Darke reports how all her friends, "a mix of Muslims and Christians from a range of professions, deeply pessimistic about the future" who are neither activists nor regime supporters (Darke, 2014, p. 11). They belong to the "silent majority caught in the middle. Their futures have been taken away from them" (Darke, 2014, p. 11). People are convinced that the situation will become worse as the country is divided between "a ruling elite fighting for its life and a poorly organised opposition increasingly taking up arms" (Darke, 2014, p. 11). This situation makes Damascus a feral city where the loss of services, corruption, and crime become widely spread. The civil disobedience started in Damascus with people stopping to pay their utility bills: "why should we pay for services we do not have?" (Darke, 2014, p. 11). This situation of having intermittent to non-existent power and water puts Damascus under the category of going feral or "red" feral city according to Norton's categorisation of feral cities. According to Norton, cities in the "red" zone would be unable to supply more than intermittent power and water" (Norton, 2003, p. 102). These living conditions in the city and Syria, in general, have a tremendous impact on the health of people psychologically and physically.

Darke also points out how environmental awareness in Syria is at the lowest level. The concept "was non-existent" to the extent that The Ministry of the Environment "was not set up until 2006 and, even then, had no clear idea what to do" (Darke, 2014, p. 32). Although there was a Ministry of Irrigation before that, its "approach was far from environmental" (Darke, 2014, p. 32). As Darke explains, land exists to be exploited which is "the Ministry's default setting" (Darke, 2014, p. 32). There is not any consideration for nature, wilderness and animals. Rather, the countryside and animals exist to provide food, "not to be nurtured and fussed over" (Darke, 2014, p. 32). With the Syrian revolution and the ongoing war, the environmental conditions are worsening. Despite all the corruption and bad economic conditions, Damascus, being the capital, seems to remain under strict control of Assad's regime unlike the case of Aleppo as represented in Lefteri's novel.

Lefteri's *The Beekeeper of Aleppo* (2019) depicts the tremendous change in the city, its people, and their life through the journey of Syrian refugee Nuri and his wife Afra from Syria to the United Kingdom as a result of the Syrian revolution. Lefteri shows how state authorities are "unable to govern" or "govern in name only" (Norton, 2003, p. 101). Besides the Assad regime, there are ISIS and vandals "claiming to be an official representative of the state" and are "competing for resources and power" (Norton, 2003, p. 101-102). After a week of fishing Firas's corpse from the river, Nuri and Afra lose their son Sami in a bombing that hit their house which also turned Afra blind. After all the tragic deaths and destructions, Afra wouldn't agree to leave Aleppo until Nuri is stopped at a checkpoint and is threatened to be killed if he does not take the side of the army: "I was stopped by the army. They held a gun to my chest" (Lefteri, 2019, p. 47). Fearing losing her husband and avoiding being called to collect his corpse, Afra agrees to flee Aleppo. People's need to flee Syria to a safer place or to secure a safe place within the country raises "criminal and individual opportunism, which would be unconstrained" (Norton, 2003, p. 102). Smugglers are among those individual criminals who would "change their rates on a whim" (Lefteri, 2019, p. 18). Fleeing the country requires money to pay smugglers and buy the necessary equipment to ride seas and avoid drowning. Hence, one's life is secured only if money is available which means that the security level is related to one's financial conditions.

Similar to Darke's book, the worsening environmental side in Aleppo is highlighted in Lefteri's novel. The narrative details how, for instance, the Queiq river has become "full of rubbish. In the winter they fished out the bodies of men and boys" amongst them is Mustafa's son Firas, "[t]heir hands were tied. Bullets in their heads" (Lefteri, 2019, p. 19). Mustafa, Nuri's cousin, and business partner beekeeper volunteers in registering the dead bodies' identities, if any are found, or writes any distinguishing features until his own son is found to be the last one to record in his black book. Having his farm and beehives burned by the "vandals", and later his son murdered by the "army", Mustafa shoots two soldiers in revenge and flees the country to join his wife and daughter in the UK. Besides the awful environmental condition in the country, the text shows the conflicting powers which make Aleppo a battlefield. The narrative shows that Mustafa's attachment to the city and what kept him behind in Aleppo is his farm and beehives. Once this attachment to the place is destroyed along with the murder of his son, Mustafa takes his decision to leave the country.

The narrator, Nuri, gives an urban description of the city before and after the revolution. Each chapter has two parts. The first part is written in the present tense as it focuses on the protagonists' struggle in the United Kingdom as refugees. The second part describes their life in Aleppo or part of their journey through Europe. Artistically, Aleppo is portrayed as an almost idyllic place where its people enjoy the warmth of family and friends, and hard work performed with respect for nature, particularly for bees. At the same time, the narrative depicts the horrific conditions and the impact of the war on the city, and how the "muezzin call[s] to empty houses to come and pray" because its people are either killed or have sought refuge elsewhere (Lefteri, 2019, p. 44). As he walks the streets, he sees "burnt cars, lines of filthy washing hanging from abandoned terraces, electric wires dangling low over the streets, bombed-out shops, blocks of flats with their roofs blown off ... It all stank of death and burnt rubber" (Lefteri, 2019, p. 45). Not only the city of Aleppo that has been turned into a gothic land, "villages [are] burnt, people flooding out like a river to get away, the women in terror because paramilitaries [are] on the loose and they feared being raped" (Lefteri, 2019, p. 45). Yet, the narrative has hints of hope. Amongst all this destruction and ugliness, Nuri finds a "damask rose bush in full bloom", closes his eyes and breathes in the smell, pretending that he has not seen "the things [he's] seen" (Lefetri, 2019, p. 45). This detailed description of the city under war emphasises that Aleppo is, indeed, becoming feral.

Lefteri symbolises the impact of feral conditions and chaos in Aleppo through the psychological status of the characters. Both Nuri and Afra experience trauma although in different forms. the obvious reason of Afra's blindness, for example, is the explosion that caused the death of her son Sami. However, it is also possible that it is "the result of severe trauma" (Lefteri, 2019, p. 246). Afra confirms that "It wasn't the bomb that blinded [her]", but that she "saw Sami die". And that when it all went black" (Lefteri, 2019, p. 248). While Afra's trauma is manifested in her blindness, Nuri's trauma is more metaphoric. While crossing the borders to Turkey and then Greece, Nuri notices a boy whose name is Mohammed and at the same age of his deceased son Sami. Nuri protects Mohammed as if he is his own son to the extent that he gives him Sami's passport, so they can be registered as a family in Greece. On the rubber boat and in the middle of the sea, Nuri notices a young woman looking at him and how he is trying to encourage Mohammed. The woman shares the same experience of losing a son which makes her aware of Nuri's fear. She tells Nuri, "I lost my son too. It's just that . . . I know. I know what it's like. The void. It's black like the sea" (Lefteri, 2019, p. 121). The void and blackness that Nuri experiences are illustrated through the character of Mohammed. Nuri keeps asking and acting as if there is a boy and he is playing with a marble. It is only toward the end of the text when Afra tells Nuri that Mohammed fell off the boat and that he does not exist anymore. Afra does not tell Nuri this earlier because she "thought [he] needed him" (Lefteri, 2019, p. 336). It is the thought of having his son Sami still alive represented in the character of Mohammed that helps Nuri stay strong to support his wife Afra during their journey until they reach the UK. Through the characterisation of Nuri and Afra, Lefteri highlights the impact of and the mutual impact of the feral conditions in Aleppo as well as the places refugees encounter on their mental and physical health.

CONCLUSION

Karachi, Cairo, Damascus, and Aleppo are just representative examples of feral cities. The risk of these cities going beyond the categories of "yellow" and "red" ferality is high. The selected texts show how the seemingly peaceful and promising life people have in postcolonial cities is not guaranteed to be permanent. Lefteri describes life in cities like Aleppo, using the metaphor of Lego house. Afra keeps the remnants of a house her late son Sami had built, imagining the house he and his family would live in when they arrive in England. He used to tell his parents that "there'll be no bombs there" and "the houses won't break like these do" (Lefteri, 2019, p. 52-53). However, Sami is killed because he "had been born into a world where everything could break. Real houses crumbled, and fell apart. Nothing was solid in Sami's world"; yet he was trying "to imagine a place where the buildings didn't fall down around him" (Lefteri, 2019, p. 53). With all the problems on the governmental, economic, moral, and environmental levels that the cities under consideration, here, suffer from, they have high potential of turning feral as discussed in the undertaken works.

Besides highlighting the bad governance of postcolonial government, the selected texts call for deeper engagement in urban planning and design processes to make it more inclusive via the choice of female protagonists. The analysis of the selected texts shows that the right to the city should not be limited to the right of living in urban areas. It is of great significance to allow inhabitants the right to participate in a city's ongoing planning and production. If the citizens are given the right to participate in the creation and production of urban planning, it is believed that the chance of enhancing the quality of life in a city and in raising the level of responsibility of its people to maintain the "health of the city". Otherwise, preventing and/or limiting people from participating in the decision-making of the urban planning of their cities leads to the creation of discriminating urban space. Consequently, people having low humanitarian living conditions will affect their quality of life not only physically but also psychologically. There is a mutual impact between the health of the city and the health of its people.

Shedding light on the postcolonial cities in this chapter foregrounds further future research. For example, the cities under scrutiny in this chapter are postcolonial and suffer from political dilemmas which increase their level of ferality. However, feral aspects in different types of cities with different political and economic statuses might exist at different levels. A multidisciplinary approach to studying urban space in different contexts would enrich and widen the study of feral cities in hope of enhancing the quality of life.

REFERENCES

Amar, P. (2013). *The security archipelago: Human-security states, sexuality, politics and the end of neoliberalism.* Duke University Press.

Brownlee, J. (2013). *Violence against copts in Egypt.* Carnegie Endowment for International Peace.

Bunker, R. J. (2014). The emergence of feral and criminal cities: US Military implications in a time of austerity. *The Land Warfare Papers, 99*(2), 1–14.

Call, C. T. (2008). The fallacy of the "Failed State." *Third World Quarterly, 29*(8), 1491–1507. doi:10.1080/01436590802544207

Darke, D. (2014). *My House in Damascus.* HAUS Publishing. doi:10.2307/j.ctt1zxsm5n

Dorman, W. (2011). Of demolitions and donors: The problematics of state interventions in informal Cairo. In D. Singerman (Ed.), *Cairo contested: Governance, urban space, and global modernity* (pp. 262–290). American University of Cairo Press.

Elyachar, J. (2003). Mappings of power: The State, NGOs, and international organizations in the informal economy of Cairo. *Comparative Studies in Society and History, 45*(3), 571–605. doi:10.1017/S0010417503000264

Group, I. C. (2014). *Policing urban violence in Pakistan.* Asia Report.

Harvey, D. (2012). *Rebel cities: From the right to the city to the urban revolution.* Verso.

Herbert, C. (2014). Postcolonial cities. In K. McNamara (Ed.), *The Cambridge companion to the city in literature* (pp. 200–215). Cambridge University Press. doi:10.1017/CCO9781139235617.017

Jordan, D. (2008). *Apocalypse: Living dangerously, population and the looming disasters of the 21st century.* Chipmunka Publishing.

Kelman, I., & Clark-Ginsberg, A. (2022). An urban governance framework for including environmental migrants in sustainable cities. *Climate (Basel), 10*(8), 121. doi:10.3390/cli10080121

Kilani, K. (2019). *Fleeing the ring road.* Al-Mahroosa Publisher Ltd.

Koonings, K., & Kruijt, D. (2007). *Fractured cities: Social exclusion, urban violence & contested spaces in Latin America.* Zed Books Ltd. doi:10.5040/9781350220225

Lefteri, C. (2019). *The Beekeeper of Aleppo.* Manilla Press.

Linz, J. (2000). *Totalitarian and authoritarian regimes*. Lynne Rienner Publishers. doi:10.1515/9781685850043

Macaluso, A., & Briscoe, I. (2015). Trapped in the city: Communities, insecurity and urban life in fragile cities. *Knowledge Platform Security and Rule of Law*, 1-15.

Norton, R. J. (2003). Feral cities. *Naval War College Review*, 56(4), 98–106.

Post, E. A. (2018). Cities and politics in the developing world. *Annual Review of Political Science*, 21(1), 115–133. doi:10.1146/annurev-polisci-042716-102405

Pourya Asl, M. (Ed.). (2022). *Gender, place, and identity of South Asian women*. IGI Global., doi:10.4018/978-1-6684-3626-4

Rafiq, A. (2016). Operation Karachi: Pakistan's military retakes the city. *National Interest*.

Rashidi, Y. E. (2016). *Chronicle of a Last Summer*. Tim Duggan Books.

Shah, N. (2022). *How do we design gender-sensitive cities? Start by listening to women and other genders. Question of Cities: Forum for Nature*. People, and Sustainability.

Sims, D. (2010). *Understanding Cairo: The logic of a city out of control*. American University of Cairo Press.

Singerman, D. (2002). The Politics of Emergency Rule in Egypt. *Current History (New York, N.Y.)*, 101(651), 29–35. doi:10.1525/curh.2001.101.651.29

Smith, C. E. (2015). State, violence, mobility and everyday life in Cairo, Egypt. *Theses and Dissertations-Geography*, 34(6), 1–178.

Solomon, E. (2012). *Darkness at noon in the mind of fearful Damascus*. https://www.reuters.com/article/us-syria-damascus-mood-idUSB RE8B30RF20121204

Tanweer, B. (2013). *The Scatter Here is Too Great*. Random House India.

Tawfik, K. A. (2008). *Utopia*. Bloomsbury Qatar Foundation publishing.

Chapter 2
Dystopia and Heterotopia:
Poetics and Politics of Space in Khaled Hosseini's *A Thousand Splendid Suns*

Jason Tan Jian Wei
Universiti Sains Malaysia, Malaysia

Moussa Pourya Asl
https://orcid.org/0000-0002-8426-426X
Universiti Sains Malaysia, Malaysia

ABSTRACT

The traditional classification of city spaces in Afghan literature in English as either utopian or dystopian overlooks the possibility of other spaces existing within the same spatial structure. This chapter argues that although Khaled Hosseini's A Thousand Splendid Suns is widely known to be teeming with exclusively dystopian elements, the novel depicts the functioning of alternative spaces within the same spatial realities. The authors use Foucault's notion of heterotopia to examine how the actuality of such different spaces throughout the novel allows the reimagining of alternate ways of life for the female characters. Drawing upon Foucault's six principles of heterotopia, the analysis underlines that despite the predominantly dystopian portrayal of the country in the novel, multiple physical and imaginary heterotopias are shown as operating whereby the characters, especially the female ones, are able to reimagine themselves away from the dreads of the chaotic reality.

INTRODUCTION

Over the past few decades, spatiality has become an important concept in literary

DOI: 10.4018/978-1-6684-6650-6.ch002

and cultural studies. It is widely perceived that the rise of spatiality as a critical theory in recent decades has been "aided by a new aesthetic sensibility that came to be understood as postmodernism" (Tally Jr, 2013, p. 3). Within the field of literary studies, space is commonly understood through the binary of utopia and dystopia, with the former being defined as an ideal place better than one's current setting and the latter being described as the worst place possible (Asl, 2020). The values associated with each term are thus in contradistinction with one another. Since World War II, popular culture has played a crucial role in the development of dystopian writing, which has served to prophesize the future of our contemporary world should negative sociopolitical practices persist. In contrast, those who oppose the dystopian trend have generally opted to explore the opposite notion of "critical utopia" that originates from a postmodern perspective (Baccolini & Moylan, 2003). Both dystopia and utopia focus on spatiality and are argued to be "two sides of the same coin" (Mustafa, 2021, p. 2). The utopian discourse pictures an ideal society that is controlled, harmonious, and favorable. In other words, a utopia is a perfect place where everything and everyone exists in an everlasting harmonious state. In short, utopianism is "a social phenomenon that is expressed in various ways, where there is a dream and desire for better life" (Mustafa, 2021, p. 2). On the other hand, the term dystopia refers to the actualization of social control for the formation of a horrifying social reality. In literary works, dystopias represent the "social fears and anxieties of humanity in an extrapolated way" which in turn speculates the "negative possibilities for the future of humanity" (Mustafa, 2021, p. 2). Hence, a dystopia is widely understood as a negative version of a utopia.

Since 9/11 events in the United States and the subsequent invasion of Afghanistan by a US-led army, the concept of dystopia has often been used as the foundational and inseparable attribute of Afghan literature in English. It is commonly argued that contemporary Afghan writers depict the landscapes or spaces of Afghanistan as purely dystopian (Fitzpatrick, 2009; Ivanchikova, 2017; Lam, 2009; Sinno, 2020). However, the classification of space as either utopian or dystopian overlooks the possibility of a different space that could exist within the same spatial reality. As the postcolonial critic, Bill Ashcroft asserts, a dystopian discourse commonly leads to the formation of utopian narrative that underscores the possibility of a "radically changeable world" caused by the hope for a better future while being in a state of dystopia (Ashcroft, 2016, p. 37). In this relation, the Afghan American writer Khaled Hosseini's novels have been similarly perceived to be of a dystopian nature as the stories often revolve around the atrocities of the wars, the cruelties of the fundamentalists, the horrors of extremism, and the oppression of individuals (Khan, 2017; Qamar & Shakeel, 2015; Shameem, 2014; Stuhr, 2011; Yeasmin, 2020). The present chapter aims to examine Hosseini's *A Thousand Splendid Suns* (2007) to demonstrate how it depicts the functioning of alternative safe spaces within the same dystopian realities. To achieve this goal, we draw upon Michel Foucault's (1986) concept of heterotopia to examine how the portrayal of such safe spaces throughout the novel provides an alternate way of life for its female characters within the confines of a dystopian reality. A close reading of the text underlines the attributes of such other places in accordance with Foucault's six principles of heterotopia, which refers to the space where there is resistance against surrounding forces of oppression. In other words, within the existing dystopias and their oppressive conditions, there is a possibility that smaller utopias can be formed that can help to change the status quo, albeit temporarily. Heterotopias, as Karkov (2020) observes, "identify multiple places that were set apart from, while still existing in, the larger world – worlds within worlds and placeless places or places out of place" (as cited in Mustafa, 2021, p. 3). In other words, the smaller utopias can act as a space which is resistant to the oppressive forces of a particular society. In what follows, the chapter will first review the related literature within the field. Then, it will elaborate on the concepts of utopia, dystopia, and heterotopia. Next, the analysis of the novel based on Foucault's principles of heterotopia will be carried out.

LITERATURE REVIEW

Dystopian Cities and Places in Afghan Literature in English

The setting of Afghanistan that is affected by war and conflict contributes to the dystopian perspectives of various authors who opt to situate their characters' lives within the contemporary conditions of the country. Scholars have pointed out that Afghan diasporic writers form their dystopian perspective through the analysis of a "war-torn Afghanistan" (Yeasmin, 2020, p. 389) caused by "foreign invading powers" (Khan, 2017, p. 86). In like manner, Banu (2016) focuses on "the tragic war and its impact on the lives of ordinary citizens" to show the intrinsically dystopian nature of such narratives (p. 180). Similarly, Dharmani and Singh (2018) and Yawari (2011) highlight the dystopian perspective by looking at the "hostile and oppressive circumstances" that the characters face in contemporary Afghan literature in English (Dharmani & Singh, 2018, p. 209). Furthermore, and in relation to the "space for discrimination, oppression and exclusion" in the novels, Kabeer and Chaudhary (2020) provide an interesting perspective through the analysis of racial and ethnic identities which play a vital role in the formation of a dystopian reality in contemporary Afghanistan (p. 1415). In short, the existing body of criticism on Afghan literature in English confirm the widespread portrayal of the country as purely dystopian, which is chiefly caused by its historical and socio-political environment and marred by years of war and conflict.

Besides, many critics have pointed out that contemporary Afghan literature in English often focuses on the oppression of women in both public and domestic places in the country. The dominance of patriarchal power and culture in Afghan society has led to an annihilating oppression of women in the society that is artistically shown by the sufferings of female characters in the stories (Agustini, 2014; Chaudhary, 2020; Dhakal, 2020; Gordan & Almutairi, 2013; Joyia, et al., 2017; Rani, 2020; Sapkota, 2020; Shabanirad & Seifi, 2015; Siahmansouri & Hoorvash, 2020; Singh, 2022; Wulandari, 2012). Feminist readings of Afghan literature in English have shown that gender oppression is deeply entrenched within the society through the patriarchal impositions of cultural values and norms, hence reaffirming the portrayal of Afghanistan as a dystopian society. However, the feminist perspective highlights a new source of plight for the female characters, who are subjected not only to the general dystopia of Afghanistan but are further oppressed by the patriarchal values entrenched within their society. This view has been dominant in feminist analysis of Muslim female characters in contemporary South Asian and Middle Eastern literature in English (Pourya Asl, 2020, 2022; Hadi & Asl, 2022; Pourgharib et al., 2022).

Within this context and in relation of Khaled Hosseini's novel *A Thousand Splendid Suns* (2007), Stuhr (2011) similarly observes the state of the country in the novel as a dystopia, where there is rampant oppression everywhere, especially for the women caused by the "devastation of wars, civil chaos, mindless cruelty, and rampant injustice" (p. 54). The country is controlled by the "whims of outside forces" and women have little influence over their own lives (Stuhr, 2011, p. 53). Shameem (2014) agrees with Sthur's dystopian perspective of Afghanistan in Hosseini's novel and further highlights the issue by mentioning the "double subjugation" faced by women "in the form of patriarchal authority and the oppression emanating from the persistent conditions of conflict" (p. 62). These authors take into account the historical, political and social factors to support their dystopian perspective of Afghanistan in the context of the novel. In addition, Shapiro (2010) also highlights the dystopian perspective present in the novel by analyzing and discussing the effects of male oppression which is socially accepted as a norm among those living there. Through the observation of male dominance in the novel which stems from a patriarchal society that greatly undermines the independence, social mobility, and educational opportunities for South Asian and Middle Eastern women, Shapiro (2010) shows how dystopian elements for the female characters are created by the male dominated society which has practiced and accepted the subjugation of women as the norm.

In relation to the dystopian perspectives which are widely shared among some researchers in their study of the novel, *A Thousand Splendid Suns*, there are others who study the dystopian perspective while focusing on the efforts to preserve the autonomy of women within the novel, thus hinting at the existence of difference spatial realities. Andrews (2016) argues that while the women in the novel remain subjugated by the patriarchal society which they live in, they do not simply succumb to the dystopian life and instead "strive for freedom in spite of the limits imposed on them by their families, religion and patriarchal society" (p. 5). The optimism and hope which are vital parts of Andrew's argument hints at the presence of a heterotopia as it shows that even women who live in oppressive environments are capable of "reinventing" their image (Andrews, 2016, p. 5). It is shown that the dystopian perspective is generally accepted by all the authors mentioned as the main perception of Afghanistan within the context of Hosseini's novel. These insights help provide a brief yet concise view of the state of Afghanistan as a dystopia in the novel.

With this critical review of the existing body of literature on spatial matters in Anglophone literature of Afghanistan and Hosseini's novel, it is now important to note the ambiguous nature of both utopias and dystopias. Utopias and dystopias are highly flexible concepts that can be wielded to serve various formal or political purposes (Asl, 2019). They are dependent on the context, or rather the social environment of the ones using such terminology to label or describe a certain space. For example, a utopia can be roughly defined as a place that is better than the current living conditions faced by a person or group of people. On the other hand, dystopias are known as the "dark side" of a utopia (Baccolini & Moylan, 2003, p. 1). Hence, it can be roughly defined as a space that is worse than the space that is currently being experienced by a person or a group. The flexible nature of these terms has given rise to various types of utopias and dystopias, developed and imagined by various authors. Critics who use these concepts in their critical readings utilize them to detect the bias or perspective that is being undertaken by the writer in their depiction of a utopian or dystopian space. Furthermore, the critical readings conducted with the concept of utopia or dystopia in mind can be related or further explored with other critical theories. For example, a popular form of utopianism is based on the idea of imperialism, where a certain power which exerts its control over everyone and everything is justified as a means to produce a utopia (Ashcroft, 2012). As such, this notion has been linked to today's postcolonial literary theory to understand the ideology and effect of postcolonialism in literary texts. In other words, the concepts of utopia and dystopia can be used as steppingstones towards other forms of critical readings by first identifying the ideology which is being used by the author to determine whether a space is classified as a utopia or a dystopia.

THEORY AND METHOD

Utopia, Dystopia, and Heterotopia: A Conceptual Framework

The main concepts that will be used in this study to analyze Khaled Hosseini's *A Thousand Splendid Suns* (2007) are the notions of utopia, dystopia, and heterotopia. The concepts of utopia and dystopia are based on the general definitions used by various authors while the concept of heterotopia is based on the six principles introduced by Michel Foucault (1986) in reference to the physical and imaginative spaces in the novel. The term "utopia" has been defined by various scholars based on their own understanding of the term. According to Sinno (2020), the term "utopia" should not to be understood based on its dictionary-based definition, which explains it as an ideal, non-existent paradise. Instead, it should be interpreted based on the context, meaning that utopia refers to places that are "founded on identifications," and its value is based on the human interactions which carry significant meaning to an individual or group, rather than "inherited religious identities or strict biological relationships" (Sinno, 2020, p. 180). More importantly, utopian places signify places that are resistant to the status quo of their environments, serving as a "mirror" which exposes the prevalent issues within the society. The understanding of utopias is vital for the overall analysis of space within the context of Hosseini's novel.

Similar to the concept of utopia, various authors have had their own unique definitions of the term dystopia, but they generally agree that dystopias are the opposite of utopias. Mutekwa (2013) defines dystopia as "nightmarish" by comparing it to the notions of heaven and hell in Christian cosmology (p. 99). Baccolini and Moylan (2003) present the notion of dystopia as "the dark side of utopia", referring to them as places which are characteristically worse in comparison to the current living spaces which we are in (p. 1). This description of dystopia is further emphasized as Baccolini and Moylan (2003) refer to these spaces also as "the realm of utopia's underside" (p. 2). These interpretations of dystopias highlight the importance of identifying dystopias within the text as its presence illustrates the oppressive environment which threatens the stability and well-being of the characters in the novel.

Michel Foucault's (1986) posthumous essay, "Of Other Spaces: Utopias and Heterotopias" introduces the author's original take on the concept of heterotopia. He states that utopias are vastly different from heterotopias, as utopias are imaginary spaces "with no real place" (Foucault, 1986, p. 24) while heterotopias are spaces which are "both plausible and existent yet possesses amazing traits that are extraneous to it or that ironically contravene its own spatial characters and configurations" (Panigrahi, 2019, p. 65). In other words, Foucault's theory of heterotopia suggests that heterotopic space is "a dubious space where both the 'real' and the 'imaginary' coexist, where an order and its violation are coeval, where a space meets both its real and mythic contestations" (Panigrahi, 2019, p. 66). According to Mustafa (2021), the term heterotopia refers to the space where there is resistance against surrounding forces of oppression, introduced by Foucault which focuses on the "cultural analysis of space" (p. 3).

Foucault's concept of heterotopic space relies on six principles which are used to identify such spaces. The first principle mentions that probably every culture in the world is capable of constituting heterotopias. However, heterotopias tend to take varied forms which are based on the culture it is derived from, thus there can be no universal form of heterotopia. Next, the second principle mentions that the function of existing heterotopias may change over the course of history. This is because while each heterotopia has a precise and fixed function within a society, it can also have other functions which are dependent on the culture in which it is based on. The third principle of heterotopia focuses on the juxtaposition of several spaces in a single real space. These several spaces, which are by themselves incompatible are juxtaposed in a heterotopic space. Furthermore, the fourth principle mentions the link between heterotopias and slices in time. Heterochronies, as Foucault has termed them, functions when "men arrive at a sort of absolute break with their traditional time" (Foucault, 1986, p. 26). Examples of such spaces would include cemeteries and museums. The fifth principle of heterotopic spaces mentions that such spaces "presuppose a system of opening and closing that both isolates them and makes them penetrable" (Foucault, 1986, p. 26). In other words, such spaces are not open to the public and require certain rites or purifications to be performed before entry is permitted. These spaces may include places such as barracks or prisons. The sixth and final principle of heterotopias is that such spaces are related to all the remaining space in terms of their function. This would include heterotopias of illusion and compensation. Foucault uses examples such as the brothel and the Jesuit colonies to illustrate the heterotopias of illusion and compensation respectively. The heterotopia of illusion is one where the reality of life becomes an illusion or fantasy which is not real. In contrast, the heterotopia of compensation "seemed to unfold the disorderly living into regulated and organized colonies" (Chowdhury, 2019, p. 6). The six principles of heterotopia introduced by Foucault will be a guide to the analysis of heterotopic spaces present in Hosseini's novel *A Thousand Splendid Suns* (2007).

RESULTS AND FINDINGS

Dystopian Places in *A Thousand Splendid Suns*

Multiple settings throughout the story can be labelled as dystopias from the perspective of the affected characters. These spaces include both the public and private spaces in the novel. One of such settings that can be identified within the novel comes from Mariam's roots, the "kolba" in which she was raised. Jalil had confined both her and Nana to the isolated space which she spent her first 15 years of life in with little to no contact with the outside world (Hosseini, 2007, p. 98). Within this secluded and isolated space, Mariam was confined to a dystopian space. She experienced constant verbal harassment, mental torture and gaslighting from her own mother who sought to manipulate her loyalty and obedience. This situation showed the nightmarish social space experienced by Mariam, highlighting the social fears and anxiety faced by her mother which was a leading factor in the formation of the mentioned dystopia.

Furthermore, another dystopian location that can be identified in the novel is Jalil's house. The setting was initially misperceived as a utopia by Mariam, Jalil's illegitimate daughter who was born to Nana who was previously a cleaner working in Jalil's house. This is because her newfound home was seemingly a better place in comparison to the space she was living in at the time. However, this fantasy was quickly shattered when Mariam stepped out of the confines of her "kolba" and attempted to visit her father in Herat. The disillusionment faced by Mariam altered the perception of the space she once sought after, corrupting the utopian glamour it once held, thus revealing the dystopian nature of the setting. The perception changed because Jalil's house had then become a place which was worse than the space she was living in. In addition to the fact that he had allowed her to disgrace herself by sleeping on the streets of Herat right outside his home a few nights before, his single irresponsible comment, "Goddamn it, Mariam, don't do this to me" which he gave in response to her one and only desperate plea for help from him, caused a lifelong rift between them from that point on (Hosseini, 2007, p. 34).

The dystopian aspect of Jalil's house is further highlighted by the forced arranged marriage which took place there, sealing Mariam's fate and tying it to Rasheed's. Due to the Afghani socio-cultural norm, a father is allowed to marry off his daughter to another man, with or without the consent of the daughter (Yeasmin, 2020). Mariam experienced this imposition from her father when she was taken in after her mother committed suicide. This shows the dystopian nature of Jalil's house as Mariam was already experiencing emotional loss and turmoil from the unexpected death of her mother which was aggravated by the forced marriage to a complete stranger without her consent. The space Mariam experiences becomes progressively dystopian, or worse than the space she was used to.

The dystopian scene continuously shifts, as Mariam trades Herat for Kabul, Jalil's house for Rasheed's. With a will "as imposing and immovable as the Safid-koh mountains looming over Gul Daman" (Hosseini, 2007, p. 47), Rasheed would dictate Mariam's life from then on. Rasheed displays obvious signs of misogyny that would translate to the oppressive environment that Mariam would come to survive in. Although Mariam's initial illusive take on her married life was one filled with optimism, it soon shattered as the reality of Rasheed's manipulative behavior comes to light. The spaces within the confines of the housing compound of Rasheed's house becomes a dystopia all on its own, separated from the dystopian state of Afghanistan beyond its gate, yet mirroring it in every single way. Rasheed becomes a symbolic representation of what Afghanistan had become within the context of the novel—a fickle minded, misogynic, and oppressive figure which only aims to beat down the less fortunate and profit off their suffering.

Midway through the novel, the warlords begin fighting one another for control over various parts of Afghanistan including Kabul, the city which the main female protagonists reside, turning the city into a dystopia filled with constant rocket fire, rape, and pillage. The "rattling of automatic gunfire" and "rockets whining overhead" were the constant melodies of Afghanistan, filling the dreams of the people "with fire and detached limbs and the moaning of the wounded" (Hosseini, 2007, p. 112). This violent setting thus becomes the norm for in the daily lives of the people of Kabul, highlighting the dystopian nature of the city which has fallen into the hands of the warlords who struggle to maintain control over it. The horror of the conflict matches the visual description of Afghanistan in contemporary Afghan literature in English (Yeasmin, 2020; Khan, 2017), where "every day, bodies were found tied to trees, sometimes burned beyond recognition. Often, they'd been shot in the head, had had their eyes gouges out, their tongues cut out" (Hosseini, 2007, p. 114).

The streets of Kabul, as one of the key spaces traversed by the people of Afghanistan on a daily basis, have also turned into a dystopia, especially for the female characters in the novel. Under the rule of the Taliban, women are not allowed to be outside their homes without a male chaperone. Laila, desperate to see her daughter whom she left at the orphanage for economic reasons could not get her selfish husband to accompany her. She was caught by the Taliban several times, resulting in a beating by an "assortment of wooden clubs, fresh tree branches, short whips, slaps, often fists" (Hosseini, 2007, p. 192). Despite the initial claims by the Taliban that order would be restored to the streets of Kabul, their presence has only reinforced the notion of dystopia in the said space, with women being the primary victims of their violent whims. Hence, the dystopian nature of the streets of Kabul is made clear through the brutally enforced rules under the Taliban control.

Public spaces related to music have also become dystopias under the rule of the Taliban. Public spaces used for the purpose of performances and entertainment are often depicted as spaces where the people can find some form of comfort from their everyday lives. However, the Taliban has banned the idea of public performances and enforced their new rules through rampant violence, quickly turning it into a nightmarish place. For example, "Khabarat, Kabul's ancient music ghetto, was silenced. Musicians were beaten and imprisoned, their rubabs tamboura, and harmoniums trampled upon" (Hosseini, 2007, p. 168). The destruction of the spaces associated with art and music by the Taliban has further increased the feelings of dystopia in the city of Kabul. In short, the private and public places, or the urban spaces in general, are all experienced and navigated by female characters in the novel as dystopian, generating in them a constant feeling of oppression, horror, and hopelessness.

Spaces of Heterotopia in *A Thousand Splendid Suns*

Within the dystopian spaces which the characters find themselves stranded in, there are spaces formed between them which can be perceived as heterotopias, alternative safe spaces which allow the characters in the novel to explore and express themselves by means of their own choosing, especially for the female characters who face not only the oppressive environment formed by the surrounding violence, but also face the subjugation of the patriarchal society of Afghanistan. There are both physical and imaginary spaces of heterotopia found within the novel's setting, which include both private and public spaces that are reconstructed and repurposed into heterotopic spaces by the affected characters.

Hosseini's depiction of Rasheed's house and the spaces within the confines of the housing compound is presented as "an incongruous pool of heterotopic spaces" (Panigrahi, 2019, p. 72) as can be seen from the different emotions and realities which characterize the separate confined spaces within Rasheed's personal, hand-crafted dystopia. One of the private spaces that can be considered as a physical heterotopia in Hosseini's novel is the yard outside Rasheed's home. The two women, Laila and Mariam are often subjected to the abuse by their husband, Rasheed. Every day, "Rasheed's demands and judgements rained down on them like the rockets of Kabul" (Hosseini, 2007, p. 137). To escape the dystopia created by Rasheed at home, the women escape to the yard, a safe space where they enjoy their nightly ritual of having chai tea. The significance of this safe space, especially for Mariam is highlighted when she faces the death penalty for the murder of Rasheed. In her final moments, Mariam had "wished she could see Laila again, wished to hear the clangor of her laugh, to sit with her for a pot of chai and leftover halfway under a starlit sky" (Hosseini, 2007, p. 224). As the characters face the inescapable violence of their husband at home, they flee to the comfort of their safe space, which plays a vital role in their survival of the dystopian setting. From the previous scenario, the yard has been repurposed and transformed into a space which is within the confines of a dystopia yet separated from it at the same time. This juxtaposition of incompatible spaces reaffirms the label of the space as a heterotopia. While it is still a part of Rasheed's home, the interaction between Laila and Mariam who psychologically and emotionally support one another in their struggle to survive their dystopian environment has altered the function of the yard from a mere open space within the housing compound to a safe haven where the characters may find a brief reprieve from the daily inescapable hostility of their dystopian world. This representation of space is in line with one of Foucault's most defining characteristics of heterotopia, where a space negates the idea that it is an entity which is "homogenous, sedentary and enclosed" (Panigrahi, 2019, p. 67).

Although the relationship between Laila and Mariam did not start off on the best of things, their eventual reconciliation in response to Rasheed's dictatorship transforms the kitchen space into a heterotopic space. As Afghan society has deemed that its women are to be responsible for domestic chores such as cooking, reinforced by Rasheed's patriarchal world view, both Laila and Mariam find themselves confined to the kitchen space on a daily basis. However, it is within this enclosed space that the initial rift between the two women is bridged as they come to an understanding that the women mutually support one another to survive their shared hardships tied to their marital vows. As the women develop a mutual respect and understanding for one another, so much so that Mariam begins to treat Laila's daughter as her own, the kitchen space becomes more than just a space where the family's food is made, but has been transformed into a fluid space that contradicts the characteristics of the house which it is located in. Although it is a space where constant labor is required, the domestic activities carried out within the confines of this enclosed space generates emotional and spiritual support for the two women, thus showing that the spatial features are not fixed and are constantly changing. This characteristic of spatial heterogeneity is in line with the Foucauldian concept of heterotopia, as the kitchen space transcends its domestic purpose to become a heterotopic space.

Next, although the general perception of prisons in any country is that of a dystopia, the prisons of Afghanistan, at least through the depiction of Hosseini's novel is that of a heterotopia instead. Ironically, the prisons have become safe spaces where the people of Afghanistan are able to take shelter from the dystopian conditions of the outside world. As the "the whistling of rockets overhead" and "the long, frantic hammering of machine gun fire" become the norm of Afghanistan, it had become much safer to be confined behind the prison walls (Hosseini, 2007, p. 162). For example, Tariq's time in the Pakistani prison had allowed him to meet Salim, a man who would be responsible for his eventual escape from the harsh life he had once endured as a refugee. Salim's spoke to Tariq, a man he hardly knew then, in a "soft, fatherly voice" in answering to his queries about his deceased mother who had passed on while he was stuck in the Pakistani prison for seven years (Hosseini, 2007, p. 204). The goodwill of the imprisoned man went above and beyond when he "gave him his brother's address and phone number", providing him with a stable job and accommodation upon his release from the Pakistani prison (Hosseini, 2007, p. 204). The ironical contradiction of the general perception of the prison space transforms it into a heterotopic space for it has become "a compressed spatial field that includes in its confines places and people that are far off and beyond the nation's boundaries" (Panigrahi, 2019, p. 71). Within the confines of the Pakistani prison, the national boundaries which separate Afghanistan and Pakistan disappear, allowing Tariq who is an Afghan citizen to become part of the larger prison community that is fighting to survive the harsh climate within the prison as well as the life they face beyond their sentence. Hence, it can be seen that the prison has become a safe space for the people of Afghanistan, a reprieve from the destruction of the outside world and a space where people come together to aid those who have suffered from the conflict.

In relation to the prison space being a heterotopia due to the nature of the outside world that is worse than the life within the prison walls, the idea is further emphasized when combined with the subjugation by the patriarchy. When Mariam was sent to the Walayat women's prison, she had expected to suffer in her final days before being sentenced to the death penalty for murdering Rasheed. Unlike the streets of Kabul where the women were unable to go out without a male chaperone, they were "free to come and go to the (prison) courtyard as they pleased" (Hosseini, 2007, p. 219). Partly due to the "celebrity" status Mariam received for her strong stand against the patriarchy, she had received a warm welcome from the other female inmates (Hosseini, 2007, p. 219). For some of the other women who were serving their sentences, the prison also served as a safe space for them from their families. For example, one of the women had mentioned that "her father had sworn that the day she was released he would take a knife to her throat" (Hosseini, 2007, p. 220). The presence of children who were also serving their sentences in the women's prison further highlighted its function as a safe space, for they spent their days running "around, making up lively games", a luxury unattainable if they had been in Afghanistan (Hosseini, 2007, p. 219). Due to the strong patriarchal values of Afghan society that has long since subjugated its women and left them without much freedom, the prison had, in comparison, become a much better space for them to live in for they were released from the heavy burdens forcefully imposed by their respective families or husbands. Despite the poor living conditions of the prison, the women were somewhat happier than they were while they were free in the outside world. The contradiction of emotions where the imprisoned women feel more freedom while serving their sentence compared to when they were free in the outside world mirrors the contradiction in the supposed purpose of the prison, where it has become a space to escape external hostilities instead of a space purely for punishment. Furthermore, the prison serves as both a closed and open system, closed in the sense that it is excluded from the outside world and not accessible by the public, but open in the sense that it permits the entering of certain individuals into its exclusive system. This can be seen from how Mariam became part of the prison system for her show of courage against the oppressive patriarchy of Afghanistan, a shared experience of the women in the Walayat women's prison. Hence, the prison becomes a heterotopia, a safe space for the women population of Afghanistan which frees them from their burdens and responsibilities imposed upon them by the strong patriarchal values of the dominant Afghan society and culture.

In addition, another physical public space which is portrayed as a heterotopia in the novel is the communal tandoor. The communal cooking space is an alternative safe space for the female characters of the novel as they are enabled and empowered within this location to enjoy their time making meals with the company of others, safe from the oppressive environment formed by the patriarchy. It is within these places that women's "high pitched chatter" and "spiraling laughs" could be heard at the communal tandoor (Hosseini, 2007, p. 44). As we are told, "[t]his endless conversation, the tone plaintive but oddly cheerful, flew around and around in a circle. On and on it went, down the street, around the corner, in line at the tandoor" (Hosseini, 2007, p. 44). Based on the happy tone presented by the female characters who are grouped at the communal tandoor, one can conclude that the place serves as a safe spot for the female characters. This is because the women are able to leave the confines of their homes and reimagine and experience a different life for themselves. For Mariam, this temporary escape was all the more significant as it meant escaping the oppressive nature of Rasheed who constantly subjugates her autonomy at home. In addition to the emotional reprieve, the communal tandoor serves as a space where women from various social backgrounds mingle with one another, setting up a diverse, miniature world isolated from the male dominated social environment of the country it is located in. Based on the understanding of heterotopia by Foucault (1986), the juxtaposition of different spaces and locations that "are in themselves incompatible" which is a key characteristic of heterotopia qualifies the communal tandoor as a heterotopic space (p. 25).

Aside from the physical heterotopic spaces which exist within the context of Hosseini's novel, there are several imaginative spaces that likewise fit the characteristics of a heterotopic space based on Foucault's six defining principles. In the first part of the novel, Mariam's limited time with Mullah Faizullah at the kolba can be perceived as an imaginative heterotopic space, for she was allowed to learn, discover, and express herself in a safe space while being engulfed by the dystopian havoc that was her first home, the "kolba". Whereas Nana oppressed and limited her autonomy, Mullah Faizullah provided opportunities for Mariam to relieve her suffering by offering her chances at education to improve herself. Even in death, Nana's presence loomed over Mariam like a shroud but Mullah Faizullah once again provided the much needed safe space for her to properly grieve her passing and ensured her that the "seed for what she did was planted long ago" (Hosseini, 2007, p. 30). This situation shows that even within the dystopian setting of her life and home, developed and sustained by her own mother's fears, Mariam has the opportunity to experience a safe space which is resistant to the surrounding oppression. The imaginative space created through the bond between the two characters adheres to Foucault's second principle, which indicates that the function of a heterotopia changes according to the functions of society. As Mariam experiences a dramatic shift from a life with her mother to one without her, the function of the imaginary heterotopic space changes from one of nurture to one of emotional comfort.

Finally, an imaginative space which can be perceived as heterotopia is the space within the company of a loved one at home. Within a dystopian location, spaces established with loved ones can resist the surrounding oppressive environment. For example, Laila experiences imaginative heterotopic space when she is with Tariq, resisting the dystopian space of Afghanistan at war and her own home. The heterotopic space shifts continuously and is not fixed to any one place but is dependent on the presence of Tariq to enable the formation of a space resistant to the surrounding oppression. Laila recognizes the pattern and seeks Tariq's companionship as it presents a safe space for her to develop herself outside the confines of her dysfunctional home and the warring Afghanistan, for Tariq's presence deters the harassment from others who have taken up arms during the conflict. The spatial heterogeneity of said imaginary heterotopic space is in line with the Foucauldian concept of heterotopia, as the space created through companionship with Tariq transcends a simple bond of companionship to become a safe space from the surrounding dystopian conditions.

CONCLUSION

This chapter aimed to examine the poetics and politics of space as represented in Khaled Hosseini's *A Thousand Splendid Suns* (2007) in light of Michel Foucault's (1986) notion of heterotopia. To this end, the study first focused on literary representations of utopian and dystopian spaces to shed light on the functioning of alternative spaces that are created by characters to escape the restricting confines of the reality. The findings reveal that despite the obvious dystopian setting of Afghanistan presented in Hosseini's novel, the narrative depicts numerous safe spaces—i.e., physical and imaginative heterotopias—in which the characters, especially the females are able to reside in and temporarily escape the violence and chaos of the outside dystopian world. In light of Foucault's six principles of heterotopia, spaces that are detected as containing the appropriate characteristics to qualify them as safe spaces include both public and private places within the context of the novel. As the social and cultural landscape of Afghanistan transforms throughout the course of the novel because of various historical events, the general dystopian elements remain consistent despite the changing forces which occupy the land. Partly due to the patriarchal nature and values of the Afghan society, the female characters are portrayed as the main victims of their dystopian environments as they face the issue of double subjugation. The hardships of the fictional characters in the novel are in line with the stereotypically Orientalist views about the contemporary Afghan literature in English that perceive them as showing the Afghan women as passive victims of patriarchy. However, such essentialist perspectives have overlooked the possibility of heterotopias which have been shown to exist within the Afghan setting in this study. For example, spaces which are often depicted or perceived as dystopias, such as prisons, have been shown to qualify as heterotopic spaces where the characters are empowered and enabled to experience growth and safety from the surrounding dystopian conditions. In other words, although the depiction of Afghanistan as dystopia in the novel is in line with the existing criticism on Afghan literature in English, there still remains unexplored spaces where the Afghan people are able to thrive within the dizzy and violent landscape. These heterotopias which come from both public and private spaces highlight the importance of acknowledging the presence of other spaces which exist within the general dystopian space of Afghanistan.

In addition, as the characters in Hosseini's novel experience the dystopian space of Afghanistan, they display a yearning for a utopia, an imaginary place better than the one they are currently living in. The attempted escape by Mariam and Laila reaffirms this idea for they seek to escape the dystopian state of their home to another place which they have deemed to be a better place. The link between utopias and dystopias within the context of the novel manifests itself in the form of heterotopias, spaces with utopian characteristics which exist within the larger context of dystopian spaces. As Foucault explains, heterotopias exist as mirrors of utopias; spaces which are "directly opposite to utopia(s) and are the experiences between the real world and the utopian world" (Chowdhury, 2019, p. 4). The acknowledgement of the existence of heterotopias presents a more optimistic view of Afghanistan which is in contrast with the Orientalist representations of the country prevailing in western societies. Such a view may help to alter the general perception of Afghanistan as dystopia and instead recognise the opportunities for positive change and developments for the people living within the country. Hence, it is vital to understand that the complexity of space within a certain narrative should be properly explored instead of simply labelling them using oversimplified definitions such as the traditional binary of dystopias and utopias.

REFERENCES

Agustini, N. W. (2014). Feminism: The cases of Mariam and Laila in A Thousand Splendid Suns. *Humanis*, 9(1), 1–8.

Andrews, A. (2016). *(Re)Defining Afghan women characters as modern archetypes using Khaled Hosseini's A Thousand Splendid Suns and Asne Seierstad's The Bookseller of Kabul* [Master's Thesis, Liberty University]. Scholar's Crossing. https://digitalcommons.liberty.edu/masters/402

Ashcroft, B. (2012). Introduction: Spaces of utopia. *Spaces of Utopia, 2*(1), 1–17.

Ashcroft, B. (2016). *Utopianism in postcolonial literatures.* Routledge. doi:10.4324/9781315642918

Asl, M. P. (2019). Leisure as a space of political practice in Middle East women life writings. *GEMA Online Journal of Language Studies, 19*(3), 43–56. doi:10.17576/gema-2019-1903-03

Asl, M. P. (2020). The politics of space: Vietnam as a Communist heterotopia in Viet Thanh Nguyen's The Refugees. *3L: Language, Linguistics, Literature, 26*(1), 156–170. doi:10.17576/3L-2020-2601-11

Baccolini, R., & Moylan, T. (2003). *Dark horizons: Science fiction and the dystopian imagination.* Psychology Press.

Banu, S. S. (2016). Discrimination, war and redemption in Khaled Hosseini's The Kite Runner and A Thousand Splendid Suns. *Language in India, 16*(8), 180–193.

Chaudhary, P. (2020). Women resistance and power relation in Khaled Hosseini's A Thousand Splendid Suns. *Journal of Xi'an University of Architecture & Technology, 12*(4), 5493–5502.

Chowdhury, S. (2019). *Understanding heterotopia: Foucault's spatial context to society.* . doi:10.13140/RG.2.2.11385.11367

Dhakal, S. (2020). Endurance of women in Afghan society in Khaled Hosseini's A Thousand Splendid Suns (Book review). *Molung Educational Frontier, 10*(1), 229–233. doi:10.3126/mef.v10i0.34088

Dharmani, D., & Singh, R. (2018). Women as nation in Khaled Hosseini's A Thousand Splendid Suns. *Language in India., 18*(1), 209–217.

Fitzpatrick, C. (2009). New orientalism in popular fiction and memoir: An illustration of type. *Journal of Multicultural Discourses, 4*(3), 243–256. doi:10.1080/17447140902972305

Foucault, M., & Miskowiec, J. (1986). Of other spaces. *Diacritics, 16*(1), 22–27. doi:10.2307/464648

Gordan, M., & Almutairi, A. S. (2013). Resistance, a facet of post-colonialism in women characters of Khaled Hosseini's A Thousand Splendid Suns. *International Journal of Applied Linguistics and English Literature*, *2*(3), 240–247. doi:10.7575/aiac.ijalel.v.2n.3p.240

Hadi, N. H. A., & Asl, M. P. (2022). The real, the imaginary, and the symbolic: A Lacanian reading of Ramita Navai's City of Lies. *GEMA Online Journal of Language Studies*, *22*(1), 145–158. doi:10.17576/gema-2022-2201-08

Hosseini, K. (2007). *A Thousand Splendid Suns*. Bloomsbury Publishing.

Ivanchikova, A. (2017). Imagining Afghanistan in the aftermath of 9/11: Conflicting literary chronographies of one invasion. *Textual Practice*, *31*(1), 197–216. doi:10.1080/0950236X.2016.1237987

Joyia, M. I., Farooq, U., Ghafoor, S., & Gull, A. (2017). Courageous women: A study of resilience of women in Khaled Hosseini's novel A Thousand Splendid Suns. *Language in India*, *17*(1), 98–108.

Kabeer, H., & Chaudhary, P. (2020). Afghan minorities and ethnic tension in The Kite Runner and A Thousand Splendid Suns. *European Journal of Molecular and Clinical Medicine*, *7*(3), 1415–1425.

Khan, R. N. (2017). Representation of the Afghan national identity in Hosseini's A Thousand Splendid Suns. *Dialogue (Pakistan)*, *12*(1), 75–89.

Lam, M. (2009). The politics of fiction: A response to new orientalism in type. *Journal of Multicultural Discourses*, *4*(3), 257–262. doi:10.1080/17447140903198496

Mustafa, W. (2021). Paradise in hell: Mapping out utopian cartographies in Margaret Atwood's MaddAddam trilogy. *SAGE Open*, *11*(4), 1–9. doi:10.1177/21582440211061571

Mutekwa, A. (2013). "In this wound of life …": Dystopias and dystopian tropes in Chenjerai Hove's *Red Hills of Home*. *Journal of Literary Studies*, *29*(4), 98–115. doi:10.1080/02564718.2013.856662

Panigrahi, S. (2019). Shadowy lines and floating spaces: Amitav Ghosh's heterotopic imagination in The Shadow Lines. *South Asian Review*, *40*(1-2), 65–76. doi:10.1080/02759527.2019.1593747

Pourgharib, B., Hamkhiyal, S., & Asl, M. P. (2022). A non-orientalist representation of Pakistan in contemporary western travelogues. *GEMA Online Journal of Language Studies*, *22*(3), 103–118. doi:10.17576/gema-2022-2203-06

Pourya Asl, M. P. (2020). Spaces of change: Arab women's reconfigurations of selfhood through heterotopias in Manal al-Sharif's Daring to Drive. *KEMANUSIAAN the Asian Journal of Humanities*, *27*(2), 123–143. doi:10.21315/kajh2020.27.2.7

Pourya Asl, M. P. (Ed.). (2022). *Gender, place, and identity of South Asian women*. IGI Global., doi:10.4018/978-1-6684-3626-4

Qamar, S., & Shakeel, R. K. (2015). Representation of Afghan institution of marriage in Khaled Hosseini's and The Mountains Echoed and A Thousand Splendid Suns: A cultural study. *International Journal of English and Literature*, *5*(1), 57–64.

Rani, E. (2020). Feministic perspectives of Afghan women in Khaled Hosseini's A Thousand Splendid Suns. *A Journal of Composition Theory*, *13*(3), 665-669.

Sapkota, B. (2020). Ideological essentialization of Afghan women in Hosseini's A Thousand Splendid Suns. *The Batuk*, *6*(1), 55–62. doi:10.3126/batuk.v6i1.32628

Shabanirad, E., & Seifi, E. (2015). Postcolonial feminist reading of Khaled Hosseini's A Thousand Splendid Suns. *International Journal of Women's Research*, *3*(2), 241–254.

Shameem, B. (2014). Living on the edge: Women in Khaled Hosseini's A Thousand Splendid Suns. *Research Journal of English Language and Literature*, *2*(4), 62–66.

Shapiro, L. B. (2010). *Middle Eastern women's issues: An analysis of a Thousand Splendid Suns and the New York Times* [Doctoral dissertation]. University of Florida.

Siahmansouri, M., & Hoorvash, M. (2020). Heroic west, villainous east: A postcolonial interpretation of narrative structure in Khaled Hosseini's A Thousand Splendid Suns. *Journal of Research in Applied Linguistics*, *11*(2), 95–106.

Singh, G. (2022). Afghan women authors' discourses of resistance: Contesting interplay between gender, place, and identity. In M. P. Asl (Ed.), *Gender, Place, and Identity of South Asian Women* (pp. 152–177). IGI Global. doi:10.4018/978-1-6684-3626-4.ch008

Sinno, N. (2020). Utopian/dystopian Lebanon: Constructing place in Jabbūr al-Duwayhī's Sharīd al-manāzil. *Middle Eastern Literatures*, *23*(3), 177–197. doi:10.1080/1475262X.2021.1917831

Stuhr, R. A. (2011). *A Thousand Splendid Suns: Sanctuary and resistance*. https://repository.upenn.edu/library_papers/79

Tally, R. Jr. (2013). *Spatiality*. Routledge.

Wulandari, S. (2012). The oppression against women in Afghanistan portrayed in Khaled Hosseini's A Thousand Splendid Suns. *Diglossia: Jurnal Kajian Ilmiah Kebahasaan dan Kesusastraan, 4*(1), 1-11.

Yawari, A. W. (2011). *The inner strength of women in Khalid Hosseini's A Thousand Splendid Suns and Alice Walker's The Color Purple* [Master's thesis, Selcuk University]. Selcuk University Digital Archive Systems.

Yeasmin, F. (2020). Khaled Hosseini's A Thousand Splendid Suns: A saga of Afghanistan. *Research Journal of English Language and Literature., 8*(3), 381–390.

Chapter 3
Gender, Caste, and Class in Transnational Urban Spaces:
A Reading of Bharati Mukherjee's Novels

Shilpi Gupta
https://orcid.org/0000-0002-6786-6656
Vellore Institute of Technology, India

ABSTRACT

Bharati Mukherjee's novels The Tiger's Daughter (1971), Jasmine (1989), and Desirable Daughters (2002) depict transnational urban spaces by situating their characters in multiple geographies from Calcutta in India to major cities in America where the female protagonists are generally shown to have multiple identities based on caste, class, race, nationality, etc. By analyzing the characters' socio-economic positions, this chapter aims to explore how women are marginalized in transnational urban spaces based on their gender, class, and caste. It also seeks to examine how the women of caste and lower class are represented in transnational urban spaces. To achieve these objectives, the chapter employs Susan Friedman's the new geography of identities, Gayatri Spivak's notion of subalternity, Tabish Khair's distinction between Babu and Coolie, and Uma Chakravarti's discussion of caste as parallel to gender and class in order to examine the silences, gaps, and obstacles as present in the selected novels.

INTRODUCTION

Bharti Mukherjee is a well-known South Asian diaspora woman writer who has written several novels, some of which are best sellers. *The Tiger's Daughter* (1971),

DOI: 10.4018/978-1-6684-6650-6.ch003

Wife (1975), *Jasmine* (1989), *The Holder of the World* (1993), *Leave it to Me* (1997), *Desirable Daughters* (2002), *The Tree Bride* (2004), and two anthologies of short stories, *Darkness* (1985) and *The Middleman and Other Stories* (1988) are her major writings. Various research works are done on her novels, considering the tremendous shift in the writing style, cultural change, and character building. However, very rarely, Mukherjee's novels have become the focus of the intersection of caste, and class together with gender reading. In one of the interviews, she was questioned regarding whom her writing emphasized especially the novel *Desirable Daughters* which was recently published. Mukherjee replied that her upbringing was from an "exclusive caste and high class where she was taught to behave a certain way, speak the same politics, have the same accent" (Martos-Hueso & García-Ramírez, 2010, p. 134). She chose to write about high class because she wanted to write about a particular lifestyle from where she comes. She feels that "it was her sense of vanishing class that did not have the right to exist anymore" (ibid). As per her statement, it becomes an intriguing point to enter her texts to see how the writer has portrayed the caste together with class and gender in transnational urban spaces through her novels *The Tiger's Daughter* (1971), *Jasmine* (1989), and *Desirable Daughters* (2002) and how the women of lower caste and class are represented in her writing.

The chapter will specifically focus on caste and class as other factors which have become the reason for the double marginalization of women within the diasporic group in transnational urban spaces. The transnational urban space, for transnational migrants, is not limited to geographically bordered space of nation-state. Rather, it questions the nation-state's geographical boundaries and enters transnational spaces which theorize the interaction between First World and Third World, and the "borders," "borderlines" and "borderlands" between two binary opposites colonizers and colonized (Anzaldúa, 1987). Theoretically, people act in multiple geographical realms, and experience and perceive space accordingly. Thus, the concept of "multiple geographies" and the space between the nation-state (or sub-national regions) and the global sphere are seriously incorporated into research based on transnational spaces (Müller & Torp, 2009, p. 610). Both individuals and collective actors simultaneously perceive, experience, live within, and actively shape, various geographical orders and carry multiple identities.

The chapter will further employ the discussion given by Susan Stanford Friedman, "the new geography of identity," to underline the existing complexity of the multiplicity of identities carried by the South Asian diaspora woman which goes beyond gender (1998, p. 26). It is "polyvocal and often contradictory" (p. 19). Freidman says that the new geography of identity is influenced by postcolonial studies where the issue of travel, nomadism, diaspora, and the cultural hybridity produced by movement through space has a material reality and political urgency as well as figurative cogency. In this chapter, the new geography of identity will help examine the debate on gender and beyond gender to class, and caste, which keeps on changing relatively and spatially. To get closer to the texts, the approach in this chapter departs from the contribution made by an Indian diaspora writer Tabish Khair where he defines "reading" literature is to read the gaps, silences, obstacles, and noise in its language and its narratives" (Khair & Doubinsky, 2011, p. 11). According to the chapter, analyzing the socio-political background present in the novels and underlining the presence of caste in the suppression of women demands to point out the gaps, silences, obstacles, and noises in the novels. The chapter will unravel the silences, noises, and gaps present in the novel in understanding the portrayal of caste, class, and gender. Silences, noises, and gaps, here, refer to the space between metaphorical and literal meanings of literature and push the limits of language in the stylistics or the aesthetics of literature to non-language, the other side of the literature and narrative (Khair, 2011, pp. 6-11).

LITERATURE REVIEW

The term transnationalism gained its currency basically in the 1990s in different fields such as anthropology sociology, human geography, and literary studies. Transnationalism came to focus when transnational migrants became visible (Schiller et al.,1995, p. 48) which covered dual lives, speaking two or more languages, having connections in two or more countries (Portes et al., 1999, p. 217). Michael Peter Smith has theoretically defined transnational urbanism as an attempt to think systematically about the ways long-distance – often transborder – connections are increasingly organized through people leading lives in two places at once, living both "here" and "there" (Smith, 2001, p. 82). The lives living in two spaces or "multiple geographical spaces" as Müller and Torp (2009) say are significant in two ways (p. 611). First, social relationships that are stretched over long distances place into question in all sorts of ways how social researchers should understand the there-ness of social interaction. Second, the spatially distributed agency implicit in such geographically stretched networks of relationship raises questions about the nature and role of cities as nodes of concentrated interaction. The concept of transnational urbanism is an attempt to place the issues of spatial distanciation at the center of how cities should be understood. Rather than thinking about cities as principally contained – and indeed easily located – sites, transnational urbanism suggests that urban theory needs from the very start to recognize that cities are constituted through the extraordinarily complex notion of what is near and what is far is often very much less than self-evident (Smith, 2001, pp. 82-83).

Crang et al. (2003) have traced transnational circuits through which ethnic entrepreneurs bring together products and materials from different home cultures to develop a new style, ways of eating and cultivating more jobs that migrant communities rely upon, the everyday infrastructure that sustains and supports the transnational social fields such as grocery, international phone stores, travel agents, money exchange services, foreign language learning schools are some examples (Smith, 2001; Friesen et. al. 2005). Thus, transnational urban spaces mostly facilitate a large number of street vendors, yard markets, home-based businesses like barbers, secondhand clothing stores, and other novel informal economic strategies that migrants brought with them. One important point to conclude here is that transnational urban spaces attract migrants (male and female) for employment (legal/ illegal) opportunities.

Within the larger panorama of transnational urbanism, the term gender, and transnational urban spaces have been interestingly described by Francisco and Rodriguez (2014) who have analyzed the oppression of Filipina domestic workers in transnational urban spaces such as New York City and Hong Kong and also talked about their strategy to survive the violence in these urban cities: by organizing transnational solidarity with and for one another across their migrant locations. Analogously, in South Asian diaspora writings, transnational urban spaces have been portrayed as a space of suppression of brown women either racially by the natives or are the victim of patriarchal norms imposed either by brown men or white men. At the same time, urban spaces have emancipated South Asian diaspora women. For instance, in Taslima Nasreen's novel *French Lover* (2003), on the one hand, she shows that Paris is a space where the protagonist struggles with the violence against her within her Indian diaspora community and a space where she is outcasted by White feminism. In Monica Ali's novel *Brick Lane* (2004), the protagonist is discriminated against by the men of her community. Nevertheless, these diaspora women writing, on the other hand, portray that transnational urban spaces especially in the First World have become a place of emancipation where they are on their own without under the control of men (Gupta, 2022; Pourya Asl, 2022). For instance, walking alone in the street, unraveling their sexual desire, and taking the decision of living alone on their income. The final lines of the novels show their satisfaction and acceptance of their lives in Paris/ Brick Lane.

Coming to the issue of caste and class together with gender, in general, there is little reflection on how popular feminist discourses from South Asian academia have silenced the diverse understanding of oppression and liberation from caste women's perspectives. Uma Chakravarti affirms that caste and gender have been seen as different entities, and still, it is in debate. Both factors are not merged as feminist women from the upper caste (mostly they) saw themselves separated from caste issues (Chakravarti, 2018, p. 2). Postcolonialism, as a theory, has focused on race, class, and gender categories and has occluded a meaningful engagement with caste and caste-like systems of subjugation worldwide. Deepika Bahri, critical to postcolonialists, writes that the visible success of border crossers like Bhabha creates a dangerous illusion about the dexterity and comfort of "hybrid people." She argues that the scores of underclass immigrants in Anglo-America and illegal border crossers cannot "make themselves comfortable" with the same ease that other postcolonials have and know that border crossing can be dangerous and potentially fatal (Bahri, 1998, p. 39). Besides, in her work *Outside the fold* (1998), Viswanathan has touched on the issue of caste and challenged that the postcolonial project remains incomplete in this respect. As far as the diaspora is concerned, Suraj Yengde states that marriage and politics are still tinged with casteist enthusiasm even at the diasporic level (Yengde, 2021, p. 4). As far as the caste issue is concerned, Simon Gikandi considers postcolonialism as a code for the state of undecidability in which the culture of colonialism continues to resonate in what was supposed to be its negotiation (Gikandi, 1996, p. 14). For Dipesh Chakrabarty, postcolonialism necessitates the re-historicizing of historicism to blast the grounds of a (received) historicism asunder, and let newer, generally subaltern, postcolonial historicities surface, replete with those life practices or forms, collected under the performative against the pedagogic, that had hitherto been consigned to what we may call non-rational nativism (Chakrabarty, 2000, p. 10). Gajjala (2019) and Mallapragada (2014) state that even digital transnational space through a deep hanging out in online spaces and in-depth and semi-structured interviews potentially takes us through a complex, layered journey of the digital space. The South Asian digital spaces were mostly occupied by a male, high caste, mostly educated, Brahmin, and upper-middle-class cosmopolitan migrants (Gajjala, 2019; Mallapragada, 2014). At the time when most of the South Asian migrants were invisible at the level of "techno-elite," some of them were at the margins within the margins. In this regard, it is crucial to question postcolonial diaspora writing regarding the representation of caste and class together with gender in their novels in transnational urban spaces.

In this chapter the choice of novels of Mukherjee is based on several reasons, first, Mukherjee is one of the pioneer women diaspora writers who is read worldwide. In her works, she has well explored the diasporic characteristics from the perspective of a woman who plays different challenging roles in the patriarchal South Asian diaspora community. Second, Mukherjee lived in her homeland for years before coming out to the foreign university and has lived a long life in the host land and that's why she is not only talking about the presence of the diaspora woman in the host land rather she produces a fine balance of writing between her homeland and host land. Third, she has not only shown the interaction between a migrant (Third World) and a native which is mostly debated in diaspora writing, but also the conflicts among Indian diasporas that can give the taste of gender disputes, class conflict, or caste among South Asian diasporas in host land. This last point is crucial for the analysis, as it presents the interaction of South Asians among themselves and their treatment of gender and caste among them. It is true that Mukherjee's novels individually cannot be studied to understand the caste system in India or outside India. A reader needs to go through the rigorous process of understanding the complexity of caste, class, and gender, which may or may not be directly discussed in Mukherjee's novels. However, the novels can be used to see the suppression based on the intersection of gender, class, and caste in transnational spaces.

THEORY AND METHOD

New Geography of Identity

In the novels, the protagonists keep on moving from one geographical space to another, one culture to another, Third World to First World, and Vice-versa, from Calcutta to the USA, from Punjab to the USA. Hence their movement is not limited to any geographical space rather they cross many physical and metaphorical borders which changes their identity(ies). Susan Friedman's new geography of identity, in this direction, delineates six related but distinct discourses of identity which are based on multiple geographical realms, experiences, and spaces. The new geography of identity has seriously undermined or complicated the understanding beyond gender geopolitically. These are the discourses of "multiple oppression," "multiple subject positions," "contradictory subject positions," "relationality," "situationality," and "hybridity" (Freidman, 1998, p. 19). As cultural formations, these discourses developed to some extent sequentially in response to the changing political landscapes geographically, academically, and in social movements around the world, especially in feminism.

"Multiple oppression" or "double jeopardy" stresses the differences among women. It focuses on oppression as the main constituent of identity. It leads to the additive naming of victimization based on race, class, religion, sexuality, national origin, ableness, and the by-now formulaic. "Multiple subject positions" intersect differently, often competing cultural formations of race, ethnicity, class, sexuality, religion, national origin, et cetera. Within this paradigm, the self is not singular; it is multiple. However, unlike the notion of multiple jeopardies, the definitional focus is not so exclusively on oppression and victimization but rather on various combinations of differences that may or may not be tied to oppression (Freidman, 1998, p. 20).

"Contradictory subject position" focuses on contradiction as fundamental to the structure of subjectivity and the phenomenological experience of identity. Thus, a woman might be simultaneously oppressed by gender and privileged by race, class, religion or sexuality, or national origin. Conversely, a man might be privileged by gender but oppressed by sexuality, race, class, or religion. The fourth discourse of positionality, "relationality," emphasizes the epistemological standpoint for identity. Identity is a fluid site rather than a stable and fixed essence. Class, race, ethnicity, religion, national origin, and gender function relationally as sites of privilege and exclusion. In sum, the relational discourse of positionality stresses the constantly shifting nature of identity as it is constituted through different points of reference and material conditions of history. "Situational" approaches assume that identity resists fixity, but they stress how it shifts fluidly from setting to setting. The sixth discourse of positional identity, "hybridity," has emerged most directly out of ethnic, postcolonial, and diasporic studies (Freidman, 1998, p. 21).

The new geography of identity addresses the meanings of gender, race, ethnicity, class, sexuality, religion, and national origin as these axes of difference constitute multiplex identities and challenge binary ways of thinking. Thinking geopolitically means asking how a spatial entity — local, regional, national, transnational—inflects all individual, collective, and cultural identities. The geopolitical axis for analysis of difference is a form of geographical imperative, requiring vigilant attention to the meanings of space as they intersect with the intentions of time in the formations of identity (Friedman, 1998, p. 110).

Coming to the novels of Mukherjee, her transnational characters are on the path of hybridity as they created the "third space" in the diasporic literature theme-wise or the complexity of the multiplicity of their identity (Bhabha, 1994). Mukherjee has prioritized sexual differences as an essential aspect of her writing. Still, "silence" and "gaps" regarding the caste presence among the South Asian diaspora community oblige that gender may no longer be privileged as the single lens for reading especially in a transnational position. The question of caste takes us deeper and beyond the notion of sexual difference.

Mukherjee lived in a cosmopolitan city, Calcutta (now known as Kolkatta), where her family maintained a high-caste and upper-middle-class conservative culture during colonial times. She studied in an anglicized Bengali school run by nuns in a recently independent India. She then moved outside India to the First World to study and then settled as a writer. Mukherjee's social, familial, educational, and economic background reminds Tabish Khair's distinction made between Indian-origin writers and Indians in his book *Babu Fictions* (2005). He has described the socio-economic and discursive position of Indian English writers where his primary focal points are gender, class, and caste. He studied Indian and Indian diaspora fiction and non-fiction writers in his analytical study. In his research, the socio-economic line of division of Indian society (especially emphasizing the Indian-origin English writers) has been conceptualized between the "Babu" classes and "Coolie" (Subaltern):

The Babus are middle or upper-middle-class, mostly urban (cosmopolitan), Brahamanized and/or "westernized," and fluent in English. The coolie classes, on the other hand, are non-English speaking, not or less significantly "westernized," not or less Brahamanized, economically deprived, culturally marginalized, and, often, rural or migrant-urban population. (Khair, 2001, pp. 9-10)

Although Mukherjee unhouses herself from her Indian social and economic status and follows the re-housement in American culture, she introduces most of her protagonists from the high-caste and upper-middle class. It is also evident from most of the protagonists that they are her autobiographical representation at some point either in positioning the socio-economic situation, her mental conflicts, in search of her identity, in her Americanization, or in balancing her past and present. Thus, she projects the complexity of her own identity where she is in-between privileges and marginalization. Besides, Mukherjee's family's socio-economic position delineates the colonial social stratification that Gayatri Spivak discusses that countries like India have witnessed at large. She affirms that "dominant indigenous groups on all India level" are "a class of persons who are Indian in blood and color, but English in taste, in opinions, in morals, and intellect. They were the colonial administrators and organizers of the colonial land" (Spivak, 1988, p. 83). Khair (2001) comments on the heterogeneity of Indians "with the withdrawal of the Englishman and growing class differences and cosmopolitanism in India, the postcolonial triangle was constructed between Coolie India, the up-start Babu/cultural coolie (That is middle class and literate but in a vernacular language) and varieties of the cosmopolitan and accomplished babu." (p. 12). The colonial babu was posited against not only the non-babu Indian but also the English man, whose poor copy he was often supposed to be.

Moreover, the histories of countries like India before colonization had a separate existence that cannot be subsumed within the colonial referent and mostly continues to extend across the period of colonization to the present and are even heavily embedded in the colonial. Caste is one of those crucial issues in pre-colonized India, colonized India, and even post-colonial India. In this context, the frequent inability to "imagine" the pre-colonial or narrate the postcolonial without depending heavily on the colonial appears damning. Postcolonialism is crucial here to understand its inability to project different factors when dealing with Third World countries in pre-colonial and postcolonial times. For instance, India's socio-economic division between babu and coolie and its complexity into a triangle of Coolie, Indian cultural babu, and cosmopolitan babu. Then in this scenario, it is necessary to put gender, as an important factor which Spivak (1988) discusses "if a subaltern is suppressed then a subaltern woman is even more suppressed" (p. 86). Chakravarti (2018) too writes that caste women (Dalit women) are the most vulnerable person in the power scale, subject to multiple forms of exploitation, by the hands of upper caste men, upper caste women, and lower caste men. Here, one can derive that caste, class, and gender can create many groups where marginalization is based on the location, situation, and relative position which can create multiple marginalisations, double marginalization, or contradictory position of the subject. Based on these theoretical backgrounds, the chapter will do an analytical reading.

RESULTS AND FINDINGS

Mukherjee's Novels from Caste, Class, and Gender Perspectives

The Tiger's Daughter

Bharati Mukherjee's first novel, *The Tiger's Daughter,* was published in 1971 in the USA. The novel begins with the background of a colonized India where upper-middle-class and high-caste Indians were allied with the colonizer. The protagonist describes her link with the colonizer as "her father used to be invited to a British club by a liberal young Englishman" (Mukherjee, 1971, p. 10). Further, she mentions that she studied in an anglicized school where she learned how British colonizers were the savior of the Indian people (ibid). In a colonial India or recently independent India, upper-middle-class and high-caste Indians were burdened with colonial attitudes, and patriarchy doubled with the colonial package for men and women whom Spivak (1988) calls "were the copy of the colonizers." They were "Indians in blood and color but English in taste, opinions, morals, and intellect" (p. 83). They were the colonial administrators and organizers of the colonial land.

The Tiger's Daughter moves on with the independent story of Tara Banerjee, the great-granddaughter of Harilal Banerjee and the daughter of the Bengal Tiger, the owner of the famous Banerjee & Thomas. The protagonist is sent to the USA, where she falls in love and marries an American. Tara crosses the border as an upper-middle-class and high-caste Indian to study in the USA. She travels back to India after seven years as an American wife. The novel's main plot is in independent India, where the focus is to show the protagonist's struggle of in-betweenness: between Indian *beti* (Indian daughter) or *Americawali* (American wife). Since the protagonist herself belongs to an upper-middle business-class family, a Brahmin Bengali, the novel also centers itself in Calcutta's middle and upper-middle-class society. However, other stories go on in the background. The novel's background, which is vital to notice, is the glimpses of the labor class protests in urban Calcutta. The narrator is not mentioning the caste differences but shows the concern toward existing class distinction among the people of Calcutta. However, she talks from the above, sitting in a luxurious car, living in a grand secured home, or looking at the laborers from the top, surrounded by the people to serve. She writes at the beginning of the novel, "while buses were burning and workers surrounding the warehouses, few come to Catelli, a five-star hotel for their daily ritual of espresso or tea" (Mukherjee, 1971, p. 4). The anger among the upper-middle-class people can be seen against the workers demanding salary hikes, and the protagonist is also sitting among them in a hotel. As the narrator writes, "these English-speaking people were locked in a private world of what should have been, and they relished every twinge of resentment and defeated that time reserved for them" (ibid).

In an independent India, the protagonist refers to a pre-colonial and colonial hangover where the high-caste and upper-middle-class enjoyed luxury and feared losing their power. At the same time, lower-class people struggle for their daily wages. Such protests are presented as the chaos of the city. Of course, these incidents are shown in a background that a regular reader will not emphasize or are the "noises" that may go unheard by the readers. However, the labor protest is a significant step in the city to break the high-class authority, for instance, by opening schools for the lower caste (here the discussion goes on the caste). This is connected to the historical moments when communism was taking birth in West Bengal, India. In the novel, such changes are marked unacceptable by the protagonist's friends and one of them said "talking of schools, Tara should see how St. Blaise's has changed! Those nuns are taking *Marwaris* by the dozens!" (Mukherjee, 1971, p. 54). Her friends are concerned about the opening of schools or public spaces for the lower caste which was earlier reserved only for the high caste Calcutta society. Certainly, most of the debates are based on the class where caste is overshadowed which can be understood through reading the gaps for example the one mentioned about *Marwaris*. Intriguingly, Tara, on the one hand, belongs to a high caste and upper-middle-class society in Calcutta where she has a privileged position, untouched by the riot, and is only a viewer of the riot as an outsider from the above.

Her caste and class privilege have given an easy access to travel outside the country and study at a foreign university. It becomes interesting the way the writer portrays her and her gender role together with her diasporic elements of being between tiger's daughter and *Americawali*. The writer has portrayed the protagonist as a woman who carries the burden of high caste and class. Although she travels to foreign countries, accepts foreign cultures, and liberal ideologies, and marries a foreigner, she is not able to come out of the patriarchal and Brahmanical culture at home. Also, the acceptance of her marriage to a white man only describes the hierarchical position of the white race. Otherwise marrying outside the caste, especially lower caste brings harsh consequences to the woman (Chakravarti, 2018). In Calcutta as the writer shows she is a good daughter, a fragile woman, and needs to be protected. Also, as a high-caste woman, she is trained to be a submissive woman where her will is not asked. In the novel, the writer shows that her feminine characteristics are shaped by her Victorian British school and Brahmanical patriarchy. For instance, the protagonist seeks her father's protection as the title says, *The Tiger's Daughter*, where she demonstrates herself as a protected daughter. She also becomes someone P.K. Tuntunwala exploited – a corporate fear, selfish energy, a national personage, an "impassive and calculating spider" (Mukherjee, 1971, p. 22). Tara's relationships with Tuntunwala suggest her passive dependence on males and an acute sensitivity towards her incompleteness. The characterization of Tara displays conventional patriarchal mindsets where a man controls power hierarchies in different societal relationships, while a woman is encouraged to live mother/wife/daughter roles in a non-agentic and non-autonomous manner.

For instance, while meeting with Tuntunwala in the annual charity carnival of the Calcutta Chambers of Commerce, she is unable to resist his peremptory gestures. She obeys him when he asks Tara to join him for a snap. Even though she did not like the peremptoriness of his gestures, she knew she would "obey without much questioning" (Mukherjee, 1975, p. 77). The weekend trip to Nayapur also allows Mr. Tuntunwala to take her sightseeing and escort her to his air-conditioned room without any protest. She is even glad of his sympathy (Mukherjee, 1975, p.196). When he authoritatively sends the maid away, she is unable to protest. She coquettishly converses with him as such behavior is traditionally linked with passive feminine charms. Her training at St. Blaise had prepared her for genteel and discreet submission; it had not equipped her with decisive survival skills. Tara never resisted when it comes to raising her voice against the violation of her sexuality. She was distressed by the incident and wanted to go back to America, but she never tried to tell the misbehavior of Tuntunwala to her parents and friends. A confused and feared Tara has no control of her body, as Katrak (2006) writes about the exile of the female body from themselves, self-censorship, or self-exile which give authority to others (p. 2). Certainly, one can understand her position in a relative form where it is a contradictory position and at the same time, she is double marginalized.

In the novel, an American wife living in India narrates the story of Calcutta where the protagonist herself is at the borderline of two distinct cultures. The city where she lives has imposed its patriarchal and Brahmanical system on her. Together with the struggle of her in-betweenness, the other factors of gender, caste, and class, class, and caste have played a crucial role in shaping the gender role of a woman. Tara often finds herself at the crossroads where her gender meets other's class. She feels privileged being on the other side, seeing the others struggling because of their class. Nevertheless, delineating the "silences" of how her gender is caste(ed) reveals that the suppression of Tara is not only based on her gender inferiority but instead linked to her upper-middle-class and high caste. Upper-caste and upper-middle-class control the sexuality of women institutionally and morally in comparison to lower-caste women such as in their teaching of chastity, motherhood, widowhood, and values of *pativrata* (Chakravarti, 2018, p. 78). Besides, her colonial and bourgeois link, her high caste privileges turn out to be the reason for her double suppression and at the same time a contradictory position when compared to the lower caste woman.

Jasmine

The novel picturizes the transnational spaces from Punjab to the USA, from one country to another, and from the Third World to the First World. Jasmine crosses the border as a lower-class widow who buys the ticket to the USA from the money she borrowed from her brothers. She travels with fake documents and wants to *sati* herself at the university where her husband was supposed to study. However, the caste to which she belongs is not discussed or mentioned in the novel. She travels to the USA as a lower-class widow without having any place to reach or return. She is one among many:

[r]efugees and mercenaries and guest workers; you see us sleeping in airport lounges, you watch us unwrapping the last of our native foods, unrolling our prayer rugs, reading our holy books...we are the outcasts and deportees, strange pilgrims visiting outlandish shrines, landing at the end of tarmacs, ferried in old army trucks... dressed in shreds of national costumes, out of season, the wilted plumage of international vagabondage. We ask only one thing: to be allowed to land, to pass through, to continue. (Mukherjee, 1989, pp. 100-101)

This character portrayal is a challenge to Mukherjee's other novels, for whom crossing the border was as easy as traveling to another city within the country. On the contrary, Jasmine symbolizes a mass of such immigrants who spends years hoping to cross the border to have a better life, job, or search for something. Jasmine belongs to the other side of Mukherjee's earlier characters, has already lived poverty and widowhood ("which is just better than the lower castes"), and is more robust, determined, courageous, and looking forward (Mukherjee, 1989, p. 97). She does not complain about the life around her because she does not have any other option. Instead, she finds ways to move ahead. She decides to travel alone after being widowed. She does not accept the fate of widowhood like her mother did and sat in the corner of a dark room. She keeps on adapting herself as an immigrant and becoming more assertive. Jasmine keeps on moving and changing herself, she does not remain as a widow crying for her husband in India, violated by an American, or as somebody's lover or wife in the USA. She takes control of her body and her sexuality to live her life.

The novel, *Jasmine*, is a new genre of diaspora woman writing where the writer, unlike in her earlier novels, has applied the sense of reincarnation to the protagonist (Mukherjee, 1990, p. 18). Mukherjee also connects herself to the same theory of reincarnation about immigration – "being murdered and reborn at least three times from the correct young woman I was trained to be and was very happy, is very different from the politicized, shrill, civil rights activist I was in Canada, and from the urgent writer that I have become in the last few years in the United States. I can't stop" (Mukherjee, 1990, p. 18). Similarly, one can see the evolution of the central character when she enters the unfamiliar American land and culture and goes through an oscillating series of painful and joyful experiences. The character believes in moving toward the future, a genetic transformation (Mukherjee, 1989, p. 222). The novel's theme coincides with the writer's life, but the protagonist has a different socio-economic background from Mukherjee, making the two lives different.

Mukherjee has successfully brought "the other" into the novel with 18 years of her writing gap. Like other protagonists, she is a woman, but her class or (caste) doubly marginalizes her. She fakes her identity and enters America as an illegal immigrant. Her class, gender, and unlawful entrance into a new land made her vulnerable to the violation. Jasmine was raped on the day of her arrival in the USA and became a murderer of her rapist. She knows she has to fight; she does not have any protector; she is not a daughter of any mighty man or a wife of any renowned businessman. She stands to challenge the cruelty against her.

There are two incidences of "multiple suppression" of Jasmine within the American society and her diaspora Indian community. First is the rape of an Indian woman (Non-American) by an American who knew the status of her immigration: an illegal lower-class Indian migrant woman. Second, her Indian community, the family of Devinder Vadhera, where she entered and lived as an Indian widow. She served them and worked in the kitchen. She was, to them (the Indian community), "a widow who should show a proper modesty of appearance and attitude; if not, it appeared she was competing with Namrata (a married woman)" (Mukherjee, 1989, p. 145). Besides, her status as a widow becomes vital as a woman who does not deserve any attention among Indian diasporas. In the novel, the narrator compares widowhood with the caste, "Mataji and I were alone in the widow's dark hut, little better than Mazbis (lowest Shikh caste) and Untouchables" (Mukherjee, 1989, p. 97). Hence in the novel, the writer shows the plight of a woman who is crossing the border, especially when she is crossing with illegal documents from the Third World. She has successfully used the class difference and portrayed the protagonists as a character who is multiple marginalized because of their class, race, and gender. The writer does not refer to the caste in her case as she has done earlier in the case of Tara from *The Tiger's Daughter*.

Desirable Daughters

Tara Lata is barely five years old when the groom dies from a snakebite on her wedding day. Her father decides to marry her to a tree so that at least she will remain a wife for her whole life. Harilal Banerjee organized a grand wedding ceremony for her daughter in 1879 (Mukherjee, 2002). This incident can be interpreted as an authorial attempt to impart its central characters' historical framework and clan continuity. Tara Chatterjee, the protagonist of the novel has a linkage to Tara the Tree-bride, becomes curious to know more about the trauma of the Tree-bride after her divorce from her husband Bishwapriya Chatterjee, and the "root search" becomes a compulsion for her till she finally yields to this most American of impulses (Mukherjee, 2002, p. 17). Hence, the novel's theme is a continuous shift between past and present, the root and route of Tara Chatterjee.

Desirable Daughters presents similar traditional gender roles, which the writer has portrayed in her first novel, *The Tiger's Daughter*. Analogously, the protagonist and her sisters have spent their adolescence in a much more affluent *bhadralok* background (high-caste and upper-middle-class society). The difference in both the novels is the space: *Tiger's Daughter* is based in Calcutta where the foreign interventions through the husband of Tara can be observed, and *Desirable Daughters*'s narration is mostly based in the USA. The second novel that narrates about diaspora in the USA shows a lot of influences from the homeland and its culture through her sisters and her family relatives which makes her an in-betweener.

The presence of the homeland, its culture, and patriarchal and Brahmanical norms were inculcated in the protagonist. As the protagonist and her sisters have already lived their youth in the homeland before shifting to the USA. In that society, they were guaranteed a privileged lifestyle. They are schooled in an anglicized environment with a conservative Brahmanical setup. Their traditional upbringing within a patriarchal design negates the possibility of assertive independence. The three daughters of the Bhattacharjee family are desired because they are trained to fulfill daughterhood politely and serve wifely duties and are protected by their father "Our father could not let either of my sisters out on the street, our car was equipped with window shades" (Mukherjee, 2002, p.29). The daughters, who came from a specific class and caste, must assure their obedience and their submission to the father and then their husband.

Accordingly, Padma is not allowed to follow her passion for becoming an actor as it does not suit a high-caste woman. She is not allowed to marry out of her caste to a Christian boy she loved and is pregnant. "Any violation of the codes, any breath of scandal, was unthinkable" (Mukherjee, 2002, p. 32). Padma is trained to be a silent and submissive wife, and she even starts preaching the same to her sister. Padma reminds Tara of the models of mythical wives *Sita* and *Savitri,* who sacrificed their lives for their husbands. "Things are never perfect in marriage; a woman must be prepared to accept less than perfection in this lifetime and model herself on *Sita*, *Savitri*, and *Behula*, the virtue wives of Hindu myths" (p. 134). Parvati, her middle sister, marries her choice, which is possible only because the boy is from the same caste. Alarmed by Tara's elder sister Parvati's love marriage, Tara is married at nineteen. "My life was one long childhood until I was thrown into marriage" (pp. 27-28). She is sent to Atherton, California, where her husband Bish tries to carve out a semblance of Indian tradition in all respect.

In the novel, Mukherjee delineates the atrocities inflicted on gender oppression, that is, women in child marriage, forced marriage, given the limited prospect of career, only carried the big name of their husbands, or burdened with upper-middle-class and high caste womanhood who should be taking care of the home and not going out to work as their husbands are enough for that. All these atrocities such as early marriage or forced marriage are the results of the fear of breaking the caste lineage. As women are seen as the carrier of the caste because of their reproductive function (Chakravarti, 2018). Even the daughters are raised to be desired by preaching to them the values of *pativrata*.

Again, the novel presents the three sisters from a high caste and upper-middle-class family, who have crossed the border as middle-class women who have catholic education and are married to reputed men living outside the country. They are living with all the privileges of middle-class women and high-caste citizens but are oppressed in their gender roles. The patriarchal system plays a very tough role for women who have other privileges. They are educated and trained to be serene and passive in their catholic school. They are taught all the wifely conduct within the conservative, orthodox family. They are taught the role of wife and mother. Hence, many institutions suppress high-caste and upper-middle-class women, unlike lower-class and caste women.

Further, Tara also becomes a point from where we can closely read the meetings of the Indian diaspora -a closed group of middle-class high-caste Indian diaspora society. They follow the same Indian patriarchal cultural norms of marriage and the role of women in marriage. Despite going outside the country, the patriarchal and Brahmanical values keep following her. She was preached the knowledge of *Pativrata* woman, the importance of a man as protector of her dignity, and living inside the community by remaining beside her husband. Tara was continuously under vigilance by her Indian community. When she was out of her marriage, she was approached by Indian diaspora men for sexual pleasure and was exploited by some of them. Also, outside her marriage, she works to meet the need of her and her son. Once outside her marriage and her Indian community, Tara can adapt to the life of the host land. After getting out of her unsatisfied marriage, she has been on her path of consciousness of gender roles and chooses her freedom over her discontent marriage. She accepts the homosexual preference of her son. Tara breaks the myth and chooses another man who suits her temperament and satisfies her sexual desires. Behind such love, one can also feel that Tara seeks love from Andy to be protected, and when he leaves her, she falls again for her ex-husband.

The Intersection of Gender, Caste, and Class

In all her novels, Mukherjee has touched on the theme of gender widely talking from the perspective of Tara from *The Tiger's Daughter*, Jasmine from *Jasmine,* and Tara Chatterjee from *Desirable Daughters*. In that, she narrates the encounter of Indian diaspora women within their community, for instance, Jasmine living with the Indian community, Tara visiting her sister, and her friends. Mukherjee also writes about women diasporas visiting India back, such as Tara of *The Tiger's Daughter* and Tara of *Desirable Daughters*. In this way, she explores the position of women diaspora in the Indian diaspora community. In her writing, she has barely talked about caste, especially in the case of Jasmine. Although she widely discusses the economic status of Jasmine and her being exploited because of her class, she never mentions her caste from where she belongs. In the case of the other two protagonists of *The Tiger's Daughter* and *Desirable Daughters,* the writer has mentioned the caste they belong to. However, there is no clear discussion on caste or caste-like suppression. In *The Tiger's Daughter,* the background discussion is mostly based on class, where the difference can be noticed between the narrator and her friend's class and the others who were protesting. Though the writer uses the term caste which overlaps with the class in her conversations, it never becomes a topic of embarrassment or exploration in the novel. Alternatively, if it is done, then in a subtle way that goes unrecognized by most of the foreign readers, non-Indian, "non-caste," or privileged Indians. Besides, the topic of caste is overshadowed by the class in the novel, which has blurred the discriminatory system among Indian diasporas. Interestingly, unraveling the "silence" about caste becomes significant, especially in the case of Tara in both novels. As both high-caste and upper-middle-class women stand in the "contradictory position" where their socio-economic status is privileged. However, class and caste intersect with gender in both cases where they enjoy the authority of their caste and class among lower caste men and women on the one side, and on the other Brahmanical patriarchal system shapes their gender where they are trained to be fragile, genteel, protected, and submissive to men. Her sexuality is organized and ordered by paternal power in the emerging class-/caste-based societies to serve the new social and political arrangements organized by men of the dominant sections of society. Patriarchy does not function alone rather it is shaped and goes hand in hand with caste and class, especially in the case of Tara. It is significant to mention here that different castes have shaped gender differently. A high-caste woman has a different role to play than a lower-caste and class woman. For instance, Vasudha Dhagambar makes a distinction that has been carried out among women of different castes: "A high caste female would sacrifice her life to her honor if contaminated by the embrace of a man of low caste whereas a woman of lower caste is considered easily accessible. Caste here is regarded almost as a natural factor in understanding notions of chastity and therefore differences, real or imaginary, in the sexuality of a woman" (Dhagamwar, 1992, p. 115).

It is significant to mention other factors that overlap with their caste and class are their marriage to an American, a "white man"/businessman, and her education, which gives them a privileged position among their friends and family. They exemplify the women who are molded through the colonial discourse, high-caste, and upper-middle-class hierarchy. These women are English educated, decent, trained in the British language, taste, thoughts (British are saviors), and conservative Brahmanical setup. They are taught to be well-behaved wives protected by their fathers/husbands. It is true from the two novels *The Tiger's Daughter* and *Desirable Daughters* that within the restricted area of Indian diaspora English fiction, the central female protagonists depicted by Mukherjee share a "Babu" standard of life and, very often, a superior degree of refinement/sensitivity and a feeling of dissatisfaction with life. Such dissatisfaction is related to the gender issue they face in their home or around. This ambivalent situation often explains their intense feeling of lack of purpose and connections: a feeling of powerlessness while situated within the proprietorial embrace of power structures. Within the limitation of her concern around gender, Mukherjee does not prioritize the complexity of gender with caste. However, in two novels, she has shown the intersectionality of gender with the upper-middle-class, and high-caste, but does not get into any discussion rather only introduces the socio-economic position of the protagonists. One cannot deny that at least she demonstrates the suppression of a woman from the position where she comes from i.e., the high-caste and upper-middle-class.

Further, both cases are different when Jasmine comes into the picture. In the case of Jasmine, Mukherjee does not declare her caste identity and talks only about her lower economic position and her daily life's economic struggle in Punjab and America. The writer shows how an economically deprived woman is more vulnerable in a patriarchal society. Jasmine symbolizes migrant women who risk their lives by crossing the border. This novel differentiates between the migration with documents and without documents, between classes, and between crossing with husband/father and without husband/father. The writer does not show the complex structures of the caste-class hierarchy, especially from below the caste hierarchy. In *Jasmine*, widows were compared with lower castes to showcase the oppressiveness of widows metaphorically. As Tabish Khair writes that "it is not that the "caste other" is completely ignored in her writing, but their presence is subsumed and marginalized. The caste other is used as filler, maybe, a symbol but seldom as a flesh-blood character who might see reality differently from his/her creator/narrator" (Khair, 2001, p. 138).

CONCLUSION

This chapter applauds South Asian diaspora writers like Bharati Mukherjee for their feminist "hybrid" diaspora writings and for breaking the quintessential theme of male diaspora where women's presence was secondary. Mukherjee becomes one of those women writers who started writing from the perspective of immigrant women, marginalized voices such as Tara and Jasmine who were not having space in male writings before. She has successfully put her protagonists in a heroic form who are emancipated and move towards empowerment in transnational urban spaces. For instance, Tara marries outside her country and caste in the USA, Jasmine decides to travel alone to the USA or Tara leaves her husband to live with her boyfriend in the USA. Urban spaces, especially in First World, have given new thoughts to the protagonists such as Tara getting to know about the liberation of women, Jasmine understanding that the ultimate desire of being someone's wife is a void, Tara too explores sexual desires while living in with her boyfriend in America. One can see in the novels that transnational urban space especially in First World became a space of self-realization and self-exploration which is not possible to achieve in their homeland and living within the Indian diaspora community.

At the same time in transnational urban spaces, such as in the USA, diaspora women have been suppressed because of their gender as they carried their patriarchal culture or lived within it. The study has prioritized the issue of caste together with gender and class which has not been given a place in postcolonial debates, especially among South Asian diaspora writings but is a need to understand the suppression of women. The chapter has analyzed the novels from the perspective of caste and class which are carried by the gendered body while crossing the border. The chapter has pointed out that the marginalization of women is not only because of one factor such as gender rather it multiplies with caste and class whether it is in Calcutta, Punjab, or the USA. The chapter has analyzed that at one point it brings the contradictory subject position where the protagonists, on one hand, are privileged of their caste and class in comparison to the lower caste and class men and women at the same time their caste and class have shaped their gender suppression. Tara from both novels has demonstrated their passive role as a woman which is doubled because of their caste and class. The *bhadralok* society demands them to serve Brahmanical patriarchal society by remaining loyal to their caste. Women are bounded to the values such as *Pativrata* dharma and treating their sexuality as the honor of the family. The diasporic situation of Tara from *Desirable Daughters* and Tara of *Tiger's Daughter* follows a hybridized culture where her training in womanhood collides with the American culture. Tara from The *Tiger's Daughter* marries outside her country and her caste. Tara from Desirable Daughter lives with someone out of her caste and country. As a result, they are treated as outsiders such as *Americawali* in the case of *The Tiger's Daughter,* and in *Desirable Daughters,* she is treated as an accessible woman. In both cases going outside the caste and not serving the caste and community are not accepted in Calcutta or the USA among diasporas.

One cannot compare the situation of these women with the ones who belong to the lower class. There are many other factors that crossover and intersect which each other and creates hierarchy and between these two binary positions, multiple positions keep on shifting relatively, locationally, and situationally; they contradict and multiply in their suppression, resulting in multiple or contradictory suppressive positions. Compared to the earlier novel, in *Jasmine,* the class difference shows a different woman and different ways of marginalization. Mukherjee has portrayed Jasmine from the other side of the class and produced a big difference, however, as we have seen in the discussion that the writer has not disclosed the caste that Jasmine carries which itself questions the representation of lower caste and class women in her writing in transnational urban spaces. Mukherjee's novels as one of the postcolonial diaspora writings have debated around class, gender, and race besides the diasporic theme but lack the discussion on caste issues which has marginalized the women who carry the caste. The absence of caste among the diaspora in the South Asian diaspora writing or its subtle presence neglects the representation of the South Asian Diaspora among its readers. This could result in misinformation or blinding the readers who are new to the Indian diaspora issues, especially white American readers, and the new generation of the Indian diaspora. Because of the negligence of intersectionality, there is a strong feeling of othering women who crosses the border with their class and caste. It can be seen as a colonial Brahmanical strategy of dividing the diaspora population based on caste where the privileged half is talked and is talking (here, the gender within the privileged caste and class is also referred to). At the same time, the other side is ghettoized and under-represented or not at all represented in the novels. The hierarchy of caste and othering caste-ed gender and gendered caste is a pre-colonial phenomenon in India and the Indian subcontinent. In post-independent India and among Indians living on the mainland or beyond the border continues to practice the outcasting of a section of people based on caste.

Thus, diaspora writing should include caste, especially from below to produce the complexity of gender with factors such as caste. Different classes have different ways of suppressing women, and geographical change has also varied their identity. Similarly, a caste-based or different caste-based debate around gender will produce a fruitful answer to the suppression of women who travel with their caste as a nanny, ayahs, or domestic maids. It will break the hierarchy and give space to the identity of caste (ed) women who are not able to connect with the existing diaspora writing which is centered on themes of gender, class, and race.

REFERENCES

Ali, M. (2004). *Brick Lane*. Black Swan.

Anzaldúa, G. (1987). *Borderlands/La frontera: The new mestiza*. Aunt Lute.

Bahri, D. (1998). Terms of engagement: Postcolonialism, transnationalism, and composition studies. *JAC, 18*(1), 29–44. PMID:9700526

Bhabha, H. K. (1994). *The Location of culture*. Routledge.

Chakrabarty, D. (2000). *Provincializing Europe: Political thought and historical difference*. Princeton University Press.

Chakravarti, U. (2018). Gendering caste: Through a feminist lens. *Sage (Atlanta, Ga.)*.

Crang, P., Dwyer, C., & Jackson, P. (2003). Transnationalism and the spaces of commodity culture. *Progress in Human Geography, 27*(4), 438–456. doi:10.1191/0309132503ph443oa

Dhagamwar, V. (1992). Law, power and justice. *Sage (Atlanta, Ga.)*.

Francisco, V., & Rodriguez, R. M. (2014). Countertopographies of migrant women: Transnational families, space, and labor as solidarity. *Working USA, 17*(3), 357–372. doi:10.1111/wusa.12119

Friedman, S. S. (1998). *Mappings: Feminism and the cultural geographies of encounter*. Princeton University Press.

Friesen, W., Murphy, L., & Kearns, R. (2005). Spiced-up Sandringham: Indian transnationalism and new suburban spaces in Auckland, New Zealand. *Journal of Ethnic and Migration Studies, 31*(2), 385–401. doi:10.1080/1369183042000339981

Gajjala, R. (2019). *Digital diasporas: Labor and affect in gendered Indian digital publics*. Rowman & Littlefield.

Gikandi, S. (1996). *Maps of Englishness: Writing identity in the culture of colonialism*. Columbia University Press.

Gupta, S. (2022). (Dis)Locating homeland: Border (home) land in Taslima Nasreen's French Lover and Monica Ali's Brick Lane. In M. Pourya Asl (Ed.), *Gender, Place, and Identity of South Asian Women* (pp. 1–22). IGI Global. doi:10.4018/978-1-6684-3626-4.ch001

Katrak, K. (2006). *The Politics of the female Body: Postcolonial women writers*. Rutgers University Press.

Khair, T. (2001). *Babu fictions: Alienation in contemporary Indian English novels*. Oxford University Press.

Khair, T., & Doubinsky, S. (2011). Reading literature today: Two complementary essays and a conversation. *Sage (Atlanta, Ga.)*. Advance online publication. doi:10.4135/9788132107750

Mallapragada, M. (2014). Rethinking desi: Race, class, and online activism of South Asian immigrants in the United States. *Television & New Media*, *15*(7), 664–678. doi:10.1177/1527476413487225

Martos-Hueso, M. E., & García-Ramírez, P. (2010). *An interview with Bharati Mukherjee*. doi:10.25115/riem.v0i1.365

Mukherjee, B. (1971). *The Tiger's Daughter*. Ballantine.

Mukherjee, B. (1989). *Jasmine*. Virago.

Mukherjee, B. (2002). *Desirable daughters*. Bentang.

Mukherjee, B., Blaise, C., Connell, M., Grearson, J., & Grimes, T. (1990). An Interview with Bharati Mukherjee. *The Iowa Review*, *20*(3), 7–32. doi:10.17077/0021-065X.3908

Müller, M. G., & Torp, C. (2009). Conceptualising transnational spaces in history. *European Review of History: Revue Europeenne D'histoire*, *16*(5), 609–617. doi:10.1080/13507480903262587

Nasreen, T. (2002). *French lover* (S. Guha, Trans.). Penguin Books.

Portes, A., Guarnizo, L. E., & Landolt, P. (1999). The study of transnationalism: Pitfalls and promise of an emergent research field. *Ethnic and Racial Studies*, *22*(2), 217–237. doi:10.1080/014198799329468

Pourya Asl, M. (Ed.). (2022). *Gender, place, and identity of South Asian women*. IGI Global. doi:10.4018/978-1-6684-3626-4

Schiller, N. G., Basch, L., & Blanc, C. S. (1995). From immigrant to transmigrant: Theorizing transnational migration. *Anthropological Quarterly, 68*(1), 48–63. doi:10.2307/3317464

Smith, M. P. (2001). *Transnational urbanism: Locating globalization.* Blackwell.

Spivak, G. C. (1988). Can the subaltern speak? In C. Nelson & L. Grossberg (Eds.), *Marxism and the interpretation of culture* (pp. 271–316). University of Illinois Press.

Viswanathan, G. (1998). *Outside the fold: Conversion, modernity, and belief.* Princeton University Press. doi:10.1515/9781400843480

Yengde, S. (2019). *Caste matters.* Penguin Random House India Publication.

Chapter 4
City, Wall, and (Feminist) Dystopia:
Urban Poetics and Narrative in Prayaag Akbar's *Leila*

Moulina Bhattacharya
https://orcid.org/0000-0001-9389-846X
Christ University, India

ABSTRACT

Prayaag Akbar's debut novel Leila (2017) is a compendium of dystopian feminism, misogyny, religious and casteist devaluation, and a post-apocalyptic portrayal of a futuristic urban India that is subjugated by a totalitarian government. This chapter aims to examine the narrative ambiguity and the unresolved problem of narrative reliability in the novel by exploring the cognitive process of the female protagonist Shalini in the context of the art of her storytelling. It is argued that the narrative pattern in this dystopian novel is mainly non-linear in spatial terms which creates a fragmented and patchy experience of reading. Using a spatial-psychoanalytical approach, the study reveals that the narrative is defied by the mental projection of the city-space and city as a gendered space.

INTRODUCTION

Dystopian literature is a speculative genre that flourished as a response to utopian literature. With a socio-politically declined setting, dystopian fiction often depicts a postapocalyptic situation with utmost chaos, instability, and the ruin of a historic past. The dystopic city, presented in the chosen narrative, *Leila*, is a rotting mausoleum of dreams and separations, divided with a wall of resistance and denial. Urban space refers to the spatiality of the city and city life, as Wolfreys states, "an emerging interdisciplinary formation centered on the problematics of 'space', 'place' and 'cultural geography'" (Wolfreys, 2002, p.180). Urban space is a microcosmic representation of an expanded world rather than just a material space and is composed of government, institutions, judiciary, and its other state apparatuses. The city, in particular, discussed here has its own government, police, and legislature even vigilantes and assailants forming a hierarchy in this urban space. In his theory of postmodern geography Edward Soja explains, "city-space refers to the city as a historical-social-spatial phenomenon, but with its intrinsic spatiality highlighted for interpretive and explanatory purposes" (Soja, 2000, p.8). In a dystopian narrative, the narrative pattern is mainly non-linear in spatial terms, hence while reading it seems like looking through a moving camera, fragmented and patchy. City-space as a geographical constitute has an intrinsic relationship with its civilians that invades their mental space like the narrator here has been a prisoner of her mental space as well as the city itself where she has passed her whole life. To explore that mental space of the narrator and her state of mind this chapter tries to critically analyze the reliability of this dystopian narrative because "This conceived space tends, with certain exceptions 'towards a system of verbal (and therefore intellectually worked out) signs,' again referring to language, discourse, texts, logos: the written and spoken word." (Soja,1996, p.67). City-space is a domineering mental space that regulates the epistemological power through the discourse of the text:

In The Space of Literature, Blanchot analyzes Mallarmé's experience and space, Kafka and space of death and Rilke from the perspective of space theory, pointing out what the writing is, what literature is, and what the space of literature is; Gaston Bachelard thinks that space is the dwelling place full of human's consciousness, rather than empty container, architecture is the poetic dwelling. In The Poetics of Space, architecture is reflected and imagined uniquely from the method of phenomenology and symbolism; Fredric Jameson maps the production of contemporary literature and art in Postmodernism, or, The Cultural Logic of Late Capitalism. (Shi & Zhu, 2018, p.229)

The psychopathology behind *reliability* is a functional part of the narration, be it an everyday conversation, criminology, or textual narrative. The whole constitution of communication lies in how consistent the speaker is with the listener or the reader. The dynamic of reliability and unreliability is a frame of reference, as Booth said, is set by an implied author's "norms" (Booth, 1961, pp. 158-59). *Leila* is a narrative fiction, advanced with a singular narrative frame by the narrator, Shalini. Shalini is a widowed mother who has lost her child and witnessed her husband's murder at the hands of the Repeaters, a gang of assassins, the accomplice of a totalitarian government in a futuristic India. She was detained in the 'Purity camp' run by a fundamentalist cult whose main objective was cleansing society using a religion-economic basis. The time narrative of the novel starts, it had been sixteen years since Shalini's husband, Riz was killed and their daughter, Leila, had been abducted. The mental condition of Shalini, projected through her narrative, makes the readers think about the whole story once they finish reading it. The margin between reality and imagination flips within a blink and leaves the readers in a state of confusion. There comes the question of narrative reliability. Getting ahead of the conventional boundaries of labeling a narrator 'unreliable,' if it could be rethought empathetically from the point of view of the narrator herself and track her train of thoughts, it would be more explainable than just labeling and inspecting under a previously set framework or qualities of reliable and unreliable narrators. To define feminist dystopia, first, the concept of feminist special criticism needs to be discussed. In feminist criticism, women have been seen as space many times, their "inner' and "outer" space, mental space, and their gender as a space, "Matter, concave, ground... Always the same metaphor; we follow it, it carries us, beneath all its figures, wherever discourse is organized" (Cixous & Clement, 1986, p.63). The oneness of Shalini and the city is a projection of spatial metamorphics in gendered space.

This research is about throwing the spotlight on narrative ambiguity and addressing the unresolved problem of narrative reliability by exploring the cognitive process of Shalini in the context of the art of her storytelling. So far, this 2017 debut novel of Akbar has been compared with *The Handmaid's Tale* as both surmount creating their dystopic world and proliferating the idea of feminist dystopia, dystopic misogyny, and so on. The existing reality and hyperreality in the fictive landscape have been researched previously.

BACKGROUND: HOW THE CITY AS *SPACE* WORKS UNDERNEATH

This chapter primarily deals with the theory of narrative reliability and rather shows that the labeling can be disproved with the theory of mind in terms of an empathic reader. While dealing with the *mind* of the narrator, the city as a space appears to be an undeniable variable. To explore the concept of urban poetics, it can be seen that city as a space, both physical and mental, surfaces as a receptacle of the lifestyle and thoughts of its inhabitants. Since post-industrialization living space has become constricted. Now to talk about dystopic city life, the construction follows a post-apocalyptic model which reflects in and out on the mind and the narration of the selected narrator of this study. Though the narrative descriptive of the setting, the readers get a sketch of it and that helps bolster the theory of mind and narrative reality. The city presented as the setting of *Leila* is a futuristic urban construction and is divided by a wall. The city is ruled by The Purity One, the Council of the fundamentalist government, that has an 'inscrutable power':

As we walk from the broad pavement to a small rectangle of grass he pulls out two candles from the satchel. Purity One, first of the sector walls, stretches out across us to the edges of the dusk, either end into the swirling ash. Gritty grey brick. Sixty feet high. Wrapping around the political quarter, sealing off the broad, tree-lined avenues, the colonial bungalows, the Ministries, the old Turkic gardens. The Council oversees the divided city from the political quarter, from behind Purity One. (Akbar, 2017, p. 9)

Shalini further describes to the readers the small rooms against the wall, the roof with a fluttering white flag, and the Council's insignia, black pyramid, white tip, blue trapezoid light, and a double door. The sectors collect their taxes. The common areas of the city are infested with rotting garbage even the air feels "black and gritty" (Akbar, 2017, p. 13) in the chest. The unbreathable situation of the city explains the project of an air-filtration dome taken by the government which will produce filtered air for the sophisticated part of the city. Apart from the wall (discussed later), the city is where the narrator has born and brought up. Each change of the cityscape defines each devastative turn of her life itself. The memory of 'home' has a permanent imprint on our memory from which comes the infliction of nostalgia. In this narrative, it comes up with her childhood memories that bring forth the comparison of the city then and now. Metaphors used for the wall, such as, murky, 'a shifting shadow' have drawn the pessimistic presence of it. The filth and grime of the city have presented it its rotting condition and the growing pessimism in Shalini's heart,

I looked up to the top of its wall, its upper reaches obscured by the murk, a shifting shadow against the sky. No one else walked here. It's the rancid smell, and the rats, big as cats, scuttling out from the garbage and scampering hairily over your feet. Most people take the long route. (Akbar, 2017, p.15)

The city is filled with flyovers hanging everywhere that might remind the readers as if the city is hovering in uncanny weather, unstable and lifeless. The Council decided to keep the women who they have brought to 'purify' out of the city. They built the Towers for them near the Southern border towards the old city gates that "look like a mouth missing its teeth, pass the landfill, the last stretch of the East

Slum, the paneer-packing plant, the puffy silver-white tents of the tulip farms." (Akbar, 2017, p.19). When Shalini got there sixteen years ago from her narrative present, when she was twenty-eight, the towers "stood in an empty basin of turmeric-yellow earth, the only relief in the vastness a row of factory sheds and the red and white stacks of a power plant in the distance. Here there were no sixty-foot walls. No sectors. Only scrubland and an empty horizon" (Akbar, 2017, p.19). The entity of the city and Shalini sometimes merge as if she is the city and the flagbearers of purity have etched their lives into a festering wound. Remembering her childhood, she tells the readers how her father once proclaimed the city as "my city" (Akbar, 2017, p.21) and they can go wherever they wanted. She often called the city 'mystical' and even after a lifelong trauma, she does not leave the city. The city is like a red-room, a much-presented literary metaphor for a labyrinthian trap. The comparison of 'turmeric-yellow earth" implies the sulfur smoke of hell which too is yellow. Her narrative fades out in the city fluorescence, at the 'center of power' of the city, the "heart of everything" (Akbar, 2017, p.173), the top of the pyramid where there is no question of impurity.

LITERATURE REVIEW

Dystopian fiction as a genre in India was not introduced until popular international publishers like Penguin and others came in around the late 1980s. The post-millennial Indian English writers tried to familiarize Indian readers with a new taste of the fictive world and bring an update to the canon (Pourya Asl, 2022). The representation of future India through Prayag Akbar's *Leila* is uniquely woven but the readers would place the book side by side with Atwood's *The Handmaid's Tale* as both have tricenarian protagonists, Shalini and Offred, are on the verge of their sanity, forcefully separated from the family and have undergone uncouth changes in life. Shalini is a progressive urban girl with liberal thinking and so has got herself into an interreligious marriage. Eventually, her image transpires as a reflection of an Indian mother. The history of fiction in India right from the start goes around the colonial sentiment, to encourage indigenous ideas and unify the nation. Postcolonial canon also has hardly come out of the colonial trans. Dystopian fictions by post-millennial writers have not discarded the existing Indianness but helped the canon break away from the colonial hangover. Das's paper on "Dystopia and Indianness in Post-Millennial Indian Fiction" (Das, 2020, p. 1) explores the psyche of the two protagonists (Shalini and Offred) alongside presenting the unique Indianness of the dystopian fiction, *Leila*.

Several review articles, including Indian newspapers, have left on the implication of the mental state of Shalini and how she shows us her reality adding with the open ending of the novel altogether, which creates an opaque idea on the whole construct of the plot. With a systematic review of the literature in the context of the theme of this selected fiction, *Leila*, an article, "From the 'Real' to the' Hyperreal': A Study of the Postmodern and Dystopian Cityscape in Ruchir Joshi's The Last Jet-Engine Laugh and Prayaag Akbar's Leila" explores the cartographic reality and the hyperreal construct of the city where the author has also veiled it as a state of mind. The discourse of the city is evaluated as a postmodern urban landscape. Moving on to the context of feminist dystopia, "The New York Times" article, 'How feminist dystopian fiction is channeling women's anger and anxiety' presents the wreck of feminism in dystopian society through the novels like *The Water* Cure, *The Handmaid's Tale*, *Hazards of Time Travel* and so on. The other prevalent theme is urban poetics which denotes modern city life and its characteristic dominance, a transformation of the geographic city into a mental space, a hyperreal escapade as well as a prison. In "Urban Poetics: a Call from (and To) the Wild" the author speaks for the poetics of the city, the urban space in the postindustrial world.

This chapter concentrates on the following research question(s),

Can an empathetic reader adhere to the theoretical norm of labeling a narrator 'unreliable'? In this context, how does the narrative of Shalini imply the ambiguity of narrative reliability?

Research hypothesis: The dystopian construct of the geo-political city and its traumatic history question the narrative reality.

METHODOLOGY (EPISTEMOLOGY AND ONTOLOGY OF THE RESEARCH)

To recalibrate the narrative with these questions, this study employs a psychoanalytic approach and examines the cognitive imprint of the narrative persona through textual analysis. The aim is to examine the narratorial voice, its flips, and turns, and find psychological interpretations behind that. Unlike other historiographic literary instances of picaresque novels like *Tome Jones* or *Tristram Shandy* or pathological liars like the narrator of the novel *American Psycho* or the inexperienced narrator in *Catcher in the Rye*, the narrator of Akbar's *Leila,* Shalini falls in neither of the categories. She is an adult narrator who is not a notorious criminal but a victim of the authoritarian mission of the dystopian government as she married out of her religion, and her child is a mixed-blood offspring of that interreligious marriage. The problem with her is that after consecutive shocks for a young, woman Shalini's mental state is questionable but cannot be typified under a 'madman' narrator, it is her disjointed narrative, verbal hallucinations, and transferred epithets that provoke the reliability issue. The discrepancy in her thought process, bipolar reaction to the same incident followed by the rage of taking revenge, and last but not least, blaming herself for everything give a clear idea of Shalini's mind. The concept of an empathetic reader mentioned in the questions as mentioned earlier is to comprehend the circumstances she has gone through from an insider's perspective. The whole narrative is not infested with her discrepant train of thoughts, it follows the "norm of the work" (Booth, p.158), a linear narrative but then takes incoherent leaps in different contexts. This paper demonstrates the norm-breaking of the conventional narratorial voice on the basis of probable causes of readers' unreliability towards the narrative persona and leaves it open to interpretation. The analysis follows the possible psychological factors to read Shalini as an unreliable narrator,

WHY IS SHALINI SUPPOSED TO BE (UN)RELIABLE?

In the first section of the paper, if Shalini (the narrator) could be assessed from the eyes of a conventional reader, the following norms can be taken under consideration to categorize her as a (un)reliable narrator. Unlike an empathic reader, a conventional reader would restrain themselves to delve into the deep psychology of the narrative persona. The concerns pertaining to the unreliability issue are:

Delusional Self of the Narrator

The opening line of the novel suggests to the readers that Shalini and her husband, Riz are having arguments in the hope of getting back their lost daughter, sixteen years after, on her birthday, "My husband thinks we cannot find her. His voice is raw from screaming". (Akbar, 2017, p.1). The arguments seem real because Shalini gives a proper frame of conversation demonstrating an auditory sense of her husband's voice which is "raw from screaming". After a bout of a lengthy conversation, she informs the readers that her husband is dead and he often appears in front of her. That clearly implies that Riz is a manifestation of her Subconscious.

Riz died the same night they took our daughter. Yet here he is, by my side, as I walk from Purity One to the huge field where our old school, Yellowstone, used to be. (Akbar, 2017, p.14)

It is not that Shalini is in denial of her husband's death and her present condition, she has accepted both the most shocking experiences of her life for craving for the balance of life and getting back to the normal chore it has made her running, "that's what all of us were like at Camp. Doing desperate little things so we could remember what was norm al". (Akbar, 2017, p. 22). Riz has become Shalini's alter ego. She places herself in Riz's self and makes the imaginary conversation thinking from his perspective, what Riz would say in those situations. Cognizance of her husband based on the past, she crafts the conversation. Hence, she also informs the readers whenever and wherever he disappears. Shalini is a sensitive human being who observes very small things she passes by; her meticulous sense of observation forms her figments of imagination. Sometimes it is hard to understand where reality ends and her imagination begins and sometimes it merges.

Auditory Verbal Hallucinations: Schizotypal Personality Disorder?

In clinical terms, people having anxiety disorder tend to have imaginary conversations with their imaginary companions, may that be their family, real-life friends, or anyone made up. Most of the population between childhood and adolescence have imaginary friends which is perfectly normal. But with adults, self-talk is more popular. Shalini's condition is self-explanatory. Her loneliness and getting barred from venting out her pent-up feelings in the Tower led her to imagine Riz by her side. These kinds of conversations are therapeutic. A study on "Neuroimaging auditory verbal hallucinations in schizophrenia patient and healthy populations" shows that the structural basis of AVH (Auditory verbal hallucinations) could not be "straightforwardly ascribed" so far but it implies that "advancing age and other illness-related contributions to brain structure possibly dilute associations with AVH" (Di Biase et al., 2019, p. 8). It also does not discard the factor of trauma exposure of the subjects under this psychosis as a reason behind it. Besides that, the Purity Camp introduced the detainers to a routine medication. Shalini used to take some pills prescribed by Dr. Iyer which appeased her trauma-struck brain from plunging into madness. She also clarifies to the readers that they were not "crazy", those pills were among their daily chores and they conciliate their ill-at ease:

We were introduced to the pills at Purity Camp. When I first got there, I felt in pieces, ensnared by the wide, open fields with the lonely gabled sheds. A single step from the brink. But we weren't crazy, we were clear about that. (Akbar, 2017, p. 22)

But the same tendency can be seen in other characters as well, for example, when Shalini follows the "Lady Police" to the forest and the mud at night, she sees her having an imaginary dinner with three other imaginary friends, setting the cutlery and serving air as food. In the last chapter, "Things that Pull Us Together", Shalini expected her deserved ending, the ending of her quest for Leila. When she got to know about Sapna, she found the silver lining of Leila being there. She pulled herself together, hoping to set for a better life ahead, leaving all the pain behind, she cleaned up for good, took a bus, and set for her destination, there again she sees her dead husband:

On the bus came a terrific surprise. As I bought my ticket, I looked up, and Riz was beaming in the last seat, in his favourite shirt, black with thin navy checks. He glowed like he'd been caught in a shard of sunlight. I went to him almost running. (Akbar, 2017, p.160)

It was a crucial moment for Shalini as she was about to get her closure that kept her cankering through sixteen years. She wanted to rest her head "on his shoulder. But I knew how it would seem to the others on the bus". (Akbar, 2017, p.160). Here is another instance of pills-induced verbal hallucination. But she is self-conscious and aware of her surroundings. But the strangest part of their conversation was when Shalini starts reminiscing about one of the conjugal conflicts they once had over Riz's late-night stay outside with another woman. In the same illusory conversation Shalini's alternative self, Riz asks her the question, why this is coming up now. The disjunction is not only visible in the narration but also influences her thoughts. The incoherent jump can be seen in almost every crook of the narration. Once she talks about following a member (Lady Police) of the Purity Camp and in the second instance she moves her depiction to the corpse of her burned husband which she knew had been thrown in the gutter. She blames herself for everything that how her husband fought and was killed where she had been cowardly when her daughter was snatched from them by the Repeaters. She confesses many times that she is scared and alone. Then she switches to the everyday life of the camp, how they were treated like a maid there.

Dramatic Monologue

The mode of narrative apparently is uni-linear. But like Browning's speakers, instances of dramatic monologue can be seen. The normal mode of narration is the narrator to the readers and Shalini can be seen to have been distant from informing the readers and start making conversation with herself. Her sudden rage for the people of the camp or seeing one of the assailants, Repeater in the face of a brown lizard. She even picks it up and tends to squeeze it to death. But Shalini, unlike a stereotypical unreliable narrator is not a pathological liar, she eventually comes to senses and understands the practicality. But her overriding emotions definitely make the narrative biased. The pill-induced verbal hallucination is evident when another character, Sapna also confirms it. Dr, Iyer's pills used to work for Shalini as a pacifier for her anxiety and the wardens of the camp made sure that they were taking them. When Shalini's anxiety optimizes to the ultimate level hitting the dead-end of finding her daughter, the first thing she did was popping Dr. Iyer's pills, and instantly she could see the manifestation of Riz. Unlike other situations, this time she converses with him in front of Sapna, "Stop it, Shalini!' Sapna says, though not loudly. I turn to her. 'Do you know you've been muttering things to that pillar for five minutes?" (Akbar, 2017, p. 172). This puts forward two notions, first, Shalini's delusional conversation with the pillar, in reality, fetched Sapna a chance to defend herself at the brim of her flamboyancy (if it is supposed that way). Or if Sapna is true, as a foil character to Shalini, she tells the readers that she is not in a correct mental state. Second, it could be just another therapeutic conversation of Shalini with her husband to calm herself down and take hold of the situation, which is evident when Shalini apologizes to Sapna for losing her cool. This in fact justifies the ending, as Shalini does not mention any other neurotic breakdown of her and has peace with the final glance of the mysterious girl's face whom both Sapna and Shalini claims to be their daughter.

Deceptive Memory Influenced by Trauma

On fading memory, the human brain has a tendency to mix it with imagination and the formation of false memory. After sixteen years Leila's memory of Shalini is a smudge. It is fidgety that suddenly come and goes. As she says, "Now the memory of Leila's face is like a skewer. Jiggling pigtails, bright shopper's lights, the green eyes twinkle. A sudden deep smile because we had come together once more". (Akbar, 2017, p.29). She remembers episodic memories of Leila, riding toy trains, and how insecure she was to let go of her. How she used to flicker with a smile once they exchanged their site. Shalini is a meticulous observer even as a mother. She loved how Leila used to copy her which brought her joy of motherhood but she was frightened that Leela would copy her anger as well. Seeing her shouting made her think her way of parenting. As a narrator, this quality of observation is rare which Shalini processes. Thus, the narrative takes its readers away from their reality to the reality the fictive world has successfully created though her. Even in the farfetched dystopic parts of the readers can get along with Shalini and their guts also wrenched with her description of the world. Shalini grew a habit of taking medication which helped her escape the stark reality for a while,

I was taking the pills Dr. Iyer gave, which was all they really cared about. Some people have reported palpitations, night sweats, a sudden inability to breathe, but the pills have helped me. I take one every night even now. (Akbar, 2017, p.19)

She has mentioned her sleep deprivation in the Towers and how she would roam around the ground chasing the trails of the bus that took them to work and came after the sunrise. With those pills she had talked about multiple times, helped to take her back to her happy days with her husband and daughter. So, her shared memory is a result of those hallucinating pill, leaves the question of reliability once again. Later in that part, she self-contradicts as she ponders that to the boy, she is probably not different from the lizard. Both of their appearances to him were sudden, confusing, and too absurd to process for a child. Shalini could see the face of a Repeater from the worst night of her life on a lizard she saw in the barren land: "The lizard's beady gaze reminded me of someone I could not place, a face from Camp, or the night the Repeaters came, a reptile fat on sadness". (Akbar, 2017, pp. 26-27). Since her first encounter, she seemed to hate the reptile, she points at its 'fat' countenance and channels her anger for her husband's murderer on it. She almost squeezes it to death. But as it is well established that Shalini is sensitive and has not toppled the brim of cruelty yet, she finally lets it go. The deformation of Shalini's past memory is instigated by her trauma,

Taking this literal return of the past as a model for repetitive behavior in general, Freud ultimately argues, in Beyond the Pleasure Principle, that it is traumatic repetition, rather than the meaningful distortions of neurosis, that defines the shape of individual lives. (Caruth, 2016, p.59)

She also states sometimes that the memory of her daughter's face has remained as nothing but a smudge. It keeps flashing and then fades out. The traumatic episodes, for her, do not end in Riz's murder and Leila's abduction. Life in purity camp and the everyday challenges to groove into the process make her history of trauma exponentially accelerating which becomes the primary causation behind her the distortion of her life and existing memories.

Narrative Sensitivity

Shalini's use of collective metaphors is one of the many qualities of a detailed narration that make readers picture the story all along. She compares her suffocation with a trapped bee. Her days in the camp was as flabbergasted as that but her escape from reality, keeping herself busy in work and following up on the surrounding and indomitable faith and effort of getting her daughter back were what kept him alive, "A bee that fights its way out of a beer first performs muddled rotations of the mug, looping wider and wider in the afternoon air. That's what all of us were like at Camp". (Akbar, 2017, p.22). She has repeatedly compared the world before the Purity Camp and after that, how the farming lands used to be there, now they are barren heaths and land of lizards and insects,

Each of the poplars, planted years ago to break the invading wind that hurtled through the crop and partnered with the sun to set off ruinous fires, had been shorn by the long summer. They grew along the side of the road like giant besoms jammed into the mud. The earth was cold against my blouse. (Akbar, 2017, p.25)

Apart from all the misery, she has gone through, Shalini's thoughtful nature appeals to the readers most. On her sleep-deprived nights when she used to go out and lie in the mud to get away from the camp, she remembers the world before the walls and what they have become. The way she perceived nature and every single thing reminded her of the past and how life would turn up in an alternate reality. Her narration is quite poetic, filled with visuals and auditory effects, how the winds hurtled, and the feeling of the cold earth against her body. This kind of in-depth account of her descriptions delineates the sensitivity of her narration.

Motherly Instincts Sways Shalini's Narration

A narrative is a fragmented reality influenced by the narrator's own judgments, infused with his/her emotional value. The entire fiction is primarily a quest of a mother for finding her lost daughter. Shalini's episodic remembrance of Leila and the narrative of her childhood show how deep of a thinker and observant mother she was. Each and every childish move of her daughter flooded her with joy. She even got worried when Leila started copying her and shouted at imaginary figures. It made her worried about her parental flaws and when she shouted at others that way so Leila had gotten to imitate her. She often asks herself if Leila remembers all those moments they spent together, questions herself if she wonders who she is and why she has abandoned her. She has read in a book that a three-year-old can not remember those memories as it is her early cognition phase. She thinks that she is like emptiness to her that she 'cannot understand but yearns to fill. No. I have left more, a glimmer at least. The blurred outline of a face. A tracery of scent. The weight of fingertips on her cheek. The warmth of her first cradle, my arms.' (Akbar, 2017, p. 12). In an article she found out that memory goes back to two and a few months, mind can place disjointed memories like a 'vast fog, discrete islands' but they do not play along in the same alignment they happened, displaced and likely to be unlinked. Leila comes into Shalini's mind like an impressionist painting, patched and brush-stroked as if she remembers every moment she had spent with her daughter, her laughter, claps, bounces, all the moves she made,

When she spotted me a light seemed to fill her face, a huge smile erupted, and then she was pointing at me, clapping, bouncing in her spot. The way she looked at me. I was filled with a golden warmth. Replete. She and me together, the track, the circle. (Akbar, 2017, p.29)

Human memory is deceptive, after a certain time the fact or the facet of an observant's reality gets mixed with his/her imagination to fill the gaps in the array of memories, and then there is confabulation or formation of the false memory. The detailed description of Leila brought by Shalini can suggest that the motherly emotion is so tactile that kept her memory not only intact but with time her past has gotten livelier in front of her eyes as she nothing but longed for her daughter, thus every day it has grown more and more. Next, when she meets the boy, Roop, on a 'sharp moonless December night', whose family was also attacked by the Repeaters rekindles her motherly spirit to protect him. She used to carry a switch knife with a wooden handle to tackle any attacker, she could handle two of them as she practiced in front of the mirror which again led her to the everlasting guilt that she could not protect her and so she was taken. After a long memory run, Shalini had a conversation with the boy, at first, she wanted to take him with her, the boy was confused and scared but she, like a mother held him dearly and told him how to get way back to his parents, she held a lizard in front of him and gave him a lesson of taking control over his fear, "The boy slowly regained breath and composure, his hands between my palms" (Akbar, 2017, P.26). For a Shalini's description of her encounter with Roop would seem sound similar to that of her memories with Leila.

The Bipolarity of Narration: Display of Anger and Hatred

The swayed judgments of Shalini are sometimes overtly vivid. Bipolarity in medical terms is defined by the inconsistency of moods, sudden switches from low to high, or the otherwise followed by fickle-mindedness and quick changes of opinions on the same matter. Her encounter with the little boy flashbacked the motherly instinct, but at once her warmth of motherhood changed into a rage, she starts calling the boy hairy and dirty and he was older than Leila when she was taken away from her. She says that it is because she had not spoken to a child for a long time, hence the peculiar feeling. These sudden flickers of mind are indications of her unsettling psyche, "This hairy, dirty boy, so many years older than my little girl. I hadn't spoken to a child in months. One moment the boy was leaning on me, breathing heavy, his whimpers throaty and wet. Then he was gone". (Akbar, 2017, p.28). She herself is confused if she was happy with the presence of the child or with him gone.

I wonder sometimes how the boy is. If they caught him that night and took him wherever it is they take our children. Why didn't I sit with him a while longer? Only a few minutes more and the Repeaters would've gone right past. Him too I did not protect. (Akbar, 2017, p.28)

Her thoughts are whimsical. While looking back at the night Shalini regrets having the boy let go, she wonders if he was safe or caught by the assailants, she plays the scene again and again in her mind with different possibilities, once with motherly worry and again with a cold detest. But she ends this thought too with her guilt that, like Leila, she could not protect Roop as well. The intersectionality of Shalini's identity as a widow, a destitute mother, a progressive urban girl, and a liberal-minded woman to whom religion and caste do not matter; she has formed a liminal space where she keeps meandering between her past and present, "The liminality of identity works as a threshold between binary identities or extreme poles of the identities wherein the subject may simultaneously hold dual identities" (Bhattacharya, 2022, p. 49). This duality can be presumed to create the bipolar dilemma in her mind which resists her as well as effervesce her *Self* at once.

Sense of Guilt

People like Shalini are the victims of the so-called 'purity' obsessed government, their false ideology of religious decontamination endorses genocidal crimes and the cleansing of mixed-blood children, keeping aside all the concerns they should have taken under consideration. As a mother who lost her daughter on the day of her birthday, Shalini's sense of guilt haunts her like a death-eater. The many times she reiterates that moment she blames on herself, "My daughter had been taken precisely because I could not protect her". (Akbar, 2017, p.25). Even though she could not have protected her daughter from those overpowering beasts, she probably regrets it because she froze. Unlike her husband she did not fight enough to end up dead, "Riz fought so that Leila wouldn't be taken. Me? I will die a coward, submissive to the last. Out of confusion. Because I'm scared. Alone. Because the Council has decreed it. I have many excuses". (Akbar, 2017, p.23). Later when she met a young boy in the same circumstance, she wanted her to protect him from the SUV full of drunk Repeaters. As they were not allowed to bring children in the Towers, she could not take him with her, instead, she helped him get rid of his fear and find a way back to his parents. As he left, she once again sank into her recurrent self-guilt, "Him too I did not protect". (Akbar, 2017, p.28), says Shalini.

THE QUEER TURN: PSYCHOANALYSIS OF DYSTOPIA

Sixteen years of her life had passed in the Purity camp, but ironically the women of the Towers did not hold the 'pure' dignity to the outsiders, especially to the Repeaters. They were treated as women of ill repute. At least twice in the fiction, she has depicted the vulture eyes of the goons on her. Before the disaster ruined her life, Shalini belonged to a rich and well-rounded family, they had maids for household help, and one of them was Sapna. Once she got to know about the presumable existence of Leila and that she might have been brought up by Sapna in a favorable environment which both Shalini and Riz wanted to give her, she corresponds with Sapna secretly and fixed up a meeting with her. The second queerly sexual encounter can be seen when Shalini was stopped for checking by the guards of Sapna's mansion. One of the women in the tent undressed her and ran a thorough checkup. The weirdness of the checking gets queerer when the woman, as Shalini says starts touching and penetrating her body in the presence of two other guards which she claims left her with no clue. This turn of the narrative topples the brim of the ethos of the story, it brings out a sadistic pleasure that once again leaves readers in a peculiar state. The way Shalini depicts the poised movements of the woman, it is hard to understand whether it reflects her pleasure principles, a slip of her unconscious or inner resistance. It too pictures a sadomasochistic facet of the narrative.

CITY AND THE OMNIPRESENT WALL

As a protruding discussion of the psychoanalytic discourse of the narratorial voice, the concept of the *wall* leaves another space for looking into the text. The architectural construction of the urban scape in Future India presented in the novel is apocalyptic. The country suffers from a water crisis and deadly air pollution. The government has divided the landscape into two, one for the slammers and another for the aristocrats. The division is "fifty-nine feet high and two feet thick" (Akbar, 2017, p.33) gigantic wall. "Some forty years after Purity One was erected there are no trees. The stunning canopy is gone. Now there are hundreds of walls, no one sure how many". (Akbar, 2017, p.33). The significant presence of walls in literature has a historical tradition. Walls have appeared many times, such as, in Bond's retelling of *King Lear*. In Bond's *Lear*, the construction of the wall was not only a means of separation and protection for his kingdom but also was the mental projection of his own insecurity and alienation. The wall here has also multitudinous meanings. In the entire narration, the word "wall" has been used one hundred twenty-nine times excluding the titular usage. In the televised version of the story, the government has been named 'Aryavartha' which is led by a Joshiji where the nation is religious acrimony, a totalitarian regime. The government is unnamed in the book even though the character, Joshiji is there in the book as well with her man Friday, Ashish, husband of Shalini's past house-help now a powerful figure in the political sector. They constructed air purifying domes only for the use of the aristocrats.

'That the walls are important. We must have them. The whole city used to be like the Outroads. Lawless. Filthy. Dirt at your doorstep. People shitting on the roads. Into the gutters. The best people could not live like that any more. We needed the walls. (Akbar, 2017, p.116)

Societal segregation is a vindication of religious and inter-caste hybridization. Not only Leila but the offspring of such marriages have been slaughtered and kidnapped in unknown locations. The wall is seen to have proliferated a deep sense of separation in Shalini's mind as well because it segregates her present life from her childhood and happy days. In the chapter, "Ma and Papa", she talks about her childhood memories,

My father detested these walls, and now that I use the Outroads every day I live with what you evict from your eyes, your minds, I must see your shit and grime, the cascading brown water, the showering refuse. Smells so thick you can taste them.

Her growing detests for the walls and the whole engineering of the structure is reasonable. Religious and economic separation is never a governmental solution to improve the nation. The figure of Joshiji is sketchy, he is based on those political figures who indulge assailants as their accomplice but keep their impression uninfluenced,

'I will take us to the pure city,' Joshi shouted, voice stretched with lust. 'Each must protect our walls, our women, the communities. Make sure they cannot break our rules any more. Go forth and do our work. Once again we will reach the pinnacle of the world!' (Akbar, 2017, p.82)

Even though Akbar's *Leila* is based on the scaffolding of dystopic feminism which is entwined with misogyny the slogan of Joshi ironically speaks of protection of the women and the walls in the same sentence, in an anticlimactic manner.

QUESTIONING UNRELIABILITY

In reply to the question regarding him being a male author creating a first-person female with motherly love and longing, which is 'relatively rare modern Indian fiction' and what came first, "the character or her story", Akbar says,

Figure 1.

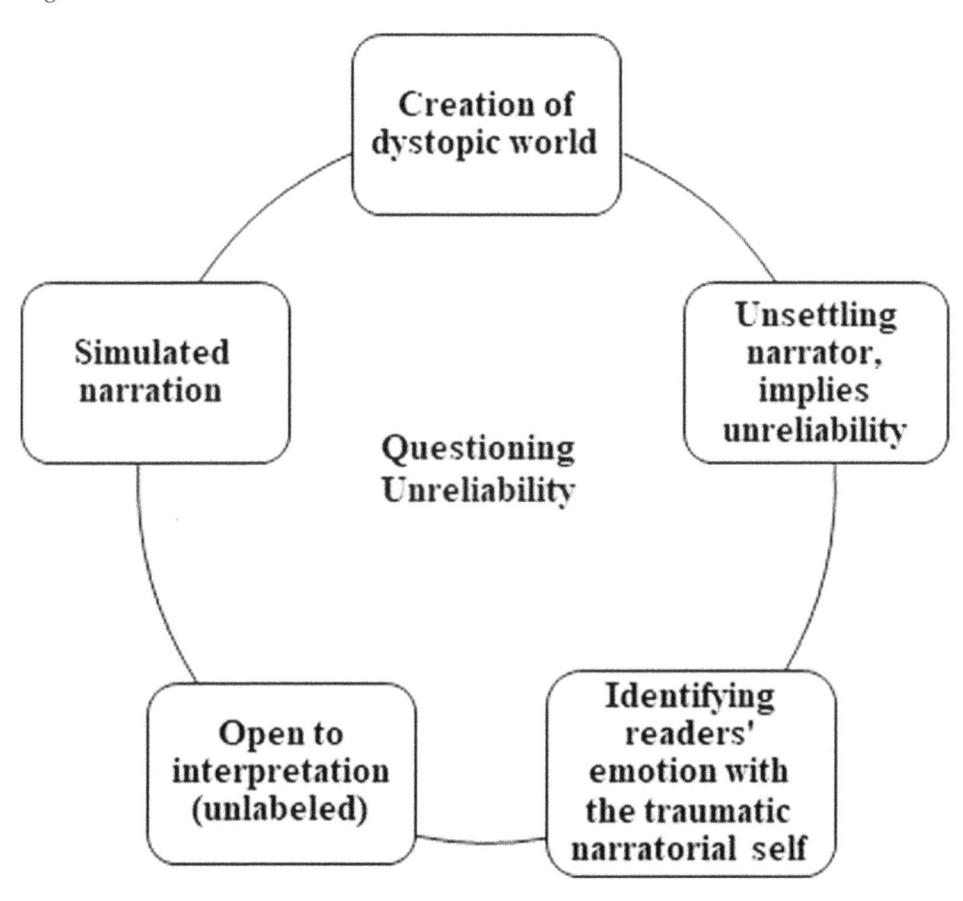

```
                    Creation of
                   dystopic world


   Simulated                        Unsettling
   narration                        narrator,
                                    implies
                    Questioning     unreliability
                    Unreliability


                                    Identifying
     Open to                        readers'
  interpretation                    emotion with
    (unlabeled)                     the traumatic
                                    narratorial self
```

Leila began with Shalini and her daughter. The dystopic elements came later. It took a great deal of effort to get Shalini to sound true, and I was glad to have an excellent editor, who managed to find each instance where I strayed, or a kind of masculinity entered, some male notion of what being a woman is like. (Guha, 2021, para. 8)

In order to create a whole new world under the dystopic veil, Akbar has been questioned many times for the influence of Atwood's *The Handmaid's Tale* and *Leila* has been compared with it too. The author himself mentions that the weaving of the fictive world has been inspired by his reading of *The Master of Petersburg, Life and Times of Michael K, Waiting for the Barbarians*. Especially the influence of Coetzee on Akbar can be noticed, which he also acknowledges in the same interview. In *Waiting for the Barbarians* Coetzee creates a frontier world surrounded by a fringed population of the natives, moreover a representation of colonial dystopia, the same harrowing frontier rule. The incorporation of trauma and torture of the government on its subjects are prevalent in both texts. Coetzee interweaves dreams in his character, a subsequent completion, and a cryptic revelation of the dream from the mid to the end of the novel. Akbar has not quite riveted the same doctrine of dream vision but he has implanted hallucination. Readers become one with the world of Shalini as she takes through it meticulously. Oatly says, "We project ourselves into the simulated world, and we may come back changed" (Oatley, 2011, p. 23). Hence readers' judgment here is compromised. If the whole text is read with the suspension of disbelief, the story comes out straight. It has got every element of a post-apocalyptic dystopic world, the voice of a female narrator, misogyny, and xenophobia creeping over the nation. But to analyze it with the cognizance of the narrator, though the theory of mind, raises all these questions,

Abnormal minds provide a perfect laboratory for examining how human characters contend with, adapt to, and overcome—or fail to overcome—obstacles to their own survival and success. Such world allows for "extreme case analysis" and provides readers with optional cognitive "playgrounds" for their own thinking and feeling brains. (Xiao-yan, 2014, p. 423)

Theory of mind recommends readers to read the mind of the narrator rather than doing a distant study of the character. The author creates his narrative persona for the ideal reader's deep understanding. Literature classics have plenty of archetypal characters who can be unfolded from different vantage points. In reference to the American sitcom, "The Big Bang Theory", it showed the universal model of supersymmetry and asymmetry are not different but the same, it just differs with the viewer's perspectives,

We have come to regard Theory of Mind (ToM) as a natural process through which readers interpret and comprehend characters in fiction. Authors such as Jane Austen or Virginia Woolf, writing books about human characters like Emma or Mrs. Dalloway, expect their readers to infer characters' motivations and feelings by assuming a similarity to the readers' own thinking and feeling bodies. (Marron, 2011, p.187)

As marron rightly points out, interpreting the characters is a task or exercise of the readers, given by the authors, "the authors often construct their characters as human beings with ToM skills similar to the reader" (Marron, 2011, p.187). Akbar here has created Shalini's strenuous journey of life, with two major shocks and immense trauma. Towards the ending when Shalini beams with hope, the readers too exhale optimism that, finally she is going to get her peace but the story, like

Lehane's *Shutter Island* (2003) leaves it open-ended. It alters from person to person, leaving it a subject to a readerly debate:

"Plays, films, short stories, and novels are about people with intentions who interact with each other. People are good at understanding processes on step at a time, but less good at understanding intersections of such processes." (Oatley, 2011, p. 21)

The unreliable narrator is a representation of a cognitive process of the implied author and to understand it a reader needs powerful imagination to fill in the gaps and interpret the story. Results of qualitative research vary on the researcher's qualitative skills and in quantitative research, it is up to the computational variables. Likewise, the interpretation of a reader depends on their knowledge and thematic preference, personal biases toward the fictional characters, etc. To a reader, the minds of narrators in "works of fiction magnify and vivify various points on the continuum of our imperfect mutual knowledge: spectacular feats and failures of mind reading are the hinges on which many a fictional plot turns" (Zunshine, 2011, p. 69). Plunging in the narrative reality it should be difficult to justify a narrator. The gradual deterioration of Shalini's mental state is vivid through the progression of the plot. That is where it becomes tough for the readers to apprehend her condition or identify themselves with her. The interweaving of imagination, hallucination and reality perplexes the viewer's minds as well,

Even though we know that there must be a mental state behind a behavior, we don't really know what that state is. That is, there is always a possibility that something else is going on behind even the most seemingly transparent behavior. (Zunshine, 2011, p. 69)

As Proust states that while reading, a reader perceives the distinction between the world he lives in and the world presented in the fiction. India, created in Akbar's novel is not the same nation in reality, by reading *Leila*, readers live a futuristic and detrimental version of it, with the mere possibilities and lots of what-could-have-been(s):

In reality each reader, when he is reading, is uniquely reading himself. The writer's work is only a kind of optical instrument which he offers the reader to enable him to discern what without this book he might not have seen in himself. (Proust, 2003, pp. 219-220)

If for once Shalini can be put under the lens of an archetype of an unreliable narrator because her narration conforms to the following attributes, "(1) It is resonated with the sympathetic reader's values; and (2) It blurs the reader's source-tracking ability. Most of unreliable narrators may have some cognitive causes for their unreliable narration". (Xiao-yan, 2014, p. 427). Considering the confounded ending of the novel, whether the girl, claimed by Sapna as her daughter was actually Shalini's Leila a reader can never know. The origin of this mystery is mapped by Shalini's cognition. She caters a legible explanation that Sapna was neither married nor with a child with Leila was kidnapped and on that cataclysmic night Leila with her, so the sudden appearance of an eighteen years old daughter is suspicious. The way Shalini depicts the story, from that it can be seen that Sapna is pointing at her mental illness and that she remembers the story wrong. Here it is hard to determine whose story is to believe. The power of Shalini's narrative does not leave much space for the readers to go with the statements of Sapna and she is seen to be fumbling. Nünning's reconceptualization of the theory of unreliability hands over the power dynamic to the reader's cognitive scheme of empathetic indulgence,

These include both textual data and the reader's preexisting conceptual knowledge of the world. In sum whether a narrator is called unreliable or not does not depend on the distance between the norms and values of the narrator and those of the implied author but between the distance that separates the narrator's view of the world from the reader's world-model and standards of normality. (Nünning, 1997, pp. 83-105)

Recalibrating the story even if the narrative scale points Shalini toward unreliability, does not portray her as a negative influence. Her side of the story is quite believable and meaningful in the bigger picture but the frame of narration and patchy clusters of incoherence makes the reader think again. The unassisted ending problematizes it even more. The first reading of the text might leave the readers exhilarated about the whole fiction but the reversed reading, after knowing the unprecise ending if Shalini seems to be more and more ambiguous character.

Determining whether a narrator is unreliable is not just an innocent descriptive statement but a subjectively tinged value-judgment or projection governed by the normative presuppositions and moral convictions of the critic, which as a rule remain unacknowledged. Critics concerned with unreliable narrators recuperate textual inconsistencies by relating them to accepted cultural models. (Nünning, 2008, p. 40)

The question of reliability, hence, is a circular trap. The interesting notion about it is that the story majorly changes on the conclusion of the reader. Reading the story without even considering the reliability variables makes the story peculiar but more in a linear structure but the other way makes the story more complex and indecisive. Either way the mystery remains unsolved.

CONCLUSION

Narrative reality is a simulated reality, sketched by the narrator. Justifying the reliability or unreliability of reality is ambiguous. Even in Platonic philosophy, the question of reliability depends on human perception and the core of it is imitation. To prove and label a narrator unreliable there must be certain factors to look into, such as incoherent fragmentation of storytelling, mismatched facts, clash of multiple realities created by the narrator, etc. In Gilman's (1981) short story "The Yellow Wallpaper", the anonymous first-person narrator is a literary prodigy of unreliable narrators. The psychopathology behind the readers' untrustworthiness toward her is her postpartum depression, a less familiar mental illness of that time. In the case of Shalini, it is her trauma-fretted brain that is subject to her biases. Other than the prominent character of the narrator, it can be thought that the character of Sapna stands as an antithesis of Shalini. If the story is read as a conspiracy theory of Sapna or if it were re-told from her perspective, it can be inferred that she is the one who makes Shalini an unreliable narrator. She consigns a different story that Leila was never there and nobody had seen her after that night. But if it is true the girl she claims to be as her daughter *was* in fact Leila, does that withdraw the question of Shalini's unreliability as a narrator? Even though it is better to leave this study inclusive because this paper itself supports the readerly perspective of interpretation and the concept of an empathetic reader.

All in all, the narrative of *Leila* is a speculative dystopian fictional writing, where the narrative is defied by the mental projection of the city-space and city as a gendered space. The lens of the narrative captures fragmented scenes. Putting them together, the narrative frame becomes spatially non-linear and multidimensional and the formation of the meaning (which is an important notion of cultural studies) depends on the reader's viewpoint, hence, it is subjective and presents many alternative perspectives. In a dystopian form of narrative, the phenomenological (philosophy of experience) aspect of human emotions contradicts the rigidity of reliability. So, the expansion of the textual discourse is stretched beyond the parameter of reliability and non-reliability. In conclusion, it can be claimed that, with the preexisting frame of the theory and the examples of classic unreliable narrators, Akbar's Shalini cannot be classified under any of the reliable or unreliable variables. She herself fabricated an axiomatic style of narration which changes with the reader's suspension of belief.

REFERENCES

Akbar, P. (2017). *Leila*. Simon & Schuster.

Alter, A. (2018). *How feminist dystopian fiction is channeling women's anger and anxiety.* Retrieved October 27, 2022, https://www.nytimes.com/2018/10/08/books/feminist-dystopian-fiction-margaret-atwood-women-metoo.html

Bhattacharya, M. (2022). The partition: A Heterotopic transcendence in self-identity of the Bengali women migrants. In M. Pourya Asl (Ed.), *Gender, place, and identity of South Asian women* (pp. 44–67). IGI Global. doi:10.4018/978-1-6684-3626-4.ch003

Booth, W. C. (1961). *The rhetoric of fiction.* University of Chicago Press.

Caruth, C. (2016). *Unclaimed experience: Trauma, narrative, and history.* Johns Hopkins University Press. doi:10.56021/9781421421650

Cixous, H., & Clement, C. (1986). *The newly born woman.* University of Minnesota Press.

Das, S. R. (2020). *Dystopia and Indianness in Post-Millennial Indian Fiction.* https://www.pwcenglish.com/2020/04/06/dystopia-and-indianness-in-post-millennial-indian-fiction/

Dashgupta, P. (2020, February). *'Real' to the 'Hyperreal': A Study of the Postmodern and Dystopian Cityscape in Ruchir Joshi's The Last Jet-Engine Laugh and Prayaag Akbar's Leila.* Melow.

Di Biase, M. A., Zhang, F., Lyall, A., Kubicki, M., Mandl, R. C., Sommer, I. E., & Pasternak, O. (2019). Neuroimaging auditory verbal hallucinations in schizophrenia patient and healthy populations. *Psychological Medicine, 50*(3), 403–412. doi:10.1017/S0033291719000205

Gilman, C. P. (1981). *The Yellow Wallpaper.* Virago Press.

Guha, K. (2021, December 5). *Prayaag Akbar on the experiences and influences that Shaped Leila.* Retrieved August 28, 2022. https://www.thehindu.com/lit-for-life/love-and-other-jihads-prayaag-akbar-talks-about-his-novel-leila/article61450463.ece

Konchan, V. (2012). *Urban Poetics: A Call from (and to) the Wild.* https://sites.lsa.umich.edu/mqr/2012/10/urban-poetics-a-call-from-and-to-the-wild/

Lehane, D. (2003). *Shutter Island.* Morrow.

Marron, O. (2011). Alternative theory of mind for artificial brains: A logical approach to interpreting alien minds. In P. Leverage (Ed.), *Theory of minds and literature* (pp. 187–200). Purdue University Press.

Nünning, A. (1997). "But why will you say that I am mad?" On the Theory, History, and Signals of Unreliable Narration in British Fiction. *AAA: Arbeiten Aus Anglistik Und Amerikanistik*, *22*(1), 83–105.

Nünning, A. (2008). Reconceptualizing the theory, history and generic scope of unreliable narration: Towards a synthesis of cognitive and rhetorical approaches. In E. D'hoker & G. Martens (Eds.), *Narrative Unreliability in the Twentieth-Century First-Person Novel* (pp. 29–76). De Gruyter. doi:10.1515/9783110209389.29

Oatley, K. (2011). Theory of mind and theory of minds in literature. In P. Leverage (Ed.), *Theory of minds and literature*. Purdue University Press.

Pourya Asl, M. (Ed.), *Gender, place, and identity of South Asian women*. IGI Global. doi:10.4018/978-1-6684-3626-4

Proust, M. (2003). *In search of lost time: Finding time again* (I. Patterson, Trans.). Penguin.

Shi, L., & Zhu, Q. (2018). Urban space and representation in literary study. *Open Journal of Social Sciences*, *06*(09), 223–229. doi:10.4236/jss.2018.69015

Soja, E. W. (1996). *Thirdspace: Journeys to Los Angeles and other real-and-imagined place*. Blackwell Publishers.

Soja, E. W. (2000). *Postmetropolis: Critical studies of cities and regions*. Blackwell Publishers.

Wolfreys, J. (2002). *Introducing criticism at the 21st Century*. Edinburgh University Press.

Xiao-yan, L. (2014). Theory of mind and the unreliable narrator. *US-China Foreign Language*, *12*(5), 422–428. doi:10.17265/1539-8080/2014.05.010

Zunshine, L. (2011). Theory of mind and fiction of embodied transparency. In P. Leverage (Ed.), *Theory of minds and literature* (pp. 56–92). Purdue University Press.

Chapter 5
"Where Do Old Birds Go to Die?":
Queer Environmental Geographies and Liminal Spaces in Arundhati Roy's *The Ministry of Utmost Happiness*

Meghna Prabir
https://orcid.org/0000-0002-2206-2814
Christ University, India

ABSTRACT

Arundhati Roy's The Ministry of Utmost Happiness (2017) addresses the question of gendered identity through the spaces that its protagonist Anjum inhabits. Applying ideas from intersectional queer ecologies, this study examines liminal spaces in the novel where the dispossessed are shown to be able to find a sense of home. It is widely believed that the novel encompasses the space of two graveyards: Anjum's graveyard, which becomes a paradise, and Kashmir, the paradise that has become a graveyard. It is argued that Roy examines contemporary India's multi-layered spaces, providing incisive observations that are deeply unsettling for the fundamentalist mind to contemplate. The non-normative geography of her literary landscape seems to posit that the liminal, in-between spaces inhabited by those with identities that transcend homogenous definitions are the spaces in which those persecuted for not conforming to acceptable norms of identity can truly find refuge and security.

DOI: 10.4018/978-1-6684-6650-6.ch005

Copyright © 2023, IGI Global. Copying or distributing in print or electronic forms without written permission of IGI Global is prohibited.

INTRODUCTION

Urbanity has almost always signified the alienation of individuals from the broader capitalist-colonialist machine. Urban spaces engender loneliness (Curtis & Han, 2022, p. 102). Individuals in such spaces also tend to be more visible than in other spaces, sometimes leading to a forced 'coming out' for those who are in gender-minority groups. For instance, transgender children in urban contexts do have the means and agency to define their own identity in some ways, especially with supportive guardians, but the question remains: "What sort of rights will they have? Who should have the power to define sex and gender?" (Schiappa, 2022, p. 48) A large city may have "a more supportive environment" than a less urban region. (Yarbough, 2018, p. 68) However, urban spaces are also rife with both epistemic and empirical violence against marginalised communities.

Arundhati Roy's *The Ministry of Utmost Happiness* (2017) begins with the question, "Where do old birds go to die?" The words take the reader back to Roy's Booker Prize-winning, *The God of Small Things* (1997), in which the precocious Sophie Mol, destined for tragedy, asks the question of adults. Sophie, the "seeker of small wisdoms," asks: "Where do old birds go to die? Why don't dead ones fall like stones from the sky?" (Roy, 1997, p. 9) *The Ministry of Utmost Happiness* addresses the question by connecting it to the deaths of vultures because of the chemicals dairy industries use:

The vultures died of diclofenac poisoning. Diclofenac, cowaspirin, given to cattle as a muscle relaxant, to ease pain and increase the production of milk, works – worked – like nerve gas on white-backed vultures. Each chemically relaxed, milk-producing cow or buffalo that died became poisoned vulture-bait. As cattle turned into better dairy machines, as the city ate more ice cream, butterscotch-crunch, nutty-buddy and chocolate-chip, as it drank more mango milkshake, vultures' necks began to droop as though they were tired and simply couldn't stay awake. Silver beards of saliva dripped from their beaks, and one by one they tumbled off their branches, dead.

Not many noticed the passing of the friendly old birds. There was so much else to look forward to. (Roy, 2017, p. 8)

Anjum, the novel's protagonist, is introduced in the first chapter as follows: "She lived in the graveyard like a tree" (Roy, 2017, p. 9). By connecting her trans protagonist to vultures and trees, Roy begins by establishing one of the book's principal concerns: how systemic oppression and hierarchical, institutionalised regulations for living have created spaces that deliberately exclude the environmental and the non-normative. Roy's passage on vultures includes the image of the many flavours of ice cream a city demands, establishing how the inherently consumerist urban imperative for families with children to go out for ice cream relates to species extinctions. Nobody knows or cares where old birds go to die; moreover, 'bird' is often a dismissively feminised term. In an ethnonationalist context, a 'lower' class Muslim transwoman has as little space as a dead bird in society's normative, rigidly regulated structures.

Based on Roy's incisive dismantling of India's hegemonic societal structures, this chapter examines how the novel, fueled by Roy's twenty years of activism, interrogates the processes through which multiple forms of othering occur in contemporary India. Women, queer communities, religious minorities, people relegated to the categories of 'lower' classes and castes, and nonhuman species are systemically degraded, their identities reduced to the utilitarian. Discourses in the fields of queer ecology, queer geography, postcolonial spatialities, speciesism, and Roy's own arguments in her essays, which critique mediatisation and systemic governmental oppressions, inform the chapter. Further, the study's key objective is to bridge the gaps between theory and application by reading Roy's fictional narratives in terms of intersectional environmentalism, which is imperative to address the current ecological crisis.

LITERATURE REVIEW

Issues, Controversies, Problems

Two of the broadest theoretical frameworks essential to this study are queer environmental geographies and feminist postcolonial spatialities. These two frameworks are discussed in the first section of the literature review.

Intersectional environmentalism today often focuses on Indigenous and colonised communities. Colonisation's cultural primitivism relegated all non-urban identities and spaces to idyllic Arcadias, positing settler colonies as 'New Edens' in which European colonisers could reinvent themselves through genocide and other xenomisic practices to gain resources and wealth. Ironically, while colonialist industrailisation led to the current ecological crisis, Indigenous ways of living are now being recognised as far more sustainable than 'civilised' economic practices. The study's key resources to understand this theoretical framework are Zsea Bowmani's essay on contemporary concerns and Greta Gaard's work establishing intersectional concerns in ecofeminism.

First, Gaard's essay "Toward a Queer Ecofeminism" (1997) introduces the notion of intersectionality through Plumwood's structures of dualist hierarchies:

culture/nature
reason/nature

male/female
mind/body (nature)
master/slave
reason/matter (physicality)
rationality/animality (nature)
reason/emotion (nature)
mind, spirit/nature
freedom/necessity (nature)
universal/particular
human/nature (nonhuman)
civilized/primitive (nature)
production/reproduction (nature)
public/private
subject/object
self/other (p. 116)

Gaard (1997) theorises that these dualistic forms of othering can be looked at "both 'horizontally' and 'vertically'" (p. 117). The terms on the left, frequently referred to as the 'A' terms, represent identity categories that are typically hegemonically in control of the 'B' terms, or the terms on the right. Several terms can be added to this list through contemporary concerns: heterosexual/homosexual, cisgender/transgender, white/BIPOC, human/nonhuman, and so on.

In *Ecofeminism: Women, Animals, Nature* (1993), Gaard states: "Ecofeminism's basic premise is that the ideology that authorizes oppression based on race, class, gender, sexuality, physical abilities, and species is the same ideology that sanctions the oppression of nature" (p. 1). Postcolonial ecofeminism also encourages examining both gender and race as means through which the marginalised, as well as the planet, are exploited by the capitalist-colonialist machine. In terms of contemporary perspectives, one may understand that a shift away from the gender binary towards perspectives from queer studies is also essential in order to dismantle systemic oppression and epistemic violence.

Further, Gaard's work is also fundamental to contemporary studies since it locates systemic oppression in a historical context that invokes the Cartesian notion of dualistic discrimination:

Many feminists and ecofeminists who have examined Western culture's hierarchical and oppressive relationship with nature date the problem of human separation from nature (the necessary precedent to hierarchy and oppression) back to 4000 B.C.E., the Neolithic era, and the conquering of matrifocal, agricultural, goddess-

worshiping cultures by militaristic, nomadic cultures that worshiped a male god. (Gaard, 1997, p. 122)

While the humanist approach insists on this separation of the human and the natural, posthumanist postcolonialism sees humans as animals rather than opposed to them. Moreover, such exclusionary perspectives see queerness as intrinsically deviant since it does not conform to binary and dualist ways of categorising identities: "In the earliest notorious example of what might today be called transgender persecution, nineteen-year-old Joan of Arc was burned at the stake as a witch in 1431, condemned to death for the sin of wearing men's clothing" (Gaard, 1997, p. 126).

A 'vertical' view of the A and B terms, consequently, investigates how women and other marginalised genders, animals, racially othered peoples, and the disabled community are all epistemic categories that are seen as inherently 'weak': "When nature is feminized and thereby eroticized, and culture is masculinized, the culture-nature relationship becomes one of compulsory heterosexuality" (Gaard, 1997, p. 131). Institutionalised oppression privileges the A terms and marginalises the B terms, beginning with processes of historical oppression and hegemony: "Colonization can therefore be seen as a relationship of compulsory heterosexuality whereby the queer erotic of non-westernized peoples, their culture, and their land, is subdued into the missionary position — with the conqueror 'on top'" (p. 131).

Gaard's work also recommends ways in which queer ecofeminist perspectives can establish ways of thought and action that can help societies begin the process of dismantling oppressive structures:

A queer ecofeminist perspective would argue that liberating the erotic requires reconceptualizing humans as equal participants in culture and in nature, able to explore the eroticism of reason and the unique rationality of the erotic. Ecofeminists must be concerned with queer liberation, just as queers must be concerned with the liberation of women and of nature; our parallel oppressions have stemmed from our perceived associations. It is time to build our common liberation on more concrete coalitions. (Gaard, 1997, p. 132)

Bowmani's essay "Now is the time for Black queer feminist ecology" (2021) locates these intersectional discourses in the context of contemporary concerns such as the Black Lives Matter movement and the issue of police brutality and other forms of institutionalised and systemic oppression:

Being a legal scholar, I am especially interested in examining how the law has facilitated these modes of domination/subordination. Because we do not lead single-issue lives, my scholarship examines intersecting issues of identity—namely race and ethnicity, gender, sexuality, human rights, and the environment. My focus on these areas [is] informed by my experience in reproductive justice advocacy (a movement started by Black women in response to their marginalization in the reproductive rights arena) and defending LGBTQ people against discrimination. (p. 4)

Bowmani's perspectives are essential to intersectional analyses since his work locates both gendered violence and environmental justice in the context of legal systems that are often directly responsible for othering and marginalisation. He examines how "the boundaries of *acceptable* and *deviant* expressions of sexuality and gender have been deeply intertwined with race and dehumanization, starting with the first white Europeans to arrive in the Americas" (p. 5, italics in the original).

Subsequently, Bowmani's work examines the A and B terms of dualistic oppression through the broader frameworks through which societal structures determine what is 'acceptable' and what is 'deviant.' Such 'deviance' is typically understood to refer to marginalised others, both human and nonhuman: animals, the environment, and people marginalised because of their gender, sexual orientation, class, caste, abilties, etc.

Further, feminist postcolonial spatialities may also be understood in terms of quotidian realities. Urban spatialities relate not only to cities as imagined constructs but also to the lived experiences of individuals (Pourya Asl, 2022). An urban space is characterised by not just its political and cultural monuments but also by slums, chawls, subways, and other markers of everyday experiences. These markers are also curiously binding: a minimum-wage worker as well as a corporate employee may take a local train or eat from a roadside food stall. In many ways, individuals' formative experiences are shaped by the quotidian rather than the extraordinary: the schedules and routines of everyday life form the spaces people inhabit most often. Modernity and urbanisation project how "the notion of nationalism relies on a political ontology of disjointed spaces and inherently antagonistic narratives" (Monterescu & Rabinowitz, 2007, p. 25). However, as Monterescu and Rabinowitz argue, the disjointedness of city-spaces, which creates a "dialectic tension between otherness and alterity," can also be understood through three ways in which it shapes public spaces: "public discourses, spatial dynamics and everyday neighborly relations" (p. 25).

When Massey talks of the everyday, she seems to create a distinction between the quotidian and the political: "'restructuring' was clearly going on, but its implications both for everyday life and for the mode and potential of political organising were clearly highly differentiated" (Christophers et al., 2018, p. 11). The context of this notion of 'restructuring' is how those with political agendas appropriate the 'local' to serve 'universal' trends and patterns. Massey's work, which popularised slogans such as "geography matters," seeks instead to examine how "not only [is] the character of a particular place a product of its position in relation to wider forces (the more general social and economic restructuring, for instance) but also that that character in turn stamp[s] its own imprint on those wider processes" (p. 12). In this, she seems to indicate that the 'small,' the 'local,' and the 'everyday' are powerful forces in their own right. The quotidian, then, is not a tabula rasa that is impacted and shaped by forces larger than itself but an active agent of change and diversity. The implications for queer and decolonised spatialities seem clear: marginalised identities need not necessarily be seen as subsumed into the mainstream but rather as powerful agents of change.

This view of the quotidian as extraordinary is furthered by Shahani's 2021 study *Pink Revolutions: Globalization, Hindutva, and Queer Triangles in Contemporary India*. Shahani (2021) examines the incursion of Hindu ethnonationalism into everyday life as "an experience of economic precarity" (p. 38). In this instance, the author is speaking specifically of the government's move to ban beef as a targeted attack against the minority Muslim community in the country. The devastating economic blow caused by this move is "not simply sidestepped; instead, it is justified through an infusion into everyday practices and logics of intimacy and desire" (p. 38). If urban spaces are inherently economic in that they embody industrialisation, then what of non-normative identities? Homonationalism may promote a superficial 'acceptance' of queerness, but the invasiveness of the capitalist cisheteropatriarchy remains ubiquitous: "mutations and reconfigurations in Hindutva's manifestations are particularly important for understanding how it might simultaneously assume the form of queerphobic threat" (p. 57). Shahani also examines the impact of the caste system on everyday realities in the country and underscores the fact that such issues are pushed to the margins of postcolonial discourses: the Hindu state posits itself as an autonomous, progressive nation: "the center-periphery models of postcoloniality that posit a monolithically defined "subaltern" in contradistinction to colonial logics actually end up having the effect of flattening epistemological and political categories (p. 232). When ethnonationalism invents homogenous historiographies for a country, it attempts to invisibilise the marginalised and the non-normative or demonise such elements as anti-nationalistic.

More Issues, Controversies, Problems

Further to the theoretical backdrop of queer ecofeminism, the literature review can further be subdivided into two categories: works that pioneered discourse analysis in terms of gendered language and contemporary South Asian theorists who locate identity politics in the realm of nationalism and performativity. First, More and Whittle's *Reclaiming Genders* (1999) is referenced here as an early work that established how gender and queer studies examine epistemic categories by reclaiming language.

... there are unfamiliar border crossings to be faced by us all. Is this obsession with all things trans in fact the manifestation of a travel sickness suffered by those so far untainted by monumental journeys in their lives? Is it that by focusing on those people who understand and have already experienced border crossings, ordinary mortal folk will face their own travels more easily? (p. 7)

This notion of "border crossings" sets up the conceptual category of liminal spaces. More and Whittle's argument indicates that society's obsessive need to regulate trans identity stems from an inherent lack in how societal structures are designed. From an 'academic' rather than 'activist' perspective, it may be theorised that all identity is queer in some way since even cisgender heterosexual people are trapped by normative regulations.

The second issue in this section is the idea of performativity, especially in terms of contemporary ethnonationalism in South Asia, and especially India. Nations are being authoritatively redefined in terms of ethnicities and religious minorities. Puar (2013) and Bharucha (2014) are key theorists in this regard, both critiquing the performativity of contemporary nationalisms. In his study of how the so-called 'Muslim terrorist' parallels the queer 'other,' Bharucha also engages with Puar's work: "The obvious theoretical point that needs to be emphasized here is that the queering of the terrorist is perhaps most convincingly read within the tropes of American popular culture" (p. 82). Hollywood's normative discourses have travelled the world, informing popular culture across the globe. Most American sitcoms portray normative cisgender heterosexuality as it pertains to privileged people in urban spaces existing within settler colonial contexts. Further, Bharucha observes that "Puar's evidence is positively virtuoso as she zeroes in on all kinds of cultural artefacts" (p. 82). Cultural artefacts within a settler colonialist context that has no geographical cultural heritage belonging to the coloniser are fabricated almost as caricatures derived from contemporary political situations. Such 'artefacts' can "rang[e] from toilet paper with Osama bin Laden's image imprinted on it, to posters which appeared in midtown Manhattan showing a caricature of a turbaned bin Laden being anally penetrated by the Empire State Building' (p. 82). As Bharucha observes, the othering of the 'Muslim terrorist' is both Islamophobic and queermisic, conflating religion, ethinicity, gender, and sexuality into a single oppressive mechanism that is easily and horrifyingly identifiable as an obvious characteristic of American popular culture today.

Moreover, it is undeniable that similar forms of nationalistic oppression also exist in India. With its military forces occupying Kashmir and the North-Eastern region, India has also ensured that its mainstream cultural conventions demonise the queer as well as the Muslim. Citizens of the country who are Muslim or North-Eastern are subjected to demands of 'Go back to Pakistan' or 'Go back to China,' with performative arenas such as cricket matches and mainstream cinema fueling and reinforcing ethnonationalist agendas. Significant—and specific to the context of this book—is the fact that almost all such culturally performative spaces are located in urban regions. Indeed, it seems almost a requirement of the urbanised life that one attend sports matches and film screenings at multiplexes.

Further, Puar (2013) analyses how nationalism in countries such as America, Israel, and India have attempted to present a 'queer-friendly' facade in order to promote its supposed inclusivity: "At times the "viral" travels of the concept of homonationalism, as it has been taken up in North America, various European states, Palestine/Israel, and India, have found reductive applications in activist organizing platforms" (p. 337). Puar observes that homonationalism is often thought of "as an accusation, an identity, [and] a bad politics" (p. 337). However, it can also be seen as a mechanism that is intrinsic to how national identities are formed and "as an analytic to apprehend state formation and a structure of modernity" (p. 337). Since notions of modernity are essential to the constructions of urban spatialities in normative and consumerist ways, homonationalism may also be seen "as an assemblage of geopolitical and historical forces, neoliberal interests in capitalist accumulation both cultural and material, biopolitical state practices of population control, and affective investments in discourses of freedom, liberation, and rights" (p. 337).

As a possible illustration, 'liberal' political parties as well as corporatised industries have enthusiastically supported homonationalism. As the term indicates, although it appears to support inclusivity, it simultaneously projects an image of the state as 'good,' as an institution that cannot possibly mean any harm to its citizens. Puar (2013) continues:

Homonationalism, thus, is not simply a synonym for gay racism, or another way to mark how gay and lesbian identities became available to conservative political imaginaries; it is not another identity politics, not another way of distinguishing good queers from bad queers, not an accusation, and not a position. It is rather a facet of modernity and a historical shift marked by the entrance of (some) homosexual bodies as worthy of protection by nation-states, a constitutive and fundamental reorientation of the relationship between the state, capitalism, and sexuality. (p. 337)

As Puar argues, homonationalism has become a means of establishing the view that some lives are worth more than others. For instance, mainstream Indian cinema often portrays feminist concerns, but such explorations are typically restricted to the opulent classes and 'upper' castes. 'Progressive' media that calls for sexual or economic freedom is usually cognizant only of economically privileged, cisgender, Hindu women. Trans characters are portrayed by cisgender actors and typically used for comic relief.

Frameworks from Roy's Non-Fiction

The final section of the literature review focuses on perspectives from the nonfiction works of Roy herself. During the two decades between the publication of her first and second novels, Roy published several compilations of essays that linked her activist work to contemporary oppressions in India. This review examines the relevance of two of her essays to the current study.

"The Loneliness of Noam Chomsky," reprinted in *An Ordinary Person's Guide to Empire* (2005), argues that "public opinion in 'free market' democracies is manufactured just like any other mass market product—soap, switches, or sliced bread" (p. 47). Roy's argument brings the culture industry and its processes of standardising not just products but also identities into sharp focus. Pointing out that "powerful people know that ordinary people are not always reflexively ruthless and selfish," Roy compares "ordinary people" to "broiler chickens or pigs in a pen": "When ordinary people weigh costs and benefits, something like an uneasy conscience could easily tip the scales" (p. 50). Roy's argument suggests that "ordinary people" exist within a controlled grid, not unlike an animal's cage or pen: "they must be guarded against reality, reared in a controlled climate, in an altered reality" (p. 50):

Those of us who have managed to escape this fate and are scratching about in the backyard, no longer believe everything we read in the papers and watch on TV. We put our ears to the ground and look for other ways of making sense of the world. We search for the untold story, the mentioned-in-passing military coup, the unreported genocide, the civil war in an African country written up in a one-column-inch story next to a full-page advertisement for lace underwear. (pp. 50-51)

Roy's observations, as her last point above indicates, are located in her broader focus, in this essay, on the ways in which the mass media are used as tools and smokescreens to distract the public's attention away from injustices and discrimination. She implies that an advertisement for 'sexy' underwear, when given as much importance as a political story, may be far more attractive to the reader.

A more recent essay, "The Pandemic is a Portal" (2020), was written during the first wave of the Covid-19 pandemic. In her essay, Roy describes the experiences of migrant labourers who were forced into exile, destitution, and death when the pandemic began: "As an appalled world watched, India revealed herself in all her shame—her brutal, structural, social and economic inequality, her callous indifference to suffering" (p. 129). Roy outlines the many ways in which privileged individuals in urban spaces, whose primary problem during the first lockdown seemed to be boredom, viewed an often-deadly virus as a mere inconvenience. The crisis "worked like a chemical experiment that suddenly illuminated hidden things" about the inequalities inherent to Indian societies: "As shops, restaurants, factories, and the construction industry shut down, as the wealthy and the middle classes enclosed themselves in gated colonies, our towns and megacities began to extrude their working-class citizens—their migrant workers—like so much unwanted accrual" (p. 129). Roy's descriptions recall the environmentalist position that what constitutes 'waste'—both literally and metaphorically—is a matter of privileged perspective. Further, Roy also compares the forced exile of migrant workers to the Partition of 1947:

Many driven out by their employers and landlords, millions of impoverished, hungry, thirsty people, young and old, men, women, children, sick people, blind people, disabled people, with nowhere else to go, with no public transport in sight, began a long march home to their villages. They walked for days, toward Badaun, Agra, Azamgarh, Aligarh, Lucknow, Gorakhpur—hundreds of miles away. Some died on the way. (p. 129)

Roy (2020) quotes from her interview with a migrant worker: "'Maybe when Modiji [Prime Minister Narendra Modi] decided to do this, nobody told him about us. Maybe he doesn't know about us,' he said. 'Us' means approximately 460 million people" (p. 130).

These perspectives from Roy's own writings are critical to understanding her significance as not only a novelist but also a political theorist today. In contemporary India, mainstream media and socio-political systems no longer recognise the notion of dissent. Any attempt to improve conditions for millions who are marginalised and oppressed is viewed as 'anti-national,' further reinforcing the dualist form of discrimination that Gaard and others have critiqued.

THEORY AND METHOD

As outlined in the literature review, the study references theoretical frameworks relating to queer studies, ecology, spatiality, and performativity. While these notions may appear discrete, they overlap in terms of the intersectional perspective that all oppressions are interconnected. Queerness is shaped and defined by perspectives and definitions that are relative to temporalities and spatialities, which are intrinsically related to how identities are performed in postcolonial contexts. Moreover, the devastation of the environment by the capitalist-colonialist-patriarchal machine makes urban spaces logical foils to natural ones, making environmentalist views integral to intersectional discourses on oppressions and inequalities.

The key concepts used to construct the study's broad conceptual framework are as follows:

- Foundational concepts from queer ecofeminism and examinations of social constructions of femininity and trans identity;
- Conflation of the notions of Muslim identity and queerness that are demonised by homonationalistic agendas;
- Roy's perspectives on the political weaponisation of mass media to reinforce essentialist and hegemonic notions of identity.

The study further uses qualitative research methods to apply these perspectives to a critical textual analysis of Roy's novel in terms of these contemporary concerns.

RESULTS AND FINDINGS

As pointed out in the chapter's introductory section, the liminal space of Anjum's graveyard is a key setting in the novel. The narrative begins and ends in the graveyard, coming full circle. In the beginning, when Anjum is subjected to transmisic remarks from the priest at the graveyard, she is represented as being as solitary as a tree. At the novel's end, Anjum's small, personal space expands into the inclusive and collective space of the Jannat Guest House, depicting "the relationship between spatial belonging and memorialization" (Essa, 2021, p. 744).

This sense of the connection between spatiality and memory is established after the loss of several of the novel's characters, both human and nonhuman. The brutality with which beloved pets such as a kitten and a rooster are killed by soldiers establishes environmentalist concerns evoked by the death of the vultures at the novel's beginning. Perhaps no other death in the novel is as impactful as that of the Kashmiri toddler, Miss Jebeen the First. When Udaya, a child of the same age, is reimagined as Miss Jebeen the Second after her arrival at the Jannat Guest House, the event seems to indicate a sense of hope and renewal, her very name memorialising the lost child.

Essa (2021) connects the sense of spatiality and memory in the novel with the concept of heterotopia, which critiques societal spaces. Ethnonationalism demonises religious minorities, and homonationalism alienates people such as Anjum; she is disowned by her parents because she is born intersex but cannot survive in their harshly regulated home that forces her to perform her gender as masculine. The fact that Anjum is born intersex is itself a blow to the essentialist notion that the gender binary is 'natural' and that everyone is 'born' either male or female. Further, Essa suggests that the novel conveys a sense of "despatialized memory": "It is through the *interplay* of alternative material spaces and connective approaches to memory that Roy's [...] novel develop[s] visions of community centering on those otherwise marginalized" (p. 744). In this, Essa's view implies that material spaces, like gender identities, are fluid and transitional rather than static and immutable.

Regarding the materiality of memory, Anjum's Godrej almirah becomes an enduring symbol of the closet. The closet, a space that has been repeatedly theorised about in academic discourses, is often used in popular culture as a simplistic image signifying the process of 'coming out.' The act is not simple by any means: the very idea of coming out implies that the space outside the closet is free from oppression, which is patently false: "the closet is a site of fantasy, a margin internalised with the secrets and possibilities of transgender identities… we walk through life carrying not the closet, but the possibility of the closet, saying, 'Shall I tell the bus driver?'" (More & Whittle, 1999, p. 2) The closet as a "site of fantasy" reinforces the idea that spatialities are hegemonically manufactured constructs that are engineered in unrealistic and normative ways; however, it also emphasises that imagining more inclusive spaces is essential. More and Whittle observe that "when you do read transpeople writing about reclaiming genders you'll recognise that it's absolute fantasy, but that fantasy is absolutely relevant" (p. 2).

In Anjum's case, Roy seems to add a unique twist to the process of coming out of the closet: when Anjum leaves the Khwabgah, the house where she lives with her trans community, she carries the almirah with her to the graveyard. This act indicates, perhaps, that she not only comes out but also carries the closet/cupboard with her. In this, Roy seems to suggest that closeted spaces are determined by their contexts: in spatially relocating her closet, Anjum defies homonormative and transnormative expectations. Her actions can also be understood in terms of the "reshaping of the queer" (Rodriguez, et al., 2016, p. 4), a reinforcement of the notion that queerness is constantly transitory in nature. Further, Rodriguez, et al. (2016) present the notion of counterpublic spatialities, encouraging perspectives through which normative spatialities can be countered, especially in urban contexts.

Roy's critique of mediatised versions of communal violence is also reinforced in the novel's exploration of the Godhra pogrom against Muslims, an event reminiscent of the 1984 attacks against the Sikh community. In August 2022, on the occasion of the Indian Independence Day, several convicted murderers in the Godhra case were garlanded by politicians and released, reinforcing the urgency of addressing the extremist forms of oppression that ethnonationalism represents today.

The police arrested hundreds of Muslims – all auxiliary Pakistanis from their point of view – from the area around the railway station under the new terrorism law and threw them into prison. The Chief Minister of Gujarat, a loyal member of the Organization (as were the Home Minister and the Prime Minister), was, at the time, up for re-election. He appeared on TV in a saffron kurta with a slash of vermilion on his forehead, and with cold, dead eyes ordered that the burnt bodies of the Hindu pilgrims be brought to Ahmedabad, the capital of the state, where they were to be put on display for the general public to pay their respects. A weaselly 'unofficial spokesperson' announced unofficially that every action would be met with an equal and opposite reaction. He didn't acknowledge Newton, of course, because, in the prevailing climate, the officially sanctioned position was that ancient Hindus had invented all science. (Roy, 2017, p. 28)

In this description of the events that triggered the pogrom, Roy depicts the crux of ethnonationalism. During the independence movement in the pre-1947 era, it was essential to construct the narrative of an ancient culture to counter colonialist arguments. However, in the contemporary context, this tired and obsolete argument is still being used: to oppress, discriminate against, and slaughter the nation's own people.

The narrative also brings an additional sense of urgency to the anti-Muslim pogrom because Anjum has travelled to Gujarat at the time, and her companions at the Khwabgah are anxious for her safety:

When flushed, animated TV news reporters shouted out their Pieces-to-Camera from the refugee camps where tens of thousands of Gujarat's Muslims now lived, in the Khwabgah they switched off the sound and scanned the background hoping to catch a glimpse of Anjum and Zakir Mian lining up for food or blankets, or huddled in a tent. They learned in passing that Wali Dakhani's shrine had been razed to the ground and a tarred road built over it, erasing every sign that it had ever existed. (Neither the police nor the mobs nor the Chief Minister could do anything about the people who continued to leave flowers in the middle of the new tarred road where the shrine used to be. When the flowers were crushed to paste under the wheels of fast cars, new flowers would appear. And what can anybody do about the connection between flower-paste and poetry?) (Roy, 2017, p. 28)

The subversive parenthetical note reinforces the ways in which Roy uses form and narrative techniques in the novel to mirror her thematic concerns. Text in parenthesis is typically considered unimportant: here, the fact that the parenthetical text refers to how the authorities are unable to completely erase the shrine's significance reinforces the notion of 'small things' from Roy's first novel. Like liminal spaces, parenthetical spaces seem to be inherently subversive.

The flowers placed on the erased shrine can also be read in terms of Khader's notion of transnational cartographies (2013). Examining spatiality through cultural genealogies, Khader examines "the poetics and politics of displacing" (p. 1), stating that "the extimate subjectivities of postcolonial women are restless not simply because, as some would argue, of modernist or postmodernist angst, but because their extimate subjectivities are inscribed within the specific socio-political conditions that mark their positionalities within the global capitalist system" (p. 6). In Anjum's case, the fact that she is entirely missing from the narrative during its depictions of the violence in Gujarat seems to indicate her absolute lack of power in the situation: she is not only a Muslim but also a transwoman, completely invisibilised by the state. Her positionality is effectively non-existent.

The narrative, however, also seems to empower Anjum in terms of both her gender and positioning. When she adopts Zainab, she counters the essentialist criticism that transwomen cannot have children. This narrative thread also seems to be paralleled by Tilo's grief at the death of the first Miss Jebeen (as well as Sophie Mol's death in Roy's first novel). All these children who die tragically or are abandoned are gendered as female, reinforcing the idea that being categorised as female is to be in danger. Anjum's defiant adoption of a child seems to counter the "price of modern national self-consolidation," which is "a straightened masculinity and the adoption of the nuclear family over against extended family and gender-segregated domesticity" (Al-Kassim, 2013, p. 344). Al-Kassim describes how nationalism promotes gender segregation in terms of domestic spaces: Anjum defies these binary constructs by not only adopting a child but also making her domestic space in a graveyard.

By extension, this notion of normative gendered relationships may also be countered by the tragedies of Roy's heterosexual lovers: "The fact that Roy places not just love, but *romantic* love, and not just romantic love but romantic love between a *heterosexual* man and woman, and not just romantic love between heterosexuals but *pre-doomed romantic heterosexual* love at the heart of her works of fiction, is significant" (Lau & Mendes, 2019, p. 6, italics in the original). Interestingly, the only lovers who remain alive and together (albeit traumatised) in Roy's novels are the twins, Rahel and Estha, in *The God of Small Things*. The fact that they are siblings makes their sexual relationship absolutely non-normative and, in the context of their shared trauma and grief as well as their psychic bond, organic. Their love survives, perhaps, because it is secret: practised in a space that contains only them, another of Roy's liminal spaces that dismantle hegemonic notions of right and wrong.

While Lau and Mendes (2019), like most analysts of Roy's novels, ignore Rahel and Estha's relationship, they do observe that non-normativity plays a significant role in her narratives:

Even Roy's non-sexual love relationships in her novels are acts of rebellion. When discussing how Anjum was spared in the massacre of Muslims at the Gujarat pogrom because she is a hijra, Roy talks of loving the fact that Anjum is saved by the very identity which excluded her. Roy says Anjum wishes to understand the world for Zainab's sake, when she becomes her mother; in Roy's words, "She [Anjum] doesn't accept this grid. She breaks it, and comes out. […] And that, for me, is so sweet" […] In most of the key relationships in the novel, there is a breaking free from what Roy calls "the grid", otherwise known as the Love Laws. (p. 10)

The Love Laws seem to exemplify Roy's view of stifling heteronormative discourses. Significantly, although Anjum's mother cannot handle the fact that her child is intersex, she takes the baby to the dargah of Hazrat Sarmad Shaheed, who was queer:

Not all the visitors to Hazrat Sarmad Shaheed's dargah knew his story. Some knew parts of it, some none of it and some made up their own versions. Most knew he was a Jewish Armenian merchant who had travelled to Delhi from Persia in pursuit of the love of his life. Few knew the love of his life was Abhay Chand, a young Hindu boy he had met in Sindh. Most knew he had renounced Judaism and embraced Islam. Few knew his spiritual search eventually led him to renounce orthodox Islam too. Most knew he had lived on the streets of Shahjahanabad as a naked fakir before being publicly executed. (Roy, 2017, p. 12)

In this description, the contrasting phrases "most knew" and "few knew" indicate the ways in which epistemologies are constructed. What is 'common' knowledge is, as the passage suggests, not necessarily true. The fact that Hazrat Sarmad Shaheed travels to Delhi from Persia because he is following his male lover also seems to imply a subversion of colonialist agendas: colonisers come to murder and loot, but he comes for love. The fact that "some made up their own versions" of his story reinforces the fluidity and construction of historiographies: if governments can invent or alter realities, so can 'ordinary' people. Anjum herself, in daring to subvert the mainstream Hindu narrative about Ram's exile by stating that the Hijra community accompanied him, aligns her story with a dominant narrative of mythology-as-history.

FUTURE RESEARCH DIRECTIONS

Bringing together the notions of human geography and liminal spaces, March (2020) writes: "Human geography has taken up a similar notion of liminality to anthropology: as a kind of in-between where life as usual is suspended, or a socio-spatial rift where new kinds of collective politics and forms of citizenship are produced" (p. 3). Since research in any discipline must address critically urgent societal needs, a study such as this one has attempted to connect perspectives in Roy's novel to communal violence and ethnonationalism in contemporary India. As Roy's writing consistently demonstrates, violence also seems synonymous with urban spaces: while instances such as the political violence in Kashmir may seem exceptions at first glance, the militarisation of the nation-state that causes such violence is an essential characteristic of the process of urbanisation.

Further, March (2020) also observes that it is necessary to see the liminal as a part of human beings' lived experiences rather than as an abstraction: "A challenge evidently exists within human geography to balance the theoretical potentials of queer conceptions of liminality with the lived realities of those who dwell in the liminal" (p. 8). As a necessary part of examining theoretical discourses through their potential for practical application, this study recommends further research along the lines of queer ecopedagogies and intersectional pedagogies.

Inclusive pedagogies are essential because texts such as Roy's are inevitably discussed in classrooms and placed on curriculums. Ironically, learners in English Studies classrooms are oppressed by colonial-era educational structures while being taught about freedom and equal rights. A text such as *The Ministry of Utmost Happiness* has immense potential to be included in studies on intersectional ecopedagogies, given its focus on the parallels between the oppression of marginalised humans as well as nonhumans.

CONCLUSION

As discussed, spatialities in the book determine the ways in which characters' identity are constructed. Where, then, do old birds go to die? Roy's novel gives her characters a space of their own at the end, a thriving space that is typically associated only with the dead. In terms of the political realities her books address, Roy's perspectives are criticised and demonised by authorities and conservative ideologies. The novel seems to subvert the binary opposition between the living and the dead, given that many of the living seem to have no value in contemporary India. Nevertheless, the novel's ending seems to be optimistic. It describes how, although everyone else at the Jannat Guest House is asleep, Guih Kyom the dung beetle is "wide awake and on duty, lying on his back with his legs in the air to save the world in case the heavens fell. But even he knew that things would turn out all right in the end" (Roy, 2017, p. 444). Roy leaves her reader with the image of a dung beetle with a personality and a name of his own. Like the vultures, the beetle brings an ecological dimension to the narrative: even the smallest of creatures appears safe in the space Anjum has created.

ACKNOWLEDGMENT

The author acknowledges the support and encouragement of the management and officials of Christ University for research work, including seed money for faculty projects. Gratitude is especially owed to Dr Fr Joseph Varghese, Director of the Centre for Research at Christ University. The Centre for Research supported the author's three-year postdoctoral research project (2017-20) on the intersections between gender studies and ecological discourses through funding for books and creating jobs for research assistants on the project.

REFERENCES

Al-Kassim, D. (2013). Psychoanalysis and the postcolonial genealogy of queer theory. *International Journal of Middle East Studies*, *45*(2), 343–346. doi:10.1017/S0020743813000093

Bharucha, R. (2014). *Terror and performance*. Routledge. doi:10.4324/9781315794488

BowmaniZ. (2021). Now is the time for Black queer feminist ecology. *Law & Sexuality*. https://ssrn.com/abstract=3795137

Christophers, B., Lave, R., Peck, J., & Werner, M. (2018). *The Doreen Massey reader*. Agenda Publishing.

Essa, L. (2021). Of other spaces and others' memories: Reading graveyards in Arundhati Roy's *The Ministry of Utmost Happiness* and Regina Scheer's *Machandel*. *Comparative Literature Studies*, *58*(4), 744–779. doi:10.5325/complitstudies.58.4.0744

Gaard, G. (1993). *Ecofeminism: Women, animals, nature*. Temple University Press.

Gaard, G. (1997). Toward a queer ecofeminism. *Hypatia*, *12*(1), 114–137. doi:10.1111/j.1527-2001.1997.tb00174.x

Khader, J. (2013). *Cartographies of transnationalism in postcolonial feminisms: Geography, culture, identity, politics*. Lexington Books.

Lau, L., & Mendes, A. C. (2019). Romancing the other: Arundhati Roy's *The Ministry of Utmost Happiness*. *Journal of Commonwealth Literature*, 1–16. doi:10.1177/0021989418820701

March, L. (2020). Queer and trans* geographies of liminality: A literature review. *Progress in Human Geography*, *45*(3), 455–471. doi:10.1177/0309132520913111

Monterescu, D., & Rabinowitz, D. (2007). *Mixed towns, trapped communities: Historical narratives, spatial dynamics, gender relations and cultural encounters in Palestinian-Israeli towns*. Ashgate Publishing.

More, K., & Whittle, S. (1999). *Reclaiming genders: Transsexual grammars at the fin de siècle*. Cassell.

Pourya Asl, M. (Ed.). (2022). Gender, place, and identity of South Asian women. IGI Global., https://doi.org/10.4018/978-1-6684-3626-4.

Puar, J. (2013). Rethinking homonationalism. *International Journal of Middle East Studies*, *45*(2), 336–339.

Rodriguez, N. M., Martino, W. J., Ingrey, J. C., & Brockenbrough, E. (2016). *Critical concepts in queer studies and education: Queer counterpublic spatialities*. Palgrave Macmillan.

Roy, A. (1997). *The God of Small Things*. India Ink.

Roy, A. (2005). The loneliness of Noam Chomsky. In A. Roy (Ed.), *An Ordinary Person's Guide to Empire* (pp. 45–74). Penguin.

Roy, A. (2017). *The Ministry of Utmost Happiness*. Penguin Random House.

Roy, A. (2020). *Azadi: Freedom, fascism, fiction*. Penguin Random House.

Shahani, N. (2021). *Pink revolutions: Globalization, Hindutva, and queer triangles in contemporary India*. Northwestern University Press.

Chapter 6

A Step Forward, Two Steps Backward:
Urbanization as Not a Gender Gap Equalizer in Indu Sundaresan's Short Story Collection

Anjum Khan M.
Avinashilingam Institute for Home Science and Higher Education for Women, India

ABSTRACT

Despite the revolutionary changes in the Indian nation's culture and lifestyle over the past few decades, the dominant attitude towards gender has not experienced a significant change. Although gender inequality and violence incited by gender identity prevail mostly in the villages, but the urban spaces are no exception to these phenomena. This chapter focuses on how Indu Sundaresan's short story collection In the Convent of Little Flowers explores and excavates the half-dead truths of gender inequality in the country concealed under pseudo modernity and social progress. It is argued that the collection includes narratives that present counter-histories of urban spaces where women confront challenges and exploitation. In pursuing this argument, the chapter uses a socio-spatial approach to demonstrate how urbanization is not a gender gap equalizer and to show how the line between rural and urban spaces is overlapping and crisscrossing.

DOI: 10.4018/978-1-6684-6650-6.ch006

INTRODUCTION

The contemporary India is a rapidly developing country with challenges engrained in its social fabric. As studies suggest, "Globally, more than half of the population resides in urban areas, while in India, only 31 percent of the total population lives in urban areas" (Baghat et al., 2021, p. 3). Further, it is observed that, "Tracing the urbanization trajectory in India, we find that by the 1950s, the urban population constituted 17% of the total population growing to a figure of 26% in 1990, 34% in 2018 and expected to touch 40% in 2030" (Kateja & Jain, 2021, p. 30). Gender discrimination in India is a present-day problem rooted in the distant past. Despite the revolutionary changes in lifestyle, the attitude towards gender has witnessed only slight change. As observed, "While violence against women is, tragically, a global problem, the situation for women in India has unique features that can pursue them at every stage of life, starting even before birth" (A. Singh, 2022, p. 5). Gender inequality and violence inspired by gender identity prevail mostly in the villages, nevertheless, the urban spaces are no exception to this. In fact, there is subtle urbanity in villages, and a part of village residing in the cities. As villagers send their children to cities for better opportunities, and the once who settle down in cities transform their standard of living, but not their attitude. Urbanity and gender inequity coexist complementing and contradiction each other.

In order to understand, how urbanity in India is still gender-biased, it is essential to recognise the interaction between gender and society, ". . . the socio-spatial approach is the explicit recognition that social life is comprised of classes and of other social divisions that are important, such as those of race and gender" (Gottdiener & Budd, 2005, p. 141). However, in India, the factors such as caste, class, and religion also define the socio-spacial methodology. Gender discrimination is aggravated by other divisions like, caste, religion, and class. As observed, "Central to the women's movement in India have been issues of caste and class that have put into question the identity of 'woman' as subject of inquiry" (Aneja, 2019, p. 11). Cities carve out opportunities to better life, however, the conformist traditions like 'honour killing' exist in the upper-class and upper-caste, well-appointed households as well. Undeniably, a literary text is a good case study to understand the society, "Like all cultural expressions, literary narratives, too, are components of social reflexivity" (J. Singh, 2022, p. 4). Indu Sundaresan's short story collection (2008), *In the Convent of Little Flowers* explore and excavate the half dead truths of gender inequality concealed under pseudo modernity and social progress. It includes narratives of counter histories of the urban spaces where women confront challenges and exploitation. The proposed chapter titled, "A step Forward, Two Steps Backward: Urbanisation not a Gender Gap Equaliser," intends to deconstruct how urbanization is not a gender gap equalizer, and the line between rural and urban spaces is overlapping and crisscrossing each other. It also exposes the ineffective interplay between progress and gender inequality with reference to the short stories from the collection.

The feminist geography has gained attention in recent years. As it is most essential to relate to female experience in the changing geography across culture and communities, the literary texts which are cultural products play a vital role. For example, "Layering feminine experience into common readings of space and the cultural concepts they stand proxy for allows us a deeper perception of both modernity and the spaces it has created" (Stauv, 2018, p. 11). Especially, today, when women are empowered to work, but are tethered to their traditional role of caring for their family as well. As a result, "The burdens of combining work and family life continue to fall more predominantly on women" (Gillis & Jacobs, 2019, p. 71). The present chapter attempts to contribute in light of gender and urbanity in India as it examines the plight of women despite progress and empowerment. It presents forth case studies from various walks of life across class and caste, where patriarchal values constantly subjugate the women.

LITERATURE REVIEW

Urbanity provides the women better and modern amenities in everyday life, however, it falls short of rendering gender equity. As patriarchy prevails in the city as in village, "More than 20 years ago I wrote an essay about women in the modern city, pointing out that the central figure of modernity, the flâneur, could only be male" (Wolff, 2010, p. 6). Undeniably, space is gendered and reflects clear patriarchal construction of the society. As observed, "Feminist geographers and urban theorists have both argued that space is gendered and that gendering has profound consequences for women" (Brassard & Joshi, 2020, p. 27). There are several articles, chapters, and scholarly literature which argues and elucidates the gendered nature of urban spaces. *Contentious Cities: Design and the Gendered Production of Space,* edited by Jess Berry, Timothy Moore, Nicole Kalms and Gene Bawden (2021), brings together interdisciplinary approaches scrutinising the representation of gender inequalities in cities all over the world. The book presents an investigation into design-led tactics along with feminist and queer theories. *Feminist Spaces: Gender and Geography in a Global Context* by Ann M. Oberhauser, Jennifer L. Fluri, Risa Whitson, and Sharlene Mollett (2018), offers an understanding of social dynamics and space by underscoring feminist approaches in examining the geographic processes. The book examines how spatial dimensions of social identity such as gender, class, sexuality, and race are rooted in unequal and historically constructed power relations that privilege some people and marginalize others. Further, there are scholarly essays, like Daphney Spain's (2014) article, "Gender and Urban Space," which examines the ways cities have reflected and reinforced gender relations in the United States from the turn of the twentieth century to the present. The article also includes a review of how women's and gay rights movements, gentrification, and planning practices play a role in gender-neutral urbanity. Malcolm Miles's (2019) *Cities and Literature: Routledge Critical Introductions to Urbanism and the City,* examines the examples of writing from Europe, North America and post-colonial countries, juxtaposed with key ideas from urban cultural and critical theories.

There are texts which concentrate on gender and other factors leading to gender injustice in India. *A Gender Atlas of India: With Scorecard* by Radha Kumar, Marcel Korff, and Karthika Sudhir (2018), broadly maps and marks India's performance from 2001 to 2016 on issues of concern for women. It examines India's performance on various aspects, including sex ratio, women's education, employment, health, political participation and representation; and prevention of crimes against women. Sujit Kumar Chattopadhyay's (2018) *Gender Socialization and the Making of Gender in the Indian Context,* observes the social measures in India that make a child conform to normative femininity or masculinity. It reveals the role of family, religion, mythology, teachers, peer group and the various media in indoctrinating this. Simran Luthra's (2021) *Gender and Education in India: A Reader,* inquires the understanding of gender and its intersections with class, caste, religion and region.

In recent times, *Gender, Unpaid Work and Care in India* by Ellina Samantroy and Subhalakshmi Nandi (2022), showcases the link between gender norms, resource rights, identities and agency in women's work in India. Similarly, Trijita Gonsalves's (2022) *Women in the Civil Services: Gender and Workplace Identities in India,* explores the personal and professional lives of women in the Indian Civil Services, and studies the undercurrents of gender and workplace identities for women in government. It brings forth major challenges that hinder the participation of women in decision-making and reveals the blockages that obstruct women's progression.

There are academic volumes examining urbanity based on literary case studies, like, *Planned Violence: Post/Colonial Urban Infrastructure, Literature and Culture* by Dominic Davies and Elleke Boehmer (2018), which Likens the spatial pasts and presents of the post-imperial and post/colonial cities of London, Delhi, Johannesburg, and Mumbai. It examines the juxtaposition between urbanity and violence in the postcolonial era. Further, Malcolm Miles's (2019) *Cities and Literature: Routledge Critical Introductions to Urbanism and the City,* inspects examples of writing from Europe, North America and post-colonial countries, put together with key ideas from urban cultural and critical theories.

There are also texts which concentrate exclusively on India, like, Subashish Bhattacharjee and Goutam Karmakar's (2022) *The City Speaks: Urban Spaces in Indian Literature,* which is divided into four sections - 'Fictions of the "Cities at the Centre,"' 'Fictions from the Fringes,' 'Staging the City,' and 'Poetics of the Cities.'

Further, Anindita Datta's (2021) *Gender, Space and Agency in India: Exploring Regional Genderscapes* which examines the links between gender, space and agency in India. It provides new views and ideas which help in connecting these links across diverse geographical contexts in India. Most recently, Dibyakusum Ray's (2022) *Postcolonial Indian City-Literature: Policy, Politics and Evolution (Routledge Research in Postcolonial Literatures)*, investigates *h*ow does the urban space and the literature depicting it form a dialogue within? How have Indian cities grown in the past six decades, as well as the literature focused on it? There are fictional texts which also reflect gender iniquity in urban India (Pourya Asl, 2022). These include works like, Shashi Deshpande's *That Long Silence*, Anita Desai's *Clear Light of the day*, Geetha Hariharan's *The Thousand Faces of Night*, and several others. The present chapter is a good addition to this scholarship, as it is an attempt to explore the gendered urban spaces with aid of literary case study. Especially when, Indu Sundaresan's *In the Convent of Little Flowers* is less explored text with ample of scope for gender studies. The chapter also elucidates the factors like, migration, caste, social consciousness, power, and it's like, which stunt the growth of gender equity.

THEORY AND METHOD

Socio-Spatial Approach

The present chapter uses socio-spatial approach as gender in India is entangled with institutions like, caste, religion, and patriarchy. *Socio-spatial Inequalities in Contemporary Cities* (2019) is one of the texts which has inspired this perspective for the present chapter. Likewise, *Socio-Spatial Theory in Nordic Geography: Intellectual Histories and Critical Interventions* (2022) and *Direction and Socio-spatial Theory: A Political Economy of Oriented Practice* (2021) also deal with socio-spatial idea. Though, there are slight variation in the explanations of the concept, they all agree that space shapes and reshapes in relation to socio-cultural factors. As observed, "Space is never neutral and reflects the structures of power that human societies are founded upon, saturating geographic locations and relations with meaning" (Tompkins et al., 2021, p. 242).

Socio-spatial approach examines the intersection between space and social factors like, gender, race, religion, and other socio-cultural identities, " . . . factors linked to variables of ethnic origin, gender, differences in sexual orientation and religion" (Mela & Toldo, 2019, p. 3). Further, "Particular understandings of space are inescapably linked to the social and our understandings of the social" (Jakobsen et al., 2022, p. 16). Space is also gendered thus- public space masculine and private space feminine. As the idea is, " . . . materially important associations remain between masculinity, public space, and the city, on the one hand, and between femininity, private space, and suburbs on the other hand" (Bondi, 1998, p. 162). The socio-spatial approach is very helpful in a multicultural society, like India. It is essential to mention that the theory also has few limitations as Hannah (2021) remarks, "Socio-spatial theory was always a rather amorphous category" (p. 10). However, the present chapter takes this approach as it illustrates the amalgam of social practices and gender regardless the nature of space.

RESULTS AND FINDINGS

It is understood that ". . . cities in literary texts (or indeed film and television) are by definition always more than just a setting for a story; rather, a version of the city comes into being by means of each act of narration" (Kinderman & Rohleder, 2020, p. 20). The present chapter makes an attempt to examine the paradigm of urban spaces through Sundaresan's narratives. Indu Sundaresan provides multiple planes of reality specked with different experience and background. She portrays educated women suffering on account of pseudo morality, and uneducated girls experiencing the despairing glam of the city. Social acceptance, patriarchal mindset, and moral capital make for these women the sense of urbanity more disputed and complicated. The attempt is to present a socio-spatial dialectic analysis of the eight short stories presented in the collection. Mostly, the setting of the short stories is Chennai, Mumbai, and unnamed cities in India.

Social Stigma

The public gaze and moral policing exists in urban societies as well. In the first story of the collection which is also the title story, "In the Convent of Little Flowers," the protagonist Padmini is retracing her childhood to the orphanage she grew up in Chennai. The convent represents a space where the social outcaste mothers or the unwelcomed children, especially girls go to live in. This appears to be a corner of consolation and refuge for the girls like Padmini who do not have the privilege of a family. The physical space plays an important role in formation of identity. The name 'Padmini' is significant in understanding the space binary of city and village. As the name means the flower lotus which is normally found in village indicates how spaces are gendered. Sister Mary Theresa recounts, "You came to us with that name. Your mother gave you the name. I am sure you have grown up to be as beautiful as the serene lotus in a village pond" (Sundaresan, 2008, p. 4). Though, the protagonist is brought up in the city and lives in another city outside India, her name fetches countryside serenity. The reference to the lilacs on the frock presented to Padmini by her biological mother restores the urbanity in the wearer's life. Sister Mary Theresa reminds, "For your sixth birthday it was a sleeveless white frock printed with purple lilacs" (Sundaresan, 2008, p. 5). The contrast between a village lotus and a city lilac is remarkable and represent Padmini's transformation from sludge to society.

A 'sense of not belonging' wraps around Padmini's gloomy narrative. As she first belongs to no one and is abandoned at an orphanage, and then she begins to belong to the Convent of Little Flowers in Chennai. This is replaced with her belonging to an American adopted family in America. She declares, "I belong no more to Chinglepet street" (Sundaresan, 2008, p. 6). It is not only change of place or scene for her, but a considerable shift in living routine.

A female's position in the society, urban or rural, is measured by social endorsement. Sister Mary Theresa's position in the orphan children's world is curious and interesting. Though the children yearn for Sister's care and kindness, they candidly and cruelly appropriates her becoming of a nun, "She must have joined the convent because no man would marry her. A smallpox-pitted face is not exactly marriage market material" (Sundaresan, 2008, p. 5). This reference to the physical appearance of Sister Mary Theresa consolidates the general Indian tendencies related to marriage and feminine beauty.

However, Sister Mary Teresa tries to save her and her ward's position by taking pride in the geographical location of their orphanage. Sister Mary Theresa is proud of their convent which is situated in a very important location in the city. She points out to the orphans' girls residing in it, "The convent was built in the shadow of the Gemini Flyover, the only road bridge in all of Chennai then, and a big landmark for giving directions" (Sundaresan, 2008, p. 6). The mere location of the convent for less fortunate girls and women becomes a point of fecundity. This 'location pride' also helps in overriding the mortification or despondency associated with the orphanage.

The orphanage is a symbol of social exclusion. The orphanage shelters the abandoned girl children who are orphaned naturally because of the death of their parents, or because of their gender. In case of Padmini, she is abandoned by her mother fearing social disgrace as she is unmarried when Padmini is born. The Convent of Little Flowers is an exclusionary place for the less fortunate women and girls. This gender exclusivity reflects gender division "At the Convent of Little Flowers, we were all either little flowers or older women—teachers and sweepers and clerks" (Sundaresan, 2008, p. 7). This gendered space represents helpless and powerless girls and women who are social pariahs. It is a private space for the socially alienated individuals.

Evidently, public sentiments are intertwined with collective morality even in urban spaces. In order to avoid public gaze and public disgrace on mother-daughter relationship, Padmini's birth mother severs all her connections with her daughter.

Sister Mary Theresa informs Padmini of her biological mother's good luck, "But do not worry, your mother married well. The indiscretion was forgotten, not made public, anyway" (Sundaresan, 2008, p. 11). This metaphor of discretion for a child represents the moral and social spaces in India, regardless the shades of urbanity.

In similar vein, Parvati the protagonist of "The Most Unwanted" also suffers the consequences of bringing a child into the world without the social sanction of marriage. Further, she also bears the brunt of her relationship with a young man from another community. "The Most Unwanted" is set in the campus of one of the biggest engineering colleges in the city of Chennai. The female protagonist, Parvati belongs to a lower-middle class family which is saturated in pseudo-morality. Her family's economic status descend on account of the three daughters they have which forces the mother to take up domestic chores. Parvati is shunned by her own father because he fears the social indignation which she has brought upon his family. It is because his grandson Krishna is born out of wedlock and Parvati is seeking refuge with her parents. Though, her father is a clerk in the premises of an educational institute, but he is unable to rise from the social and traditional lines.

Undeniably, the society is wired with patriarchy, "Society is dominated by social relations of male power. The masculine and the feminine, as cultural qualities, are related to each other in the form of superordinate/subordinate relations" (Gottdiener & Budd, 2005, p. 61). The patriarch of the family always enjoys privileges irrespective of social and economic background. Nathan being the patriarch enjoys all the privileges. He is treated as a king who spends time leisurely smoking and getting the best share of meals. He is waited upon by his wife and daughter, "Nathan's wife has spread a knitted jute pai on the concrete floor, and set out just one stainless steel plate and a steel tumbler with boiled water. This is because Nathan will eat alone—the women of his family have never joined him in the meal; they are there to serve him and then to eat after he has had his fill" (Sundaresan, 2008, p. 53). This demonstrates the female position and female placement in the order of Indian household.

The equation of gender, education, and urbanity is also based on the economic factor. Nathan grudgingly sends his daughter for school as he is all the time worried about their dowry. He is unable to think more for his daughters, "The three girls went to the campus school. . . . What use was it to educate girls? He had himself never learned to read and write too much and yet he managed at his job well enough. All the girls were fit for was to cook and clean and bear children. His wife could teach them that" (Sundaresan, 2008, p. 54). Sundaresan draws parallel between Mrs. Rao's daughter who comes from a well-to-do and educated family and Nathan's daughter who are her foil. Nathan's attitude towards his daughters' education represents the collective attitude of many who live in cities but still in their minds live in ancient times, "In Mrs. Rao's world, her daughter had to have a college degree to be married. In Nathan's world, if his daughters were too learned, they would not find a husband.

Eighth standard was enough, and they could even read and write and speak some English" (Sundaresan, 2008, p. 55).

Parvati is a victim of patriarchy, casteism, and classism. Nathan also suffers from the caste and class conflict, and he attributes this to his economic status. He intends to class and caste appropriation because he is poor, so he is unable to afford modern lifestyle, crossing the caste lines. He forbids his daughter mingling with Raja who hails from a lower caste, "Not just for the class matter, but also they were of a different caste. For Nathan this was very important. It defined who he was, and stepping out of the caste was something only the rich and famous and indifferent did" (Sundaresan, 2008, p. 56). Nathan, Parvati's father is so obsessed with his family's reputation, that he does not even offer his grandson a name. However, Parvati stands up for herself and for her son, and gives him a name, "She did not ask Nathan or his wife permission for the name; they would not have given it anyway. Preferring to let the child be nameless, for giving him a name would mean putting a name to their shame" (Sundaresan, 2008, p. 51). This moral penalising and reluctance to accept, affects Parvati both emotionally and socially. She becomes an outsider in her own house, in her own family. She is judged by the society, her family included, nonetheless, Raja being a man, is spared the past and finds a bright future. This patriarchal reality always imposes onus on women, "In the context of sexual encounters in the modern city, it becomes the primary responsibility of women to uphold these principles of distancing and separation between male bodies" (Tyagi & Sen, 2019, p. 13).

Gender, Poverty, and Migration

Sundaresan's short story, "3 and a Half Seconds" reappropriates the antipastoral nature of city life and its challenges on the rural immigrants. Bombay, the peak of urbanity and metropolitanism is the setting of this story which unfurls the gloomy confession of a suiciding elderly couple. The narrative begins thus, "But no one wakes in the flats. No lights come on, no heads stick out of windows, no fists are shaken in disgust. They all still sleep. Tomorrow they will know, Meha thinks. Tomorrow they will see what Chandar and she have done. Time enough for that" (Sundaresan, 2008, p. 13). The tightly-knit apartment sleeps in oblivion as the desperate elderly couple jump to their deaths. The clamour of the city drowns the 'cries of help' of the elderly couple.

Tension and transformation are associated with urban migration for the rural immigrants. Meha the female protagonist lives half of her life in the countryside and the rest of the life in the city. Her life in the countryside is marked with happiness and contentment, whereas, her later life in the city is saturated with desolation and woes. Despite the criticism and back-breaking toil, village proves a better place for Meha. The village being the heartland of patriarchy sentences Meha for delay in the child birth. However, her husband chandar is untouched by the shadow of this ordeal, "No one dared talk with Chandar, of course" (Sundaresan, 2008, p. 13). Meha is crushed down with insults and humiliation. Until, "The questions, the snickers, the looks in the village stopped as Meh''s stomach grew" (Sundaresan, 2008, p. 15). Further, after the birth of Bikaner, a son, Meha's other tribulations begin.

Migration of livelihood from countryside to cities characterises economic progress among others. Meha represents economic migration from villages to city in search of livelihood and better opportunity of life. Meha and Chandar after enduring two long years of misery and pangs of hunger in their village, finally decide to survive by moving to city. They head towards city with meagre belongings, "Chandar finally decided that they must head to the big city in search of work And so they packed their belongings: one extra set of clothes each, which was all they had; a handful of rice; four handfuls of atta from the communal bin to knead for chappatis; a brass pot; an old pink talcum powder tin with the top cut off and filled with chili pickle; fifty rupees rolled into a tight wad and tied to the pallu of Meha's sari" (Sundaresan, 2008, p. 18). Urbanity is expensive and complicated. As meha is stricken by the cost of everything in the city, "Meha can remember being horrified at paying five rupees for the panipuri" (Sundaresan, 2008, p. 19). Meha is disturbed by hunger and sense of homelessness of her family. She with her husband and son is hardly able to find a sleeping spot under the open sky on the footpath, "They spent the night on the footpath, anonymous among other huddled and covered forms. Meha looked around her, unable to sleep. In the village, in their compound, she had always slept outside on hot nights, but then she knew everyone around her. In Mumbai, the noises from the street were strange, so many cars and taxis and scooters and buses. And the people were rude" (Sundaresan, 2008, p. 19). She is also troubled by the strangeness and lack of familiarity of the place.

Meha also suffers from mortification and disgrace in the city. As she hails from village and a patriarchal set up, she is accustomed to gentle bashfulness and self-possession. She feels violated in the city when she feels any new gaze or touch upon her, "There were so many people who pushed and shoved and yelled, 'Behenji, move out of the way.'. . . In the village, the men of other families barely looked at her, or stood aside as she passed, knowing she was not of their family. Here, already, one man had put his broad hand on her back" (Sundaresan, 2008, p. 19). Chandar and Meha find themselves trapped in the hopeless state of finding daily sustenance. Meha is so helpless that she is forced to pick the leftovers, "Every morning as Meha and Bikaner fought on the street for food scraps, as they dug through the dustbins for leftovers, he greeted the manager at the bank, 'Find me something, sahib'" (Sundaresan, 2008, p. 20). Meha and her family find themselves on the wrong side of the city dreams. They find themselves in the centre of the urban nightmare which deprives them of familiarity in addition to food and shelter. This representation of urban spaces is global, "the city is the place where deep class divides, social injustices, violence, and repressive forces struggle and clash with seemingly unlimited opportunity, creativity, and production" (Duff, 2014, p. 11).

There is a shift in social status and position based on economic standing. Meha's dignity is also bartered for food when she accepts to become a menial domestic help. She is demoted from a landowner's wife to a domestic help. Meha find no respite even after Chandar's newly found job. She is unable to make both the ends meet and decides to earn by domestic labour. She reasons with her husband who believes that it is emasculating that his wife should participate in earning the livelihood, "The money still was not enough. The bank job brought in only a few rupees, barely enough for food. One night as they lay on the footpath looking up at a cloudy sky, Meha said to Chandar, "Geeta said her memsahib's neighbour lady needs a bai" (Sundaresan, 2008, p. 20). However, this desperation of Meha unsettles Chandar who is shocked. He protests, "My wife will not be a maidservant. We are a proud people, Meha. What will the village elders think if they knew? I forbid you to go; you will not be a bai like Geeta" (Sundaresan, 2008, p. 21). However, Meha's misery grows as a result of shrunken space. She is unable even to privately talk to her husband. She is constantly under the public scrutinising gaze. The metaphor of street dogs aptly describes Meha's condition, "What pride was there in living like pariah dogs on the street? She slid an arm over his chest. A man passing on the street snickered, then stood over them watching. They stayed very still and soon he wandered away" (Sundaresan, 2008, p. 21). Finally, Meha is able to get the job of a domestic servant and starts helping with their livelihood.

Meha is lost and defeated by the urban economy and urban life. She finds it difficult to migrate from the slow economy of village to the fast economy of city where the cost of living is higher, "Uniforms and chappals were required and so Meha went to the bazaar near Dadar station and bought them, watching the rupees dissolve in her hand. But she understood that it was necessary for Bikaner to go to school. At home in the village, it would not have been necessary, but here even a peon was an Intermediate pass, or at least had appeared for the exams" (Sundaresan, 2008, p. 21). In addition to tackling the livelihood crisis, Meha is also weighed down by problems of her difficult son, Bikaner. Bikaner is not only uncaring towards his family, but also bad-tempered and clingy. He transfers his difficulties and humiliations to his mother. He suffers in the school because of his village background and less standard of education.

Another struggle for the poor immigrants is housing, "Accessibility to adequate housing is a critical issue for the urban poor" (Gottdiener and Budd, 2005, p. 56). Shelter becomes the principal challenge for Meha and her family. They are unable to find a place to be. They live like 'dumped population' of the city which is move around by the administrators. The difficulty of being removed from one place after other increases Meha's unease and distress, "They were moved a few times. Each time the good citizens of Mumbai considered the footpath-dwellers a blight on the landscape, they moved. From one footpath to another, in another street, in another part of town" (Sundaresan, 2008, p. 22). Meha's pastoral dreams are replaced with urban nightmares. She yearns to find a stable place and the basic amenities. Her longing embalms her scars of urban abuse, "As she walked on the street between the huts of the jhopadpatti, Meha would look up at the flats towering above them and think of mosaic floors, concrete walls, a toilet that flushed, water out of taps" (Sundaresan, 2008, p. 22). Eventually, her hard work enables her to live her dream of a small house. She and her husband are able to purchase a small house with help of bank loan. Urban space is characterised by limited land space, and vertical space. "The tall building was not a contribution of a particular place, but is viewed, rather, as an evolutionary innovation resulting from the unique city aspect of limited locationally valuable land" (Gottdiener & Budd, 2005, 9). Meha's movement from ground to height is also noteworthy. Meha is anxious about the heights; she has always lived and loved the ground. She distrusts the height, "It frightened her to live so far above the earth that she loved. She did not look down from the balcony for many years" (Sundaresan, 2008, p. 22). Height and technology ruffle Meha's calm and comfort. This is another fear she learns to live with in the urban haven.

Another urban conflict arises when Bikaner proposes to marry his female colleague from work belonging to a different cast. Caste system is an inevitable order of social life in India and this casteism is especially intense in rural India. The cities glorify cosmopolitan way of life and casteism is less prevalent. This declining and modern caste system in the city disturbs Meha. She is unable to reconcile with this urban reality, "Even after seventeen years in the city, Meha and Chandar were not used to living shoulder-by-hip with people from all castes. Things were simpler at home where they rarely met or saw other communities. Everything had an unquestioned system—the village well, the patshala, the vegetable market timings, but.. Bikaner was going to bring home a bride who was not Kshatriya, not of their warrior caste" (Sundaresan, 2008, p. 23). Thus, Meha's struggles are multiplied by a complete shift in lifestyle, values, socio-cultural practices, poverty, social downfall, and strange ways of the cities.

Gender and Aging

Aging is another aspect which intersects with gender and urbanity. "As recent research has shown, crimes such as domestic violence, acquaintance violence and elder abuse also have a role to play in the construction of fear" (Pain, 2001, p. 3). Meha grows weak, powerless, disillusioned, and fearful. Her manifold troubles are augmented as her grown-up son takes out his frustration on his parents. Meha has tried to help her son earlier when he was a small boy, but later, she finds herself helpless and her son overpowering. His failure to accept the truth transforms into ugly anger and abuse, "He said calmly, 'I would be an officer if you were not a chowkidar at the bank. Do you think they 'don't know that you are my father? Why do you think I have not passed the exam? Because I am a farmer's son—worse yet, a chowkidar's son'" (Sundaresan, 2008, p. 25). Meha not only helps herself and her family to adapt in the urban reality, but also, is forced to absorb her son's failings and losses in the course of life.

Bikaner's metamorphosis into an inhuman son is one of the gloomiest aspects of Meha's life. She is oppressed by the overwhelming starkness and injustice which she finds in her life after coming to the city. Bikaner's abuse of his parents is partly the result of his self-loathing and failure to reconcile with his let-down. Instead of being grateful to his parents for their efforts and sacrifices, he abuses them for his incapacities and lower social standing. Meha and Chander relapse into their bad phase of life, but this time they are broken from inside and out. They are forced out of their living places to balcony where they live as invisible and unwanted beings, "They were moved out of the kitchen to the balcony, huddling in one damp corner during monsoon nights. Bikaner's voice and his beatings just grew louder and wilder" (Sundaresan, 2008, p. 26). Meha finds herself lost and all alone with her husband in the antagonistic social system. She endures silently by shedding tears, but lacks the courage to seek help as it would mean exposing her family matters to the strangers. This engrained attitude of pride and honour make things worse for her and Chandar. Ageing coupled with physical and emotional abuse weakens her resolve to live on. "But where would they go? Whose eyes could they meet anymore?" (Sundaresan, 2008, p. 26).

The betrayal of her own flesh and the shocking treatment she and Chandar received at the hands of their son shakes Meha's existence. She is overwhelmed with pity and hurt, and this is augmented by the space they are forced to confine in. Meha is confined to the balcony which is both closed and opened. Conceivably, the son does not want to have his parents inside the home and also he is unable to send them completely outside. He confines them in balcony which is a metaphor of confinements and freedom which eventually Meha and Chandar seek by jumping from it. Possibly Bikaner intended this fatal downfall of his parents and that is why he forced them on to the balcony which would facilitate their jumping to death. His corporal punishment is just a procedure or operation to attain this end. However, Meha does not surrender to the fate very easily and she tries to salvage her condition by reaching out to one of her relatives, "But finally it got to be too hard to stay outside on the balcony all the time. . . . Meha wrote to one of Chandar's brothers, digging deep inside herself for words to call him to Mumbai, to tell him to look after them"

(Sundaresan, 2008, p. 27). However, she is found, and Bikaner punishes badly her parents for this transgression.

Meha breaks her silence by making a statement. She not only ends her life with her husband, but begins her narrative, "Before they left Meha wrote out their story, in her broken English, using the language Bikaner had taught her. The papers lie folded in Chandar's kurta pocket, now already stained with his blood. But people must know, Meha thinks, that their lives were once worth something" (Sundaresan, 2008, p. 28). She leaves her story behind to be known by others. Her feeble attempt to write and broken English with which she tries signifies her last attempt to snatch a piece of past. The city has made her a woman of iron will, where she has learnt to accept insults and agree with unconventional ways of life.

Similarly, the short story, "Bedside Dreams" presents the interplay between gender and aging in urban spaces. It projects the rude reality of changed times when the elderly parents are left to fend for themselves in care homes and hospices. Comatose Kamal and his paralysed wife exist merely as bodies which are tampered by the medical hands for clinical care. The narrator, Kamal's wife who is only bodily paralysed is drowned in her sweet-bitter memories, revisiting the past and thinking of alternate presents. She describes her present life in the confines, "My eyes cast over the chalky whitewashed walls within my range of vision and then to the beds lined in a military row along the sides of the room. Twelve to each side. This has been our home for the last twenty-three years, from the day Kamal retired from the Indian Railways as chief engineer" (Sundaresan, 2008, p. 73). This Western concept of elderly homes both hurts and helps the elderly couple. Though Kamal's wife is shocked initially when she is informed about their living arrangement, but she reconciles, "What was that? I asked in apprehension. And I was right to be frightened of this Western concept that had invaded our existence. Kamal and I moved into this dormitory twenty-three years ago and haven't left it since" (Sundaresan, 2008, p. 77).

The elderly female protagonist suffers more as she is conscious of her condition and state. She is able to feel the agony of being abandoned by her twelve children, among which most are sons. She relives both happy days and regrets, time and again in her paralysed state. Her disability disables her from not only moving, but also, from enjoying the oblivion. Unlike her husband, she carries on with the burden of loss and neglect . The present-day society of urbanity weakens her chances of care and family, "In other words, the circumstances of older women are the outcome of (1) their social and class positions; (2) institutionalised discrimination that women experience throughout their life; and (3) age discrimination" (Vera-Sanso, 2012, p. 325). The narrator's pain is greater as it contrasts with the glory of her young life and olden days.

Gender and Punishment

Sundaresan portrays gender-based violence which is inflicted under the guise of social practice and beliefs. "The Faithful Wife" is set in an Indian village named, Pathra, representing two female characters – Ram's elderly grandmother who is brave and makes an effort to stop the unthinkable tradition of Sati; and the twelve-year-old young girl who is merely a child, set on fire in the funeral pyre of her diseased husband. The young girl is too young to defend herself and submits to the cruel fate. However, Ram's grandmother is undeterred to make a difference and she is unable to directly interfere with the old tradition, she writes a letter to her grandson, Ram who is a journalist, wishing that he would stop it or at least report about it. Here, the urbanity is limited to Ram who works as a journalist in the city and his grandmother finds courage in this. Ram's grandmother intends to rescue the helpless young girl and she knows only one way, that is to inform her grandson. In fact, Ram knows this when he sees his grandmother who silently and secretly wishes that Ram does something, "Ram would never have heard of this but for one incident. The village code, extending strictly even to minor things, was broken by a woman who all her life followed the rules society laid down for her in rigid lines. All her life, until now. When she opened the door for him this morning, in her eyes he had seen fear but also, in that grim glance, defiance" (Sundaresan, 2008, p. 29). This courage and defiance is translated into words on a piece of paper and sent to her grandson. Though, she is from a traditional village where women are confined within domestic restrains, she has acquired little literacy and lot of resistance. Ram is astonished at his grandmother's daring letter as Is always seen his grandmother meek and extremely traditional, "Nani has always followed the rules. Yet there was the childish scrawl on the scrap of paper tucked into an old envelope. . . . Inside she has not asked him to come—she rarely asks for things—but has simply said, Beta, there will be a Sati here in two days, the child is only twelve, her husband, whose body lies on a block of ice in his home awaiting the cremation, is the man we talked of when you were last here" (Sundaresan, 2008, p. 32).

Similar to Meha, Ram's grandmother uses her limited literacy to convey the deep-seated secret and defy the traditional bonds of shame and timidity. Both women who are not formally educated, use the meticulously earned skill to voice out and let the world know. Even if the grandmother is unable to interfere with the tradition of Sati and save the young girl's life, she strongly hopes that Ram would report about it in his newspaper and let the entire country know about it. Only when people learn about this, they will condemn and stop it from happening in other places to other widows. The grandmother wants to use this urban device called mass media to make this known and draw public attention. Ram's grandfather directs, "'What will you do about this, Ram?' his grandfather asks. 'Will you rage against it? Or will you do something? Write about this. Tell the world; break the silence that hangs over this village. Do what your grandmother wants you to do.' He slants his head toward the other end of the courtyard where his wife has stopped pounding the wheat and listens instead to his voice" (Sundaresan, 2008, p. 34). Ram's Grandfather also gives his implicit approval and does not reprimand his wife for challenging the traditions. However, Ram with his urban system is unable to stop the sati from taking place. The twelve-year-old girl who is set on fire alive, represents both child marriage and sati. Though, the sati is taking place in a village, Ram's grandmother wishes to use the urban space to translate the practice into news.

Similarly, the short story, "Fire" reveals the horror of honour killing in an urbanising setup. It is a short story built around three women who suffer as a consequence of imposed tradition and morality. It exhibits the intensified social and religious confrontations. Religion is an important factor in Indian society, "Contemporary India is a key context for considering social change and religious community interaction" (Stroope, 2012, p. 4). It also typifies the generation gap despite shifting times and transformed spaces. The story takes place in urban setup. Payal describes the spatial arrangement of the house which is traditional and urban in its nature. The house stands for the crisscrossing family network and morality. She describes, "It is an ancestral home, cavernous-looking on the outside, inside squirreled with small, limewashed rooms. Like a maze. To get from the front door to the back, there are seventeen different ways. I know. I counted them as a child" (Sundaresan, 2008, p. 37). The system of joint family is mostly rural, but it is found in some of the traditional urban houses also. Payal also describes the nature of family system they had. Her family is a combined family occupying a large bungalow like house with a handful of servants to attend their chores. This symbolises both opulence and conservatism. She observes, "In my childhood, we were twenty-one people in the house. My mother and father, of course, and aunts and uncles who were not terribly good at having or keeping jobs, and their even more useless children. And the servants" (Sundaresan, 2008, p. 38). Payal's family enjoys the privilege of city and materialism. They have servants to wait upon them. The family exhibits a microscopic view of class and social hierarchy. This status and attitude in the society makes them pseudo-moralists. When the female servants are exploited, they are just sent away, "Then there were the three maids who lived in a shack in the back garden, who swept and wiped the house each day, and spent the rest of the time on the steps, their voices delicious with gossip. They seemed to disappear a lot, one after another, leaving with heavy stomachs, made pregnant by the mali or the chowkidar, or even once, the chauffeur" (Sundaresan, 2008, p. 38). The house looms over like a gargantuan patriarchal structure promoting gender and class hierarchy.

Payal's grandmother is the antihero who represents stark orthodoxy and merciless social and religious intolerance. She is the matriarch of the family, enjoying the power and authority of her subjects – the individuals living under her roof. Though, she has all the power vested upon her, but she operates in the patriarchal way. She oppresses the female member of the family with morality and customs. She maintains her dignity and power both physically and emotionally. However, when she is very sick, her power ebbs away, but she tries to keep a strong hold on her grace, "Everything is white around her: the sheet that covers her body; her blouse, through which gaunt arms protrude like sticks; the pearls she always wore; and her sari, of course. White, pure, spotless. To show she is a widow. To show she is faithful to 'her husband's memory, to show that she does not consider it worth her while to preen in gold and coloured silks for another man" (Sundaresan, 2008, p. 38). Payal's grandmother being an agent of patriarchy sentences her grand daughters' transgressions. She is so entrenched in male-controlled order, that she closely examines their every move and behaviour. She chides Payal, "Payal, come down from the champa tree. Girls do not climb trees" (Sundaresan, 2008, p. 39). This is a metaphor for, how women are forced to stay low and are not allowed to climb up in life. However, Both Payal and Kamala are rebellious and cross the threshold of their grandmother's kingdom in their own way. While Payal does well in education and goes outside India for her prospects, Kamala breaks away from her family's traditional order by falling in love with a man of different religion and class.

However, both Payal and Kamala revolt and use the opportunity of going out for education to break away from the family tradition. Payal is undeterred and she makes her way out to America as a gesture of defiance and confrontation. The grandmother and others relents to her aggressive approach, "It was hard, sending away one of ours to a foreign land. But you insisted, yelled to get your way, left us here alone" (Sundaresan, 2008, p. 41). Payal does not stop just there, and her dissidence stretches and continues. She defiles the sanctity of her family tradition and name by indulging what was prohibited and immoral. She admits, "I had spent seven years in America without coming back here. After graduate school, I got a job editing a newspaper in New Jersey. I partied at night, downing my tais with a vengeance. I opened my legs for a few men; the American men were always kinder than the Indian men afterward when we broke up. For I always broke up. I did not care enough to be a good girl" (Sundaresan, 2008, p. 43). Payal registers her defiance by asserting her eating habits. She challenges her grandmother who is proud of her Brahmin heritage and the reason she hated Kamala and Aziz. Payal taunts her grandmother, "I eat cows, I say. In America I have eaten many many cows. American cows are not that different from Indian cows. I eat cows. Steaks, hamburgers.... It slides down my Brahmin throat, into my Brahmin stomach" (Sundaresan, 2008, p. 44). Payal challenges both her gender and her caste.

Education empowers women who become equipped to challenge the traditions. Payal arms herself with English language and higher education. She confronts her grandmother, "How can you even ask, bitch? I speak in English, a language she is not comfortable with, but I know she understands. I will not give her the pleasure of speaking in Tamil, even though what I have to say will be so much more effective, so much more terrible in that tongue. I use antiseptic English" (Sundaresan, 2008, p. 40). Appearances and passing become essential requisites of urbanity as women try to pass as modern in their looks. Payal describes the modern ways of her family despite the morality coated ways. Evidently, their modernisation is limited to their hairdo, "We all grew up modern. The aunties cut our hair short, bangs in the front, a straight sweep just above the shoulders in the back, but Kamala, dreamy, tranquil Kamala, would not let them touch her head" (Sundaresan, 2008, p. 40). However, Kamala proves her modern attitude by not adhering to her elders and doing what she wished and preferred.

Payal rebels and protest more boldly than Kamala who is silent and she uses her silence to confront her family. She tries to help her sister, Kamala by yelling at others on her behalf, "I did all the yelling and screaming on her behalf" (Sundaresan, 2008, p. 41). There is restraint even on expressing affection in Payal's urban yet traditional family. Payal confesses when Kamala tried to express her gratitude and fondness for her sister, "Then she came in, reached up from the floor, put her little arms around me and laid her cheek against mine. We did not kiss much in this house; neither of us would have known how to do so. But that one embrace was enough. It was never repeated again" (Sundaresan, 2008, p. 41). Kamala demonstrates her insubordination by acknowledging her Muslim lover in public. She does not care about her family's disgrace, "She knew, Kamala knew it would be Aziz. She never hid anything from the people at the house. Met him openly. Talked with him outside the shop where anyone passing could see her, always standing away from him" (Sundaresan, 2008, p. 44). However, Kamala meets her brutal and fatal downfall in the guise of 'honour killing.'

Kamala's gender, class, caste, and the patriarchal conscience of her family lead to the capital punishment. The grandmother justifies the honour killing of her granddaughter, Kamala and her lover, Aziz, "I had to, she says. I had to show everyone what was right. I had to tell' them. Aziz's blood could not mix with the blood of this house. Not with the blood of a daughter of this house. They had been missing for forty-eight hours. Who knows what they had done, and where they had done it? No good Brahmin boy would ever marry her. Or marry a daughter of the house if we had not done what we did. It was right" (Sundaresan, 2008, p. 45). Similar to the sati girl, Kamala is also sacrificed for the upkeep of patriarchal values.

Gender and Sexuality

Another point which proves the gender inequality in urban spaces is the juncture between gender, sexuality and free will. The lives of well-educated rich women are also demarcated by gender inequality. "The Key Club" is about a modern couple who attempt to construct their dream reality and assume different roles and new names. This story limns the lives of rich and so-called modern family picking at the fruits of urbanity and autonomy. They relate urbanity to forged reality where they prefer different names and new identities. The fake life routine is:

On this night, once every four months, they change their names to Ram and Sita. They begin to think of themselves by these names from the moment the servant maid knocks on their bedroom door at 10am and says, 'Kapi thayaar' (Coffee is ready). The club always meets on a Saturday night, and on Sunday, Ram and Sita each go to their yoga class, their meditation class, the five-star gym at the Temple Palace Hotel with its shimmering Olympic-sized swimming pool, and end the day with a Laugh Class in Clyde Park where they learn to laugh from the bottom of their bellies until their eyes tear. (Sundaresan, 2008, p. 62)

Sita tries to play a dutiful hostess as it is deemed as one of the roles of an urban upper-middle class wife. She waits upon their so-called friends, focusing on the food, "They were twelve at the table, the dinner had been cleared away, Sita was delicately scraping the last of the mango ice cream from the white bowl in front of her, a few of the men and some of the women had leaned back in their chairs to light cigarettes" (Sundaresan, 2008, p. 63). Their choreographed lives only tell their urge to live a dream. Sita plays her role very well, almost like a puppet. "And she will say, as she always says, 'Sure'" (Sundaresan, 2008, p. 67). Sita acts and speaks to please her husband and his guests.

The husbands design a game where they exchange their sexual partners for a night which they spend in a hotel or its like. Ram and his friends initiate this idea in order to quench their latent sexual desires, and to reduce the boredom of their marriage. All the men are its members and their wives' mere guests. According to the key club game, the wives pick lots which are numbers from inside an envelope, and in that order they choose the car keys of the men which are placed on the table top. The owner of the car key which is picked becomes the sexual partner of the woman who played the turn. The key club downgrades its female members to mere objects, while the male members to keys. Though, it is the men who are literally reduced to keys it is the female members who are metamorphosised into trading currency. "The women draw lots from another envelope. Sita's number is seven" (Sundaresan, 2008, p. 72). The wives are also reduced to numbers and games.

The short story, "Hunger" is again depiction of the sophisticated lives inside the hart of urbanity where women enjoy the din of gathering and prosperity of shopping. However, they still route for their male partners and repress their desires and dreams in order to align their lives as per the code of social morality. Sheela, Jai's wife and Nitu, Prakrit's wife are the main female protagonists who are positioned in the society and in their apartment building based on the position of their husbands. Though, they are both lesbians, in order to be part of the larger social order, they suppress their individuality. The patriarchal organisation of the any house or home is important to understand the gender division, "The fact that housing, the primary workplace for social reproduction, is also the major asset for many people tends to reinforce the single-family, patriarchal shape of housing and neighbourhoods" (Curran, 2018, p. 4). Both Sheela and Neetu are educated and professionally capable, however, as married women, they are reduced to their husbands' keepers. "The head of the household is generally still unthinkingly presumed to be a man, supposed to be capable of catering for the material needs of wife and children, while the wife and mother provides nourishment and nurturance" (Pilcher & Whelehan, 2004, p. 81). Nitu serves her husband and her children as she is required by the dictates of the patriarchal society.

Both Sheela and Nitu are like Sita and other wives from "The Key Club" who trade their free will for status of wife. Similar to cars and symbols of prestige, wives are also exhibitory tokens, as Nitu narrates, "'He looks at me in the mirror.' 'All the managers are going with their wives. The MD wants to see me there. Wear something nice. Not Indian. Western'" (Sundaresan, 2008, p. 94). Nitu feels lost and alienated in the festivities not because she does not like and she is very traditional, but it is because, she is forced to participate. She suffocates, "Strobe lights in blue, green, red, and purple puncture the darkened room. A silver ball glitters in the centre of the ceiling. The music, cacophonous, is a thud of teclmo-funk. Boom. Boom. Boom. Over and over again. No other rhythm, no voices, no singing. Just a guitar and a heavy set of drums. We cleave through wedges of people; I see Prakrit's back appear and disappear" (Sundaresan, 2008, p. 96). The grandeur of the party widens the chasm in Nitu's troubled mind.

The conflict between female free will and patriarchal authority resolves by submission or resistance. Nitu is forced into submission, and her identity fractures. Prakrit believes that he owns Nitu and when she longs to visit her parents, he just refuses to let her go, "Even this is familiar. He does not want me here because he wants me here. But because I am a fixture in this flat. A wife. A symbol of status" (Sundaresan, 2008, p. 101). Nitu discovers her sexual identity when she meets Sheela, and when the conflict reaches the peak, she with her children decides to embark on her own journey this time.

CONCLUSION

The socio-spatial approach towards the literary case study, *In the Convent of Little Flowers*, demonstrate the varying degree of gender injustice in contemporary urban spaces in India. The spaces range from house to social clubs which delineate women from different classes and communities. Further, there are marginalised spaces like, orphanage, slums, and socialising spaces like clubs, hotels- which all show the subjugated situation of the women. The women get education, but no justice like Kamala who is murdered by her own family for choosing her life partner, and Parvati who is shunned by her own family for begetting a child out of wedlock. Some of the reasons are the societies exists in the cities, but, lives in their traditional past, and unfortunately, the traditions are dangerously patriarchal in nature, like sati and honour killing. Further, even in highly educated upper-class societies, old patriarchy is replaced with urban form of patriarchy – where, wives become object of showcasing and exhibition to assert social standing. Like Nitu who is highly educated but is enslaved by her husband, and Sita who lives with a crew of servants but is sexually demoralized by her husband and his friends.

The eight different narratives examined here, set against diverse social backdrops, share the theme of gender inequity and social injustice against women in cities and suburbs. There are range of challenges the women come across, to list out a few – social stigma, migration from village to city, aging, disability, sati, honour killing, and sexual expression. The furnish analysis and discussion reaffirm, how urbanity is not a gender gap equaliser, and the women suffer on various grounds. Despite urbanisation, issues like, communalism, casteism, unwed mothers, child marriage, widows, and lesbian relations, challenge the lives of Indian women. All these short stories demonstrate the victimised position of women across economic and caste lines. Privileges and patriarchy are synonymous and, the men harness women in their ordeal while women struggle all alone. Orthodoxy suits patriarchy, and as a result men govern modernity also. Urbanity seems to affect the gender roles and gender equity only marginally.

REFERENCES

Aneja, A. (2019). *Women's and gender studies in India*. Routledge.

Baghat, R. B., Roy, A. K., & Sahoo, H. (2021). *Migration and urban transition in India*. Routledge.

Berry, J., Moore, T., Kalms, N., & Bawden, G. (Eds.). (2021). *Contentious cities: Design and the gendered production of space*. Routledge.

Bhattacharjee, S., & Karmakar, G. (Eds.). (2022). *The city speaks: Urban spaces in Indian Literature*. Routledge. doi:10.4324/9781003323761

Bondi, L. (1998). Gender, class, and urban space: Public and private space in contemporary urban landscapes. *Urban Geography*, *19*(2), 160–185. doi:10.2747/0272-3638.19.2.160

Brassard, C., & Joshi, D. U. (2020). *Urban spaces and gender in Asia*. Springer.

Chattopadhyay, S. K. (2018). *Gender socialization and the making of gender in the Indian context*. Sage Publications. doi:10.4135/9789353280628

Curran, W. (2018). *Gender and gentrification*. Routledge.

Datta, A. (2021). *Gender, space and agency in India: Exploring regional genderscapes*. Routledge.

Davies, D., & Boehmer, E. (2018). *Planned violence: Post/Colonial urban infrastructure, literature and culture*. Springer.

Duff, K. (2014). *Contemporary British Literature and urban space: After Thatcher*. Palgrave. doi:10.1057/9781137429353

Gillis, M. J., & Jacobs, A. T. (2019). *Introduction to women's and gender studies*. Oxford University Press.

Gonsalves, T. (2022). *Women in the civil services: Gender and workplace identities in India*. Taylor and Francis. doi:10.4324/9781003193630

Gottdiener, M., & Budd, L. (2005). Key concepts in urban studies. *Sage (Atlanta, Ga.)*.

Hannah, M. G. (2021). *Direction and Socio-spatial Theory: A political economy of oriented practice*. Routledge.

Jakobsen, P., Jonsson, E., & Larsen, H. G. (2022). *Socio-Spatial Theory in Nordic geography: Intellectual histories and critical interventions*. Springer. doi:10.1007/978-3-031-04234-8

Kateja, A., & Jain, R. (Eds.). (2021). *Urban growth and environmental issues in India*. Springer Nature.

Kinderman, M., & Rohleder, R. (Eds.). (2020). *Exploring the spatiality of the city across cultural texts*. Springer. doi:10.1007/978-3-030-55269-5

Kumar, R., Korff, M., & Sudhir, K. (2018). *A gender atlas of India: With scorecard*. Sage Publication. doi:10.4135/9789353287832

Luthra, S. (2021). *Gender and education in India: A reader*. Taylor and Francis. doi:10.4324/9781003191612

Mela, A., & Toldo, A. (2019). *Socio-spatial inequalities in contemporary cities*. Springer. doi:10.1007/978-3-030-17256-5

Miles, M. (2019). *Cities and literature: Routledge critical introductions to urbanism and the city*. Routledge.

Oberhauser, A. M., Fluri, J. L., Whitson, R., & Mollett, S. (2018). *Feminist spaces: Gender and geography in a global context*. Routledge.

Pain, R. (2001). Gender, race, age and fear in the city. *Urban Studies (Edinburgh, Scotland)*, *38*(5), 899–913. doi:10.1080/00420980120046590

Pilcher, J., & Whelehan, A. (2004). *50 key concepts in gender studies*. Sage Publication. doi:10.4135/9781446278901

Pourya Asl, M. (Ed.). (2022). *Gender, place, and identity of South Asian women*. IGI Global. doi:10.4018/978-1-6684-3626-4

Ray, D. (2022). *Postcolonial Indian city-literature: Policy, politics and evolution (Routledge research in postcolonial literatures)*. Routledge. doi:10.4324/9781003166337

Samantroy, E., & Nandi, S. (2022). *Gender, unpaid work and care in India*. Taylor and Francis. doi:10.4324/9781003276739

Singh, A. (2022). *Gender, violence and performance in contemporary India*. Routledge.

Singh, J. (2022). *Feminist literary and cultural criticism: An analytical approach to space*. Springer. doi:10.1007/978-981-19-1426-3

Spain, D. (2014). Gender and urban space. *Annual Review of Sociology*, *40*(1), 581–598. doi:10.1146/annurev-soc-071913-043446

Stauv, A. (2018). *The Routledge companion to modernity, space and gender*. Routledge.

Stroope, S. (2012). Caste, class, and urbanization: The shaping of religious community in contemporary India. *Social Indicators Research*, *105*(3), 499–518. doi:10.100711205-011-9784-y

Sundaresan, I. (2008). *In the Convent of Little Flowers*. Washington Square Press.

Tompkins, K. W., Aizura, A. Z., Bahng, A., Chávez, K. R., Goeman, M., & Musser, A. J. (Eds.). (2021). *Keywords for gender and sexuality studies*. New York University Press.

Tyagi, A., & Sen, A. (2019). Love-Jihad (Muslim sexual seduction) and ched-chad (sexual harassment): Hindu nationalist discourses and the ideal/deviant urban citizen in India. *Gender, Place and Culture*, *27*(1), 104–125. doi:10.1080/0966369X.2018.1557602

Vera-Sanso, P. (2012). Gender, poverty and old-age livelihoods in Urban South India in an era of globalisation. *Oxford Development Studies*, *40*(3), 324–340. doi:10.1080/13600818.2012.710322

Wolff, J. (2010). Urban spaces keynote: Unmapped spaces — gender, generation and the city. *Feminist Review*, *96*(1), 6–19. doi:10.1057/fr.2010.12

Section 2
Self-Representation and the Re-Mapping of the Urban Geography

This section is concerned with autobiographical stories of women's daily experiences of city and city spaces in South Asia. The section explores the processes of reimagining urban spaces and redefining identity constructs and studies the significance of women's activism and resistance practices in everyday life as documented in selected eyewitness accounts by women writers from the region.

Chapter 7
Reshaping Existing Discourses on Urban Spaces:
Women's Socio-Spatial Activism in Indian Autobiographical Narratives

Kiron Susan Joseph Sebastine
 https://orcid.org/0000-0002-0621-0303
School of Arts, Humanities, and Commerce, Amrita Vishwa Vidyapeetham, Kochi, India

ABSTRACT

Activism can occur in urban spaces independent of their spatial proportions. This chapter analyses the representations of women's activism as observed in their autobiographical works. The study focusses on women's activism documented in life writings by Nalini Jameela titled The Autobiography of a Sex Worker (2007) and Kiran Bedi's Dare to Do! For the New Generation (2012). The chapter draws upon the sociologist Mario Diani's deliberations on the different types of grassroot activism and social movements that can be understood as a manifestation of the right to the city struggle. Through a comparative analysis of the texts, the chapter examines how city spaces can become arenas of transformation, and the myriad ways people can come together to propose a common agenda and conjointly act to accomplish their goals.

INTRODUCTION

Activism can occur at different planes. Activism can take various forms. Activism can occur in urban spaces independent of their spatial proportions. Although factors such as caste, class, creed and community segregate individuals from each other, there are elements that bring together the activists and the victims of a human rights violation thus making space for their concerns politically, symbolically, and materially. Activism can make itself present through people situated in different social structures. It can evolve from an effort in claiming an identity. In the present age of social media, we come across activistic groups, seeking to express and establish their racial, ethnic, and transnational identities through online networks. (Lai, 2022, p. x). Rooted in-between the private and public spheres, urban activism grows from concrete challenges like density, diversity, and an imbalance of power among urban stakeholders. (Domaradzka, 2018, p. 3). Women's activism is no different in this regard. An urban civil sphere is developed including place-oriented, democracy-oriented as well as 'quality of life'-oriented forms of social engagement and collective action (Domaradzka, 2018, p. 3). Activism is a collective performance which brings a group of people to the forefront and others to rally around them thereby unanimously proposing the significance of certain ideologies and rights. The rights frame calls attention to the disadvantages created by an unequal and prejudiced society that tend to create an inferior class of citizens rather than positioning rights as a personal trouble (Carey et al., 2020). It can easily be related to social movements and is often initiated by individuals who are dissatisfied with the existing system of values, principles, methods, and actions. They optimistically look forward to bringing about radical changes to the structure of the existing scheme of things. The past experiences of the activists play a vital role in the themes of their activism. These experiences urge them to strive towards disconnecting themselves from the existing system and proposing a reformed system. The activists set well defined goals for their organisation, and as they seek to accomplish these goals, they are faced with demanding threats from the spaces in which they operate. The greatest challenges in activism or in social movements are the resistances to a transformation. Hurdles are placed before the movement by powerful vested interests who may be politically or otherwise motivated. Urban spaces contribute largely towards the initiation and sustenance of activistic movements and the activism in urban spaces is subject to the various stimuli invariably prevalent in the city spaces. Scholarly works on activism mention that historians have examined the "urban and industrial roots" of certain forms of activism and have shown how cities and workplaces were often key sites of the struggle (Ward, 2022, p. 9). Activism can resultantly evolve into an integral part of an urban narrative. The urban setting could be of multiple proportions and variant traits. Correspondingly activism can be embedded within an autobiographical narrative. According to Chatterjee (2008), the autobiography would seem to be obvious material for studying the emergence of modern forms of self-representation. The members of an activistic movement participate in a mirroring of themselves through the collective action that develops within the politics of the urban spaces and may choose to construct a narrative founded on their exercises. Christina Leza, author of *Divided Peoples: Policy, Activism, and Indigenous activities on the U.S.-Mexico Border*, states that the term activist may be less problematic and a useful label to better connect to a variety of individuals working for shared causes (Leza, 2019, p. 143).

An autobiographical narrative has the potential to represent activism irrespective of whether it is a collective performance or individually operated. Narratives on the challenges faced by activist movements can be analysed taking the support of scholarly works on activism as well as social movements. Activism can be corelated to the thoughts shared by Herbert Blumer in his essay titled *Social Movements* which forms a part of the critical work, *Social Movements: A Reader*. He proposes that social movements can be viewed as collective enterprises to establish a new order of life. He adds on that they have their inception in a condition of unrest (Blumer, 2008). According to Blumer the background of social movements is constituted by gradual and pervasive changes in the values of people which can be termed as cultural drifts which stand for a general shift in the idea of people concerning themselves, their rights, and their privileges (Blumer, 2008). This chapter focuses on a study on women's activism as represented in the autobiographical works by Nalini Jameela and Dr. Kiran Bedi. A police officer marked by innovation and participative approach to bureaucratic administration, Dr. Bedi runs two non-governmental organisations, namely *Navjyoti India Foundation* and *India Vision Foundation* during her career as an officer in the Indian Police Service and post her retirement from service. The organisations effectively handle the social and economic maladies that adversely affect present-day society in areas such as domestic problems, women's issues, addiction, juvenile matters, and crime. Nalini Jameela, a former sex worker, sex work activist and author belongs to the state of Kerala in the south of India. She is the coordinator of the Sex Workers Forum of Kerala and an active member of five non-governmental organisations. Under her leadership the SWFK has held protest marches to draw attention to the plight of street-based sex workers within the city spaces of the state of Kerala in India. Nalini Jameela's book, *The Autobiography of a Sex Worker* (2005) is one among the two works selected for analysis in this chapter. Originally written in her mother tongue Malayalam, the book was translated into English by J. Devika. The second autobiography chosen for the study is *Dare to Do! For the New Generation* (2012) by Dr. Kiran Bedi. The work primarily focuses on an analysis of Dr. Bedi's role as an activist who was able to contribute towards variant forms of activism through her efforts towards the control of drug related crimes and the rehabilitation of the related offenders and through her prison reforms at the Tihar jail situated in the capital city of India, New Delhi. Since the 1970s, "new social movement" theorists discussed on how new movements tried to oppose the intrusion of the state and the market into social life, reclaiming individuals' right to determine their own life projects and identities, against the omnipresent and manipulative systemic apparatuses (Porta & Diani, 2015, p. 4). This chapter draws upon the sociologist Mario Diani's deliberations on the different types of grassroot activism and social movements that can be understood as a manifestation of the right to the city struggle. The chapter examines how city spaces can become an arena of transformation, and the myriad ways of how people can come together to propose a common agenda and conjointly act to accomplish their goals. Along with other scholarly works, the chapter takes support from the critical perspectives of Vanhoose and Savini who state that activism focussed on structures identified with urban spaces need to be built upon a careful analysis of the existing scheme of things and followed on with essential transformation of the system inclusive of its participants.

LITERATURE REVIEW

The study of social movements and activism has developed into a major area of research interest in the 20th century. Further on the study developed at an unparalleled pace into a major area of research. Presently the study of social movements is solidly established, with professional associations, specialized journals, and book series. According to Lalitha (2008), author of the essay *Women in Revolt: A Historical Analysis of The Progressive Organisation of Women In Andhra Pradesh*; in the early days of women's movements, during the discussions that women held among themselves, they felt that initially they had to understand the different trends in the women's movements before they would be able to identify with one. Activistic movements or social movements can be studied as an organised process, its participants being individuals with exemplary leadership skills and commitment towards the cause. They must persistently encounter resistances and frictional forces working against their course in the spaces in which they operate. In the work titled *Contested Cities and Urban Activism* the notion of 'urban activism' is described as the conventional expression to capture sustained mobilisations and protests that challenge consolidated power structures in relation to the production and transformation of urban spaces (Yip et al., 2019). Social and political events over the past decades have hardly rendered the investigation of grassroots activism any less relevant or urgent. To the contrary, social movements, protest actions, and, more generally, political organizations unaligned with major political parties or trade unions have become a permanent component of world democracies. The importance of urban settings for social and political mobilization is not a new phenomenon; the civil rights movement in the United States in the 1960s, urban protests in Hong Kong in the 1980s, and the global justice movement in the 2000s, are examples for this (Andretta et al, 2015). Malala Yousufzai in her memoir titled *We are Displaced: My Journey and Stories from Refugee Girls Around the World*, shares her experiences as an international activist and the stories of other refugee students who have been displaced into urban spaces situated in their host countries. Their survival stories develop within the politics of the host city spaces (Yousufzai, 2019). According to the prominent scholarly works and critical perspectives in the subject area, social movements developing within city spaces can no longer be described as unconventional (Diani & Porta, 2006). Past social movements were linked to meta social principles, but they opposed themselves to domination of tradition and natural principles while new social movements are threatened by utilitarianism as they defend the self and its creativity against interest and pleasure (Diani, 2008).

Urban narratives have the potential to accommodate the theme of activism within their narrative structures. There exists negligible distinction amongst fictional and non-fictional narratives in this regard. George Villanueva in his text *Promoting Urban Social Justice* states that communication is a key to reimagining stigmatized urban places through nuanced narratives that reflect everyday people fighting for both daily survival and collective community change (Villanueva, 2022). Life narratives of individuals who have invested themselves in activist movements to devise a change in the existing structures within the urban spaces can be critically analysed taking the necessary support from scholarly works. In literary narratives the resistance is registered by women's identities in different forms using both similar and dissimilar symbolic elements (Pourya Asl, 2022; Singh, 2022). American Chicana Feminist and community organiser Sutherland Martínez's writing career is characterised by the transnational identification and resistance to US political and cultural hegemony which she expresses through her works (Perez, 2018).

Social movements or activist movements are complex and highly heterogenous network structures (Diani, 2003). They are shaped by the connectivity established amongst its participants. They attempt to address a range of issues, from child labour's exploitation by global brands to deforestation, from human rights in developing countries to military interventions by powerful nations. They do so in a myriad of forms, from individual utterances of dissent and individual behaviour to mass collective events. (Diani & Porta, 2006). The internal organization and the way cohesion and authority are (self) structured within the group is a determining factor in appreciating the democratic value of these forms of active citizenship (Vanhoose & Savini, 2017). The various critical perspectives on the discourse of urban activism reveal that social movement groups or activist groups are built on specific principles of 'reflexivity of organization and action' and they honour a system of membership that is fluid in nature. They address the power hierarchies existing within the urban spaces and strive towards a collective identity. Discrimination and harassment are other contributing factors that have resulted in the growth of activism within urban spaces (Beriss, 2018, p. 20). Although the membership to the movement is by no means formal, it is socially constructed within the group through practices of peer control (Vanhoose & Savini, 2017). While activistic movements appear to be organized fluidly, or even volatile, from the outset, they feature highly structured networks, albeit in their own informal way (Vanhoose & Savini, 2017). For the empirical study of the internal organisation of activist groups, two dimensions can be identified namely the construction of a common identity and purpose as well as the maintenance of group integrity. The individuals who belong to an active movement are to be strongly linked through a common identity and purpose. A shared purpose or meaning for action is to be essentially established and the reliance of one individual on others is crucial. This happens alongside the power struggles exemplary of the urban spaces. Maintaining the group integrity is equally important for the long-term sustenance of an activist community, as the characteristic informality has the potential to break down the internal structure of the movement (Vanhoose & Savini, 2017). It has been understood that a certain uncertainty exists in the politics of urban spaces and within these spaces, organising and resistance emerge largely in response to a shifting range of intensifying pressures that are increasingly felt at the level of everyday life (Bunce et al., 2020). There exists an awareness that activists and organisations must work together across boundaries and spaces to inform and galvanise intersectional forms of equity and justice (Bunce et al., 2020).

THEORY AND METHOD

Activism occurring at the grassroot level as well as at the highest echelons of power and politics relate themselves to urban spaces. Grassroot activism makes itself visible as an entity involving the ordinary people in a society or an organisation. The urban spaces evolve themselves into spaces of participation where people from different social structures confirm to a single identity under the umbrella of activism. How the urban spaces respond to activism and social movements can be studied and critically analysed. Urban spaces are traversed by people from different socioeconomic backgrounds. They constantly attempt to identify themselves and negotiate with each other. It is inevitable that these negotiations prompt them to reach a common point of agreement through social movements that arise and develop in the urban spaces. Urban spaces may geographically take the form of big cities, small cities, large and small towns. Kiran Bedi's autobiographical work is set in the backdrop of the capital city of India, New Delhi whereas Nalini Jameela's work is set in the urban spaces within the southern state of Kerala, in India. Dr. Bedi's narrative has been created based on the seeds of the ideology of activism that she nurtures through the convictions that she had received through her upbringing and education. Her personality abounds in exemplary leadership qualities. She has always led from the front and has faced all obstacles head on. Simultaneously as a responsible leader she has believed in and been supportive of her colleagues in their judicious decision making and corresponding actions. Throughout her career Bedi has carried a message of rehabilitative and correctional approach for the community (Bedi, 2012). Bedi's activism can be recognised as activism being integrated into and performed, in her role as an administrator. In the autobiographical work that has been selected for study Bedi presents the specific facts and figures in a very methodical manner. Her narrative has the attributes of an autobiographical work as well as that of a scholarly article. There are instances where critical perspectives and scholarly insights are well embedded within her narrative. When she was appointed as the DCP North District, she came to the realisation that the sale and consumption of drugs was the focus of criminal activities happening in the city. She narrates that as she became determined to check drug-related criminality, she got socially involved with the problem (Bedi, 2012). It was quite apparent to her that drugs and crime went together, and she became intent on pursuing the subject of cause and effect even academically (Bedi, 2012). Dr. Bedi delves into books on the subject and her findings revealed that most drug abuse cases led to crime in the form of domestic violence including verbal abuse, mental torture as well as physical violence. She writes that the violence was directed towards the female family members of the male addicts as they happen to be the soft targets (Bedi, 2012). In his Introduction to the text *Social Movements and Networks: Relational Approaches to Collective Action*, Mario Diani mentions that social movements cannot be reduced to specific insurrections or revolts, but they resemble strings of connected events, scattered across time and space and that they cannot be identified with any specific organization. According to him they consist of groups and organizations, with various levels of formalization, linked in patterns of interaction which run from the centralized to the totally decentralized, from the cooperative to the explicitly hostile. He adds on those persons promoting and/or supporting their actions do so not as atomized individuals, possibly with similar values or social traits, but as actors linked to each other through complex webs of exchanges, either direct or mediated. He finally states that social movements are in other words, complex and highly heterogeneous network structures (Diani, 2003).

It is imperative that at this juncture there exists the need to analyse Dr. Kiran Bedi's role as an advocate of women empowerment. She agrees that women's empowerment is one subject that has been endlessly discussed and debated in numerous fora and in many books and other publications. She emphasises on the constant vigil that a woman needs to maintain the movement towards being empowered. Dr. Bedi argues that educated and professional women who are normally considered as empowered can be willingly or unwillingly disempowered by their own actions, without realising the short- or long-term impact (Bedi, 2012). She exhorts women not to lower their guard at any point of time in becoming disempowered. Despite being an officer of the Indian Police Service, she was confronted by groups of people who constantly wanted to humiliate her in the service and thereby the gender (Bedi, 2012). In her work she candidly narrates her own experiences to depict how she ensured and sustained her own empowerment essentially by refusing to get disempowered and by overcoming all the frictional forces that she had to encounter (Bedi, 2012). Undoubtedly, in many situations, a woman is disempowered by circumstances beyond her control, but in many others, she becomes disempowered by her own actions, without herself realising their short or long-term impact. Such disempowerment is even more surprising in the case of 'educated and professional' women, whom we normally consider 'empowered' (Bedi, 2012, p. 241).

RESULTS AND FINDINGS

The works taken for an analysis in this chapter are texts which are marked by the powerful and intrepid characteristic traits of its authors. The authors share the same nationality, yet they belong to different social structures and occupy distinct positions in the social spectrum. The common thread that links them together is the doctrine of "activism" that develops through the politics of the spatial structures existing within the urban spaces. Dr. Kiran Bedi's autobiographical work has been written largely in the third person. This can be contributed to the reason that the author would like to look at her own self and her life achievements from the perspective of a third person. This allows for greater flexibility in the writing and an expansiveness in presenting the events in one's life. The work is composed of thirty-eight chapters of which the last three chapters are written in the first person as is commonly observed in autobiographical works. Apart from this in chapter 25 which is titled '*We Are Orphaned': Tihar after Kiran*' the author switches over to the first person in her narrative. The text is a special and exclusive edition, for the new generation, of Kiran Bedi's autobiography *I Dare!* (1995) and the text stays much close to it except for the inclusion of a few additional chapters.

The second autobiographical work chosen for study in this chapter is a text translated from Malayalam, the Dravidian language spoken in the state of Kerala in India. The language has the status of the official language in the state. The work was translated into English by the Indian academician Dr. J. Devika who is also a historian, a feminist, and a social critic. The French translation of the text was done by Sophie Bastide-Foltz. The work was subjected to condemnation by the conservative segment of the society and by the feminists as they alleged that it glorified sex work. In her foreword to the text, J. Devika mentions that Jameela's autobiography reveals the exclusions of the dominant, home-centred, self-controlled feminine ideal and challenges the prototype of the prostitute (Jameela, 2005). This gets reflected in the very title of her work as she attempts to claim the dignity of her profession. Nalini Jameela's autobiographical work is marked by the presence of both a 'Foreword' by the translator J. Devika and an 'Afterword' which is an interview of Jameela by the translator. In the interview that comprises the Afterword, Jameela admits that the last chapter of her work is quite weak as she was in a hurry to publish the work since she had wanted to remedy the damage caused by the first inadequate draft that was published. She confesses that she was extremely concerned about reclaiming her previously published autobiography that she could not provide the required focus (Jameela, 2005). Although unapologetic, Jameela states that if she had another chance, her last chapter would be an appeal to the community of sex-workers, encouraging them to be less reticent, to enter public life, and to be of service to the public. She also states that she would have taken the chance to speak to young girls belonging to other communities who happen to be the victims of sex rackets (Jameela, 2005). The narrative follows a story-telling mode. Nalini Jameela's narrative is built upon her life experiences and significantly the displacement that she undergoes traversing through the urban spaces.

Empowerment necessarily precedes activism, and it enables the individual to bring people together towards a common goal and a collective action. An empowered woman successfully dons the role of an activist. Bedi makes her perspectives on the concept of an empowered woman very clear in her writing. She defines an empowered woman as the woman who can make her own decisions and face their consequences. An empowered woman shows a sense of responsibility as well as a sense of maturity. She will be able to contribute towards addressing the politics of urban spaces transforming them into spaces of empowerment. Bedi believes that empowerment is not solely economic empowerment. Empowerment comprises of mental maturity, self-dignity, and the ability not to look down on oneself. (Bedi, 2012). In the year 2008 Dr. Bedi had published a text titled *Empowering Women.... As I See....* (2008). The book envisions her definition of women empowerment where she states that being a woman is both an asset and a liability. She also mentions that a woman is a huge asset when she is self-dependent and possesses the awareness and choice of being interdependent. Bedi further writes that a woman is totally a liability for herself when she is psychologically dependent on others (Bedi, 2008). According to Dr. Narendra Prasad author of the text *Women and Development* (2007), the term empowerment in its simplest form means the manifestation of redistribution of power that challenges patriarchal ideology and the male dominance, and it is found to be a process and the result of the process. He adds on that the major strategies of women empowerment include – social empowerment, economic empowerment, and gender justice (Prasad, 2007).

Dr. Kiran Bedi who has been acknowledged as a field person was convinced that the menace of drug abuse could be controlled only by establishing centres for the therapeutic treatment of drug abusers. She put forth the concept of *Navjyoti* in this regard. As a visionary leader she believed in community participation in her activism. She appealed to the community for support in establishing these centres and the community responded enthusiastically by contributing towards the cause in form of beds, blankets, rugs, televisions, fans, doctors, yoga teachers, medicines, and food (Bedi, 2012). A call for activism prompts the city space to evolve itself into an arena of participation which further leads to an inflow of positive responses from individuals. The formation of *Navjyoti* led to the commissioner of police becoming its first president and Dr. Bedi the founder general secretary. Due to the popularity of the *Navjyoti* centre, five more such centres were developed within a year. Of the nineteen police stations under her charge, six were running drug abuse treatment centres (Bedi, 2012). The *Navjyoti* programme had made an impression internationally for its pioneering work in drug abuse treatment. The programme was honoured by several national and international awards, which encouraged in the burgeoning of drug victims' treatment centres all over India. Kiran Bedi takes her activism to a superior level as she pursues her doctoral studies on drug abuse and its impact on criminality. In September 1993 she was awarded the doctorate for her thesis on "Drug Abuse and Domestic Violence" from the Indian Institute of Technology (IIT), Delhi (Department of Social Sciences) (Bedi, 2012, p. 85).

During her variant postings Kiran Bedi firmly believed in resorting to her time-tested method of seeking community participation for preventive policing. A good leader ensures a harmonious participation of the society in the proposed corrective and preventive measures and mobilise them towards a common goal. According to her for an officer in the Indian Police Service, a prison assignment is regarded as a 'dump' posting (Bedi, 2012, p. 113). In her work, Bedi narrates that in the early 1990s the Tihar jail was completely shrouded in secrecy. She writes that the entire area was closed to the outside community for fear of being exposed on how the inmates were being treated. She further mentions that the prisoners were treated like street animals, and they were uncared for, disorderly and possessed a mob mentality (Bedi, 2012). As the Inspector General of Prisons Kiran Bedi faced challenges of great proportions. When looking at the opponents of social movements, we can start observing that they can be either institutional or noninstitutional actors. (Diani & Porta, 2006). She mentions about an inhibiting factor that most of the staff members at Tihar were not used to serving under a woman officer and therefore felt that they could not communicate with her as they would with a man (Bedi, 2012). In *The Oxford Handbook of Social Movements*, Klaus Eder mentions that social movements can be regarded as devices that irritate the social systems (Eder, 2015, p. 41). Large efforts are to be devoted to gain a positive response from the surrounding community. The staff members were unable to understand the prisoners and they could not offer solutions for the prisoners' problems, and inadvertently became a part of the problem. She realised that it is only a team that can work collectively, and collective effort was the need of the hour (Bedi, 2012). The basic thrust of Kiran's prison reforms could be summed up as delegating powers to hitherto neglected prison officers and making them accountable for their actions (Bedi, 2012). The story of Tihar and Kiran Bedi's reform movement at Tihar is a classic illustration activism happening in the government machinery and an example of what can be achieved by a sensitive, humane, and benevolent leadership (Bedi, 2012). She believed in participatory management along with her staff and the community. Bedi sought the support from the media to project the efforts of participative community support. Narratives on activism can stimulate scholars to examine the mechanisms in which some resistances concentrate in certain places, harness energies and countervailing powers, and grow into large mobilizations that have the potential to cross over and sometimes alter the administrative practices and rationalities of modern nation states. (Nichols & Uitermark, 2017).

Bedi started off her work at the Tihar jail with the staff of the jail. The staff were trained, and regular checks were made to control the drug smuggling into the prison. The staff members who required treatment were sent to the *Navjyoti* clinics for treatment. Prisoners were taken for treatment to the treatment centres situated within each jail. A proposal was sent to the Ministry of Health, Government of India for establishing treatment centres like *Navjyoti* within the prison premises. The funds allocated from the government could be utilised for employing a team of homeopaths, vocational trainers, yoga instructors, social workers, and psychiatrists for the benefit of the prisoners. Bedi was driven by her strong conviction that a professional and humane police service is one of the strongest safeguards of democracy. Her activism in the field of administration took a defined form and shape as she implemented pathbreaking reforms in the Tihar jail. For her the prison was to be the last place for crime prevention and correction and the prison itself was not a place for continuing punishment. Being an activist in the administrative body of a democracy was most arduous for Bedi as she had dared to persistently challenge the old order against all odds, despite facing envy and sabotage at virtually every step of her career led activism (Bedi, 2012). Resistances may be everywhere that power is enacted, but all places do not provide the support needed to grow resistances into tangled and disruptive political mobilizations. We also know that certain environments furnish more resources than others. Resistances may arise in places where specific government powers are enacted but not all places provide sufficient conditions to grow small seeds into big mobilizations (Nichols & Uitermark, 2017).

The activities related to the Tihar jail captured the attention of not only the national media but the foreign media as well since it possessed a human rights angle. They started to show keenness in special culture-based reform programmes that were unique to Tihar and the Indian ethos, such as the Vispassana meditation, spiritual discourses, yoga, community support to total literacy, the petition box system, drug abuse treatment, keeping of small children with their mothers and how the prison could accept being a no-smoking zone (Bedi, 2012). The Tihar jail was aptly renamed as Tihar Ashram by Dr. Bedi indicating that it was a place of reform. Meanwhile she had secured the prestigious Jawaharlal Nehru Fellowship during her tenure as the IG (Prisons) at the Tihar jail. Activism has always been lauded as a collective action with individuals marked by good leadership skills at the helm. Dr. Bedi's efforts in activism at the Tihar jail in New Delhi, India in the form of prison reforms captured the attention of the governments of almost all countries. Further on regular international conferences took place and are continuing to take place as well as several committees were formed in various nations to look into the state of affairs in prison management in their respective nations (Bedi, 2012). Dr. Bedi firmly believed that in whatever condition, and in whatever place we may discover the human being his or her rights must be recognised and appreciated. She adds on that the working material was human and any system not permeated by humaneness would not, and could not be expected to work (Bedi, 2012). Despite the success of the reform movements implemented by Dr. Bedi as the IG(Prisons), her efforts were observed as a breach of civil service officers' code of conduct by the then government of Delhi and an enquiry was asked to be made into her mode of functioning as the head of Tihar for her acts of omission and commission (Bedi, 2012). Social movement actors are engaged in political and/or cultural conflicts meant to promote or oppose social change. By conflict it is meant that there exists an oppositional relationship between actors who seek control of the same stake – be it political, economic, or cultural power – and the process of making negative claims on each other (Diani & Porta, 2006).

During her stint at the Narcotics Control Bureau, she was exposed to the drug scenario at both the national and international levels. She was working at the national level and attending a lot of seminars and talks on the problem. She was also interacting with international agencies like the Interpol and various countries' drug liaison officers and the picture of the narcotics trade and drug abuse became clearer in her mind. The *Navjyoti* programme was working wonders and had made an impression internationally for its pioneering work in drug abuse treatment. This programme was honoured by several national and international awards which encouraged the mushrooming of drug victims' treatment centres all over India. The feedback from many of these centres helped in keeping her attention focused on the treatment programme (Bedi, 2012). Inside the prison walls, however, the atmosphere belied all such fears. Strains of religious hymns and songs greeted you as you entered the prisoner's barracks. All around were groups of persons sitting and studying in regular classes. Every barrack had its own library where you could see the inmates engrossed in reading newspapers, magazines, and books. Everyone was occupied with something or the other, be it studying, or exercising, or practising yoga, or repairing television sets, or knitting, or sewing or performing a variety of other activities. The inmates did not appear tensed or worked up but like any other member of society, were busy with their daily work-a-day life (Bedi, 2012).

To make Tihar a correctional institution, most of the reforms that were to take place, successively and successfully eliminated the criminalizing traits in its inmates. Their need for and access to sensory stimulation was to be almost eliminated. Most of them were soon occupied in acquiring self-monitoring skills. Progressively they began developing decision-making abilities and were thus to attain a position to exercise accountable responsibility. Procurement of basic life skills was to give most of them some hope for future. And all this was to help them greatly in achieving better control over their emotions (Bedi, 2012).

But the most important step Kiran took, which perhaps was all she could do within the ambit of her powers, was to free the woman constables from their 'imprisonment'. These constables were lodged at the centre (where they were undergoing training) and were permitted to go home only on weekends- that too as a special favour. Kiran allowed them to go back to their children (i.e., those women who had left behind their children without a reliable support system) after the training at the police station for the day was completed. Without their asking, Kiran gave them what they needed the most to ensure that they put in their best-efforts during training and learn as much as they could. For Kiran, each one of them is an investment for the future, near and far (Bedi, 2012).

Crime prevention was always top priority for Dr. Kiran Bedi wherever she was posted. Her track record is replete with measures taken to prevent potentially negative and harmful situations from developing. Her approach has all along been to anticipate events and guide their course towards a positive goal and her energies have been channelised towards proactive prevention rather than after-the-event reaction. Dr. Bedi's first community project in crime prevention became visible during her posting in 1980 as deputy commissioner Delhi (west), where she used her powers, in a benign way, to persuade an erstwhile criminal tribe of bootleggers in Delhi to abandon their ways of selling illicit liquor and take up acceptable, non-criminal ways of making a living. She was successful in her mission (Bedi, 2012).

Nalini Jameela's autobiography is filled with descriptions on displacement through urban spaces from the very beginning of the narrative. The author employs a linear narrative style initially but later shifts into a non-linear narration whereby moving between the early past and the near past. The text begins as a memoir as the author tries to recollect the earliest memories of herself along with those of her paternal grandmother, her brother, and her parents. Having to discontinue her education and taking up various odd jobs as a teenager, Nalini Jameela convinces herself that life is a great struggle and to live one must fight incessantly. Jameela started sex work in a struggle to fight poverty and provide for her young children who were supported by her mother-in-law after her husband had passed away (Jameela, 2005). She narrates that like any other job, the job of a sex-worker too had been tiring at times and after the responsibility of her children had ended, she began to think of other options including that of leaving the trade. It is in chapter four that the author mentions about contacting *Jwalamukhi*, an organisation that worked for rights of sex workers. She further mentions that the office was located at Ancheri, five kilometres from the city of Thrissur and the members of the organisation were called as '*Jwalamukhikal*' (Jameela, 2005). After hesitantly joining the organisation, Jameela mentions that there was a class about AIDS being conducted by a college professor. Experiences were shared by sex workers and there were free discussions about the way the police interfered in sex work and about different types of clients (Jameela, 2005). It is with a tone of strong conviction that the author narrates that by the time she had attended the second meeting at *Jwalamukhi*, she had become a part of the organisation and an activist. She felt that it was a platform where problems were shared but suitable solutions to the problems were not put forth by any member. Jameela pointed out to the group the fact that if the sex-workers were offenders, then the persons or the clients who had participated in the act of sex were offenders too. But they hardly ever got caught by the police. She proposed that if a sex-worker got arrested the organisation should come to the aid and bail them out (Jameela, 2005). It was discussed that public meetings should be conducted to gather the attention towards the afore mentioned concerns and Jameela volunteered to make the speech (Jameela, 2005).

A person with a strong sense of self-respect, Nalini Jameela was not ready to accept a secondary status in her life and has regarded herself as the spokesperson of the sex workers. Her commitment to the cause of the sex workers reflects in her unbiased perspectives as expressed in her autobiographical work. In her narrative Jameela judiciously acknowledges the selfless efforts of other sex-workers who were activists associated with other social movements. In urban areas social and political boundaries are less rigid and more fluid than on reservations since the membership is not tied exclusively to a charter of blood-quantum or genealogical criteria, nor is there a formal over-arching political structure, equivalent to a tribal council that governs the entire urban community (Lobo, 2009). She mentions about Ammu who had taken part in Medha Patkar's agitation against the Sardar Sarovar Dam. Ammu, along with another sex-worker named Usha were part of the twenty-five-member group that had gone to the national capital New Delhi to take part in the protest march (Jameela, 2005). She utilises her autobiographical narrative as a tool to give credit to other sex-workers who had involved themselves in some form of activism. Ammu had also spent time amongst the local tribal people in Narmada and was arrested for her protest against the Chief Minister of Maharashtra (Jameela, 2005). There has been considerable fluctuation in the intensity of collective action over the years as there has been in its degree of radicalism, its specific forms, and its capacity to influence the political process (Diani & Porta, 2006).

Dr. Kiran Bedi's narrative primarily focuses on the urban space of the city of New Delhi, where the power structures persistently experience frictional forces as they operate through the spaces. As observed in her work, her form of activism develops as she attempts to control the urban criminality by resisting and controlling the malice of drug abuse. Further on in her capacity as the Inspector General in charge of prisons, she introduces reforms in the Tihar jail, Delhi and transforms it into an estimable correctional facility. She traverses through innumerable interactions and negotiations during her course of action in these urban spaces. Her vivid descriptions and her lucid style of writing provide an expressive image of her earnest efforts occurring within the urban space of Delhi. According to Anna Domaradzka, urban activism has been increasingly considered an important part of urban governance processes as local activists participate in urban politics and influence decision-making through legal tools and participatory practices (Domaradzka, 2018).

Nalini Jameela's text is marked by her transparent and candid narrative style. She is adept in narrating her own observations of the myriad urban spaces that she explores in her profession as a sex-worker in the city of Thrissur in Kerala. While urban development brings huge social, economic, and environmental transformations, nowhere is the rise of negative social processes clearer than in urban areas, where enclaves for the rich often coexist alongside ghettos of the disempowered poor (Domaradzka, 2018).

There are many factors involved in deciding the degree of freedom one has with a client. The area from which one is operating is one of the most important. I have operated from almost all areas. Those who stand near the Thrissur KSRTC bus stand are considered the lowest class. The district hospital is very close to this, but those who hang around there get VIP treatment. If, by any chance, you happen to meet a client near the KSRTC stand and start laying out your conditions to him, immediately the comment will follow that you're playing high-hat despite being low class. The same conditions can be easily put forward by a woman standing by the District Hospital. I have had both experiences early in my career, so I don't negotiate with clients in either of these places. I talk to them away from these places, and then I am able to talk frankly (Jameela, 2005, pp. 148-149).

Jameela narrates that if a sex worker stands near a certain bus station, then she is sure to be taken as low class and it doesn't matter what she looked like. She continues that the standard of a sex worker depends on the area you hang around in and even if it's a regular client, these prejudices are sure to surface in their dealings if you are picked up at the wrong place (Jameela, 2005). According to Henri Lefebvre, the concept of city no longer corresponds to a social object and an image or representation of the city can perpetuate itself, survive its conditions, inspire an ideology and urbanist projects (Lefebvre, 2003). Jameela observes that in many of Kerala's cities, it is the female construction workers who usually move into sex work as they are sexually exploited by their supervisors. and that most of them do so realising that they do not have to do both construction work which brings in poor wages and sex work (Jameela, 2005). It is the sexual exploitation that she attempts to resist through her activism in *Jwalamukhi*. She believes that sex work and sexual exploitation are two different entities, and it is the sex workers that they bring under the umbrella of their organisation. Inspired by Goffman's (1974) 'frame analysis' Diani asserts that individuals forge their own 'schemata of interpretation' which allow them to make sense of the world surrounding them. Frames render events meaningful and interpretations possible functioning as guiding philosophies for action. For individuals to take part in social movements their interpretive frameworks must coincide with those possessed by the movements they join; frame alignment processes conjoin participants' expectations and organization objectives (Diani, 2008).

If a woman is found on the streets, the organisation first conducts a counselling session to find out whether she chose the sex trade or came into it by accident. They help the women who want to move out. If the sex worker is facing any domestic or professional issues Jwalamukhi reaches out to help them. Jameela poses the question of the meaning of the term rehabilitation to the readers. She states that 'sex workers' doesn't refer to a group that stays the same all the time and they keep changing. While some women move out of the profession, others move in (Jameela, 2005). Social movements are distinct social processes, consisting of the mechanisms through which agents or activists or actors of the movement are engaged in a collective action. The activists are involved in conflictual relations with clearly identified opponents. They are linked by informal networks, and they share a distinct collective identity (Diani & Porta, 2006). As an activist and a leader of the organisation Jwalamukhi, Nalini Jameela puts forth the demand in public that sex work be decriminalised. She presents her own version of decriminalising that if two people want to have sex by mutual consent and if this is in no way a nuisance to others, then it should not be questioned (Jameela, 2005).

Nalini Jameela always demonstrated the strength of a leader while giving her voice to deliver justice to the sex workers. When a senior police officer claimed during a television talk show that the sex workers were never harassed by the police, Jameela cited an incident in which twenty-six sex workers were arrested and put behind bars which was apparently provoked by the fact that a sex worker had stood next to a magistrate's wife at the bus station (Jameela, 2005). In activism, individuals are strongly linked through a common identity and purpose. When a shared purpose or meaning for action is established, the strong ties made possible by bonding social capital maintain and reinforce this common goal. For activist communities, the reliance of one individual on the others is crucial as the movement transforms into full-fledged social political movements (Vanhoose & Savini, 2017). Urban spaces are persistently denied to the marginalised as they are being dislodged from these spaces. The individuals living in the fringes of the society make a continuous struggle getting accepted in urban spaces. The most accurate description of urban movements is inclusive of activities that range from advocacy and service provision to political representation, as well as down-to-earth problem solving at the neighbourhood level (Domaradzka, 2018). A collective identity and solidarity are the necessary features of an activist movement. There exists a continuous process of realignment and negotiation amongst the participants of the social movement or the activist movement (Diani, 2008, p. 268). Nalini Jameela's life experiences were good eye-openers about the prejudices that even highly motivated political activists carry around. Jameela narrates about the slow, yet steady progress attained by the Jwalamukhi over the years in upholding the interests of the sex workers in the society. Different forms of urban mobilization, united under the right to the city umbrella, are examples of how solidarity can be generated through skilful framing and introducing new norms (Domaradzka, 2018). Jameela writes that although the media was generally hostile to Jwalamukhi in its early days, gradually their experiences caught the attention of the media. Newspapers and magazines commenced reporting the activities of Jwalamukhi and thereby acknowledged their efforts (Jameela, 2005, p. 134). To be considered a social movement, an interacting collective requires a shared set of beliefs and sense of belongingness (Diani, 2008). This forms the driving force in their endeavours towards a challenge. It could also be associated with a common fate that the members are willing to share. This is essential in being regarded as a part of the movement.

Yet another milestone that Nalini Jameela achieved in her activism was turning into a film maker. This helped her in echoing the much-subdued voices of the sex workers. Her very first documentary was titled *Jwalamukhikal* and the second one was *Nishabdarakkapettavarilekku Orettinottam* which can be translated as *A Glimpse of the Silenced*. The theme of this work was the police atrocities towards the sex workers. Besides capturing the experience of sex workers, the documentary film had Jameela's personal interviews with an advocate, a doctor, a police officer and an autorickshaw driver. (Jameela, 2005). Her documentaries were screened in Thiruvananthapuram, the capital city of Kerala by the Russian Cultural Society and at the international festival of films on sexual minorities in Mumbai. She was invited as a guest on the Malayalam TV channel, Asianet's News Hour when it was shown in Thiruvananthapuram. In Mumbai she was treated as a VIP being the director of a documentary. (Jameela, 2005). Apart from being a filmmaker Jameela along with her team members organised camera workshops for the sex-workers. It is the shared collective identity that moulds the foundation upon which activism is built upon. According to Mario Diani, activist movements or social movements consists of a process whereby several different actors be they individuals, informal groups, and or organisations, come to elaborate through either joint action and or communication, a shared definition of themselves as being part of the same side in a social conflict. Diani mentions that by doing so they provide meaning to otherwise unconnected protest events or symbolic antagonistic practices and, make explicit the emergence of specific conflicts and issues. This dynamic is reflected in the definition of social movements as consisting in networks of informal interaction between a plurality of individuals, groups, and /or organisations, engaged in a political and/or cultural conflict based on a shared collective identity (Diani, 2008). Activist movements pertaining to urban spaces inspired by ideas of self-organized, self-led and engaged urbanism has become increasingly salient in cities across the globe. As expressions of broad socio-political movements within cities, such practices reveal a peculiar type of urban activism. Often oriented towards the modification of urban space at the micro-local scale and led by highly motivating individuals with exceptional leadership skills, the activities often reflect the urgency of groups of individuals concerned with specific, spatial problems in the living environment. Over time, these practices have the capacity to extend to broader city-regional scales.

CONCLUSION

The urban spaces persistently engage themselves in encounters and negotiations. These structural developments within the urban spaces often lead the members to forming a collective identity and a resultant activistic movement or a social movement. The presence of shared beliefs and solidarities allows both actors and observers to assign a common meaning to specific collective events which otherwise could not be identified as a part of a common process. Social movements or activist movements condition and help constitute new orientations on existing issues and the rise of new public issues (Diani, 2008). The movements are led by individuals with immense self-respect, an innate sense of justice and exemplary leadership qualities. These individuals become the voice of the movement they are associated with, and they believe in the inclusivity of individuals and in spaces where the marginalised can be easily accommodated. They uphold their identities to motivate the participants of the movement and lead the collective movements towards achieving a goal. Activists transform themselves into change agents of the society and administrative system.

They are motivated by a sense of community and democracy within the spaces that they navigate through.

Activism as expressed in women's autobiographical narratives provides a myriad of insights on activistic movements and social movements occurring within the premises of bureaucracy, power, society, and profession. The autobiographical narratives of the individuals involved in activism in a participative or a leadership role, reveal the different layers in the power structure that exists within the spaces in which they operate. Activism can resultantly evolve into an integral part of an urban narrative, the urban setting being one of multiple proportions and variant traits. They serve as eye-witness stories that contribute material for studying the emergence of modern forms of self-representation. The members of an activistic movement engage in a mirroring of themselves through the collective action that develops within the politics of the urban spaces, and they may choose to build a narrative based on their participation in the movement. Urban spaces transform themselves into an arena of participation that flourish on positive responses from individuals. The numerous scholarly perspectives on the discourse of urban activism reveal that social movement groups and activist groups are constructed upon entities such as the reflexivity of organisation and action. They also honour a system of membership that is fluid in nature. These groups address the power hierarchies existing within the urban spaces and strive towards a collective identity. Although the membership to the groups is by no means formal, it is socially developed and constructed within the group through practices of peer control. While activistic movements appear to be organized fluidly, or even volatile, from the outset, they feature highly structured networks, in an informal way.

Activism can occur in an urban space regardless of its spatial proportions. Its socio-political impact need not necessarily take shape from the contemplations on the persona of the activist. Different types of grassroot activism and social movements can be understood as a manifestation of the right to the city struggle. The individual leading an activistic movement ensures a harmonious participation of the society in the proposed corrective as well as preventive measures and mobilise them towards a common goal. The city spaces become avenues of transformation where people come together to propose a common objective and conjointly act to accomplish their goals.

REFERENCES

Andretta, M., Piazza, G., & Subirats, A. (2015). Urban dynamics and social movement. In D. D. Porta & M. Diani (Eds.), *The Oxford handbook of social movements* (pp. 200–215). Oxford University Press.

Bedi, K. (1995). *I dare!* Hay House (India) Publishers Pvt. Ltd.

Bedi, K. (2008). *Empowering women...As I see....* Sterling Paperbacks.

Bedi, K. (2012). *Dare to do: For the new generation.* Hay House (India) Publishers Pvt. Ltd.

Beriss, D. (2018). *Black skins, French voices: Caribbean ethnicity and activism in urban France.* Routledge. doi:10.4324/9780429502040

Blumer, H. (2008). Social movements. In V. Ruggiero & N. Montagna (Eds.), *Social movements: A reader* (pp. 64–72). Routledge.

Bunce, S., Livingstone, N., March, L., Moore, S., & Walks, A. (2020). Conclusion. In S. Bunce, N. Livingstone, L. March, S. Moore & A. Walks (Eds.), Critical dialogues of urban governance, development, and activism: London and Toronto (pp. 297-305). UCL Press.

Carey, A. C., Block, P., & Scotch, R. K. (2020). *Allies and obstacles: Disability activism and parents of children with disabilities.* Temple University Press.

Chatterjee, P. (2008). Women and the nation: The trouble with their voices. In M. E. John (Ed.), *Women's studies in India: A reader* (pp. 309–316). Penguin Books.

Diani, M. (2003). Introduction. In M. Diani & D. McAdam (Eds.), *Social movements and networks: Relational approaches to collective action* (pp. 1–18). Oxford University Press. doi:10.1093/0199251789.003.0001

Diani, M. (2008). The concept of social movement. In V. Ruggiero & N. Montagna (Eds.), *Social movements: A reader* (pp. 266–271). Routledge.

Diani, M., & Porta, D. D. (2006). *Social movements: An introduction.* Blackwell Publishing.

Domaradzka, A. (2018). Urban social movements and right to the city: An introduction to the special issue on urban mobilization. *Voluntas, 29*(4), 607–620. Advance online publication. doi:10.100711266-018-0030-y

Eder, K. (2015). Social movements in social theory. In D. D. Porta & M. Diani (Eds.), *The Oxford handbook of social movements* (pp. 31–49). Oxford University Press.

Jameela, N. (2005). *The Autobiography of a Sex Worker.* Westland Ltd.

Lai, J. S. (2022). *Asian American connective action in the age of social media: Civic engagement, contested issues, and emerging identities.* Temple University Press.

Lalitha, K. (2008). Women in revolt: A historical analysis of the progressive organisation of women in Andhra Pradesh. In M. E. John (Ed.), *Women's studies in India: A reader* (pp. 32–41). Penguin Books.

Lefebvre, H. (2003). *The urban revolution (R. Bononno, Tran.)*. University of Minnesota Press. (Original work published 1970)

Leza, C. (2019). *Divided peoples: Policy, activism, and indigenous activities on the U.S.-Mexico border*. The University of Arizona Press. doi:10.2307/j.ctvrf89pr

Lobo, S. (2009). Urban clan mothers: Key households in cities. In S. A. Krouse & H. A. Howard (Eds.), *Keeping the campfires going* (pp. 1–21). University of Nebraska Press. doi:10.2307/j.ctt1dgn4sz.5

Nichols, W. J., & Uitermark, J. (2017). Cities and social movements: Immigrant rights and activism in the United States, France and the Netherlands, 1970-2015. John Wiley & Sons, Ltd.

Perez, A. (2018). "Tu Reata Es Pi Espada": Elizabeth Sutherland's Chicana formation. In D. Espinoza, M. E. Cotera, & M. Blackwell (Eds.), *Chicana Movidas: New narratives of activism and feminism in the movement era* (pp. 245–260). University of Texas Press. doi:10.7560/315583-015

Porta, D. D., & Diani, M. (2015). Introduction: The field of social movement studies. In D. D. Porta & M. Diani (Eds.), *The Oxford handbook of social movements* (pp. 1–30). Oxford University Press. doi:10.1093/oxfordhb/9780199678402.013.61

Pourya Asl, M. (Ed.). (2022). *Gender, place, and identity of South Asian women*. IGI Global. doi:10.4018/978-1-6684-3626-4

Prasad, N. (2007). *Women and development*. A P H Publishing Corporation.

Singh, G. (2022). Afghan women authors' discourses of resistance: Contesting interplay between gender, place, and identity. In M. Pourya Asl (Ed.), *Gender, place, and identity of South Asian women* (pp. 152–177). IGI Global. doi:10.4018/978-1-6684-3626-4.ch008

Vanhoose, K., & Savini, F. (2017). *The social capital of urban activism: Practices in London and Amsterdam city*. http://rsa.tandfonline.com

Villanueva, G. (2022). *Promoting urban social justice through engaged communication scholarship: Reimagining place*. Routledge.

Ward, B. M. (2022). *Living Detroit: Environmental Activism in an age of urban crisis*. Routledge.

Yip, N. M., Martinez López, M. A., & Sun, X. (2019). Introductory remarks and overview. In N. M. Yip, M. A. Martinez López, & X. Sun (Eds.), *Contested cities and urban activism* (pp. 3–24). Palgrave Macmillan. doi:10.1007/978-981-13-1730-9_1

Yousufzai, M. (2019). *We are displaced: My journey and stories from refugee girls around the world.* Little, Brown, and Company.

Chapter 8
Inside and Outside the Hijab:
An Urban Utopian Study of Samra Habib's *We Have Always Been Here: A Queer Muslim Memoir*

Sandhya Devi N. K.
Presidency University, India

Kirankumar Nittali
Presidency University, India

ABSTRACT

The plight of Pakistani women has been normalized under the hegemonic patriarchal rule. As public and urban spaces are gendered, women are normally confined to domestic and private spaces. This chapter explores Samra Habib's autobiographical narrative We Have Always Been Here: A Queer Muslim Memoir (2019) to examine the ways in which the spaces and spatialities in South Asian and Western urban spaces are portrayed. Drawing upon the theoretical perspectives of feminist and queer geography, the chapter argues that the Western urban spaces function as a space of utopia that overcomes the exclusionary practices of Pakistani society. Feminist geography attempts to include women as the primary subjects in the public space, and queer geographies delineate how queer individuals have been ostracized by Pakistani society in public and private spaces. Further, the study reveals that Western urban spaces liberate and provide a normative non-discriminatory environment that empowers women and queer individuals to celebrate femininity and sexuality as it did in the case of Samra.

DOI: 10.4018/978-1-6684-6650-6.ch008

INTRODUCTION

The plight of Pakistani women has been normalized under the hegemonic patriarchal rule (Karmaliani et al., 2012). Pakistani culture and Islamic Fundamentalism amplify their adversity by hindering and suppressing women from living a liberated life (Hadi, 2017; Nittali & N.K, 2021). Pakistani women's harrowing living conditions demonstrate the sufferings of these women as they are silenced, oppressed, and forced to be docile (Hadi, 2017). Their ability to live and survive depends on how far they are prepared to conform to the patriarchal culture that rules both rural and urban areas. Pakistani women are constrained from opinionated behaviour and individualization in urban spaces (Borovoy & Ghodsee 2012). Karmaliani et al. (2012) posit that Pakistani women face "poor health, domestic violence and lack of empowerment" (p. 820). The Aurat Foundation (2011) observes that women are often subjected to gender-based violence including acid attacks, honour killings and domestic violence. Since in most cases, the offenders are family members, the victimized women refrain from filing complaints to the concerned authorities. The traditionally male-dominated spheres of politics, religion and economics cripple women and reinforce the oppression by preventing them to be financially independent. As patriarchy and religion regulate the spatialities of gender, it constricts women from forming non-traditional and unorthodox values to hinder their emancipation thereby emphasizing the rigidity of the binary structural restraints that control women's spaces (Hadi, 2017). Further, queer sexualities and expressions are undermined since Pakistani and Islamic culture only morally approves of the dominant heterosexual marriages and childbearing. Being a Muslim and being queer is traumatic and highly challenging. Many times, such individuals are persecuted, rejected, and closely monitored by society and family. The relationship and the interconnectedness between space, society and the environment are some of the main concerns related to geography (Massey, 2013). When gender binary dichotomy is combined with geography it forms the feminist geographical analysis (Little et al., 1988). Feminist geography is defined as:

Socio-economic, political and environmental processes create, reproduce and transform not only the places in which we live, but also the social relations between men and women in these places and how, in turn, gender relations also have an impact on these processes and their manifestations. (Little et al., 1988, p. 1)

Therefore, feminist geography aims to explore how gender division is a social construct and that spatial environments are constructed based on gender, especially dictated by men. Spaces such as domestic labour and waged labour; home and work are divided spatially. This includes private and public spaces that are designed based on the performances of men and women. Historically, since geography is constructed and designated to men, consequentially women are excluded in the public space. But feminist geography attempts to locate and include women as primary subjects. Women do not fit into a man's daily routine as they play the role of chief breadwinners who go to work and occupy the public space. Women are restricted to function in the private space as homemakers and in the public space as waged labourers. These systematic and diurnal duties may lead to systematic physical or psychological oppression. Male-dominated places, such as knowledge spaces, political and cultural spaces, force women to perform the gendered roles, such as the prescribed roles of mother and wife, in order to discriminate and oppress them as inferior.

Furthermore, while eastern urban spaces force women to accept the disadvantaged and exclusionary position, western urban spaces can be liberating and inclusive of female participation rendering female independence, public and political participation, economic autonomy, and self-empowerment. In Samra Habib's *We Have Always Been Here: A Queer Muslim Memoir* (2019) it can be easily analysed that resultant gendered and patriarchal practices of urban Pakistan push women to the private space and excludes them in urban public space. This study uses the portrayal of the protagonist Samra Habib to bring about the concept of feminist geography and queer geography in urban spaces to examine the spatialities of gendered and sexual oppression. The aim is to discuss how moving to western urban spaces can be liberating and helps provide an inclusive, non-discriminatory environment to women and queer individuals. Additionally, this study also attends to analyse how women negotiate urban spaces in terms of patriarchal norms, forced marriages, gender bias and sexuality in a conscious effort to become more assertive against the structures of oppression in Pakistan.

LITERATURE REVIEW

Gillian Rose in her book *Feminism & Geography: The Limits of Geographical Knowledge* (1993) posits that geography and spatiality are "masculinist" (p. 11). Le Doeuff (2007) notes that masculinist spatial studies is the "work which, while claiming to be exhaustive, forgets about women's existence and concerns itself only with the position of men" (p. 42). This sheds light over how women's experiences are erased in every aspect of society. Little et al. (1988) observe how there are few females in academics. Conventionally, knowledge has been marked as a man's domain where man is the creator of knowledge, and his views and opinions are standardly accepted. In the United Kingdom, until 1913, except for a handful of women, the Royal Geographical Society did not elect women (Rose, 1993). Only 2.6 per cent of women had participated in writing in *Annals of the Association of American*

Geographers between the year 1921 and the year 1971 and only 6 per cent actively contributed to Economic Geography.

Spatial theory can be utilised to articulate and reveal female oppression, allowing for an examination of various facets of gender and female disempowerment. Appleby (2005) observes that Spatial theory is used to understand the spatial workings of English Language teaching and its connection with gender. Price-Chalita (1994) discusses how lesbians, women of colour, and poor women experienced displacement and underwent obstructive and negative spatial experiences because they associated space as a non-place. Also, when women discuss about spaces, they speak of helplessness, voicelessness and being "peripheral" or "outsiders" (p. 238). Mohanty (1984) illustrates the patriarchal hegemony that renders women, in "East" as secondary to their male counterparts whose positions are irrefutably centralized. In her 1987 semi-autobiographal book, *Borderlands/La Frontera*, Gloria Anzaldua writes from between the borderlines of Mexico and the United States to deliberate over the identities of Chicana, woman, lesbian, and language. Borderlands delves into the artificial boundaries that exist between Latinas/os and non-Latinas/os, men and women, heterosexuals and homosexuals, and other groups. Anzaldua shifts between Spanish and English using a technique known as code-switching. Regarding her spatial position and identity, she remarks how women like her are "nothing, no one" in the borderland conflict (Anzaldúa, 1987, p. 63). Correspondingly, De Lauretis (1990) relates how the term "lesbian" is understood to be "meaningless" implying that a woman's position with whatever identity she may carry is maintained at a subsidiary position.

Many notable academicians, female writers and feminist scholars such as the likes of Judith Butler and Janet Bowstead discuss terminologies such as displacement, de-centralized position, and homelessness for describing the despairing state of women devoid of their families, children, largely ostracized by society as they were struggling to become independent or while they come out as a lesbian. Additionally, spatiality and geography studies include pre-existing work on areas such as landscape and sexuality, humanist geographies, feminist geography, post-structural theories and new cultural theories (Pourya Asl, 2022). Davies et al. (2017) observe how gendered washrooms have been used to police transgender and alternative genders. Joelsson and Bruno (2022) examine gender spatiality by discussing how in Sweden young children have to negotiate and renegotiate between safe and unsafe places through concepts of space, time, gender and violence. Even in the traditional experiments of spatial abilities, men are observed to perform better and hold privileged positions. Likewise, spatial theory is used to map out the different levels of oppression, and poverty experienced by women in urban spaces. Furthermore, Kaur (2022) observes that spatial theory can bring out how young women's outdoor physical activity is based on safe and unsafe environments, cultural, mental, and societal factors that restrict their movements. Socio-spatial theories also seek to describe and elaborate on how hegemonic ideologies arise (Kaur, 2022).

Feminist geography, that strives to include insights on racial, social, intellectual, and sexual identity in the study of geography is a consequence of social exclusion. It is similar to queer geography which also births from the same (Knopp, 2007). While feminist geography is a result of feminist theories and female oppression, queer geography is a consequence of Queer theories and queer oppression. Although feminist geographies discuss the ostracization of women, queer geographies discuss how normative sexualities marginalize and demonize queer communities. Queer geographies attempt to find the connection between space and queer experiences. As queer individuals are subjected to marginalization, verbal, physical and psychological abuse, they feel socially alienated which compels them to move to considerably inclusive urban spaces. Moreover, queer geographies try to bring out the heterosexualized spaces that are demeaning and oppressive to queer individuals., Queer geographies discuss how queer individuals bargain spaces that are unwelcome to them. Since dominating settings are deemed heterosexual spaces, queer geographies seek out places that promote flexibility and different sexualities. In this manner, queer geographies recreate and reclaim spaces for the LGBTQ community.

Kazi, et al. (2006) posit that the oppressive gendered social conditions and relations in urban Pakistan result in depression among Pakistani women. Women are also prevented to gain personal freedom and educational opportunities in urban Pakistan (Ali et al., 2011). On walking practices, Warren (2016) astutely notes how urban Pakistan genders the walking space for women. Masood (2017) discusses how women are forced to renegotiate and challenge societal, patriarchal, and capitalistic restrictions especially on women's accessibility to the roads. Additionally, mobility rights including transportation and driving challenge the pre-constructed gender identities. Anwar et al. (2018) observes how masculine mobilities and spatialities limited, immobilised, and oppressed female spaces. Female domestic workers undergo rampant discrimination due to inconvenient domestic labour arrangements which compel women to dependent on a market-based wage system (Zulfiqar, 2019). Mustafa et al. (2019) link between the experience of violence faced on a day-to-day basis and global war terror to be gendered and politicized in the states of Islamabad and Karachi. Pakistani women are forced to be submissive and work according to the managers in garment factories, thereby gendering the workplaces in Karachi. Married women in Urban Pakistan undergo educational and economic marginalization, following the gender and private nature of spatial tasks (Chatha & Ahmad, 2020). Restrictions on education, economic dependence, and gender spatial tasks of the private space leads to domestic violence for married women in Urban Pakistan (Chatha & Ahmad, 2020). In their 2020 study, Hussain and Jullandhry, posit that in their survey, most of the women indicated reduced empowerment, restricted decision-making opportunities, restricted mobility and were restricted from using familial savings or acquiring paid services.

There are multiple studies concerning urban literature in India. But the existence of studies pertaining to Pakistani urban areas is minimal (Chambers, 2014). The cities of Lahore, especially in Pakistani Punjab and Karachi are portrayed in the novels written by Bapsi Sidhwa and Moshin Hamin where women are portrayed in demeaning characterization in urban Pakistan. Bapsi Sidhwa in her novel *The Crow Eaters* (2000) discusses the portrayal of women as prostitutes in Urban Pakistan. Also, Sidhwa's *A Pakistani wife* (2008) displays how women wearing gaudy dresses and excessive make-up danced. Moshin Hamid's *How to Get Filthy Rich in Rising Asia* (2014) describes Lahore where women are subjected to domestic work where women carry pots of water, and milk buffaloes and perform diurnal domestic duties. Hamid's *Moth Smoke* (2012) portrays the protagonist being the head of a brothel in the urban sectors of Pakistan. This novel describes how young women expose their feminine body parts, sold their bodies for sex and were assaulted by men. Hamid in *The Reluctant Fundamentalist* (2009) points out how men were the main inhabitants of the city. In Sidhwa's *An American Brat* (2012), Sidhwa describes how challenging, oppressive and difficult it was for women to even walk in the city. Additionally, while some women were unveiled, many were veiled as they frowned upon unveiled women. Yousafzai's autobiography *I am Malala* (2013) portrays how Malala and her friends were shot by the Taliban when she was part of the activism for Female Education. The fictional works display how in urban cities, everyday life was wrought with challenges and oppression. In her autobiographical work, Durrani et al. (1995) describes how Western spaces provided her with opportunities that allowed her to be independent and attain self-empowerment as she struggled to come out of her oppressive marriage, even though she lost custody of her children and is disowned by her parents. Khan (2021) describes the conflict between Pakistani and British identities, as she attempts to come out of the confines of gender inequality, gender segregation and patriarchal beliefs. Furthermore, she attempts to find her identity, as she learns to be individualistic and assertive.

The urban arena of Pakistan side-lined women by pushing them to the confines of the private space as their deserving space. Additionally, access to public sections of the urban society was dangerous and oppressive hindering them from self-empowerment. Women performed professionally as sex workers or dancers thereby rejecting autonomy over their bodies and minds. Additionally, in the contemporary scenario even though women may not choose demeaning jobs, they still have reduced autonomy as to availing services or making household decisions. Due to this, migrating to Western urban space becomes liberating especially for Pakistani women which helps them to come out of the mandatory spatial practices of Pakistan to a more liberating spatiality that promotes self-empowerment (Afshar,1989). Samra

Habib's *We Have Always Been Here: A Queer Muslim Memoir (2019)* is employed to expose how urban Pakistan fails to accommodate women from empowering themselves, autonomy towards spatialized tasks, and restricts educational, and employment opportunities. The city spaces segregates "rights" of women since urban spatial oppression continue to exist. Additionally, the public urban space of Pakistan continues to restrict women from mobility and opportunities that is spatialized in the public - urban spatialities of Pakistan.

This study aims to highlight the fact that Pakistani women continue to struggle for empowerment and improved living opportunities even in the modern day. By highlighting the lack of opportunities to foster individuality and to pursue long-awaited ambitions and objectives that are free from sexism and oppression, the study contributes to feminist geography and spatial studies. Additionally, Muslim women are still persecuted, sexually abused, and humiliated for coming out of the limiting nature of the hijab. The study reveals how the hijab itself is a confining spatiality in South Asian and Middle Eastern countries as a result of the oppression they experience in both private and public settings, as well as the fact that they are forced to undertake private-related spatial activities. This study is pertinent because it tries to assert a simple and compelling notion that women do not have to suffer in South Asian private and public places that emphasise the constraints of the hijab's spatiality. As a result, the work contributes to feminist geographies and spatial literary studies.

THEORY AND METHOD

The academic discipline of geography has been dominated by men (Rose, 1993). Even in the field of geography, women have undergone verbal and sexual abuse, and are provided with medium or low-paying jobs (Lindsey, 2020). Since gender is a major criterion, space is divided into male and female spaces which are based on the spatiality of occupation and lifestyle. Mackenzie (2002) defines "women's space" which is related to "private space" is the space that is restricted to domestic responsibilities (p. 109). The public space occupied by men, reverberated superiority and power, in contrast to the private spaces that historically undermined and controlled women from exercising autonomy. Women were excluded from productive work and thus pushed women to occupy the home that did not provide academic and economic freedom and restricted mobility (McDowell, 1983; Sasidharan & Prasuna, 2022).

Public spaces are located in cities and outside private spaces that provide access to community centers, parks, streets, etc. The divide between private and public spheres plays a significant role in interpreting urban spaces (McCasland et al., 2018). The private/public binary is similar to other binaries such as inside/outside, light/dark, inclusion/exclusion, movement and stasis (Vaiou & Kalandides, 2009). As a result, urban public space incorporates symbols, social codes, cultural and organisational regulations that identify where a person or which area a person belongs. As public spheres imply opportunity, tangible achievements, and practical endeavours, public space obtains autonomy, undercutting private spaces. Due to this, segregation occurs between public spaces whose members are recognized as the insiders and the private space whose members are recognized as being outside of the public space (outsiders/periphery). Even though public space may symbolize inclusivity, exclusivity is prominent as the insiders move freely and dismiss the outsiders (Beebeejaun, 2017; McCasland et al., 2018).

Additionally discriminatory practices against women and girls are common occurrences in public spaces including places such "as streets, parks, markets, public transport and other public venues" (McCasland et al., 2018, p. 9; Vaiou & Kalandides, 2009). This prevents women from attaining education, employment, mobility, relaxation, and recreational activities, thereby restricting their ability to enjoy the benefits of the city and equal citizenship. As a result, urban-public land use sequences and transit networks create movement barriers for women with children, particularly daughters, bolstering gender disparity. Subsequently, many women refrain from entering public spaces and occupy private spaces which is also a source of oppression (Fenster, 2005).

Women's space is geographically divided such that men's workplaces remain separated from women's spatiality. Therefore, women are doubly oppressed both in public spaces and private spaces (Bondi & Rose, 2003; Mackenzie, 2002). The purpose of feminist geography is to highlight the connection between patriarchy and the constraints of the private space. Similarly, Patriarchy governs the confines of the family where women are pressurized to perform gender-specific roles (Joseph Sebastine, 2022; Lindsey, 2020). These roles regulate male domination since men are economically independent and are considered to be superior to women (Karmaliani et al., 2012). But feminist urban geography attempts to resist and extend these shackles of confinement thereby expanding and reshaping women's spaces. By tearing down these gendered spaces, feminist geography aims to empower women by reinterpreting the division of gender roles.

Additionally, the movement towards the western urban spaces eventually enables women to be independent and free of patriarchal shackles. Women aspire to establish themselves in western public metropolitan settings even while they actively participate in household activities. By becoming wage earners, they take on dualistic roles in both the private and public/economic institutions which results in recreating and ungendering urban spaces. As mobility begins so do educational and professional experiences for many women. Therefore, newer urban feminine movements, urban organizations, and structures are recreated. Urban space provides a new dimension where women experience increased liberation from gender bias and seek new opportunities (Bondi & Rose, 2003). Thus, cities will aid in the overthrow of discriminatory practices and conventional roles in order to promote independence and self-empowerment. Urban spatialities subvert the hegemonic patriarchal and capitalist structures, encouraging and supporting women by providing them with decent-paying jobs that free them from the binds of household duties and patriarchal normative institutions (Markusen, 1980). Cities become primary locations for women because they help to transform their constricted living arrangements into freer and safer environments.

Urban spaces not only provide new opportunities for women but encourage and accommodate alternative sexualities. Queer identities and spaces undergo multiple levels of tensions, and contestations in private as well as public spaces. The patriarchal and cultural perspectives of queer individuals as "deviants" leads to discriminatory practices. Queer individuals are compelled to remain hidden because they face stigma heteronormative spaces like home and society.

Western urban spaces play a major role in accommodating queer sexualities, and queer spaces (Brown, 2008). Bech (1997) posits that cities promote homonormative lifestyles that support queer individuals to be a part of the queer community and assimilate into queer culture. Activism and resistance can lead to increased queer visibility. Additionally, urban spaces can provide psychological, social and legal aid that may assist queer individuals to fight homophobia and gain access to urban spaces (Gamrani et al., 2021).

Urban spaces help dismantle heteronormative practices by employing urban spaces subsequently making private sexualized spaces as public (Sibalis, 2002). Halberstam (2005) observe that cities disregard the negative and strict heteronormative norms of the private space by providing socialising opportunities in queer-friendly communities, thereby facilitating identity disclosure. Urban spaces encourage homosexuals to express their homoerotic inclinations in public spaces. By unifying queer identity to the self, Western urban areas enable them to relinquish their heterosexual identity. Mobilities from rural to city spaces also help to seek an alternative accepting urban locality as it provides access to residential, political, organizational, and commercial spatialities. Valentine (1993) observes that urban spaces allowed increased emergence of queer networks and public spaces (Podmore, 2001). Queer geographies discuss how "spaces are produced through embodied social practices", and cultural, political, and ethnic practices (Brown et al., 2017, p. 3). These practices govern, influence, and prescribe how the sexualized body, private and public space, and the closet should and should not function. Spatialities such as bodies, the closet space, and private spaces such as homes are also investigated using queer geography. Urban spaces allow women to overcome and contest male domination and heterosexism. Migration to western urban cities empowers them and allows them to reveal their sexuality. They become wage-earners, and they may engage in activism while also sustaining their families.

RESULTS AND FINDINGS

An Abridgment of Samra Habib's *We Have Always Been Here: A Queer Muslim Memoir* (2019)

The autobiographical novel, *We Have Always Been Here: A Queer Muslim Memoir* (2019) is based on Samra Habib's life and experiences. She is a photographer, writer, and activist through which she supports the plight of Queer Muslims. In her memoir, she writes about oppressive experiences due to gender segregation and the private spatialized practices of Pakistan. Due to Ahmadiyya intolerance[1] in Pakistan, Samra and her family migrate and resettle in Canada. Her father's moderately prospering business and the selling of their house help them to move to Canada. The money provided by Canadian welfare, and the menial jobs of Nasir and her father help her to acquire an education. At sixteen, she is forced to marry her cousin Nasir. As her marriage becomes a source of unhappiness, she divorces Nassir and moves out of her house. Additionally, she also realizes that she is queer and explores her sexuality and comes out to her family. Her education as well as the exposure she receives by reading the works of numerous feminist authors help her to become more assertive and independent. She comes out of the shackles of structural inequalities and becomes a photographer voicing the stories of queer Muslims.

Exploring Gendered and Sexualized Spatialities

Samra Habib's *We Have Always Been Here: A Queer Muslim Memoir* (2019) discusses how patriarchal institutions and gender dichotomies demote women in the urban space of Pakistan. Patriarchy and gendered spatial structures provide a clear divide between public and private spheres where public spheres are male-dominated while private spheres are reserved for women. In Pakistan, urban space subjugates and pushes women to private space, limiting mobility and thereby forcing women to forgo their personal needs and desires. Habib (2019) describes how her life and her mother's life were affected by patriarchal conventions and religious traditions and exemplifies the harrowing conditions of women who were physically and psychologically abused. Also, Samra's forced marriage denied her the opportunity to explore her burgeoning sexuality. But migrating to Canada enables her to overcome the restrictive gender spatial practices of urban Pakistan and Islamic religious institutions and allows her to be self-sufficient and independent. Western urban spaces help break societal injustices by facilitating liberatory practices that allow women to explore their femininity and sexuality (Bondi & Rose, 2003).

Women existed only to be trapped and to abide by the demands of their husbands and society as the traditional gender roles and expression have been continued by many "generations, that came before them, by their parents and grandparents" (Blackstone, 2003, p. 338). Pakistani women were not allowed to vocalise their feelings and could not take part in conversations in the public space. Additionally, they only accompanied their husbands in their cars since driving or talking with outsiders was considered immodest behaviour. This is indicative of how women were expected to follow and depend on men in public spaces and adjust their behaviour according to the traditional roles. At her mother's marriage, her mother became entitled to her father as her name was changed without her consent and knowledge (Karmaliani et al., 2012). The institution of marriage required that her mother play the role of a pious wife and mother forcing her into the private space and performing gender-assigned roles. Such a subdued position also eventuated in occupying reduced public space and increased private-related spatial activity (Baenninger & Newcombe, 1989). Women were indoctrinated that performing attentive and submissive roles would permit them to enter *Jannat*[2]. Samra's mother undergoes multiple miscarriages since gender discrimination, exhaustive household duties and caring for the husband cause excessive stress for pregnant women that leads to miscarriages (Stepanikova et al., 2020). Furthermore, the birth of three girls eventuates depreciation and lamentation by her family and relatives. In Pakistani society bearing female children was considered a burden since daughters had to be married off by paying huge dowries and needed extra protection (Habib, 2019). Also, women are denied access to mobility in public spaces, movement between private and public spatiality, transportation, and occupation (Coutras & Fagnani, 1978). Spatial movement into the public space meant being permitted by male figures such as fathers/brothers/husbands (Habib, 2019). While men could look after their parents, women were forced to leave their parents and move to the husband's family which was unfamiliar and constituted them to follow restrictive rules while curtailing their freedom.

Samra observes how her mother and female relatives maintained gendered spatial skills by attending knitting classes which were also only held after their husbands went to work. Since the private space is controlled by men, Samra's father bars dancing, singing, or playing music, traits that were considered to be exhibited by bad women (Brohi, 2006). Religious beliefs and elderly familial authority were also used to make women obey the gender spatial roles. Furthermore, appropriate behaviour and gendered submissive roles were maintained by the patriarchal and gender power structures as this limited their decision-making power and autonomy over their body and mind. Unrestrained behaviour was only seen in the absence of male figures. At a young age, Samra is made to look after her sisters, as she is expected to take on the role of nurturer. In childhood, gendered stereotypical and spatial behaviours are taught and trained to develop a strong gendered typical self (Saeed Ali et al., 2017).

When I finally found my mother and told her what had happened, she took me into the bathroom, her body trembling under the black fabric of her burka, her kajal-lined eyes displaying horror at the possibility of her worst fear being a reality. She examined me with the careful precision of a surgeon. Despite the sweltering heat, her touch felt cold and clinical. Once she determined that my hymen had not been broken, she uncovered her face by taking off her burka; finally, she could breathe as deeply as she needed to. She was too mortified to take me to the doctor, even though in the aftermath I couldn't stop coughing. My father was the only other person who could be trusted to know what had happened. She didn't dare discuss it with friends and family for fear of people speculating whether I was still a virgin, the worst possible outcome. (Habib, 2019, p. 15)

Molestation or physical coercive acts, and domestic abuse are daily occurrences to Pakistani women (Ali & Gavino, 2008). When Samra is molested by her father's male friend, her mother thoroughly examines her only to find out if Samra's hymen is intact. The marital prospects were highly important due to which such a horrific incident is kept a secret. This was because the ideal Pakistani woman was expected to be a modest and decent Muslim woman (Ellick, 2010; Khan, 2021). Samra keeps modest and self-contained behaviour because her chastity was more valuable to her family than her well-being and psychological trauma. Violence and subjugation against women in urban spaces are due to the naturalization of patriarchal institutions, "socio-cultural, political, legal, and economic factors" since these spaces maintain and concede to the particular rules and conditions of the society that dictate how women should access public/urban spaces (Karmaliani, 2012, p. 820). Coping and managing such spatial inequalities and gendered spaces become extremely challenging for women (Grant, 2010). In urban Pakistan, if women are unable to birth male children or refuse their private spatial duties and disregard their husbands, they were subjected to severe punishment (Zulfiqar & Hasan, 2012). Additionally, Khattak, (2014) observes how women were not only humiliated and killed for giving birth to female children but they were subjected to incidents of honour killing and murder due to domestic violence and sexual violence. Many women were also abandoned by their husbands because of minor physical deformities and were subjected to domestic violence, assault, rape, or even murder for not adhering to the harsh patriarchal rules of society and family. Habib (2019) highlights how "countless women are found dead in alleyways and on the sides of dirt roads, their bodies discarded because they were not able to conceive children, particularly boys" (Habib, 2019, p. 16).

Habib (2019) recounts how physically harassed wives huddled together in the absence of their husbands to discuss how they were assaulted for the simplest errors and blunders. As a result, women were forced to abandon their desires and longings and strictly adhere to gender-segregated and gender-typical spatial activities to avoid severe repercussions. Zulfiqar and Hasan (2012) posit that this resonated with the insecurity that Pakistani men faced leading to excessive control over women's bodies. Their insecurities also are used to legitimize acts of control and punishment to render that these men were the defenders of decency and chastity in society. Gender norms are dependent on the allocation of power, and thus the distribution of private and public space. This also locates how certain behaviours, roles, and characteristics maintain the private space and public space both being systematically gendered by male domination and patriarchy.

Mobility is also a crucial aspect of urban spaces that symbolizes the empowerment of an individual. City spaces of Pakistan are dominated by natural claims and rights of the men and also the gendered power relations and patriarchal claims (Zulfiqar & Hasan, 2012). However, women's mobility between private and public spaces may be regarded as a kind of defiance against gendered norms and male dominance. While men are free to move freely in public spaces, women are restricted and must be supervised by a man. Eastern urban spaces portray different socialization experiences and also promoted gender typical masculine and feminine experiences in public and private spaces (Eccles et al., 1990). This is specially done to preserve the sanctity of male domination in public and urban spaces. Masculine-related activities promoted spatial skills; feminine activities only needed social skills (Caplan & Caplan, 1994). Such highly gendered and male-dominated spaces encourage discrimination and violence against women in South Asian urban spaces. When women try to access such highly masculinized urban spaces, they are forced to rely on strict gendered norms to effectuate safety and security. Habib's mother forces her to cover her hair and to wear a hijab for her protection even though she is merely a child. After Samra's molestation, she is confined inside the quarters of her house and is constantly under surveillance either in the presence of her parent or nannies. She is not permitted to walk outdoors on the streets or play with her friends, limiting her access to public spaces. Lever (1976) observes how boys play outside while girls choose games like dolls or board games. Such indoor activities are preferred for girls since they limit "body movement and vocal expressions". Also, the girl's preferred games can be called "private affairs" whereas boys' outdoor games are "public" spatial activities (Lever, 1976, p. 480). She was also taught that being quiet was a necessary and appreciated virtue in her culture to refine gender-specific spatial skills (Reilly & Neumann, 2013).

Male harassment is also another reason that pushes women to private spaces. In public spaces, women are under the threat of the male gaze. They are objectified and sexualized, which causes shame, dread, and anxiety, driving them even further into the security of their private space. Samra discusses how men tease and pass comments when women walked outside:

They hissed and murmured "Bohat pyari gori hai"—what a beautiful fair-skinned woman—at my mom as her grip around me and my toddler sister tightened, and she raised her burka to ensure that only her dismissive eyes were visible. It seemed that no matter how much her burka covered her up and hid her silhouette, nothing could protect her from the vulgar comments and predatory eyes of neighborhood men. (Habib, 2019, p. 10)

Thompson (1994) observes how women in public spaces are vulnerable "to overt observation, evaluation, and verbal commentary by male strangers" (p. 315). Such teasing may include pointing to a woman's physical form and may be sexualized as women may suffer "wolf-whistles, leers, winks, grabs, pinches, catcalls, and rude comments" (Kissling & Kramarae, 1991, p. 75). Since these types of harassment is demeaning and threatening in nature, women choose to stay in their own spaces, preventing them from reaping the benefits of the city or relaxing from household tasks. Furthermore, this may prevent women from using public transportation or participating in public spaces, limiting their occupational prospects (Anwar et al., 2018; McCasland et al., 2018). Also, girls in adulthood in public places provoke tensions and anxiety. Habib (2019) discusses how the stories in the newspapers were crafted to convince women to be docile, obedient and to be spiritual so that their behaviours and needs adhered to the private space.

Habib (2019) discusses how men were allowed to act violently if their wives did not follow their demands or did not appease them or birthed girls. Saeed Ali et al. (2017) posits that husbands believed that it was their right to punish and correct their wives by assaulting them to render them spaceless. Additionally, such gendered violence and gendered behaviour were regulated by peers, parents, husbands, spousal families and media (Martin & Ruble, 2004).

The area designated for women while the men prayed in the airier and more welcoming space above—was where I would ask Allah for guidance, just as my mother did. There was a kinship among the women who occupied that space together, as many of them resented being treated as second-class citizens within their own faith. Our only access to any ideological dialogue about the verses of the Quran came by way of a TV screen projecting what male elders deemed worthy of our discussion.

Women were not asked to share their thoughts on how the teachings of the Quran played out in their lives. (Habib, 2019, p. 97)

The spatiality of the mosque is also segregated according to gender (Habib, 2019). The women had to occupy smaller and more uncomfortable spaces and the men had larger "airier and more welcoming space" (Habib, 2019, p. 96). Religious sectors in urban Pakistan also dictated spatial practices for women. She claims that chapters from the holy Quran were exclusively discussed by men who could openly express their ideas and engage in religious debates. Women, on the other hand, were not permitted to debate or express their views. Women managed spatial inequality both in private and urban spaces by utilizing strategies by avoiding urban spaces, covering themselves with hijab, speaking softly, repressing opinions and desires, and maintaining non-confrontational and non-provokable behaviour (Anwar et al., 2018). These constraints were expected of all women but mainly targeted younger women in Pakistani urban spaces.

Samra, her sisters, her mother and her first cousin, Nasir move to Canada due to Ahmadiyya intolerance in Pakistan. In Canada, as financial stress increases Samra subverts the gender norms of her community and her parents by selling roses. Samra faces parental disapproval and is rebuked as the public space is unsafe, especially for young girls and women. Clearly, the gendered non-conformational behaviour is not tolerated even though Samra's act was intended to help her needy family.

At the age of thirteen, news about her marriage is given through a letter from Nasir. She realizes denied the right to choose her husband or marriage. Pakistani women are also met with immense resistance by familial, societal, and religious factors and spatial gender norms for entering and coming out of marriage. Additionally, they are not given the power to decide on whom they should marry or when (Critelli, 2012). Women's rights towards their marriage are also subverted even though Islamic law and civil law claim to support women (Malik, 1996). Most South Asian cultures consider societal and familial approval for marriage and deem personal preferences insignificant (Jilani, 2000). Rejection, independent choosing of spouse or divorce may result in being exiled from family and society (Critelli, 2012).

The urban western space that she is a part of allows her to engage in non-conforming behaviour. She departs from the private space and proceeds to explore new frontiers in the urban space. Samra subverts her family, society, and patriarchal forces. She constantly transgresses the gender codes and norms as she watches movies that are forbidden and attempts to lose her accent. She begins to admire TV characters with rebellious flare. She reads Virginia Wolf and Noam Chomsky as she is interested in academics and feminism and removes her hijab. She frequently deceives her parents and attends parties. Nevertheless, she is policed by her parents, Nasir, and the Muslim community in Canada. She is called *Azaad* which has a gendered meaning that symbolizes a wild woman who cannot be controlled. The word can also mean an insult to any woman who shows a small amount of independence which meant devaluing the men in her family (Habib, 2019). At the same time, she begins to wear lipsticks to impress girls and look at the girls' changing rooms.

Her marriage at sixteen is consented only to respect her parent's honour and to maintain familial harmony. Samra's life is designed on conformity, and traditionalism to adhere to the gender binary structure and patriarchy. Bem and Lenney (1976) observe that such conformity to hegemonic spatial structures is because gender-typed individuals have internalized gendered norms. After marriage, Nasir (her husband and cousin) begins to monitor and condition her as she believes that books polluted her mind and promoted independence. Her mother and Nasir confront her since literary books had words like "sex, kissing and love" (Habib, 2019, p. 58). Intellectual skills are considered incompatible with private spatial gender roles and gender-tying skills (Eccles, 2007). Her persistence in attaining intellectual independence drives her to hide the books and read only after locking her bedroom. However, constant subversion against the private spatial practices and patriarchal norms puts her which puts her at risk for physical abuse from her husband because Pakistani society considered physical abuse from a husband to be acceptable (Saeed Ali et al., 2017). Additionally, she realizes that she would not receive parental support above spousal authority as her parents refuse to help her (Karmaliani et al., 2012).

She starts a romantic relationship with Peter, a classmate. She attempts to commit suicide because she is so desperate to leave her marriage. Eventually, she confronts her parents and Nasir and divorces him. Even though she is out of her trapped marriage, her parents control her as she defied the familial and societal institutions. Furthermore, she is rejected by the Muslim community as she is labelled as a rebellious daughter for defaming the status of her family and is called a bad Muslim. As she leaves her house, she removes her hijab as a rebellious gesture. Rejecting hijab is Samra's way of rejecting the gendered and patriarchal rules that dominated and controlled her and leaving behind the traits that confined her to private spatiality. Additionally, Iranian women have been burning their hijab marking their stance against the strict gender codes and especially dress codes that patronize women. Wearing the hijab loosely is considered as immodesty which may result in warning from authorities, arrest, and police brutality as in the case of Mahsa Amini (Cherain, 2022). Samra removes her hijab to describe the trauma she underwent inside the hijab when she was continuously forced to conform to the strict gender rules of Pakistani culture. The influence of the western urban space allows her to be assertive, independent, and strong when she steps out of the confining environment in which she was raised. The public space bestows her with a life of self-empowerment and without the dictates of the male figures. Moving out of the private space and into the western urban space helps her to gain self-respect, dignity and increased freedom that helps to chase her personal goals and dreams (Gaye & Jha, 2011). She continues her education and becomes economically independent. She is also able to come out of the unchanging generational gender oppression that corners women to private spatial duties and marriage.

Her mother also steps out of the confines of the private space in Canada. Samra's mother breaks free from the diurnal chores of the private sphere by opening a beauty salon. She empowers other women by hiring other Pakistani women. Thus, western urban space allows many Pakistani women to break out of their strict gender roles and repressive private space to create a space on their own. Here they are unreserved, opinionated, speak loudly, make decisions, and take care of each other. Economic autonomy also supports female-headed households where they lead a role of empowerment.

In Pakistani culture, women lack the power in making choices and decisions pertaining to their marriage and sexuality (Critelli, 2012). Even contemporary society still arranges a marriage between two families. This hinders individuals from properly maturing and exploring their sexuality. Samra realises in her mid-twenties that her sexuality does not conform to heterosexual orientation and that she may be queer. She understands she has a non-heterosexual sexual identity and seeks to explore it by attending queer parties and admiring lesbian and gay relationships. Coming from a heteronormative patriarchal background, queer culture makes her feel as though she does not belong in the queer community. As Islamic culture does not recognize queer sexualities and adheres to heterosexual and procreative practices, Samra faces a myriad number of challenges as she confronts her sexuality (Siker, 2007). She also faces confusion as she has to face her heterosexual identity and integrate a queer identity. Additionally, pre-existing shame related to her divorce forces her to rethink repeatedly of her queer sexuality. Such dominating influences cause further hesitancy as she yearns to accept her sexuality and engage in same-sex relationships. Even though she was attracted to her childhood female friend, Sonia and in high school she often glimpsed at girls' bodies in the changing room, Samra was not able to identify her growing non-normative sexuality. Her sexualized body, which is heavily policed by patriarchal and heteronormative rules, prevents her from accepting her identity wholly. She breaks up with Peter after realising she is not sexually interested in him.

Johnston and Longhurst (2010) observe that the body is the "primary space in which and around which we construct our subjectivities" (p. 39). She concludes that her body had been performing like a puppet under strict gendered roles. Samra attempts to realise that her body does not need to cater to heteronormative marriage and reproduction but rather prioritises personal preferences. Due to the intricacies of her sexual orientation, her family and the Samra grow apart as she strives to break free from the deeply established orthodox culture and tradition. To explore her sexuality Samra travels to Japan and experiences queer nightlife and visits Ni-chōme which is Tokyo's gay district (Habib, 2019). She struggles with her sexuality and faces anxiety as she attempts to come out of the closet. The closet is also a spatiality that performs confusion regarding sexual identity and disclosure (Gorman-Murray & McKinnon, 2015). Her struggles due to her ethnic, sociocultural, religious and familial influences curb her from exploring her sexuality. Her inherited culture had pushed her into a closet that forced her into performing normalized gender and sexual roles. The closeted spatiality is thus marginalized by many markers (Gorman-Murray & McKinnon, 2015). Even though the continued discrimination persists in urban spaces, her movement into the urban city makes her experience acceptance of her gender and sexuality in the city-built environment (Angeles & Roberton, 2020). She questions herself as she realizes that she seeks complete acceptance of her gender and her sexuality so that she may never waver from who she is or how much she was exploited for her gender and private spatial skills.

Maybe being a woman could be a source of power for me. What would it feel like to walk through the world daring to present myself without apology? Why had I never given myself permission to marvel at my body and appreciate how resilient it had been? How it had gently carried me through pain and trauma, and how for years I hid it under layers of shame. Because my femininity had often been exploited by others, used as justification for controlling and monitoring me, I didn't want it to be looked at or acknowledged. Now, looking at myself as if for the first time, I understood how showing off my curves could allow me to take back the power from those who had stripped me of it. My body could be a source of joy and pride. It was for me and for me alone. (Habib, 2019, p. 87)

As travelling to various urban spaces helps her to embrace her sexuality, she accesses urban opportunities such as online dating to explore her sexual identity. Her journey to numerous urban cities allows her to meet with individuals with varied queer identities, queer-friendly communities and engage in relationships with individuals who are lesbians, trans and non-binary.

She reconciles with her Muslim identity with her queer identity by joining a progressive mosque that accepts queer Muslims (Habib, 2019, p. 99). These mosques were unpublicized and kept a secret to allow queer Muslim experience. Many individuals who visited these mosques were exiled or self-exiled from Muslim countries in fear of persecution. Samra finds her deeply absent culture and unbiased spirituality with similar experiences of rejection in the urban space of Canada. Here individuals who were not conforming to the orthodox traditions on dresses, hairstyles, non-gender binary structure and non-heteronormative sexualities were accommodated and accepted (Yip et al., 2010). She also meets multiple women with stories of exhaustive and threatening private spatial practices, violence, and rape. The urban mosque did not segregate gender and provided a space to practice non-conformist queer behaviours and expressions. Western urban space also provides queer spiritual spaces and queer empowerment since non-normative sexual expressions were accepted and encouraged. Internal homophobia was also addressed in this spiritual space (Yip et al., 2010).

She also becomes a photographer to document the discriminatory experiences of Queer individuals and coloured and Muslim queer individuals. Because Islam forbids photography, the experiences of Queer Muslims through pictorial representation are invisible. Through photography, she creates a newer space for Queer Muslims to be both Muslim and gay. In Samra's case, western urban space not only allowed queer visibility, but it also allowed Queer Muslim visibility.

She also comes out publicly in the newspaper, *The Guardian*. Further, urban space provides her access to political and public segments of the urban society by oration and writing in various newspapers and magazines about different queer experiences. Also, she is able to contest normative heterosexual practices and patriarchal beliefs. Urban culture supports her to disclose her sexual orientation to her family. Additionally, queer geographies through urban spatiality reveal how the spatiality of closet and private spaces are deeply entrenched with normative structures and politics. City spaces also allow public acceptance and provide public access and legal reform (Gorman-Murray & McKinnon, 2015). Migration also helps in moving from a space of conditioning and discrimination to a place of liberal and modern culture that include individuals who do not fit the normative gender and sexuality (Gorman-Murray, 2007). Despite the fact that there is still discrimination in city spaces, the upgradation of liberal attitudes promotes women and sexual collectivities.

CONCLUSION

The private and public spatialities of male-dominated Urban Pakistan are oppressive and objectify women thereby pushing them to perform private spatial tasks. They are also coerced to endure societal injustices and inequalities all the while enduring unparallel psychological and physiological trauma. Consequently, they lose control over their minds and bodies, as well as their ability to access public areas, which limits their political, economical, cultural, and personal freedom. Additionally, religious tensions, sociocultural beliefs and familial reservedness restrict women to private space and hinder them from exploring their sexuality. As Samra's family is from Pakistan and has an uncompromising, steadfast conventional lifestyle, severe religious views, and gender norms, self-empowerment and admitting her sexuality becomes difficult because she must reconcile contradictory gender roles, ethnic values, and familial belonging.

Western urban spaces attempt to ignore the strict normative spatial practices of eastern urban settings. Migration and displacement to western urban spaces also dismantle traditional gender roles allowing individuals to pursue lives that enable self-empowerment and queer visibility. While some women try to resist and change the restrictive norms of patriarchal structures, others create their own space that subtly uplifts their subjugated position. City spaces also help in reimagining and recreating gender roles that allow access to public spaces. Bech (1997) posits that modernized types of living, customs, cultures, and sexualities emanate because of urban spatialities. Eastern spatial traditions are destabilized in order to create a liberating space in western metropolitan spaces for women and queer sexualities. These spaces liberate people from histories of shame, violence, and conservatism that have characterised gendered and queer experiences. Urban spaces become ungendered and utopian when women become urban agents, eliminating hegemonic sexism and privatizing gender roles. Western urban spaces provide alternative and empowering visions of urban life, enabling political and economic opportunities. Urban city spaces have an essential part in providing education and employment, which aids in decision-making skills and the development of progressive connections with family and community. Urban spaces also provide people with more freedom in their choices and emphasise personal well-being. Western urban spaces provide more flexibility for queer expressions and gender practices, as well as a desire to oppose prejudice, hatred, and violence in order to celebrate, solidify, and redefine predetermined private spatial patterns. Urban spaces thus become a safe space - a utopia to engage in spatial practices that support women's empowerment and queer tolerance.

ACKNOWLEDGMENT

This research received no specific grant from any funding agency in the public, commercial, or not-for-profit sectors.

REFERENCES

Afshar, H. (1989). Gender roles and the 'moral economy of kin' among Pakistani women in West Yorkshire. *Journal of Ethnic and Migration Studies*, *15*(2), 211–225. doi:10.1080/1369183X.1989.9976111

Ali, P. A., & Gavino, M. I. B. (2008). Violence against women in Pakistan: A framework for analysis. *JPMA. The Journal of the Pakistan Medical Association, 58*(4), 198. PMID:18655430

Ali, T. S., Krantz, G., Gul, R., Asad, N., Johansson, E., & Mogren, I. (2011). Gender roles and their influence on life prospects for women in urban Karachi, Pakistan: A qualitative study. *Global Health Action, 4*(1), 7448. doi:10.3402/gha.v4i0.7448 PMID:22065609

Angeles, L. C., & Roberton, J. (2020). Empathy and inclusive public safety in the city: Examining LGBTQ2+ voices and experiences of intersectional discrimination. *Women's Studies International Forum, 78*, 102313. doi:10.1016/j.wsif.2019.102313

Anwar, N. H., Viqar, S., & Mustafa, D. (2018). Intersections of gender, mobility, and violence in urban Pakistan. In J. E. Salahub, M. Gottsbacher, & J. de Boer (Eds.), *Social Theories of Urban Violence in the Global South* (pp. 15–31). Routledge. doi:10.4324/9781351254724-2

Anzaldúa, G. (1987). *Borderlands/La Frontera: The new mestiza.* WorldCat Discovery Service.

Appleby, R. J. C. (2005). *The spatiality of English language teaching, gender and context* [Unpublished doctoral dissertation]. University of Technology, Sydney.

Aurat Foundation. (2012, February 15). Aurat Foundation launches report on violence against Women. *Pakistan Today.* https://www.af.org.pk/AF%20in%20Media%20-%201/Violence%20aga inst%20women%20%20News%20clipping%20PDF/Aurat%20Foundation%2 0launches%20report%20on%20violence%20against%20women,%20Paki stan%20Today.pdf

Baenninger, M., & Newcombe, N. (1989). The role of experience in spatial test performance: A meta-analysis. *Sex Roles, 20*(5), 327–344. doi:10.1007/BF00287729

Bech, H. (1997). *When men meet: Homosexuality and modernity.* University of Chicago Press.

Beebeejaun, Y. (2017). Gender, urban space, and the right to everyday life. *Journal of Urban Affairs, 39*(3), 323–334. doi:10.1080/07352166.2016.1255526

Bem, S. L., & Lenney, E. (1976). Sex typing and the avoidance of cross-sex behavior. *Journal of Personality and Social Psychology, 33*(1), 48–54. doi:10.1037/h0078640 PMID:1018227

Blackstone, A. (2003). Gender roles and society. In J. R. Miller, R. M. Lerner, & L. B. Schiamberg (Eds.), *Human Echology: An Encyclopedia of Children, Families, Communities, and Environments* (pp. 335–338). ABC-CLIO.

Bondi, L., & Rose, D. (2003). Constructing gender, constructing the urban: A review of Anglo-American feminist urban geography. *Gender, Place and Culture, 10*(3), 229–245. doi:10.1080/0966369032000114000

Borovoy, A., & Ghodsee, K. (2012). Decentering agency in feminist theory: Recuperating the family as a social project. *Women's Studies International Forum, 35*(3), 153–165. doi:10.1016/j.wsif.2012.03.003

Brohi, N. (2006). *The MMA offensive: Three years in power 2003–2005*. Action Aid International.

Brown, G. (2008). Urban (homo)sexualities: Ordinary cities and ordinary sexualities. *Geography Compass, 2*(4), 1215–1231. doi:10.1111/j.1749-8198.2008.00127.x

Brown, G., Browne, K., & Lim, J. (2017). Introduction, or why have a book on geographies of sexualities? In K. Browne, J. Lim, & G. Brown (Eds.), *Geographies of Sexualities: Theory, Practices and Politics* (pp. 15–32). Routledge. doi:10.4324/9781315254470

Caplan, P. J., & Caplan, J. (2015). *Thinking critically about research on sex and gender*. Psychology Press. doi:10.4324/9781315662374

Chambers, C. (2014). 'The heart, stomach and backbone of Pakistan': Lahore in novels by Bapsi Sidhwa and Mohsin Hamid. *South Asian Diaspora, 6*(2), 141–159. doi:10.1080/19438192.2014.912463

Chatha, S. A., & Ahmad, D. K. (2020). Socio-economic status and domestic violence: A study on married women in urban Lahore, Pakistan. *South Asian Studies, 29*(1), 229–237.

Cherain, J. (2022, October 6). Anti-hijab protests rage across Iran after death of Mahsa Amini. *Frontline India's National Magazine*. https://frontline.thehindu.com/world-affairs/autumn-of-discontent-brews-in-iran-with-anti-hijab-protests-after-mahsa-amini-death-in-custody/article65949425.ece

Coutras, J., & Fagnani, J. (1978). Femmes et transports en milieu urbain. *International Journal of Urban and Regional Research, 2*(3), 432–439. doi:10.1111/j.1468-2427.1978.tb00760.x

Critelli, F. M. (2012). Between law and custom: Women, family law and marriage in Pakistan. *Journal of Comparative Family Studies*, *43*(5), 673–693. doi:10.3138/jcfs.43.5.673

Davies, A. W. J., Vipond, E., & King, A. (2017). Gender binary washrooms as a means of gender policing in schools: A Canadian perspective. *Gender and Education*, *31*(7), 866–885. doi:10.1080/09540253.2017.1354124

De Lauretis, T. (1990). Eccentric subjects: Feminist theory and historical consciousness. *Feminist Studies*, *16*(1), 115–150. doi:10.2307/3177959

Durrani, T., Hoffer, W., & Hoffer, M. M. (1995). *My feudal lord*. Random House.

Eccles, J. S. (2007). Families, schools, and developing achievement-related motivations and engagement. In J. E. Grusec & P. D. Hastings (Eds.), *Handbook of socialization: Theory and research* (pp. 665–691). The Guilford Press.

Eccles, J. S., Jacobs, J. E., & Harold, R. D. (1990). Gender role stereotypes, expectancy effects, and parents' socialization of gender differences. *The Journal of Social Issues*, *46*(2), 183–201. doi:10.1111/j.1540-4560.1990.tb01929.x

Ellick, A. B. (2010). *Necessity pushes Pakistani women into jobs and peril*. https://www.nytimes.com/2010/12/27/world/asia/27karachi.html

Fenster, T. (2005). The right to the gendered city: Different formations of belonging in everyday life. *Journal of Gender Studies*, *14*(3), 217–231. doi:10.1080/09589230500264109

Gamrani, S., Reidel, M., & Tribouillard, C. (2021, June 28). Cities with pride: Inclusive urban planning with LGBTQ + people. *Ciudades Sostenibles*. https://blogs.iadb.org/ciudades-sostenibles/en/cities-with-pride-inclusive-urban-planning-with-lgbtq-people/

Gaye, A., & Jha, S. (2011). Measuring women's empowerment through migration. *Diversities*, *1*, 1–13.

Gorman-Murray, A. (2007). Rethinking Queer Migration through the Body. *Social & Cultural Geography*, *8*(1), 105–121. doi:10.1080/14649360701251858

Gorman-Murray, A., & McKinnon, S. (2015). Queer geography. International Encyclopedia of the Social and Behavioral Sciences, 19, 759-764. doi:10.1016/B978-0-08-097086-8.10212-0

Grant, U. (2010). *Spatial inequality and urban poverty traps*. Overseas Development Institute.

Habib, S. (2019). *We Have Always Been Here: A Queer Muslim Memoir*. Penguin Random House.

Hadi, A. (2017). Patriarchy and gender-based violence in Pakistan. *European Journal of Social Sciences Education and Research*, *10*(2), 297. doi:10.26417/ejser.v10i2.p297-304

Halberstam, J. J. (2005). *In a queer time and place: Transgender bodies, subcultural lives*. NYU Press. doi:10.18574/nyu/9780814790892.001.0001

Hamid, M. (2009). *The Reluctant Fundamentalist*. Anchor Canada.

Hamid, M. (2012). *Moth Smoke*. Penguin.

Hamid, M. (2014). *How to Get Filthy Rich in Rising Asia: A Novel*. Penguin.

Heimer, K. (2000). Changes in the gender gap in crime and women's economic marginalization. *Criminal Justice*, *1*, 427–483.

Hussain, S., & Jullandhry, S. (2020). Are urban women empowered in Pakistan? A study from a metropolitan city. *Women's Studies International Forum*, *82*, 102390. doi:10.1016/j.wsif.2020.102390

Jilani, M. J. T. H. (2000). Discrimination–Pakistan: The right to marry. *Amicus Curiae*, *2000*(24), 25–28.

Joelsson, T., & Bruno, L. (2022). Proximal or peripheral: Temporality and spatiality in young people's discourses on gender violence in Sweden. *Gender and Education*, *34*(2), 167–182. doi:10.1080/09540253.2020.1860199

Johnston, L., & Longhurst, R. (2010). *Space, place, and sex: Geographies of sexualities*. Rowman & Littlefield.

Joseph Sebastine, K. S. (2022). Construction and reconstruction of space and identity: An analysis of Jasvinder Sanghera's shame travels. In M. Pourya Asl (Ed.), *Gender, place, and identity of South Asian women* (pp. 178–195). IGI Global. doi:10.4018/978-1-6684-3626-4.ch009

Karmaliani, R., Pasha, A., Hirani, S., Somani, R., Hirani, S., Asad, N., Somani, R., McFarlane, J., Hirani, S., & Cassum, L. (2012). Violence against women in Pakistan: Contributing factors and new interventions. *Issues in Mental Health Nursing*, *33*(12), 820–826. doi:10.3109/01612840.2012.718046 PMID:23215983

Kaur, N. (2022). Gender, caste, and spatiality: Intersectional emergence of hegemonic masculinities in Indian Punjab. *Gender, Place and Culture*, *1*(19), 1–19. Advance online publication. doi:10.1080/0966369X.2022.2122945

Kazi, A., Fatmi, Z., Hatcher, J., Kadir, M. M., Niaz, U., & Wasserman, G. A. (2006). Social environment and depression among pregnant women in urban areas of Pakistan: Importance of social relations. *Social Science & Medicine, 63*(6), 1466–1476. doi:10.1016/j.socscimed.2006.05.019 PMID:16797813

Khan, S. (2021). *The Roles We Play*. Myriad Editions.

Khattak, A. K. (2014). Female Infanticide and Killing Women for Giving Birth to A Baby Girl. A Case study of Pakistan. In *Proceedings of SOCIOINT14-International Conference on Social Sciences and Humanities* (*Vol. 8-10*, pp. 321-328). Academic Press.

Kissling, E. A., & Kramarae, C. (1991). Stranger compliments: The interpretation of street remarks. *Women's Studies in Communication, 14*(1), 75–93. doi:10.1080/07491409.1991.11089751

Knopp, L. (2007). On the relationship between queer and feminist geographies. *The Professional Geographer, 59*(1), 47–55. doi:10.1111/j.1467-9272.2007.00590.x

Le Doeuff, M. (2007). *Hipparchia's choice: An essay concerning women, philosophy, etc*. Columbia University Press.

Lever, J. (1976). Sex differences in the games children play. *Social Problems, 23*(4), 478–487. doi:10.2307/799857

Lindsey, L. L. (2020). *Gender: Sociological perspectives*. Routledge. doi:10.4324/9781315102023

Little, J., Peake, L., & Richardson, P. (1988). Introduction: Geography and gender in the urban environment. In J. Little, L. Peake, & P. Richardson (Eds.), Women in Cities (pp. 1-20). Palgrave. doi:10.1007/978-1-349-19576-3_1

Mackenzie, S. (2002). Women in the city. In R. Peet & N. Thrift (Eds.), *New Models in geography* (pp. 125–142). Routledge. doi:10.4324/9780203036358

Malik, I. (1996). *State and civil society in Pakistan: Politics of authority, ideology and ethnicity*. Springer.

Maqsood, A. (2017). *The new Pakistani middle class*. Harvard University Press.

Markusen, A. R. (1980). City spatial structure, women's household work, and national urban policy. *Signs (Chicago, Ill.), 5*(S3), S23–S44. doi:10.1086/495709

Martin, C. L., & Ruble, D. (2004). Children's search for gender cues. *Current Directions in Psychological Science, 13*(2), 67–70. doi:10.1111/j.0963-7214.2004.00276.x

Masood, A. (2017). Negotiating mobility in gendered spaces: Case of Pakistani women doctors. *Gender, Place and Culture*, *25*(2), 188–206. doi:10.1080/0966369X.2017.1418736

Massey, D. (2013). *Space, place and gender*. John Wiley & Sons. doi:10.2307/4065933

McCasland, H., Travers, K., Sanchez, S. L., Brum, L., Dannatt, M., Justo, L., & Shaw, M. (2018). *Safety and public space: Mapping metropolitan gender policies*. Metropolis.

McDowell, L. (1983). Towards an understanding of the gender division of urban space. *Environment and Planning. D, Society & Space*, *1*(1), 59–72. doi:10.1068/d010059

Mohanty, C. T. (1984). Under western eyes: Feminist scholarship and colonial discourses. *Boundary 2*, *12*(3), 333. doi:10.2307/302821

Mustafa, D., Anwar, N., & Sawas, A. (2019). Gender, global terror, and everyday violence in urban Pakistan. *Political Geography*, *69*, 54–64. doi:10.1016/j.polgeo.2018.12.002

Nittali, K., & NK, S. D. (2022). Uncovering the veiled experiences: Women, memories, and the Bangladesh Liberation War. In M. Pourya Asl (Ed.), *Gender, Place, and Identity of South Asian Women* (pp. 211-231). IGI Global.

Podmore, J. A. (2001). Lesbians in the crowd: Gender, sexuality and visibility along Montréal's Boul. St-Laurent. *Gender, Place and Culture*, *8*(4), 333–355. doi:10.1080/09663690120111591

Pourya Asl, M. (Ed.). (2022). *Gender, place, and identity of South Asian women*. IGI Global. doi:10.4018/978-1-6684-3626-4

Price-Chalita, P. (1994, July). Spatial metaphor and the politics of empowerment: Mapping a place for feminism and postmodernism in geography? *Antipode*, *26*(3), 236–254. doi:10.1111/j.1467-8330.1994.tb00250.x

Reilly, D., & Neumann, D. L. (2013). Gender-role differences in spatial ability: A meta-analytic review. *Sex Roles*, *68*(9–10), 521–535. doi:10.100711199-013-0269-0

Rose, G. (1993). *Feminism & geography: The limits of geographical knowledge*. University of Minnesota Press. doi:10.22201/ffyl.poligrafias.1996.1.1589

Saeed Ali, T., Karmaliani, R., Mcfarlane, J., Khuwaja, H. M., Somani, Y., Chirwa, E. D., & Jewkes, R. (2017). Attitude towards gender roles and violence against women and girls (VAWG): Baseline findings from an RCT of 1752 youths in Pakistan. *Global Health Action*, *10*(1), 1342454. doi:10.1080/16549716.2017.13 42454 PMID:28758882

Sasidharan, S., & M. G., P. (2022). Identity, roles, and choices within the space of the "Home" in Vijay Tendulkar's Kamala. In M. Pourya Asl (Ed.), *Gender, place, and identity of South Asian women* (pp. 68-88). IGI Global. doi:10.4018/978-1-6684-3626-4.ch004

Sibalis, M. (2002). 'La lesbian and gay pride' in Paris: Community, commerce and carnival. In L. Cairns (Ed.), Gay and Lesbian Cultures in France (pp.51–66). Verlag Peter Lang.

Sidhwa, B. (2000). The Crow Eaters. Academic Press.

Sidhwa, B. (2008). *The Pakistani Bride*. Milkweed Editions.

Sidhwa, B. (2012). *An American Brat: A Novel*. Milkweed Editions.

Siker, J. S. (2007). *Homosexuality and religion: An encyclopedia*. Greenwood Press/Greenwood Publishing Group.

Stepanikova, I., Acharya, S., Abdalla, S., Baker, E., Klanova, J., & Darmstadt, G. L. (2020). Gender discrimination and depressive symptoms among child-bearing women: ELSPAC-CZ cohort study. *EClinicalMedicine*, *20*, 100297. doi:10.1016/j.eclinm.2020.100297 PMID:32300743

Thompson, D. M. (1994). The woman in the street: Reclaiming the public space from sexual harassment. *Yale Journal of Law and Feminism*, *6*, 313.

Vaiou, D., & Kalandides, A. (2009). Cities of "others": Public space and everyday practices. *Geographica Helvetica*, *64*(1), 11–20. doi:10.5194/gh-64-11-2009

Valentine, G. (1993). (Hetero)sexing space: Lesbian perceptions and experiences of everyday spaces. *Environment and Planning. D, Society & Space*, *11*(4), 395–413. doi:10.1068/d110395

Warren, S. (2016). Pluralising the walking interview: Researching (im)mobilities with Muslim women. *Social & Cultural Geography*, *18*(6), 786–807. doi:10.1080/14649365.2016.1228113

Yip, A. K. T., Browne, K., & Munt, S. R. (2010). *Queer spiritual spaces: Sexuality and sacred places*. Routledge.

Yousafzai, M. (2013). I am Malala: The girl who stood up for education and was shot by the Taliban. Hachette UK.

Zulfiqar, G. M. (2019). Dirt, foreignness, and surveillance: The shifting relations of domestic work in Pakistan. *Organization*, *26*(3), 321–336. doi:10.1177/1350508418812579

Zulfiqar, H., & Hassan, R. (2012). Level of awareness regarding domestic violence comparison between working and non-working women: A case study of Lalazar, Rawalpindi, Pakistan. *Journal of Peace, Conflict and Development*, *19*, 32–42.

ENDNOTES

[1] Due to the doctrinal difference, Ahmadiya Muslims were discriminated by mainstream Muslims since they believed that Ahmadiyyas as non-Muslims.

[2] The prized heaven.

Chapter 9
Reconstructing Urban Spaces in Sushmita Banerjee's *Kabuliwalar Bangali Bou*:
The Memoir as a Narrative of Marital Migration in the South Asian Context

Monali Chatterjee
https://orcid.org/0000-0002-7993-090X
Gujarat Arts and Science College, India

ABSTRACT

This chapter explores Sushmita Banerjee's memoir titled Kabuliwalar Bangali Bou (1997) that portrays the horrors of displacement and city life in the South Asian context. The memoir poignantly chronicles the experiences of an urban Bengali woman who marries an Afghan businessman for love and migrates to Afghanistan during the rule of the Taliban. The objectives of the study are four-fold: 1) to establish the relationship between the vitality of urban space and the nature of social conventions that migrants are expected to follow; 2) to observe how such social and urban conventions and geopolitics affect migration, migrants, and diasporic communities; 3) to examine the reconstruction of urban spaces by women within the Taliban-governed nation of Afghanistan; and 4) to examine their narratives of urban space in the light of Foucault's dichotomy between private and public space as well as Heterotopia, Soja's notion of the third space, and Lefebvre's maxim about social space.

DOI: 10.4018/978-1-6684-6650-6.ch009

INTRODUCTION

The diasporas of India often feel the urge to reconstruct or experience urban spaces and this is detrimental in stimulating the international relations as well as the intellectual and societal capital of India. However, the grief and distress of losing the security of family and motherland, the trials of isolation, adaptation, acculturation, and reconciliation are faced by migrants to negotiate urban spaces in varying capacities. The anthropological, historical, political, religious, economic, and sociological aspects of urban spaces and migration are captured within a substantial bulk of literature that now exists as fiction, biographies, autobiographies, memoirs, diaries, poetry, content on the social media, films as well as academic works.

This research aims to: a) establish the relationship between the vitality of urban space and the nature of social conventions that migrants are expected to follow, b) observe how such social and urban conventions and geopolitics affect migration, migrants and diasporic communities, c) examine the reconstruction of urban spaces by women within the Taliban-governed nation of Afghanistan, and d) examine their narratives of urban space in the light of Foucault's dichotomy between private and public space as well as Heterotopia, Soja's notion of the third space and Lefebvre's maxim about 'social space' among others. This paper attempts to bring new perspectives about migration from urban space and emotional reorientation, particularly in Afghanistan and the relevance of its context in the present day.

For the last few decades, it has been recorded that:

Afghanistan faces a huge humanitarian challenge due to war and drought related displacements. Thousands of families have abandoned their homes. The situation is critical for refugee returnees and displaced persons, many of whom are living in open spaces and in urban informal settlements facing eviction and violence (Boulaich, 2019).

Though this research centres on a singular case of a migrating bride in the form of a memoir, the nuances of its depiction and description may be relatable across the borders of culture, space and time. In this memoir called *Kabuliwalar Bangali Bou* (A Kabuliwala's Bengali Wife; 1997), Sushmita Bandyopadhyay, also known as Sayeda Kamala (1964-2013), recounts some of the crucial occurrences that took place as a part of her experience as an immigrant in Afghanistan in vivid detail. The text documents the incidences of this a woman from India who marries an Afghan businessman, Janbaaz Khan, for love and migrates to Afghanistan during the rule of the Taliban. The protagonist, Sushmita Bandyopadhyay (or Banerjee) from Kolkata, India, is a thirty-two-year-old Indian woman who had only travelled to Afghanistan with her husband "to visit" her in-laws but became almost "socially imprisoned" in Sarana, Afghanistan for eight long years.

Migration entails the dyads of both movement and settlement to a different place, change and permanence and establishment and displacement. In this light, it would be interesting to focus on some of the apprehensions and ambiguities of urban diaspora spaces and cultural customs. The poignant memoir examines the encounters between a 'migrant bride' and religious practices 'misrepresented' as authentic cultural customs as well as the debatable issues concerning the generation gap, family, gender, and religion imposed as accepted norms in society. In terms of its social-political and historical context, the memoir is a pivotal text that audaciously records untold miseries and atrocities within the framework of urban space. Banerjee's memoir captured immense attention from the media. The memoir brings fresh insights about migration and emotional reorientation and the relevance of its context in the present day. This memoir was later made into a film *Escape from Taliban* in 2003 starring Manisha Koirala and Nawab Shah directed by Ujjal Chatterjee (livemint, 2013). Yet, its implications are to be researched through various lenses.

Sushmita Banerjee was a writer and activist from India. She risked her life as an Indian who wrote about life in Afghanistan. (Versey, 2021) Her major works in Bengali include *Kabuliwalar Bangali Bou* (1997) *Talibani Atyachar—Deshe o Bideshe* (Taliban atrocities in Afghanistan and Abroad), *Mullah Omar, Taliban O Ami* (Mullah Omar, Taliban and I) (2000), *Ek Borno Mithya Noi* (Not a Word is a Lie) (2001) and *Sabhyatar Sesh Punyabani* (The Swansong of Civilisation). (Ibid.) She is known for her bold proclamations about the pitiable predicament of the people of Afghanistan under dire political strife. During her tragic immigration from Kolkata to Kabul, Afghanistan, Sushmita Banerjee (henceforth, referred to as Banerjee) is beleaguered by the Taliban militants for repudiating their commands and mandates such as converting to Islam. The candid and incisive memoir depicts the petrifying account of her survival in Afghanistan, the precarity of her third space and her continual struggle at the edge of death. Narrated in the first person, the work gives a first-hand experience of how she escapes the fanatics of the nation and the Taliban to return to her homeland, refusing to compromise with her terms.

She is unable to find any ethnographic explanation or justification behind savage actions like imposing certain restrictions on women or domestic exploitation and violence on women and children. Her courage sets an immortal example as an ordinary woman who braves the violence of terrorizing forces that thrive even today. Banerjee's memoir *Kabuliwalar Bangali Bou* (A Kabuliwala's Bengali Wife), recounting her escape from the Taliban in 1995 and published after two years, became a bestseller in India (PTI, 2013). The memoir demonstrates the notion of the "spatial turn" which "fosters researches that explore a sense of locality combined with a sense of hybridity and mobility" (Chiesa, 2016, p. 1) through the local inhabitants of Afghanistan and the protagonist.

The interplay of Afghanistan and the feminist theorizing of urban space demands a keen understanding. It has been rightly observed:

Though feminist debates have catalysed new ways of thinking about gender and gender relations, the limitations of planning's understanding of the complexity of gender militate against an extended conversation about the gendered and dynamic nature of space that might enable stronger linkages to feminist, antiracist, or queer scholarship (Beebeejaun, 2017, p. 324).

Kovačević and Malenica (2021) claim that "The realities of everyday life of the local population, … are countered by the reality of migrants rushing towards … security and abundance" (p. 79) and the urban space becomes the arena for binaries of the local and migrant population, particularly if the migrants are woman, as a result of a marital migration. Judith Butler writes, "Gender ought not to be construed as a stable identity or locus of agency from which various acts follow; rather; gender is an identity tenuously constituted in time, instituted in an exterior space through a stylized repetition of acts" (Butler, 1990, p. xvi). Taking this idea of space and gender further, Wrede proposes that:

Effectively, the junctions of space and gender have gradually moved more and more into the feminist critical purview, including the relation between gender and movement and the gendered public/ private binary, to convey how space itself can become a form of control, of limitation of women's mobility—but also a site of women's actualization, of breaking out of gender constraints, and of achieving power. (Wrede, 2015, p. 10)

HISTORICAL AND POLITICAL CONTEXT

Gulbuddin Hekmatyar (also called Engineer Hekmatyar), was the fanatic leader of the Isbi-Islami-Afghanistan Party warring against Dr. Najibullah and Soviet Russia since 1979. When in 1990, the Najibullah government fell, a pact was made between Mojaddedi and Burhanuddin Rabbani for coming to power as the government of Afghanistan for two years. First Mojaddedi would rule for two years and then Rabbani would come to power for the next two years and Mojaddedi would probably rule after that. Everything was peaceful during this time Mojaddedi's time when he ruled for the first two years. After Rabbani's rule for two years, when Rabbani refused to give up his power as the government, then (the self-proclaimed patriot) Hekmatyar declared a Civil War against Rabbani. Due to this, whatever economic developments Rabbani had created, got destroyed. Hekmatyar started mass killings to protest Rabbani. People started saying that the Najib government was far better. It was decided that Hekmatyar would become the Prime Minister, Rabbani, the President and Massud Ahmed Shah, Chief of Defence. Hekmatyar vowed never to start a war again but broke it the next month to remain in power. This is the true picture of the Mujahids. (Banerjee, 1997, p. 58). Hekmatyar had been crusading to establish his Islam in Afghanistan since 1979. Due to Hekmatyar's initiated war, the Taliban militants entered the country. People prayed for Najib's freedom so that he could come back to power.

The Taliban militants started their activities in 1993 in Ghazni, Afghanistan. Once the villages and police stations came within the power of the Taliban, they mandated many religious practices. Growing a beard, and going to the mosque for Namaz for men, the hijab for women became compulsory. The Taliban became dictators, inducing the fear of Islam within the people. Soon, the Taliban conquered Kabul. Rabbani challenged the Taliban. Mozaddidi from the USA asked Rabbani and Taliban to stop waging a war but the Taliban did not budge (Banerjee, 1997, p. 58).

By 1996, the Rabbani Government had hardly a quarter of the territory of Afghanistan under its control. On the other hand, the Taliban had captured Qandahar, Heart, Eastern Pashtun, Jalalabad, Dostum's areas and the Shia (Hazara) areas in the centre. Though Hikmatyar joined the government of Rabbani and Massoud, as Prime Minister and conglomerated his troops to Kabul to crusade against the Taliban, the latter's social and political control over the territory had become immensely powerful (Barnett, 1997, p. 283).

When Banerjee came to Kabul in 1988, it was heavily patrolled by armed Russian soldiers. At that time a man aged between 18 and 38 could not go to the city from the village, otherwise, the Russians would force him into a prison and later he would be absorbed into the Russian force. Otherwise, the Afghans would have to brave the bullets of the Russian firing squad. On the other hand, they would never be allowed to return to their village. In the village, the Mujahid group had been revolting against Russian forces since 1979. The Mujahid regarded the Soviet government as well as their puppet Dr Najibulla as they are the prime enemy. So, they are Khalki (traitors). Najibulla allegedly became a minister and surrendered his country, Afghanistan to the Soviet Union. So Najibulla's followers were also considered to be traitors by the Afghans. On the other hand, the Mujahids want to perpetuate Islamic rule in the country. Therefore, the Mujahid followers were considered loyal patriots of the country. During this political upheaval when people dreaded coming to Kabul, Banerjee arrives there with Janbaaz.

TRENDS OF MIGRATION

Migration is an adaptation strategy adopted by individuals' households or communities to enhance their livelihoods (Haan, 2000; Pourya Asl, 2022). India has a long history of highly skilled migrants (both working professionals and students), specifically to developed nations, causing the 'brain drain' to become an issue of concern. The number of Indians living abroad has burgeoned to 17 million at present according to a recent report by the United Nations Department of Economic and Social Affairs (UN –DESA). The proliferation of migrants shows the significance of migration and how international migration profoundly influences not only societies and economies but also our emotional bonds and human relations.

The structure of India's economic system thrives on the prolonged sustenance of capitalism and neo-liberal policies that seek economic growth by promoting consumerism and competition. The solidarity of the corporate with the government further gives them both a disproportionate share of benefits at the expense of the poor. During the migration women migrant workers frequently face a drawback due to gender-specific influences and have diverse experiences on account of gender stereotypes and the division of labour between the two genders (Gender and International Migration, n.d.). Very meagre data seems to be available about Indian women migrants in Afghanistan and even there the sources are not dependable. So, the memoir had to be depended upon for information. In the context of this memoir, the migration of the protagonist and another Indian woman, Kakoli is driven by marriage. Unlike women migrant workers, marital migration has a much greater degree of vulnerability since immigrant brides are often unemployed and financially dependent upon their husbands. Marital migration also entails several social expectations. Critics document this conditioning in considerable detail:

Yet despite the ubiquity, and hence vast scale, of marriage migration, it has rarely been studied with the degree of attention it warrants. Perhaps because they regarded wives and their work as 'uneconomic', census officers categorized such migrations as 'casual'. In truth, they were anything but. Migration to a husband's household was a profound and permanent transition, for which girls not only in Bengal but all-over North India, were assiduously prepared from childhood. A young girl would be typically regarded as a temporary visitor in her father's home. Since her birth, then, she was an 'always-already' migrant. Both Hindu and Muslim brides, on arrival in their *shashur-bari* (in-laws' home) were expected to learn their duties and responsibilities as wives, mothers, daughters-in-law, and household workers. They had to adopt the ways and conduct (*niyomkanon*) of their husbands' 'lineages'. A young bride would be instructed in these duties by *shashuri* (mother-in-law) in an initiation no less intimidating than modern citizenship tests and in an acculturation process no less demanding. She could return to her father's house, but only at times preordained, such as the birth of her first child. If widowed, she would stay on in her late husband's home, but she would be treated as an 'inauspicious' person, with little authority or no autonomy. She could perhaps migrate again, as a pilgrim to a holy place, and many Bengali Hindu widows did end up in Banaras (Alexander et al., 2016, pp. 41-42).

SOCIAL CONTEXT

The social backdrop of the memoir is closely documented as witnessed by Sushmita Banerjee. The memoir opens with Banerjee's honest disclaimer, expounding that her work is not an indictment of any country or intended to slander any religion, community or group of people. However, her bitter criticism in this work is directed against those who engage in fanaticism or terrorism in the name of religion, who cause communal differences in the name of religion, who seize the liberty of women and push them into the darkness of their harems, who easily murder and annihilate others or engage in mass killing. She mentions that her open crusade is not against religion but religious superstitions and fundamentalism.

She witnesses in Afghanistan, a distorted practice of Islam religion. She also wishes to warn that those who migrated from India to Afghanistan, suffer unbearable pain in life and may never return to India. She would not have been able to return if she did not have reckless courage and patience. She is fondly grateful to the few benevolent individuals who help her to combat her challenges. According to her, torturing women, neglecting children and ignoring senior citizens are the quintessential situation of the people of that country. She had been imprisoned there for eight long years. She eventually escapes to Pakistan. Her humiliation by the Indian Embassy in Pakistan has been duly recorded in her writing. (Banerjee, 1997, p. 8) In an economy of globalisation within a neoliberal frame, diaspora and cultural hybridity have set in motion hybridized social structures. Sushmita Banerjee is the by-product of such a complex social structure that is already highly conservative, and the Taliban mandates further aggravate the condition for Banerjee.

LITERATURE REVIEW

According to Foucault, the present epoch will perhaps be "the epoch of space" (Foucault, 1994, p. 1) which juxtaposes "the near and far, of the side-by-side, of the dispersed" (Foucault, 1994, p. 1). Foucault further proposes, "The space in which we live, which draws us out of ourselves, in which the erosion of our lives, our time and our history occurs, the space that claws and gnaws at us, is also a heterogeneous space. (Foucault, 1994, p. 3) This heterogeneity is determined by the binaries between private space and public space, between family space and social space, cultural space and useful space, and between the space of leisure and work. This bipolarity is conspicuously evident in Banerjee's transition from her parents' home in Kolkata, India to Sarana in Afghanistan. Kolkata is a metropolitan city and a melange of cultural interactions, religious ideologies and social approaches.

Foucault's notion of Heterotopia is relevant here. Heterotopia refers to real places like "counter-sites", simultaneously "representing, contesting, and inverting all other conventional sites" (Sudradjat, 2012, p. 32). For Banerjee this marital migration from Kolkata to Sarana is Heterotopia. Heterotopias can enable one to both confront illusions and create new illusions of the utopias we cannot have. One of the chief reasons which prompts Banerjee to regret arriving in Afghanistan was the lack of conformity to the existing geographies and socio-urban spaces that she was acclimatized within her homeland, Kolkata. Her illusion of the utopia of her in-laws' house has been disappointing for her. Banerjee, therefore, endeavours to reconstruct this lost urban space of Kolkata by developing several habits and practices that are contrary to the social conventions of Sarana but benefit the people, particularly the oppressed women in the vicinity. These urban practices include her desire to offer generous medical aid to those to need them and her charity with whatever scanty resources she possesses.

Foucault was convinced that heterotopias exist "in a society and give way to otherness, and otherness subsequently opens a door to plurality and heterogeneity" (Sudradjat, 2012, p. 32). Banerjee's upbringing in the urban space of Kolkata had given her enough mental and emotional resilience to accommodate the differences in cultural, social, and geographical changes in her life. Foucault describes heterotopia with verbs like 'mirror', 'reflect', 'represent', 'designate', 'speak about' all other sites, but at the same time 'suspend', 'neutralize', 'invert', 'contest' and 'contradict' those sites. He supports his thesis by offering a list of ideologies with a wide range of illustrations. (Johnson, 2016) Concerning migrants, heterotopia, third space and social conventions are the practices that migrants use and adapt to get acclimatized to a new environment, as is the case with Banerjee.

Banerjee must migrate as a result of her marriage despite parental resistance from Kolkata to Afghanistan. Her parents were against this matrimonial alliance, fearing that Banerjee's life could be engulfed by the atrocities of socio-cultural and religious differences. However, Banerjee was ready to embrace the new culture for the sake of her beloved, Janbaaz. At this point, understanding the history and the usual predicament of a migrant wife is relevant here.

It may be difficult to agree with demographers who support that 'in marriage migration females genuinely predominated in the past as they do in the present (Alexander et al., 2016, p. 41). Marriage, then, was in the migration of more final than most, but because of its submersion into the realm of 'culture', it has been seen as such. It is remarkably difficult to find the migrant wife in the historical record (Alexander et al., 2016, p. 42). Henri Lefebvre's maxim that 'social space' is produced through 'social practice'' encourages us to recognize that the social distance the migrant bride travelled was vast and that her experience as a migrant is worthy of research. (Idem.)

With such expectations in the backdrop, Banerjee migrates to Afghanistan in the hope of finding a family. However, over time this migration only leads to displacement, dispossession and consequent disappointment and frustration since she witnesses not only the erosion of territorial liberties under the Taliban governance but also the sudden and cruel disappearance of her freedom for an indefinite period. Even her husband moves away from her to India and seems to have abandoned her in Afghanistan. Banerjee states that crossing the threshold of a house for a woman in Afghanistan is very challenging. (Banerjee, 1997, p. 9). This threshold is determined by the existence of spaces and places that are differentiated as: "Our daily lives take place under established patterns of action within conventional places and spaces while migrants' lives take place within *places* and *spaces* of counter-sites (Kovačević & Malenica, 2021, p. 76). Her concerns about cultural differences and displacement, stemming from the difference in urban spaces begin to surface in Afghanistan when she states that she had never thought that would encounter such a dreadful reality (Banerjee, 1997, p. 10). The Soviet occupation of neighbouring Afghanistan allowed the military regime to exploit the Afghan security situation to gain domestic and foreign support.

As a migrant wife, Banerjee's hopes of finding her in-laws amicable and hospitable are replaced with apprehensions of continual hostility and violence she gradually faces. This fear is generated by the mental and social conditioning of her upbringing in Kolkata. She misses the vitality of the urban spaces that Kolkata afforded her. Vitality in urban space can be defined as "a safer, more desirable, and more attractive space which has the capacity for offering more choices for social activities as well as being a place for cultural exchanges" (Jalaladdini & Oktay, 2012, p. 665).

Transnationalism, defined as the process by which migrants forge and sustain multi-stranded relations and create transnational social fields, was described as a constant traversing of national boundaries by processes of communication and exchange, such as capital expansion, the Internet, and other telecommunications (Portes et al., 1999, p. 220). The only way Banerjee communicates with her family in Kolkata is by using audio cassettes which contain voice recordings of her family members. These she receives once in a blue moon and sends forth her recorded messages to her family even more rarely. The exchange of cassettes and her attempts to escape from Afghanistan is the only transnational activityshe engages in. This is Banerjee's attempt to resurrect the memories of the activities she engaged in within the territory of her homeland. It is the memory of this "remembered space" or "conceived space" that helps her to reinstate her identity in the light of her changing circumstances.

In contrast, much of the action of this memoir takes place in the suburbs of Afghanistan. Sarrimo rightly points out, "The word "suburb" has even become a metonymy in media discourses telling the "entire" story of deprived childhoods and marginalization" (Sarrimo, 2020, p. 56). Banerjee stays with her in-laws in Sarana, the capital of the province Paktita. Yet, the mode of living and livelihood is far from being modern; they are rather primitive and basic resources like food and medicines are often scarce.

THEORY AND ITS APPLICATION TO THE MEMOIR

When she first lands in Afghanistan in July 1988 from Kolkata, she travels with Janbaaz to the village, Sarana, which takes eighteen hours from the city of Kabul. Her resolute desire to meet her in-laws compels her to come to this place in West Asia where the darkness of medieval superstitions had not been dispelled. She wonders how she would find her in-laws and how would they find her as a Hindu Bengali woman (Banerjee, 1997, p. 9).

Amidst the isolation of being a lonely wife, separated from her husband, Janbaaz's audio cassettes would convey to Banerjee that he would come to her as soon as the roads were opened after the war. He knows that she never receives any news about the crisis in the country and so she would have to believe him. These cassettes are the only companion to her life as a lone suffering prisoner (Banerjee, 1997, p. 15). Before the wedding, she never had much time or opportunity to know Janbaaz. They would stealthily meet once a week within a very limited time since Banerjee knew that her parents would object to the relationship.

URBAN SPACE IN THE MEMOIR

Banerjee's sense of displacement looms large when she points out that she misses her homeland, particularly Kolkata, walking through the crowded streets, having savouries in Curzon Park, being drenched to the skin in the rain, day-dreaming about gloomy days and afternoons shopping at Park Street or Grand Arcade. She misses these memories (Banerjee, 1997, p. 17) Here, Kolkata, as an urban space assumes the role of a character. Henri Lefebvre radically states that "people who use the city – who live, trade, walk there – create it themselves, both at the mental and material levels. The city, he believes, serves only as a starting point triggering spatial situations which transform and create the diversity we need so much" (Nadolny, 2015, p. 33). Park Street and Grand Arcade are highly frequented urban public spaces that promote the exchange of several cultures and social practices. Though Kolkata may have afforded her sufficient cultural diversity, the hope that the cultural diversity of Afghanistan would bring her greater positive experiences, drove Banerjee to explore the spatial dimensions of another country. However, upon her arrival in the country, she notices that the earthen houses in rural Afghanistan are enclosed by enormously high walls projecting the insular nature of some people in the country.

People in Banerjee's new household in Afghanistan call her Sahib Kamal; her original name also becomes the memory of a past album six years old. It is observed, "Migrants tend to arrive in new places with baggage: both in the physical sense of possessions or belongings, but also the less tangible matter of beliefs, traditions, customs, behaviours and values. This can have consequences for the ways in which others may or may not make migrants feel 'at home' or arrive in a new place" (McLeod, 2011, pp. 211-212).

In his seminal work *La Production de l'espace* (1974) Lefebvre proposed that space is a socially constructed multi-dimensional entity. According to him, space has three dimensions. The first dimension is the 'physical' spaces of daily life in a society, such as workplaces, places of leisure and private space. The second facet of space represents a conceptualized space, as space is denoted in symbolic systems. The third dimension of space is representational space, also known as lived space, which can be owned and altered (Lefebvre, 2007, p. 39). Building on this theory, distinguished political geographer and urban planner, Edward Soja further categorized them as first space, second space and third space. In his ground-breaking work, Soja proposed a 'third space' as a place to generate counter spaces (Soja, 1989, p. 71). Noted economic geographer, David Harvey established the relationship between urban space and power (Harvey, 2003, p. 5).

The dichotomy between the public and private space has attracted plenty of debates within gender dynamics since it relates closely but challengingly to dissimilarities and partitions between women and men. The projection of the public and private space as related by the memoir is supported by the prevalent social practices of the local inhabitants of the urban spaces of Paktita province. As a result, this urban space becomes more of social space through these social practices as mentioned above (Lefebvre, 2007, p. 15). Social (mal)practices like domestic violence, gender inequality and casteism (which Banerjee braved for eight years) are exercised within the private space of her household but are endorsed by male patriarchy throughout the society in the country, particularly by the people who are under the surveillance and control of the Taliban. The encroachment of spaces by the Taliban, the coalition of a new government and the new socio-political diktats caused an inevitable infringement of Banerjee's personal space and individual rights along with the other inhabitants of the country.

Harvey perceives the dynamic between the public and private space as an arena of constant change. He points out, "Societies change and grow, they are transformed from within and adapt to pressures and influences from without" (Harvey, 1990, p. 419). Similarly, when Banerjee arrives in Afghanistan, she witnesses the onslaught of social and religious conventions by external agencies like the Taliban and the Russian armed forces. The urban space of Sarana had to adapt to new pressures just like Banerjee was trying to adapt to the societal pressures within and without her household.

Banerjee's memoir is replete with instances of domestic violence inflicted upon the protagonist by her in-laws. In the absence of Janbaaz, his brothers torture her and deprive her of food and sleep. They even beat her like brutes. They are inhuman and they treat her like a slave. Sushmita Banerjee recalls that most women are like slaves in this country and the entire country is like a prison. She had never imagined that her life would be fraught with so much suffering and she would never see the free sky again (Banerjee, 1997, p. 16). Through her ruminations, she brings out the crucial question of an individual's fundamental rights and the law. Spatial laws refer to:

'if-then' laws that say that if we place an object here or there within a spatial system then certain predictable consequences follow for the ambient spatial configuration. Such effects are quite independent of human will or intention but can be used by human beings to achieve spatial and indeed social effects. Human beings are bound by these laws because they form a system of possibilities and limits within which they evolve their spatial strategies. But human agents decide independently what their strategies should be. Like language, the laws are then at once a constraining framework and a system of possibilities to be exploited by individuals (Hillier, A Theory of the City as Object or, How Spatial Laws Mediate the Social Construction of Urban Space , 2001).

Banerjee elaborates in the preface to her book and the subsequent chapters that following such spatial laws resulted in torturing women, neglecting children and ignoring the senior citizens in the hands of the Taliban or the Mujahids who wanted to perpetuate Islamic rule in the country (Banerjee, 1997, p. 8). Moreover, during Ramzan, Asam Uncle, the brother of her father-in-law insists that she must fast and humiliates her for being a Hindu and denigrates Janbaaz for marrying a Hindu "Qafir" which means an atheist (Banerjee, 1997, p. 55). Banerjee proclaims that she does not understand the differences in religion. For her, love for mankind is the best religion. Migration and translocality aid creating transient urban spaces. Moreover, migrants "live, move, interact and communicate across contiguous or distant physical spaces; as a result, they shape distinct social spaces and contribute to social change" (Bork-Hüffer, 2016, p. 124). Banerjee also contributes to such a social change.

Banerjee meets a woman called Kakoli Roy from North Kolkata, currently living in Afghanistan. The latter discreetly travels ten miles with her relative to share the tale of her agony with Banerjee and asks her to convey a message to her family. She knows that Banerjee would soon be able to escape from the place. So, she wants Sushmita to tell Kakoli's father in Kolkata that her (Kakoli's) husband's brother stays in Kolkata; if he gets Kakoli's brother-in-law in Kolkata arrested, Kakoli's in-laws would be forced to release her. Her brother-in-law stays close to the locality in which her father stays (Banerjee, 1997, p. 17).

Her family members hold her almost as a hostage. Like Banerjee, Kakoli too had felt attracted to Nawab when he had come to Kolkata, married him against the wishes of her family and eloped with him to Afghanistan in March 1986. She arrived in Kabul amid war, violence and corpses lying on the roads and was received coldly in Nawab's house: nobody was prepared to accept a foreign wife for Nawab. An elderly lady who seemed the most infuriated on seeing her was Nawab's wife with whom he was married for the past ten years. On learning about Kakoli, Banerjee observes that destiny has brought the two women (Kakoli and Banerjee) to a strange point of circumstances. Their point of irony is different but the centre is very similar (Banerjee, 1997, p. 23). Kakoli was further told to share the bed with Nawab and his wife, Arana. She was heartbroken with shame and embarrassment. She had only two conjugal nights with her husband in Delhi on her way to Kabul after which her head reeled with the shock and disappointment of the barbaric polygamy that she witnessed. The next night Nawab lay down in his bed, flanked by his wives Arana and Kakoli on either side of him. Kakoli found this so disgusting that she turned away and slept while Nawab slept with Arana. Kakoli's woes do not end with this humiliation inflicted upon her in her household by her in-laws.

This spatial violation of the two women, Arana and Kakoli subjects them to tremendous emotional oppression. While each wife is alarmed to learn about her co-wife, Arana accepts the change easily after her brief altercation with her husband. Kakoli soon realizes that Residents of a locale raise boundaries through the control of their territories as a response to their emotions, requirements and their technical diligence or capacity. Therefore, territorial boundaries represent the characteristics of residents. Therefore, spatial justice is conspicuously usurped and the sudden loss of social security (that is received through rights exclusively from one's husband) is bitterly experienced by Kakoli (Banerjee, 1997, p. 24).

Being at grips with immigrant anxieties and material constraints in the host society, the diasporic patriarchy, as represented by her in-laws, endeavours to impose gender norms of the host country and domestic violence and seclusion on women under its domain. They seek to control and restrict their movements during every moment of their life and expect unquestioned compliance of the same. The focus of the memoir shifts to the kind of violence that occurs in the private sphere or within the confines of the household, often known as 'domestic' violence. Even though the phrase domestic violence incorporates a violent demeanour towards children, women, elders and those who are ailing, feeble or incapable of defending themselves, this memoir restricts itself to domestic violence against the female gender. It projects how among the many expressions of violence; domestic violence is one of the most severe: it occurs in a seemingly secure ambience and is inflicted by someone who is expected to be a protector.

Both Kakoli and Banerjee, fall prey to violence inflicted by the male members of their own family who are their in-laws. In most cases, these are instances of physical violence. For example, Banerjee is reluctant to offer medical care to someone in the neighbourhood who requires saline. This is because she would have to return home alone in the late evening and thereby garner the unwarranted attention of the Taliban who forbid women from moving alone in the streets. However, her brother-in-law who urges her to do so but refuses to accompany her or help her, punches her in the face and Banerjee bleeds and groans in pain. (Banerjee, 1997, p. 119) It is the sheer inclemency of such psyche of those in the family that forces her to lose faith in the ties of her family. Like the immigrant women Kakoli and Banerjee, the domicile women of Afghanistan, as represented by Banerjee's extended family, Gulguti, Pabloo Chachi and Guncha—are continually oppressed by the men of the house or the Taliban. Negative energy for women pervades not only in the household but becomes part of the teleology affecting all those who are tortured to varying degrees. Lefebvre justifies this through the ideas of Hoyle:

Hoyle looks upon space as the product of energy. Energy cannot, therefore, be compared to content filling an empty container. Causalism and teleology inevitably shot through with metaphysical abstraction, are both ruled out. The universe is seen as offering a multiplicity of particular spaces, yet this diversity is accounted for by a unitary theory, namely cosmology (Lefebvre, 2007, p. 13).

According to Soja, space is generally an outcome of urban life. (Soja, 1989, p. 72) The way in which outdoor and indoor spaces are built can impact behavioural diversity among their occupants. This is evident in the memoir when Banerjee observes the unusual architectural practices of the houses near the city of Ghazni were enclosed within the high walls (Banerjee, 1997, p. 27). The settlement seems comparable to the insular social and cultural psyche of the people who were not open to new ideas. A newly wedded bride is welcomed by sprinkling sugar upon her and bullets are fired into the air. This latter practice startles Banerjee but she was assured that since firecrackers are not available, gunshots are used for the celebration. Banerjee wishes if any of those bullets had shot her, she would have been spared from facing the terrible situations she later underwent (Banerjee, 1997, p. 27). However, celebrating with gunshots may also lead to catastrophic accidents. During a wedding, gunshots are fired into the air and during one such firing, the groom fired a bullet that lands back, lodges into his head and kills him instantly. These practices seem eccentric to Banerjee and reinstate her predicament of alienation in the host country.

Banerjee's sense of displacement and dispossession are evident when she feels that being an educated woman in a civilized world, she was gradually adapting to the changes around her. She is completely severed from the awareness of the occurrences of the outside world. Secondly, she loses her self-esteem. In the absence of newspapers, TV or radio, she claims to have lost the sense of time (Banerjee, 1997, p. 28). Durkheim has pointed out that space and time are social constructs. In the absence of any personal fulfilment, Banerjee could not find any liberty in controlling her personal space and time. At the age of thirty-one Banerjee reserves a great deal of motivation to mingle with all the members of her in-law's family. She begins to learn their language. Language contains an ideological baggage (Whorf, 1956, p. 112). While she does so, it is ironic that Janbaaz is made to separate from his family because he has married a foreigner like Banerjee. Thirdly, she bitterly observes that while the children of her country, India, are trained to write at a young age, those of Kabul grow up with guns in their hands (Banerjee, 1997, p. 28). A news report mentions that in the year 2000,

Sources of the UN have estimated that over 95 per cent of Afghan children do not go to school, which depicts the total collapse of the education system in the war-ravaged country. According to reports as a result of 21 years of war, an entire generation of Afghan children is growing up without education." (News Reports from Afghanistan, 2001)

Diaspora unlocks new cultural territories beyond the borders of one's homeland and host land (Kenny, 2013, p. 31). As a part of such a diaspora, Banerjee shifts the focus from the process of migration to the endeavours that enterprising migrants like her from abroad engage in and the types of culture they create. Banerjee tries to offer amateur but genuine medical aid to women who are deprived of basic healthcare products and medical attention. For instance, to consult a doctor one needed to travel to Mushkhel, where there were no professional doctors but quacks. Several weeks after Banerjee reaches Sarana, she cannot eat and feels nauseous and giddy. Some members of her in-laws undertake to accompany her on her dangerous journey to Mushkhel. Everybody is frightened of going to Mushkhel from Sherekala (Banerjee's village) as there lay huge open ground between these two places which was overseen by Russian helicopters. At Mushkhel, a forty-year-old doctor in a Khan's white dress diagnosed Banerjee with jaundice but prescribed calcium and vitamin tablets. This makes her realize how imperative the need for medical help is in the locality. There were no lady doctors in the vicinity for a vast stretch of Sarana. There were only quacks who gave the same prescription for dental problems and endometriosis. In the face of terror, oppression and superstition, Banerjee's urban upbringing prompts her to enkindle the light of knowledge. A long time, after her strange experience in Mushkhel she sets up a medicine store and altruistically gives medical help to many women day after day. This was against the social conventions of her immediate locality (Banerjee, 1997, p. 29). However, following the urge to create her "third space," she starts working as a health worker in Paktika and had been observing the lives of the people within this urban space.

Human territoriality assumes a colossal magnitude in the memoir. Dr. Najibullah's soldiers came in a Russian helicopter and dropped bombs on the villages. So, nobody lights up their houses at night, even if they want to celebrate an occasion. The nation's land is full of land mines. At the end of 1989, Janbaaz's uncle, Gafar Khan, along with his son, was travelling in a lorry illegally to Angurhata, near the border of Pakistan. Angurhata was in the possession of the Russians and Najibullah. Later Mujahids conquered and seized possession of the place. At this time, the lorry ran over a mine. The news came home, and grief overtook the bereaved family. The family members set off for that place and happily returned the next morning with Gafar and Ammajan. Nobody thought that they would return safely. Such death traps are spread out everywhere, some belonging to the Russians and others to the Mujahids (Banerjee, 1997, pp. 28-29). Banerjee writes that usually, in a civilized country, people are unarmed but here every household has arms. Mines are planted everywhere. The ambience of terror becomes more pronounced when Banerjee comments that cannons can be heard firing all night. The air is thick with the smell of ammunition. The night of darkness, terror, war and distrust never seems to end. (Banerjee, 1997, p. 29)

Moreover, Banerjee observes the prevalence of some unique practices in society. If a wife dies, it is very unfortunate as marrying a woman costs a man twenty thousand Afghanis and if she has a child with him before their wedding then the man must pay another twenty thousand Afghanis to the bride's family. An Afghan man never divorces his wife, but practises polygamy for want of a child, if he is childless. Banerjee recalls that in India the bride's family pays the groom's family a hefty dowry and yet there is no assurance that the bride will not be abandoned or divorced by the husband. She is unable to decide which country has a better practice and leaves this to the discretion of the reader. Moreover, the identity of a woman in Afghanistan is that of a companion, cook and child producing-machine—three in one (Banerjee, 1997, p. 33). If a woman cannot bear children in Afghanistan, then she would have to share her husband with a co-wife who can bear children. Thus, a woman has no individual identity of her own nor can she exercise any freedom in her decisions or actions. It has been observed that:

The prospect of sustainable development is like a utopia that seeks to inhabit the planet otherwise, in the hope of developing a new society, more responsible, accountable and inclusive. As an urban model, the sustainable city seeks to go back and restore the role of the city as a place to live and not as an area to stack people. The principles of this model are about interaction and interdependence (Kettaf & Moscarelli, 2010, p. 230).

However, the above-mentioned facts about the social system of Afghanistan are a flagrant contradiction of this paradigm.

The trust in women's sense of integrity is also very low: For instance, when Banerjee and Janbaaz were going to visit their ailing relative, Gulguti, in Pakistan, it is assumed that Banerjee would never return but escape to India from there. Janbaaz's uncle challenges Banerjee that if she returns without escaping to India, then he would offer his wife as a gift to Janbaaz. Banerjee finds such poor humour disgusting and embarrassing (Banerjee, 1997, p. 37). One's wife is treated like a lifeless property instead of a self-willed individual. This is a threat to both spatial as well as social security of a woman.

Bringing up the issue of communal unrest and violence, the protagonist points out that the riots in India in 1992 during the Babri Masjid dispute in Ayodhya caused the Hindu and Muslim fanatics of both religions to indulge in bitter clashes. But the communal riots are vain and futile, and man will never be free of such hypocrisy (Banerjee, 1997, p. 56). Being continually oppressed by her family and the Taliban for proselytising her, Banerjee would often wonder if she could ever escape from the primitive nation, driven by male chauvinists and fundamentalists and return to the individualistic nation of her own (Banerjee, 1997, p. 60). It has been rightly remarked:

'Talibanization,' the destabilizing export of Afghan-style radical Islam, maybe a new term in the American political... lexicon. But in Central and South Asia, the repercussions of the super strict Taliban rule of Afghanistan have been widely felt... behaviour of Afghanistan's new leaders is no longer a local affair. More and more, chaos in Afghanistan is seeping through its porous borders. The ongoing civil war has polarized the region, with Pakistan and Saudi Arabia backing the Taliban regime while Iran, Russia, India, and four former Soviet Central Asian republics support the opposition Northern Alliance. The confrontation is producing enormous economic disruption throughout the area, as the Afghan warlords' dependence on smuggling and drug trafficking grows insatiable (Rashid, 1999, p. 22).

Within such a backdrop, "traditionally-gendered domestic relationships have been central" (Formes, 2005, p. 467) to the life of the protagonist. Much of the religious fanaticism projected by the Taliban is a misinterpretation of the religion of Islam. For instance, according to Banerjee, Islam does not propound that if a man does not offer his prayers or grow a beard, he should be beaten or a woman cannot survive independently or run her own business (Banerjee, 1997, p. 65). The Taliban impose severe restrictions upon women claiming that it is prescribed in Islam. A news report mentions: "Since the Taliban militia captured the capital of Afghanistan in September of last year, women and girls have been severely oppressed. Women are barred from work, school, and even walking the streets, without a male relative. Women are also forced to wear head-to-toe covering (including mesh over the eyes and some have been stoned to death" (Feminist Majority and Avia, 1997, p. 4). They torture women: they grab hold of women in the streets and even beat them. They stare at Banerjee as she is in a *Salwar Kameez* and not in an Afghani *Ghaghra* as is the custom for women to wear. (Banerjee, 1997, p. 86) Fear and terror percolate everywhere but she does not lose hope of a possible escape.

The modern urban social structure is founded on a multifaceted amalgamation of schemes of penalty, order, and security. Researchers, drawing from Foucault's observation of the art and justification of authority, have discovered how urban social orders are increasingly built on the "governance of space rather than on the discipline of offenders or the punishment of offences" (Merry, 2001, p. 16). In this context it has been aptly pointed out:

The capture of Kabul by the forces of the Taliban (Islamic student) movement on 26 September 1996 quickly realigned political forces within both Afghanistan and the region. The Taliban's repressive policies, especially against women, attracted international media attention for the first time, now that they were carried out in the capital city.' Their brutal public castration and execution of Afghanistan's last communist president, Najibullah, who since his downfall in April 1992 had lived in the sanctuary of the Kabul UN office, consolidated their brutal image, especially since Najibullah's past responsibility for torture and executions had faded, at least in the memory of non-Afghans. The Taliban's restrictive policies played a role in preventing states from recognizing them as the new government of Afghanistan, despite their control of the capital and most of the country's territory and population (Rubin & R., 1997, p. 283).

It can be justly derived that: "Afghanistan and neighbouring states are finding it hard to challenge the influence of non-state actors that threaten the traditional order and stability of the nation-state." (Akhtar, 2008, p. 50) As a result of globalization, "more Indians have migrated to foreign lands in the past sixty years than in the 6000 years before that. But in the last six years they have been returning home in spirit and body" (Rajghatta, 2006- 2007, p. 116).

CONCLUSION

After making several attempts to escape from Afghanistan, Sushmita Banerjee finally reaches the Indian Embassy in Pakistan. However, the Indian Officer only makes her an indecent and offensive proposal in return for the favour of granting permission to cross the border. This is due to the supreme authority over border security of a territory that is granted to each nation:

In international law, the notion of territory is of key concern, for within its national territory each state is supreme. Therefore, subject to certain special rules (e.g., concerning diplomats and responsibilities under certain international norms and expressly accepted treaties, including the United Nations Charter), each nation has complete control over persons, things, and events within its territory (Taubenfeld, 1969, p. 1).

It is only after many more attempts that she finally reaches India and subsequently to her city Kolkata safely after suffering a great deal of trauma and agony. She returns safely to India from Afghanistan only after eight long years of suffering and struggle. The memoir, *Kabuliwalar Bangali Bou*, ends at this point on a note of relief from the continuous threat to her life and security. However, in reality, a few years later, she goes to Afghanistan with her husband and is summarily shot dead in Paktita by the Taliban militants who avenge her neglect and disobedience of their diktats. Sushmita Banerjee is still remembered far and wide for her courage and refusal to accept the atrocities she has once been compelled to face. The memoir helps to understand the dire predicament of Afghan women under the Taliban by casting a political and sociological perspective to highlight the patriarchal bent of gender and social alliances, deeply rooted in Afghanistan's ethnic and traditional society. The work demonstrates the progression of spatial reorganization and the anxieties stemming from the rigidity and resilience of human territoriality that the protagonist experiences in a new urban space.

REFERENCES

Akhtar, N. (2008). Pakistan, Afghanistan, and the Taliban. *International Journal on World Peace*, *25*(4), 49–73. https://www.jstor.org/stable/20752859

Alexander, C., Chatterji, J., & Jalais, A. (2016). *The Bengal Diaspora: Rethinking Muslim Migration*. Routledge.

Banerjee, S. (1997). *Kabuliwalar Bangali Bou*. Bhasha O Sahitya.

Barnett, R. R. (1997). Women and pipelines: Afghanistan's proxy wars. *Asia and the Pacific, 73*(2), 283-296. https://www.jstor.org/stable/2623829

Beebeejaun, Y. (2017). Gender, Urban Space, and the Right to Everyday Life. *Journal of Urban Affairs*, *39*(3), 323–334. doi:10.1080/07352166.2016.1255526

Bork-Hüffer, T. (2016). Migrants' agency and the making of transient urban spaces. *Population Space and Place*, *22*(2), 124–127. doi:10.1002/psp.1891

Boulaich, K. (2019). The silent revolution of public spaces in Afghanistan. Clean and Green Cities (CGC) Programme-United Nations Human Settlements Programme (UN-Habitat).

Butler, J. (1990). *Gender trouble: Feminism and the subversion of identity*. Routledge.

Chiesa, L. (2016). *Space as Storyteller: Spatial Jumps in Architecture, Critical Theory, and Literature*. Northwestern University Press. doi:10.2307/j.ctv47w5px

Feminist Majority and Avia. (1997, October). Afghanistan. *Off Our Backs, 27*(9), 4.

Formes, M. (2005). Post-colonial domesticity amid diaspora: Home and family in the lives of two English sisters from India. *Journal of Social History: Kith and Kin: Interpersonal Relationships and Cultural Practices, 39*(2), 467–482. doi:10.1353/jsh.2005.0134

Foucault, M. (1994). Des espaces autres [1967/1984]. In Dits et Øcrits. 1954–1988 (Vol. 4, pp. 752–762). Gallimard.

Gender and International Migration. (n.d.). Retrieved from United Nations: https://sitreport.unescapsdd.org/gender-and-international-migration

Haan, A. (2000). Migrants, Livelihoods and Rights. The relevance of Migration in Development Policies, Social Development, Working Paper No.-4.

Harvey, D. (2003). *The new imperialism*. Oxford University Press. doi:10.1093/oso/9780199264315.001.0001

Hillier, B. (2001). A Theory of the City as Object or, How Spatial Laws Mediate the Social Construction of Urban Space. Proceedings: *3rd International Space Syntax Symposium*, (p. 2). Atlanta.

Johnson, P. (2016). *Brief history of the concept of heterotopia (revised)*. http://www.heterotopiastudies.com

Kenny, K. (2013). *Diaspora: A very short introduction*. Oxford University Press. doi:10.1093/actrade/9780199858583.001.0001

Kettaf, F., & Moscarelli, F. (2010). Understanding public space concepts as key elements of sustainable urban design. *Sustainable Architecture and Urban Development, 3*, 229–244.

Kovačević, V., & Malenica, K. (2021). Heterotopia and postmodern community in the context of migration and relationship towards migrants. *Italian Sociological Review, 11*(1), 63–86. doi:10.13136/isr.v11i1.415

Lefebvre, H. (1974). La production de l'espace. *Anthropos*.

Lefebvre, H. (2007). *The production of space* (D. Nicholson-Smith, Trans.). Blackwell Publishing.

livemint. (2013, September 5). *Indian writer Sushmita Banerjee shot dead in Afghanistan*. Retrieved from livemint: https://www.livemint.com/Politics/VjV6CNEl5wptQRgdTS9fGP/Indian-writer-Sushmita-Banerjee-shot-dead-in-Afghanistan.html

McLeod, J. (2011). *Beginning postcolonialism*. Viva Books.

Merry, S. E. (2001). Spatial governmentality and the new urban social order: Controlling gender violence through law. *American Anthropologist, 103*(1), 16–29. doi:10.1525/aa.2001.103.1.16

Nadolny, A. (2015). Henri Lefebvre's concept of urban space in the context of preferences of the creative class in a modern city. *Quaestiones Geographicae, 34*(2), 29–34. doi:10.1515/quageo-2015-0012

News Reports from Afghanistan. (2001, November). *Images of sexuality and reproduction: services: Meeting women's needs*. Retrieved January 13, 2020, from https://www.jstor.org/stable/3776142

Portes, L. E., & Landolt, P. A. (1999). The study of transnationalism: Pitfalls and promise of an emergent research field. *Ethnic and Racial Studies, 22*(2), 217–237. doi:10.1080/014198799329468

Pourya Asl, M. (Ed.). (2022). *Gender, place, and identity of South Asian women*. IGI Global. doi:10.4018/978-1-6684-3626-4

PTI. (2013, September 6). *Indian author Sushmita Banerjee, who wrote about her dramatic escape from Taliban shot dead in Afghanistan*. Retrieved from India Today: https://www.indiatoday.in/world/rest-of-the-world/story/sushmita-banerjee-shot-dead-in-afghanistan-escape-from-taliban-book-210014-2013-09-04

Rajghatta, C. (2006-2007). Across the black waters. *India International Centre Quarterly, 33*(3/4), 116–127.

Rashid, A. (1999). The Taliban: Exporting extremism. *Foreign Affairs, 78*(6), 22–35. doi:10.2307/20049530

Rubin, & R., B. (1997). Women and pipelines: Afghanistan's proxy wars. *Asia and the Pacific, 73*(2), 283-296.

Sarrimo, C. (2020). Mapping a postmodern dystopia: Hassan Loo Sattarvandi's construction of a Swedish suburb. In K. Malmio & K. Kurikka (Eds.), *Contemporary Nordic literature and spatiality*. Palgrave Macmillan. doi:10.1007/978-3-030-23353-2_3

Soja, E. W. (1989). *Postmodern geographies: The reassertion of space in critical social theory*. Verso.

Sudradjat, I. (2012). Foucault, the other spaces, and human behaviour. *Procedia: Social and Behavioral Sciences, 36*, 29. doi:10.1016/j.sbspro.2012.03.004

Taubenfeld, H. J. (1969). *Outer space: The "territorial" limits of nations-Article 9*. Fordham University Press. https://ir.lawnet.fordham.edu/flr/vol38/iss1/9

Versey, F. (2021, August 18). *Essay: She couldn't escape the Taliban - On Sushmita Banerjee, author of A Kabuliwala's Bengali Wife*. Retrieved from Hindustan Times: https://www.hindustantimes.com/books/essayshe-couldn-t-escape-the-taliban-on-sushmita-banerjee-author-of-a-kabuliwala-s-bengali-wife-101629314082282.html

Whorf, B. L. (1956). *Language, thought and reality* (J. B. Corroll, Ed.). MIT Press.

Wrede, T. (2015, Spring). Introduction to special issue--Theorizing space and gender in the 21st century. *Rocky Mountain Review, 69*(1), 10-17. https://www.jstor.org/stable/24372860

Section 3
Ethnographic Representations of Gendered Geographies and Geographies of Gender

The subject matter of essays in this section is women's active participation and agency in reclaiming their right to the city in countries like Iran, India, Bangladesh, and Egypt. Issues that are discussed in the four ethnographic studies in this section include women's alliance and solidarity across borders, women's agency in resisting against spatial injustice and gender inequality, women's active opposition to patriarchy, and women's active participation in re-designing urban spaces with the aim of reasserting their identities and subjectivities.

Chapter 10
Transnational Urban Solidarities:
A Political-Geographical Study of Contemporary Iranian Feminists' Activism

Maryam Lashkari
York University, Canada

ABSTRACT

In theorizing solidarity among women, feminist scholars often ask what is it that can unite women in their fight against misogynistic social, cultural, and political structures, without reinforcing a victimized discourse and subjectivity. This chapter addresses the question by examining solidarities among Iranian feminist and women's activists in light of the existing dynamics between urban and virtual spaces. To this end, the study examines eye-witness accounts obtained from semi-structured interviews with activists, scholars, and policymakers, and conducts a content analysis of organizations' websites, journals, and documents. The findings indicate that feminist solidarities are moving across geographical scales ranging from the body, neighborhoods, cities, and beyond nation-state borders. Furthermore, although virtual spaces have provided significant tools for shaping feminist solidarities for Iranians, platform biases and authoritarian interventions have posed challenges against feminist activities and agendas.

DOI: 10.4018/978-1-6684-6650-6.ch010

INTRODUCTION

The economic, political and military conditions in the Middle East are rapidly changing. Perpetuated conditions of war, political contestation between neighbouring countries, state authoritarianism, and superpowers' interventionist policies have significantly impacted civilians' lives in the region. Women are among those who experience state and geopolitical violence in various ways. The imposition of compulsory hijab on Iranian women since the 1979 Islamic Revolution, sexual assault against Yazidi women by ISIS, and prosecution and imprisonment of feminist activists across countries of the region have demonstrated how women's demands and bodies have become a domain for ideological and political contestation by ruling elites. In the face of hostility against feminism, Iranian activists, among other feminists in the region, have utilized virtual and urban spaces to claim their rights and agencies and built solidarities based on shared lived experiences and mutual resources and strengths.

Drawing on feminist scholars' engagement with the notion of solidarity (Hooks, 1986; Butler, 2004; Butler, 2016; Yuval-Davis, 2016), this chapter adopts a geographical lens to argue that Iranian feminist solidarities have increasingly taken a transnational and multi-scalar characteristic. Two case studies have been selected to demonstrate varieties of strategies and tactics that are employed by activists to respond to gendered discrimination such as denying the right to one's body, sexual harassment in public space, and state's gendered violence. First, it will be argued that rather than building solidarity based on an essentialist and objectified definition of "oppressed woman"-i.e. the social construction of the category of woman according to which to be a woman, by definition, is to be in an oppressed situation (Butler, 2004)- feminist solidarities are articulated through mutual strengths, resources and values. Secondly, it will be shown that feminist solidarities go beyond racial and national divisions and identities, and instead use mutual living experiences as a source for building strategies and defining goals in fighting against gendered violence. This is made possible through a conscious understanding of the potentials and challenges that are associated with the physical and virtual space. Thirdly, in addition to crossing national boundaries, the scale of feminist solidarity ranges and moves between individual bodies to the neighbourhood and the city and beyond nation-state boundaries. By focusing on transnational and multi-scalar aspects of feminist activism, this study contributes to theoretical literature that put the space at the centre of feminist practices (Amir-Ebrahimi, 2006; Arjmand, 2016; Asl, 2022; Bagheri, 2014; Fariman, 2022; Golabi, 2022; Khatam, 2009; Ooryad, 2020; Mokhles & Sunikka-Blank 2022; Shahrokni, 2014; Shahrokni, 2019; Shaban, 2021). Spatial practices adopted by women can overcome racial and ethnic divides by relying on localized tactics and resources to lay claim to space. Moreover, as will be shown in the subsequent sections, online space has further reinforced connections across geographical boundaries and has assisted women to think and act collectively to fight against various forms of gendered violence and discrimination.

Although virtual and urban spaces are used creatively and effectively by feminist activists, over the past decade scholars have shown how "social media platforms have gone from being praised as 'liberation technologies' to being lambasted as tools of repression", across the Middle East (Leber & Abrahams, 2021). Censorships, content moderation and manipulation, and cyberbullying by state and non-state actors and users are some of the tactics that have negatively affected emancipatory features of social media. "Networked authoritarianism" (Mackinnon, 2010) and "digital orientalism" (Alimardani & Elswah, 2021) exemplify some of the obstacles faced by Iranian feminists whose activities are more focused on online platforms. In the face of accelerated state's restrictive policies on cyberspace and social media companies' inabilities in addressing those issues, feminist activists across geographies will benefit much from continuing to bridge the gap between virtual and the "real" urban space.

LITERATURE REVIEW

Feminist Solidarity and Geographical Perspectives

Feminist scholars have previously theorized solidarity by examining transnational pedagogic models, political commitments, and common interests and oppressions (Rahbari et al., 2021). Yuval-Davis (2016) uses the notion of transversal politics as a form of "cosmopolitan dialogical politics" in which participants while being engaged with "other" belongings to collectivities across borders and boundaries, do not act as representatives of identity categories (p. 12). She explains the strengths of such forms of solidarities lie in the construction of "common epistemological understandings of particular political situations". In this sense, transversal politics is different from "rainbow coalitions" which are built upon a set of political strategies and actions rather than a specified, common value system. Moreover, the trust that is formed based on shared values is what differentiates it from the Habermasian notion of deliberative democracy where individuals disregard their socio-economic differences and subjectivities to engage in public affairs. Hooks (1986) cautions against a form of feminist solidarity that is shaped around collective victimization and common oppression. Instead, she suggests feminist movements should encourage solidarity that is built upon mutual strengths and resources. She remarks that the failure of the global sisterhood movement in the 1970s was due to assuming universal oppression directed against all women led by white bourgeois feminism (Naghibi, 2007). Similar to Yuval-Davis, she argues to experience solidarity, there must be a community of shared interests, goals and beliefs that "requires sustained, ongoing commitment" (Hook, 1986, p. 64).

Judith Butler (2004) notes feminist discourse has often mistakenly relied on the category of women as "a universal presupposition of cultural experiences" (p. 523). Therefore in their effort to combat the invisibility of women as a subject, feminists run the risk of rendering visible a category that may or may not be representative of lived experiences of women. She argues there is no unifying term to cover "all" forms of dispossession that could link minority politics, nor there should be one. What is necessary, she writes is that "those engaged in such coalitional efforts be actively involved in thinking through the category of the "minority" as it crosses the lines that divide citizen from non-citizen" (Butler, 2016, p. 147). As such, she advocates for "coalitions" that are not based on subject position or reconciling differences of those positions, rather they should be built upon overlapping aims and strategies.

While there is an overwhelming focus on successful cases of feminist solidarity works across the globe, feminist scholars have highlighted potential risks and threats in specific historical and geographical junctures that negatively affected efforts for achieving gender equality and justice. Nima Naghibi (2007) refers to the case of the feminist movement in the early days of the 1979 revolution in Iran and argues that the movement was defeated due to a distorted perspective of universal sisterhood which drew upon the binary of Western versus anti-imperialist discourse. She argues that interventions of feminists from Western societies, advocating for what they perceived as an anti-imperialist sisterhood were hijacked and appropriated by revolutionary forces to suppress the Iranian women's movement against religious dogmatism. This misguided understanding of global sisterhood, she notes, assisted ruling elites to portray feminism as a Western phenomenon and counter-revolutionary for pushing their political and anti-Western agenda. Under such conditions, "Iranian feminist activists were thus forced to choose between the two sides of a false binary: the West and Iran" (p. 101). To overcome dichotomies that are informed by an essentialist view of West versus East, Zine (2006) proposes an agenda for fighting against overlapping and multiple forms of racism, patriarchy and imperialist dominations in order to develop a solidarity framework that is inclusive of all diverse forms of feminist politics and activisms.

With the growing use of communication technologies as well as increasing cross-national migrations, feminist solidarities have faced new challenges and opportunities. Rahbari et al. (2021) examine transnational solidarity by and for Iranian women, from a diaspora perspective. They draw on cases of hijab-related campaigns, to argue that showing solidarity with "Muslim women in non-Muslim contexts" requires taking a responsible and sensitive approach in choosing means and strategies for the shared commitment. They suggest rather than viewing hijab as either a symbol of repression or empowerment that is central in activities by some online campaigns, "a nuanced contextual approach to women's political struggles, a deep understanding of power differences and politics of location, and a commitment to intersectionality should be at the heart of any transnational campaign that seeks to build feminist solidarity across differences" (p. 21). While virtual space has been utilized effectively to forge transnational feminist connections, without taking into account the diversity of women's experiences, they fail to address specific configurations of power, inequality and injustice in specific contexts. Therefore, to avoid representing a unified, homogenous image of Iranian women as a basis of transnational feminist solidarity work, it is necessary to pay attention to the ways in which the virtual and real spaces construct each other. A geographical perspective toward feminist politics, that takes into account similarities and differences across global space, can effectively strengthen an inclusive and intersectional approach to feminist solidarity.

In the past century, a growing body of literature has emerged to draw attention to the significance of space within the formation of identities and politics (for example see Pourya Asl, 2022). Geographical perspectives have illuminated ways in which women in Iran interact with space to claim their rights and subjectivities (Amir-Ebrahimi, 2006; Arjmand, 2016; Asl, 2022; Bagheri, 2014; Fariman, 2022; Golabi, 2022; Khatam, 2009; Ooryad, 2020; Mokhles & Sunikka-Blank 2022; Shahrokni, 2014; Shahrokni, 2019; Shaban, 2021). In her book *Women in Place: The Politics of Gender Segregation in Iran*, Sharokni (2019) examines gender segregation in the city as a fluid space rather than a fixed reality and argues that an exclusive focus on the religious dimension of gender segregation overlooks social, political and cultural development of the state within globalization effects. In order to unpack the politics of space in the case of gender segregation, she argues multifacetedness of the state must be taken into account. Such an analysis, she notes, helps to better understand negotiations, tensions and struggles between the state and women that unfold in the everyday space of the city". Bagheri (2014) further highlights the complex interaction of women with urban spaces by looking at urban spaces in Tehran. She argues that women often use semi-privatized modern spaces of the city to extend their sense of freedom, which is often restricted in traditional urban locations. Despite encountering daily limitations and controls over their spatial behaviours, women's everyday experience in semi-private spaces challenges generated binaries in the use of urban space. This study builds upon literature on gendered perspectives on urban space, by highlighting the transnational and multi-scalar characteristics of feminist activisms. Theoretically, it draws on feminist geopolitics scholarship, that problematizes space and scale as fixed notions in order to better understand political practices enacted by women outside the formal space of the nation-state and government institutions. By focusing on spatial practices by feminist activists, not only the everyday aspect of politics and its significance will be emphasized and theorized, traditional ways of understanding politics is challenged in order to see a more diverse and dynamic network of actors that fight against unjust dominant social and political structures in all its shapes and forms.

THEORY AND METHOD

Feminist geopolitical scholarship bridges the gap between feminist and political geography by establishing a theoretical and political framework where geopolitics becomes a more "gendered" project that "represents more accountable and embodied political responses to international relations at multiple scales" (Hyndman, 2004 p. 307). In this way, feminist geopolitics has offered conceptual tools to go beyond the nation-state as the only unit of analysis for the articulation of counter-politics and transnational activism. While geopolitical literature has conventionally emphasized the rationalization of dominant power and efforts of powerful nations to control the global, critical and feminist geopolitics question traditional understandings and practices of peace, war and violence within the state system to understand how power circulates within a diverse range of geographical scales (Hyndman, 2004; Pratt, 2020). A feminist-political geographical perspective entails redefining the boundaries of formal political spheres and spaces, to take into account transformative politics enacted by individuals, groups, and actors at various scales (Staeheli & Kofman, 2013).

By taking the body as the subject and object of geopolitics, feminist geopolitical studies not only have reformulated conventional and narrow views on violence, security and borders (Hyndman, 2004; Smith, 2012; Mayer, 2013; Staeheli & Kofman, 2013), they effectively reconceptualize international politics to include the personal and the everyday as important sites in the exercise of and resistance to geopolitical power (Pratt, 2020). Mayer (2013) describes how hierarchical and static notions of geographical scale have been challenged by women's activism during the Bosnia-Herzegovina war in the 1990s. She explains that although the war was fought within the boundaries of the former Yugoslavia, interventions by international women's organizations turned war crimes into a global matter. By providing Muslim women with a space to share their embodied and personal experience of war violence, for the first time in 1996 rape became categorized as a crime against humanity. She argues that the significant impact of international bodies in mitigating violence against women illustrates the fluidity of geographical scales in that mobilization did not take place at one scale or another, "rather it occurred at all scales at once". The present study builds on a fluid understanding of scale and space, as theorized by feminist geopolitical scholars, to frame how Iranian feminist activists create a site for transnational solidarity by using urban and virtual space.

Drawing on two contemporary cases of feminist activism, *Girls of the Revolution Street* and *Harraswatch,* it highlights transnational and multi-scalar characteristics of Iranian feminist activism.

Methodologically, this chapter draws on discourse analysis of 22 semi-structured interviews with feminist activists, scholars and policymakers inside and outside the country between March to August 2022. The majority of interviews, except for one in English, were conducted in Farsi. Due to the growing persecution of feminist activists by the Islamic Republic security forces, many feminists residing in the country were less willing to participate in the research therefore only 6 activists at the time of interviews were those living in Iran. Following the theoretical framing of the research, interview questions revolved around feminists' defined objectives, adopted strategies, usage of online and urban space, and their targeted audiences. The majority of research participants living outside of Iran were in countries of the so-called Global North, including the U.S, Canada, Australia, Germany, France, the U.K. etc. Other methods of data collection included conducting a thorough online ethnography of feminist social media accounts, as well as analysis of parties' and organizations' websites, journals, and documents. Two case studies have been chosen as examples of feminist activism: *The Girls of Revolution Street* campaign and the *Harraswatch* collective which focus on compulsory hijab and sexual harassment in public spaces. These two cases were selected to showcase how activists' solidarity is formed by utilizing resources available in the space; how spatial practices by women transcend national borders and identities; and how the scale of their activities does not remain fixed at one level and constantly moves from individual bodies to the streets of the city and beyond.

RESULTS AND FINDINGS

Anti-hijab campaigns are among the most enduring attempts by Iranian women and activists to oppose compulsory hijab law. Shortly after the 1979 Islamic revolution, when Khomeini declared that women should wear hijab when appearing in public spaces, many women went onto the streets to protest against the law. With the increasing use of communication technologies, however, anti-hijab protests in the past few decades have taken a variety of other forms. One of the earliest instances was the *White Wednesdays* campaign, where women put on white scarves on Wednesdays as a sign of protest against mandatory hijab. Another example was *My Stealthy Freedom*, during which women posted their selfies without hijab in public spaces, on their social media using the same hashtag. *Girls of Revolution Street* was and is one of the most important movements against compulsory hijab. It started in 2018 when protests against economic mismanagement and high rate of inflation after the re-imposition of sanctions by Trump were taking place all over the country. During the protest in Tehran, Vida Movahed took off her scarf while waving it on a stick and standing on top of a utility box in Enghelab (which means "revolution" in Farsi) Street, located at the central part of the city, the focal point of protests at that time. The act took much media and public attention, and in the next days and weeks, many other girls and women started doing the same act in other parts of the city and country. Subsequently, over 30 women were arrested for publicly removing their headscarves to express their protest against the compulsory hijab law (Hashemi, 2018).

In 2017, a group of feminists started *Harasswatch* "to fight against gendered violence in public spaces". Their objective according to their website (harasswatch.com) is to "publicize women's safety in public space". They produced educational content focused on gendered violence in public spaces of the city such as taxis, shops, streets, metro stations etc. to raise public awareness about ways in which women experience unsafety while using urban spaces. They created an interactive online map, where users from across the country could map and describe incidents of sexual harassment that they experienced or witnessed. By doing so, they brought attention to restrictions and risks that are associated with women's day-to-day presence in the city. In addition to online activities, the group published posters to be put in city spaces, to further publicize and visible sexual harassment as an issue that should be addressed by all members on a day-to-day basis.

Feminist Solidarity and the Urban

These cases demonstrate feminist solidarity that is built upon mutual living experiences of gendered oppression and discrimination i.e. compulsory hijab and sexual harassment. However, rather than using victimizing discourses to define solidarities, feminist activists and participants utilized common resources available in city spaces to claim their agencies and rights. Solidarities, therefore, were constructed through overlapping aims (Butler, 2004) to challenge social, political and cultural patriarchies and lay their claims on the public space of the city. In the *Girls of Revolution Street* campaign, participants used urban objects, namely utility boxes as a stage for their deficient performance. Ooryad (2020) argued the symbolic performance of taking off the hijab gave utility boxes political meanings as integral elements of the protest. By creatively using seemingly banal urban objects, women "reclaimed public spaces and cultivated political kinship within their local resistance collectives" (p. 130). While participants in the protest did not know each other personally, they build on their mutual demands and grievances to forge a kind of solidarity that is focused on claiming the body as well as the space. The topic of hijab has often been minimized as a marginal feminist issue within public debates, the movement, however, made it

Figure 1. Girls of Revolution Street
Source: Iran Human Rights (2018)

visible by bringing it to urban public spaces. Similarly, the *Harraswatch* group used urban material resources to spread knowledge and awareness of sexual harassment as a significant challenge faced by women in their day-to-day encounters with city spaces. As such urban spaces provided a site where not only women could take back their bodily autonomy and perform their subjectivity, it initiated a conversation that address the society as a whole, to actively take their part in creating a safe space for all. Therefore they expanded the boundaries of formal political spheres (Staeheli & Kofman, 2013) by bringing gendered discrimination and violence into the public spaces of the city.

Transnationality of Feminist Solidarity

Another significant characteristic of these two cases of feminist solidarity is their transnational dimension. Transnational activism has been made possible through the wide usage of social media and online platforms. In the first case, Iranians outside the country used *Girls of Revolution Street* hashtags on their social media accounts to show their solidarity and support with those inside Iran and their discontent with the compulsory hijab law. As such, while not immediately affected by mandatory hijab law themselves, Iranians in the diaspora used their online platforms as a tool for forging sisterhood bonds that transgress national borders. The Transnationality of

Figure 2. Posters of Sexual Harassment by Harraswatch
Source: Harraswatch (2022)

feminist solidarity was also evident in activities by the *Harraswatch* group. In tackling the issue of sexual harassment, the *Harraswatch* group drew on the experience of Egyptian feminists and the differences and similarities between the two socio-political contexts in terms of women's rights. One of the members of the group explained:

They had a long experience and a lot of research has been conducted. Therefore, many elements were already provided. They had a lot of similar challenges to us. They were [also] under pressure for their activities. Between being radicals and at the same time having minor impacts, or being in the middle and having a wider impact, they also had a similar challenge. It is like us. I mean we have the same challenge in Iran, where the government is sensitive to networking activities, regardless of the content. [Interview conducted in June 2022]

Instances such as these demonstrate how transnational perspectives have come to the benefit of feminist activists. By building a network of solidarity that crosses national borders and racial divides, feminists across the region created a space to inspire each other and learn from the challenges that they face in fighting against patriarchal structures. Oosterlynck et al. (2016) have discussed the shortcomings of nationalistic views toward solidarity which do not take into account the complicated ways that people engage and relate to one another. As such they argue that the theoretical framing of the concept of solidarity, often defined according to cultural homogeneity and spatial boundedness by nation-states, can be enriched "by solidarities that develop in the different spatio-temporal register of everyday place-based practices". Feminist practices of solidarity, showcased in the case of *Girls of Revolution Street* and *Harraswatch*, demonstrate how "innovative forms of solidarity" are articulated through "shifting our perspective from the spatio temporal register of the nation state to what diverse populations do, learn and collectively engage in here and now" (p. 765).

Multi-scalar Dimension of Feminist Solidarities

As discussed so far, women have variously used the space to claim their rights and forge solidarity across geographies. What is common in both of these cases is that woman's body is at the center of spatial practices. In other words, women drew on their embodied and everyday encounters with the space to build a network of solidarity and a collective subjectivity to dismantle dominant forces of social and political patriarchal structures. However, these spatial practices do not remain at the level of individual bodies. By making themselves visible and performing their political subjectivities in virtual and urban spaces, these networks of solidarities extend and encompass larger scales, from the neighborhood, city, country and even beyond. Participants in anti-hijab campaigns were inspired by Vida Movahed's brave and powerful act of defiance, which was captured and circulated widely within online space, and took the same tactic to extend the network of feminist solidarity and support across the city. In this sense, they integrated personal and everyday matters to exercise power and resistance against the misogynistic structure of the Islamic Republic. Similarly, by situating women's embodied interaction with the city, the *Harraswatch* group highlighted how patriarchal structures are not limited to state policies and practices but have purred into all aspects of daily urban life. After the group was launched and started its activities of producing educational content against sexual violence in Tehran, subsequently they were contacted by volunteer individuals and groups in other parts of Iran to publish those posters to be put on in public spaces of their cities. Therefore, they made a case for the "rescaling of geopolitics" to challenge and dismantle patriarchal discourse and policies that dominated the space at a whole variety of scales (Smith, 2001). As exemplified in these cases, practices of feminist solidarity are not possible "at one scale or another; rather, they occurred at all scales at once" (Mayer, 2013, p. 164).

Table 1. Characteristics of Feminist Solidarities

Spaces of feminist solidarity	Girls of Revolution Street	Harraswatch
Shared lived experience of discrimination	Compulsory hijab	Sexual harassment in public space
Transnational urban solidarities	-Using social media to connect Iranians inside and outside the country	-Learning from the experiences of feminists in other countries
Transgressing scale boundaries	Individual bodies	Neighbourhoods and cities

Challenges in Using Online Space

Although social media and online platforms have turned into effective tools for feminist activism, authoritarian states have also used a wide variety of strategies to restrict, manipulate and influence those activities to their benefit through censorship and restricting access to the Internet, cyberattacks and cyberbullying. MacKinnon (2010) describes such tactics as networked authoritarianism which refers to states' adaption to change brought by digital communication technologies to maintain their power in digital space. Tactics of networked authoritarianism were employed recently in a series of cyberattacks against Iranian feminist Instagram accounts with a large number of followers. While it is not certain who is behind those attacks, in a conversation between *Article 19*, an international human rights organization to promote freedom of expression, and feminist activists, many of them believed they are concerted efforts by the Iranian state to overwhelm their accounts through bots or to bring down feminist accounts' reach and engagement. Following those attacks, 23 international and specifically MENA regional human rights and women's rights organizations signed a statement condemning online attacks and urged *Meta*, Instagram's parent company to work with Iranian civil society to ensure the safety of Iranian women's human rights defenders online.

In addressing online cyberattacks against Iranian feminist accounts, platforms' policies and strategies of content moderation in Farsi, are not as effective as it is in dealing with English and European languages. As explained by an activist and researcher of *Article 19*:

They [Meta] have different resources for non-English or non-European languages. We don't see the same precision as those that are applied in English. For example, a feminist activist might get threats and harassment in English and the platform will remove that immediately. But if it comes in Persian, it is quite cumbersome and difficult for the platform to remove. Because often, they might not have the proper resources to be able to assess those language nuances. [Interview conducted in June 2022]

Alimardani and Elswah (2021) describe such forms of biases as a new kind of orientalism in online platforms or "digital orientalism" that lead to the removal of pro-democracy content, limiting data access, and restricting and deleting accounts of activists due to insufficient resource and knowledge on languages spoken in the Middle East within institutional frameworks. Drawing on Edward Said's notion of Orientalism which describes stereotypical and discriminatory Western perspectives of non-Western cultures and societies, they argue that this framework has been central in defining policies and actions by social media companies in the West to the disadvantage of internet users and democratic forces in the Middle East.

Instances such as these demonstrate the dual repressions that feminists activists under authoritarian regimes such as Iran are facing in their online activism: first, they have to deal with restrictions, censorships and online harassment inflicted by states and their agents and secondly, they are faced with biases and deficiencies of social media companies and platforms that put limits on their online activisms. As such, it is of crucial importance to be cautious of challenges and risks that are associated with increasing and exclusive dependency on online space as the only available source of connection and communication amongst activists. Therefore, in the face of accelerated state's restrictive policies on cyberspace and social media companies' inabilities in addressing those issues, feminist activists will benefit much from continuing to bridge the gap between virtual and the "real" urban space.

CONCLUSION

Perpetuated conditions of war, political contestation between neighbouring countries in the Middle East, state authoritarianism, and superpowers' interventionist policies have significantly impacted civilians' lives in the Middle East. Under such conditions, transnational feminist solidarities have made possible collaborative works that effectively utilized both online and urban spaces for fighting against gendered violence and injustices. These forms of solidarities not only reject an essentialist categorization of "oppressed woman", but they have also successfully built on mutual strengths and resources to claim women's rights and agency against social, political and cultural patriarchies. Furthermore, rather than defining feminist solidarities based on unified national and racial identities, feminist solidarities developed through "the everyday places and practices in which people engage across ethnic and cultural boundaries" (Oosterlynck et al., 2013).

Establishing online and urban networks of solidarity have allowed Iranian feminist activists to create a space for practicing politics that is both finer and larger than the scale of nation-states in the region (Hyndman, 2004). The scale of the feminist solidarity practices ranges from the intimate space of the body to neighbourhoods, cities and beyond national borders. By putting women's bodies and embodied experience of the city at the centre of their political interventions, participants in anti-hijab campaigns and members of the Harraswatch group politicize the everyday and lay claims in urban spaces. While virtual space has been an effective tool to strengthen solidarity urban networks, censorships, content moderation and manipulation, and cyberbullying by state and non-state actors and users have negatively affected emancipatory features of social media. Networked authoritarianism and digital orientalism exemplify some of the obstacles faced by feminists whose activities are more focused on online platforms. Therefore, in the face of accelerated state's restrictive policies on cyberspace and social media companies' inabilities in addressing biases, feminist activists will benefit much from continuing to bridge the gap between the virtual and the "real" urban space.

REFERENCES

Alimardani, M., & Elswah, M. (2021). Digital orientalism: #SaveSheikhJarrah and Arabic content moderation. *POMEPS Studies 43. Digital Activism and Authoritarian Adaptation in the Middle East*, *43*, 69–76.

Amir-Ebrahimi, M. (2006). Conquering enclosed public spaces. *Cities (London, England)*, *23*(6), 455–461. doi:10.1016/j.cities.2006.08.001

Arjmand, R. (2016). *Public urban space, gender and segregation: Women-only urban parks in Iran*. Routledge. doi:10.4324/9781315603025

Asl, M. P. (2022). Gender, space and counter-conduct: Iranian women's heterotopic imaginations in Ramita Navai's City of Lies: Love, sex, death, and the search for truth in Tehran. *Gender, Place and Culture*, *29*(9), 1296–1316. doi:10.1080/0966 369X.2021.1975100

Bagheri, N. (2014). Mapping women in Tehran's public spaces: A geo-visualization perspective. *Gender, Place and Culture*, *21*(10), 1285–1301. doi:10.1080/096636 9X.2013.817972

Butler, J. (2004). An essay in phenomenology and feminist theory. In H. Bial (Ed.), *The Performance Studies Reader* (pp. 154–165). Routledge.

Butler, J. (2016). *Frames of war: When is life grievable?* Verso Books.

Fariman, M. A. (2022). Closedness and openness in Tehran: A feminist critique of Sennett. *Gender, Place and Culture*, 1–22. doi:10.1080/0966369X.2022.2092074

Golabi, M. (2022). Aesthetics of invisibility in Iranian women's identity and their domestic space during the 1980s. *Gender, Place and Culture*, 29(11), 1616–1638. doi:10.1080/0966369X.2022.2056146

Harraswatch. (2022). *It has nothing to do with your coverage.* https://harasswatch.com/news/1908/

Hashemi, K. C. (2018). The girls of Enghelab Street: Women and revolution in Modern Iran. *IMEIS Annual Conference*.

Hooks, B. (1986). Sisterhood: Political solidarity between women. *Feminist Review*, 23(1), 125–138. doi:10.1057/fr.1986.25

Hyndman, J. (2004). Mind the gap: Bridging feminist and political geography through geopolitics. *Political Geography*, 23(3), 307–322. doi:10.1016/j.polgeo.2003.12.014

Iran Human Rights. (2018). *"Girls of the Revolution Street" Challenging 39 Years of Repression.* Iran Human Rights. https://iranhr.net/en/articles/3215/

Khatam, A. (2009). The Islamic Republic's failed quest for the spotless city. *Middle East Report (New York, N.Y.)*, 250, 44–49.

Leber, A., & Abrahams, A. (2021). Social media manipulation in the MENA: Inauthenticity, inequality, and insecurity. *Digital Activism and Authoritarian Adaptation in the Middle East*, 48.

MacKinnon, R. (2010). *Networked authoritarianism in China and beyond: Implications for global internet freedom.* In Liberation Technology in Authoritarian Regimes. Stanford University.

Mayer, T. (2013). Embodied nationalisms. In L. Staeheli, E. Kofman, & L. Peake (Eds.), *Mapping women, making politics* (pp. 154–168). Routledge.

Mokhles, S., & Sunikka-Blank, M. (2022). 'I'm always home': Social infrastructure and women's personal mobility patterns in informal settlements in Iran. *Gender, Place and Culture*, 29(4), 455–481. doi:10.1080/0966369X.2021.1873743

Naghibi, N. (2007). *Rethinking global sisterhood: Western feminism and Iran.* University of Minnesota Press. doi:10.5749/j.cttts4mn

Ooryad, S. K. (2020). Conquering, chanting and protesting: Tools of kinship creation in the girls of Enghelab Street (non-)movement in Iran. In G. Bauer, A. Heise-von der Lippe, N. Hirschfelder, & K. Luther (Eds.), Kinship and collective action in literature and culture (pp. 129–149). Academic Press.

Oosterlynck, S., Loopmans, M., Schuermans, N., Vandenabeele, J., & Zemni, S. (2016). Putting flesh to the bone: Looking for solidarity in diversity, here and now. *Ethnic and Racial Studies, 39*(5), 764–782. doi:10.1080/01419870.2015.1080380

Pourya Asl, M. (Ed.). (2022). *Gender, place, and identity of South Asian women.* IGI Global. doi:10.4018/978-1-6684-3626-4

Pratt, N. (2020). Embodying geopolitics: Generations of women's activism in Egypt, Jordan, and Lebanon. University of California Press.

Rahbari, L., Dierickx, S., Coene, G., & Longman, C. (2021). Transnational solidarity with which Muslim women? The case of the my stealthy freedom and World Hijab Day campaigns. *Politics & Gender, 17*(1), 112–135. doi:10.1017/S1743923X19000552

Shaban, N. (2021). *The Influence of Geopolitics on the Resistance Movement Against Compulsory Hijab in Iran* [Unpublished doctoral dissertation]. University of Colorado at Boulder.

Shahrokni, N. (2014). The mothers' paradise: Women-only parks and the dynamics of state power in the Islamic Republic of Iran. *Journal of Middle East Women's Studies, 10*(3), 87–108. doi:10.2979/jmiddeastwomstud.10.3.87

Shahrokni, N. (2019). *Women in place: The politics of gender segregation in Iran.* University of California Press.

Smith, F. M. (2001). Refiguring the geopolitical landscape: Nation,'transition'and gendered subjects in post-cold war Germany. *Space and Polity, 5*(3), 213–235. doi:10.1080/13562570120104418

Smith, S. (2012). Intimate geopolitics: Religion, marriage, and reproductive bodies in Leh, Ladakh. *Annals of the Association of American Geographers, 102*(6), 1511–1528. doi:10.1080/00045608.2012.660391

Staeheli, L. A., & Kofman, E. (2013). Mapping gender, making politics: Toward feminist political geographies. In L. Staeheli, E. Kofman, & L. Peake (Eds.), *Mapping women, making politics* (pp. 1–13). Routledge. doi:10.4324/9780203328514-11

Yuval-Davis, N. (2016). Power, intersectionality and the politics of belonging. In W. Harcourt (Ed.), *The Palgrave handbook of gender and development* (pp. 367–381). Palgrave Macmillan. doi:10.1007/978-1-137-38273-3_25

Zine, J. (2006). Between orientalism and fundamentalism: The politics of Muslim women's feminist engagement. *Muslim World Journal of Human Rights, 3*(1), 1-24. doi:10.2202/1554-4419.1080

Chapter 11
Re-Making the City for Women:
A Case of New Kolkata

Srestha Chatterjee
St.Xavier's College, India

Anushyama Mukherjee
St. Xavier's College, India

ABSTRACT

A city is a place that consists of several diverse categories of individuals surviving together. In such a setting, the creation of cooperation and equal opportunity of competence is expected in order to excel or progress towards a level of sustenance and development. However, if the level of equal access to spaces and resources are not validly applied to all individuals, then that city requires a change of lens and perspective. Building an inclusive city involving all its inhabitants is a crucial starting point. Re-imagining a city from the lens of the silenced requires an active step towards remaking the manifesto of constructing spaces. Through the perspective of a feminist lens and the theory of "Right to the City," this chapter seeks to explore an attempt to re-make the city of New Kolkata.

INTRODUCTION

This chapter analyzed Indian women's understanding of a city followed by their perspective of restructuring it. The basic idea was to understand how women could bring in changes in the way neighborhoods or streets of a city are experienced by them, by reimagining the way how women look at the city. Women in Kolkata from the pre-colonial times have had to face restrictions in using public spaces either due to reasons of caste-based responsibilities or discriminations. Women have always had to contest their right to city space because they hardly get the opportunity to voice their concerns. The narratives built around public space that were constructed for women was bound to produce fear among themselves (Roy & Bailey, 2021). This position contradicts with the idea which was developed by Lefebvre on the "Right to the City" (1996) of how individuals inhabiting a city would enact the right to appropriate urban space and have a central role in decision making processes (Fenster, 2006 as quoted in Biswas, 2019 pg. 16). Women had to face the major consequences of being subjugated and barred from having basic rights which have been expressed in the works of Ashapurna Devi, and later on through works of Arundhati Roy and Anita Desai. Their works have portrayed how women fought the hinges of patriarchy in order to have a particular voice of their own (Sharma, 2016). These works prove how integral it is to understand autoethnographic narratives which highlights the perspective of women, of how they look at the world and how they perceive a slice of freedom distanced from the constant pressure of being unheard and uncounted for. The autobiographies of Manikuntala Sen (2001) and that of Santisudha Ghosh (1989) also portrays the complexities of constructing a woman's self while learning to break free from the stereotypes of colonial Bengal and adjusting to the struggles of independence and incoming of modernity while constructing her distinctive identities in the public and the private (Ghosh, 2010). This research brings in these narratives of certain women in Kolkata in order to understand how they would want to imagine a New Kolkata and shape it according to their benefit. The ideal conditions of survival in a society are hardly possible to be incorporated in one single setting (Franck and Paxson, 1989 as quoted in Day, 2011), yet it becomes important to integrate the opinions of those who are mostly marginalized – including the voices of women. Women experience and understand the city differently and are even habituated in taking up lesser space (Mozingo,1989 as quoted in Day, 2011). Therefore, to have a feminist lens situated in the process of planning and designing a city would enhance the useful experience and enjoyment of spaces by the women who actively struggle to participate. Urban planners are yet to integrate the gendered perspectives in the planning process in India because there is a lack of narratives available of the journeys of everyday life of women (Roy & Bailey, 2021). Having a feminist lens might be helpful as it tries to engage with alternative possibilities of imagining spaces and places from the vantage point of women (Beebeejaun, 2017).

Why Restructuring a City?

The planning of a city involves inclusion of the social, economic and political influences of structures on the relations of individuals living in that city. This was why it was made prominent in the "Right to the City" by Lefebvre (1996), where he distinctly informs the involvement of active participation of citizens in the way a city is being imagined (Biswas, 2019). To have an active participation in the way a city is being planned would also eventually include the right to have a say in how infrastructures could be constructed. Feminist urban planners have seen that involvement of women in the core of city planning would help in challenging gender roles and altering social systems (Visakha, 2021). Concerns like transportation safety has severe consequences in workforce participation of women, because of which safer mobility becomes a crucial aspect (Kumari, 2022). Problems of sanitation and unhygienic toilets have created health problems for women as well, which was proven to be in terrible conditions according to a three-month study by Ishita Bagchi on the public toilets of Kolkata (Bagchi, 2020). Building a city thereby might be an all-inclusive process in order to bring in the balance in power relations as well as environmental sustainability. A city which meets the demands of all its inhabitants is determined to be a progressive asset for the development of a nation. However, the exclusion of any section's voice might defer the chances of such progress. This has been the case with representation of women in the process of planning or constructing their own living spaces. Predominantly, however, men have been the contributors in the field of architecture and planning.

This was one of the compelling reasons why the authors took on the aspect of studying the experiences of women while using public infrastructure in Kolkata. The inherent idea behind the study was to explore the way women would react to the concept of participatory planning and of having more female planners and representatives in the urban planning sector. It further compiled up into the idea of exploring in totality the idea of feminist urban planning and its possibilities in the city of Kolkata. Kolkata as a city has consecutively been selected as the safest city for the recent couple of years (Ghosh, 210), which shows the possibility of it having a better chance of turning into a feminist city. Kolkata itself has seen a dip in the rate of crime cases to an extent of 10%, according to the National Crime Record Bureau (NCRB) 'Crime in India 2021' report. However, it was not the case between the years 2008 - 2012 when there were higher cases of molestation and rape reported around all parts of Kolkata (Dey & Modak, 2015 as cited in Roy & Bailey, 2021). The NCRB data of 2019 even reiterates for the same about how Kolkata has been the safest cities in India among the nineteen cities (Basu, 2020). Even for the purpose of usage of city space, women have mostly considered daytime to be safer than nighttime in Kolkata, because of the public space being unsafe for them, interestingly although, working women preferred all times of the day to be accessible to travel in believing in equal access to spaces for both and women (Kerketta & Maiti, 2021). This study also mentioned how women who mostly feel unsafe in the city are the ones who have newly moved to the city in comparison to the ones who have lived in the city for more than 10 years (Kerketta & Maiti, 2021). However, Kolkata's incapacity to be a sustainable and inclusive city has been accentuated by uncontrolled expansion, plan violations, municipal waste mishandling, environmental deterioration, traffic congestion and unsafe public areas (Haque, 2019). Due to these circumstances, this research was taken up by the authors in order to understand the areas in which Kolkata could bring in changes in order to re-imagine itself through a feminist lens.

Greed (1994) mentioned in one of her books, that women were usually compelled to believe in the fact that they are not good enough for taking such "rational" decisions which involves matters of practicality. Women are more accustomed to the abstract world, or the academia where the practical issues are hardly dealt with. Therefore, abstract ideas may look good on paper, but they hardly matter when it comes to important decision-making instances which men are well versed with. Men are more of "bureaucratic" planners than women being just "visionaries". The bureaucratic planners are more efficient in implementing jobs, rather than having a vision of their own (Greed,1994, p.29 -30). Therefore, the cause of incorporating more female urban planners becomes yet more essential.

The fact that infrastructures were constructed with a prioritization suited for the needs of men implies sharply for the possible situations which women might face because of inconvenience, improper structuring, and limited visibility of public facilities for women. Women have limited usage of the public space also because of restricting factors like demarcating areas as forbidden and restricted, unsafe, and unhygienic because of which they must navigate and map the city in a different way. They have faced difficulty with issues such as problems in accessing transport at certain times of the day, getting access to safer streets, problems in getting good access to hygiene-related infrastructures like public toilets etc.

A city space cannot be fulfilling in nature unless it provides an equitable opportunity for all its users. However, this has not been the case as city spaces are generally designed in a way that are mainly beneficial for men (Pourya Asl, 2022). This is confirmed by many feminist critiques of urban planning and theory established in the year 1970 (Beebeejaun, 2017). Hence to make this restructuring a success, feminist means of urban planning could be sufficiently incorporated as a process which would help in the process of "un-gendering" happen a lot quicker.

INFRASTRUCTURE RESTRUCTURING: A CASE OF 'NEW KOLKATA'

One of the primary means of livelihood in a city is through transportation and networking among many. This transportation would not become possible without well connected roads which make up one of the many important public infrastructures. Proper infrastructural planning is a big responsibility in constructing and planning a city. Proper urban planning makes the area livable and sustainable for the citizens. It ensures the efficiency of a city is increased and no infrastructural gaps are created amongst communities (George, 2020). However, there are different socio-economic levels of inequality based on usage of infrastructure. As a result of these: disparities exist on the basis of housing, sanitation, water supply, land, etc.

The main area of concern lies here with the way women have been able to access and use the public infrastructures like public toilets and streetlights. Accessing the city in a safe and secure manner has been one of the crucial challenges for women, as the generalized notion about them being unsafe in the public sphere remains strong, especially in the Indian society.

The city of Kolkata is no different, where women from various social and economic backgrounds have faced harassments of different kinds on the streets and even within public transports. Kolkata as a city had developed after the liberalization process with the prevalence of middle-class mentality, which dominated the ideology of many individuals and the reflections of which still could be felt, even in the 21st century. This ideology has presumed the fact that women have "genuinely" achieved a lot of rights and powers, so they do not need more of it. Yet it is interesting to also note the fact that women who have progressed in every field, including fields like politics and entrepreneurship, have not been able to feel safe and comfortable navigating the streets of the city. "Male gaze", a concept by Laura Mulvey (1975) an important feminist terminology analyzed that women are viewed in an objectifiable manner by men, so that men feel empowered to control and enjoy the power to control women (Loreck, 2017). Women feel uncomfortable due to poor design of infrastructure and lack of "eyes on the street" to help them be vigilant and act as a helping hand under troubles of the "male gaze".

Women are invigilated upon many a times when they are out in the public by onlookers and bystanders which adds an essence for their safety. Even to some extent women feel unsafe because of stereotypical societal behavior of judgement which comes with the views of neighbors and even passers-by who do not always have to be men. It also remains a heavy doubt as to how women feel unsafe under the gaze of men, yet with the same male population being most prevalent on the streets, they could feel safe under the "eyes". With the experience of women already skewed in the private or domestic sphere, the proportion of women commuters in metropolitan cities which includes Kolkata never rises above 20%. Even according to 2011 Census, only 17% of those commuting to work are women (Goel, 2018).

For instance, women of Delhi even complained of having faced rude behavior while using public transport which is another reason to feel unsafe on the streets (Lathia & Mahadevia, 2019). The problem of navigation comes mainly at night when women tend to become more unsafe. It stands to reason that if women perceive public space to be uncontrollable and dangerous, they will avoid and limit their mobility (Weisman, 1992, p.70). Infrastructures like streetlights have been considered essential by several women who have had troubles navigating the city at night. According to the National Women's Commission, there were 23,722 reports of crimes against women in 2020, the highest number in six years. Streets, markets, public transport, parks and other public spaces are not represented equally to women, adding to the widespread misunderstanding that public spaces are inherently unsafe for women. In Mumbai, the so-called "safest" city for women, only 28% of people in public were women at a time (Bhandari, 2021). Even according to the NCRB data, 75% of the women who had reported facing harassment claimed to have faced that on the streets, whereas 19% of them faced harassment at the bus stop. 25% of the women were harassed once in every week regularly (Joshi & Singh, 2021). At these points, building of proper and sustainable infrastructural facilities would ensure some form of safety and give women equal chances of feeling comfortable and unanimous with the general population.

METHODOLOGY

The authors have performed qualitative research on six women respondents of South Kolkata, where the women were asked about their experience on the streets of Kolkata. The locations used under the study included the public toilet which is situated near Silver Point School and closer to Kasba Rathtala Minibus stand, on Banku Bihari Chatterjee Road, South Kolkata and the Bosepukur Bus stand opposite Bosepukur Shitolamandir. These two areas fall under Ward Number 91, East Kolkata Township. The immense amount of traffic congestion and no place for women to walk through, less access to seats on bus stands, hustling in public transports and low lighting of certain parts of her neighborhood compelled her to work on this matter. Focused, face-to-face, in-depth interviews were carried out on six women through purposive and later snowball sampling methods. Due to restriction of time and mandatory maintenances of distance due to Covid, the number of responses recorded was limited.

Description of the Field Site

The public toilet is a "pay and use" toilet, where both men and women have access to the services from 8 a.m. to 10 p.m. The toilet was situated near a huge group of apartments. The area remains mostly clear around the toilet. The toilet is constructed directly over the street and has been situated there since 11th October 2007. The bus stand falls under Ward number 67 opposite the Bosepukur Shitalamandir location. The bus stop has a shade over itself, with no proper name plate and sitting arrangements. The main road is separated by a divider which is filled with greenery and even has a Kolkata Traffic police booth inserted in front of the divider. There were shops spread out at night which were not open in the daytime, opening at 3p.m. till 9 at night. The road is mostly busy during the office hours (9a.m. to 7 p.m.), and the bus stop remained crowded. Men were seen waiting in the bus stop more in comparison to women according to the observation period.

Un-Gendering of Local Spaces Within a City

To construct a space where everyone gets an equal opportunity to imagine a space requires a rigorous elimination of biases. Removal of biases might be possible with the proper application of feminist methods of urban planning and design, which basically is responsible for determining how women's identities have a good amount of influence in determining their environment. It helps in bringing forth some radically "private" issues within the purview of public discussion and debate in order to make spaces livable for women (Day, 2011). Having a feminist viewpoint could only help in bringing equal opportunities to the desk and further help in un-gendering the very process of constructing a city through its infrastructures. To un-gender, the very first thing would be to fill in the gaps which are compelling thinkers and researchers to opt for a feminist perspective or to make the vision a little accommodative for women as well, at par with men. Feminism is not only for facilitating women but challenging the system which has kept women in the margins of the society and has made them into docile, submissive creatures who are better suited or limited in the domestic and emotional spheres of life. The process of feminist urban planning inculcates within it the ways or means of making the city accessible in an equal manner for all individuals. It allows for assessing the fields where women are left behind and increases their chances of being included. Inclusivity increases with the incorporation of such mechanisms of planning, and it would also require inclusion in representation. Representing women as planners and having an equal participation in the process of planning infrastructures could help in improving lot of facets in building a better city.

According to the concept of "Right to the City" by Henri Lefebvre (1991), every single citizen who resides inside the city has the right to reconstruct spaces and reform the underlying power-relations in the society (Purcell, 2002). Un-gendering these processes would mean making sure that no privileged viewpoint is used to construct a city, instead it would be a city which is accessible and advantageous for all sections of society. Therefore, clarity is required through a gender-specific approach which would further bring out the drawbacks of planning and make the infrastructural arrangement suitable for all, devoid of any form of discrimination for any section of society. This process might help in further challenging the societal biases and social norms that have disturbed the social cohesion and stability of our society. This methodology also focused on the means of participatory planning which would help in bringing forth the bottom-up approach, which helps in incorporating marginalized or silenced voices in the process of planning at smaller to larger scales (Escalante & Valdivia, 2015). These processes further ensure that women could also enjoy the same amount of anonymity as men at any time of the day, which certainly lacks in the present times. Women planners could thereby be considered an essential part of city planning process in order to ensure that the "Right to the City" is restored for women and men equally.

Now this whole process of restructuring would become applicable in case of Kolkata, which is supposed to be a city that is regarded to be one of the safest cities for women, according to the National Crime Record Bureau (Pathak, 2021). A city which has liberal outlooks and having such strong political opinions has been lacking in the field of urban planning. Kolkata has a chance of becoming a sustainable city, yet it had somehow faltered with the increasing amount of population and lack of proper planning of spaces, which have been resulting in limited physical movements and increased amount of environmental trouble including problems of the municipalities.

Women from all socio-economic classes avail the infrastructures yet their opinions were not included while planning. Women are largely represented on the streets, yet they are hardly seen unaccompanied (Basu, 2017). Some of these issues are a part of their everyday life therefore it is important to examine the issues that they experience in a city. For instance, the respondents reportedly claimed that the streets genuinely become unsafe for them at night because of certain conditions like improper neighborhoods, unruly people, passersby passing comments, etc. For instance, Priyam, a 28-year-old domestic help, mentioned:

Women are always followed at night in our locality, by some young teenagers who eve-tease and pass inappropriate comments on women, which I also had to face once. This is why women are never safe on the streets.

Even the mere fact that women were somehow unsafe on the streets were made to be believed and internalized as an integral information by the over-powering patriarchal society. Women respondents who had travelled on the street near Ward 91 claimed them to be very much safe for travelling, but when asked further about their preference for walking back home or taking any form of conveyance, they preferred to choose conveyance. Shanti Mondal, a 33-year-old school bus helper, mentioned:

I usually would prefer taking a taxi or autorickshaw to return home. Even if a street is safe or not, at night I cannot take risk, especially when a child is with me.

The mere reasoning behind using public or private transport was related to safety of themselves and safety of their family members. Some of these women have even informed that their neighborhood had proper infrastructures. This brought the authors back to the assumption that women were forced to believe somehow it is unsafe to dwell on the streets after a certain time period.

The demand of enough patrolling and availability of cleaner footpaths were the popular opinions of the research. This proves the point of rethinking the city infrastructure might ensure proper planning of the streets and enough patrolling safety. Further that shall enable women to access the streets sufficiently instead of looking for any form of conveyance for covering even shorter distances at night. Digitally the matter of ensuring street safety had however been started by the SafetiPin app, with the help of which women could navigate on the streets with assurance through checking of street congestion and lighting facilities of each street, provided through thorough navigation technologies. However, it was realized that disparities do not die down in the socio-economic front as many women might have to walk down darker alleys without their choice. Therefore, the whole idea of restructuring through the bottom-up approach is necessary.

The use of public toilets is another form of infrastructural drawback that women faced in Kolkata where accessibility was limited. Municipalities have constructed public toilets for its citizens; however, women have not always preferred to use it because many times it was unhygienic and unsafe. ActionAid India 2017 research pointed out that 35% of the 229 toilets surveyed in Delhi lacked a distinct portion for women, 53% lacked running water, and 45% lacked mechanisms to lock the door from the inside (Patel, 2021). The case of public toilets in Kolkata has been rather problematic as a result of which many women chose to use toilets in shopping malls and cafeterias. Women have complained of being harassed while using public toilets, because of which many do not prefer to use it at night. For instance, Priyam, a 28-year-old domestic help, mentioned:

Once at night I was returning from a fair when I had to urgently use the public toilet, but I could not because the guard charged me extra money which was not there with me at that moment. When I complained, he verbally abused me and made a scene, because of which I could not use it.

It has also been mentioned in a case study conducted in Delhi that women usually do not prefer to use the community toilet because men keep standing there under a banyan tree just in front of the toilet so that they can harass every single woman who uses the toilet (UN WOMEN, 2013). Public toilets are supposed to be made accessible for women 24/7, yet many of them are closed at an earlier time which makes it difficult for women working night shifts to use toilets.

The feminist planning mechanism is supposed to alter these situations and restructure the entire environment of safe and hygienic public toilets for women to use. Women who use these public toilets could also be interviewed by the local municipal bodies and necessary actions could be followed to ensure better maintenance. The un-gendering of these infrastructural developments and further un-gendering the city would require using the gendered lens to understand how women could come at par with men in experiencing or using the varied city spaces. Proper sanitation facilities and better hygienic conditions are pros for women who work daily and travel a lot.

For instance, Mita Chatterjee, a 51-year-old private tutor, mentioned:

I think public toilets are both unhygienic as well as unsafe; unsafe because the doors are sometimes not working properly and it has been dysfunctional for quite some time, until one week back it was fixed, and unhygienic because the latrines are kept unclean and they smell disgusting.

Nalini Mukherjee, a 42-year-old business owner, mentioned:

I do not use public toilets that very often, I use it when it is absolutely necessary. I believe that more than feeling unsafe, it is more unhygienic, as the one time I used it out of emergency I had UTI (Urinary Tract Infection).

Also reiterated by Shanti Mondal, a 33-year-old school bus helper:

Most of the times the public toilets are very unclean, and hence increases the risk of infections for us. Proper development of trash cans should be set up inside public toilets and they must be cleaned properly.

These women as citizens claimed the public toilet of Ward 91 to be safe yet unhygienic because of the lack of proper cleaning, no proper locking facility of doors and even no availability of soaps and sanitary napkins. The public toilet even lacked any form of waste disposal bins inside the structure. These conditions are already pointing towards the disadvantages that women have, and above that it risks their health, with increased chances of having UTIs (Urinary Tract Infections). Women in the study, belonging to the upper-middle class claimed that they do not prefer to use public toilets unless emergency with no other options available.

For instance, Jyoti Ghosh, a 35-year-old shopkeeper, mentioned:

It was a very bad experience. And since then we have got a small bathroom installed behind the shop so that I do not have to use the public toilet. The toilet is really dirty and not well maintained at all.

This also shows the level of disparity and the privilege of choice amongst women themselves. Feminist planning methods could become a quintessential element in fixing these gaps in framing better laws and policies to close these disparities, to ensure that everyone deserves equal opportunities and facilities. Maintenance and planning of these infrastructures and the accompanying facilities could increase the involvement of women in levels of administration to ensure their representation is acknowledged.

Restructuring of these structures would ensure that the experiences of women change and help in building an environment which do not require any gendered lens to look for improvements and growth. The infrastructural developments might further also ensure that women could navigate and communicate throughout the urban arena in a much more confident and assertive fashion. Involvement of women in important roles would facilitate the development of a city from all arenas – including economy, social impact and environmental sustainability. Sometimes the soft skills that women are supposed to imbibe far more in comparison to men, might help in sustainable usage of resources, better redistribution and better structuration of not only the city but also the country at large.

Male city planners particularly those at the top were primarily concerned with the largest, fastest, and most expensive projects. Men from privileged backgrounds were generally overrepresented in decision-making positions in our cities (Wyckoff & Pilat, 2018). Gendered understanding of infrastructural inequalities might be helpful in channeling the primary focus of planning a city which would be to guarantee that women do get to access public infrastructure as much as men do. Women deserve to enjoy and construct the city according to tastes and distastes equally as men do. The problem of restructuring could begin at the very basic level – by making local government bodies efficient enough to handle important situations and duties.

The government could be made responsible for making sure these facilities are used by men and women regularly with ease. It would be better to consider that the burden of responsibility might not solely be of civil society organizations to maintain such public infrastructures. Including everyday experiences is an integral process of developing infrastructures. Restructuring always requires understanding of mistakes which the existing infrastructure has not been able to provide, and it further helps in including more ideas which could help in improving the condition and environment of the area where the infrastructures are built. Construction of such infrastructures could cover, ideally, all possible arenas which includes being sensitive towards the minority communities like the sexual minorities who also face a lot of troubles while using toilets in every public place.

This shall be ensured once a feminist outlook and a gendered lens could be attached in the process of planning and infrastructural development which would not only eye on building higher skyscrapers but even ensure that equality is reached at its peak. As a result, when the balance could be restored, and everyone would be able to enjoy facilities thoroughly, the lens of planning and development could finally become un-gendered.

A City for Women by Women

The process of restructuring becomes easier when citizens are included in the decision-making process. This would ensure that women would have the empathetic touch and shared feeling of understanding for taking further actions in the planning process. Patriarchal privilege and influence in the process of planning had become a major drawback in the process of bringing overall development and it even failed to build an imagination which could be sustainable and egalitarian, if not utopian.

Building a matriarchal city is obviously not a good option either. But what we can do is ensure that no one of the groups would have to make decisions on behalf of the entire population. Women city planners have also been missing from the scene in many developing countries where the sexist mentalities dominate the belief systems of several men along with women as well. Yet the possibilities of bringing about some form of change to this system were possible with the help of a step towards equal representation and opportunities. There have been instances where women architects have proven to be efficient enough.

While conducting field work, the researchers noticed that women currently access spaces that were considered unsafe for them, such as, eating alone in a restaurant or local food stalls. This might have happened due to an increase in the dissolution of public-private divide, which used to restrict women within the domestic sphere and gave her legitimacy only based on the attachment to male kins (Ray. 1991). Women do not play such major roles in the public arenas like tea shops or small eateries because they are supposed to be preoccupied with the domestic front and sitting alone in such spaces could lead to drawing of unnecessary attention towards herself.

By-lanes and streets – everything seems to be unsafe for women because of which they might not be suitable for any part of the city. Women might even feel like having excursions in the city, but restrictions always come in – whether be in the form of unsafe localities or for being extremely dirty. Women also require others to accompany her and make her feel safe. So, if a city is not even made in the vision of a woman's perspective or imagination how can we expect them to participate and be representative equally? For this to happen some form of a logical experiment could be undertaken. This might include a democratic approach where women themselves would approve for more women being represented at the front of decision-making processes. This might be a form of women uplifting other women's situation where the ideology of feminism also stands tall.

Respondents from the study undertaken in Kolkata, Ward 91 had to add some of their inputs as to how women could be represented more in the area of planning.

Priyam Ghosh, 28-year-old domestic help suggested:

Women should definitely be more involved in the planning process and they require fair amount of representation in the ward offices, so that while conducting surveys, which is another thing hardly done, we would be comfortable enough to share our problems.

Shanti Mondal, a 33-year-old school bus helper suggested:

Not only better public toilets, but also separate public toilets should be set up for women.

Mita Chatterjee, a 51-year-old private tutor suggested:

I believe women must definitely be an equal part of the planning process and as per my personal opinion there should be a system whereby, we can have specific gender vehicles, only for women with female drivers in localities that are marked as dangerous or unsafe for women. Bus stands must also be well lit, well-spaced and female conductors should also be employed.

A dissimilar voice was of Baishali Basak, a 63-year-old shopkeeper who opined:

See I believe that women should have their say and equal representation, but men should always accompany them, because they are nothing without each other's support.

Considered so, it is the agency that has to be shared through equal access to resources for both men and women which would stop this dependency on one side and make it mutual thereby fulfilling the part of un-gendering of decision making.

Gender sensitive urban planning includes the very basic step of including the voices and problems of men and women both, but the weightage had always been in favor of men which is the only thing that stops the entire process of un-gendering. Restructuring a city would be initially a daunting task with this amount of prejudice ingrained and stored within the minds of not only men, but women as well. This system of planning and development would be essential in incorporating an inclusive system of acquiring opinions from the women debarring any sort of discrimination based on caste, class, economic position or race.

Engaging women in such planning projects would ensure that women find a certain form of agency within themselves. This would also require awareness generation programs to be held consistently by the civil society organizations as well as government funded agencies like the local government bodies. The local government bodies could employ women and make them volunteers in order to acquire better information from the residents of an area, because many a times men and women both are comfortable in expressing their opinions to women. Places like Tunisia and Liberia have already implemented such projects where women are involved at the very base of participatory decision-making processes and have helped in building gender sensitive environments including improved infrastructures (Kitchi et al., 2022). However, in these processes several political implications and influences are involved which might make matters worse for women.

The issue of representation in important roles like administration and city planning processes might uplift the barrier in the unequal divide of equitable representation of both the genders. Problems like not availing dustbins inside public toilets and not having facilities of getting sanitary napkins could not be always communicated to men. Therefore, communication might improve, and problems would be sorted with ease.

One of the respondents also shared that women have a certain quality in themselves which has been ingrained as a result of societal trainings according to gender norms. Nalini Mukherjee, a 42-year-old businesswoman, mentioned:

As in a family, women take care of the whole house and make sure that everyone remains in good health, similarly I believe that making more women a part of the planning process would ensure the city becomes safer and healthier with the incorporation of ideas from women which are less heard of.

Women are made multitaskers from the very beginning, and they take on responsibilities to take care of every single individual in the family. This quality of women helps them to understand and analyze several problems at one go, and it also makes them sensitive enough about the interests and disinterests of people. This quality could be used up for taking important decisions even in local government bodies and channeling that quality into something which could be useful for this society. This type of management skill is a soft power which women could use for the benefit of themselves. This would help in further empowering themselves.

Women do carry with them a set of experiences that teaches them the importance of caregiving roles and the aspect of nurturing the needs of every member within the family. The way women are socialized involves being more driven towards the domestic world while men are taught to be more outgoing, less homebound. The priorities in expected roles differed in case of men due to which the experiences and viewpoints of men and women differ. A city managed by women has the potential to bring people of various gender identities, skills, ages, and ethnic backgrounds together around the common goal of respecting women and girls (Zimmerman, 2017).

Increasing female traffic police officers would help in raising the accountability on the road for women's safety and help in lodging complaints more reasonably if there is any kind of harassment on the road. Being bus drivers, auto drivers and cab drivers could help women not only sustain themselves but also build their confidence in taking decisions and making their voices felt heard. The pink taxi service was started in Kolkata, but unfortunately could not succeed in bringing out profitable results for women. The main problem with this system involved women taxi drivers not being able to use public toilets because police inspectors did not allow them to park in front of the public toilet (Singh, 2019). The added values of shame and honor attached to a woman's identity somehow still fully stops her from exploring her potential.

A survey conducted in Bangalore revealed that women were highly underrepresented in Apartment Management Committees, because of which their decision-making power gets reduced. Similarly, women's representation in the ward offices are negligible despite their political position because the representation was done by husbands. This gives us an added dimension in understanding why concerns that were raised by women were neglected. Their opinions and voices were hardly taken into consideration in the process. Amplification of voices is a bigger necessity than merely adding the voices of women. (Navya, 2021).

Decentralizing the decision making in the sphere of gender dimensions and equally charting out administrative strength to both men and women would work out the issues that women face not only in planning, but also governance. Enhancing the process of governance also includes making sure public infrastructures were properly maintained and innovative methods were used for improving the facilities.

Another important measure was taken while conducting this research on the respondents of Kolkata ward number 91 which was about women's perspectives in restructuring their own neighborhoods.

One of the respondents, Nalini Mukherjee, 42-year-old businesswoman, did come up with some innovative means like putting dustbins around their neighborhood which would be within every 3 to 4 kilometers:

Dustbins should be installed within 3 to 4 kms and they should be coded blue and green in colors, which would ensure the wastes are properly managed. The locality where I stay, in Chetla, is really ill-maintained by the municipality.

For instance, Mita Chatterjee, 51-year-old private tutor, recommended:

Our neighborhood should install security cameras on or near the lampposts and the entire neighborhood should be participating in its maintenance. This would ensure community participation and accountability to help maintain the safety and security of a neighborhood.

This method would involve participation from men and women alike in the whole neighborhood to reduce criminal activities. The ideas of restructuring their own neighborhood vary according to the socio-economic background and accessing the infrastructure.

For instance, Priyam Ghosh, 28-year-old domestic help, lived in a slum wished to change tap water to sweet water (drinkable water) which was promised by the state.

If I am allowed to bring about any changes it would involve changing the water supply system in the slums. It is because we were promised to get sweet water taps installed near our colony, yet all we get is salt water which cannot be healthy for kids to consume.

Water in the slums had high concentration of salt and iron which was not only bad for health but also can increase pollution. Sustainable means of living like cleaner roads and better water supply connections were a necessary means of livelihood for all the people living in the slums.

Joyti Ghosh, a 35-year-old shopkeeper, demanded that public bus services should be improved, and some buses should only have female conductors which would be covering many routes throughout Kolkata. Having accessible public transport facilities is another major help for women to access the city space with ease and comfort, having an equal footing as that of men.

Priyam Ghosh, 28-year-old domestic help urged for having proper and hygienic toilets for women in local trains. Stricter checks in female compartments of local trains were also claimed by her, as in many cases men wrongfully enter those compartments to harass women. Maintenance of these services would ensure traveling could be healthier, safer and cheaper for women.

For instance, Mita Chatterjee and Nandita Majumder, both were working women and opined that female police officers should be recruited more who would be made responsible for patrolling duties:

Women police officers must be recruited to do the patrolling services at night, especially in locations where women are more prone to danger. This type of system should be made frequent so that girls and women both could feel a lot safer on the streets. This would make them feel comfortable in complaining as well.

Involving women in local administration and volunteering could encourage other women to come up front and open up about their problems, which might lead to fruitful discussion and better solutions could be gathered. The bottom-up approach helps in these circumstances which might not only be the priority of civil society organizations but also of the government who are equally accountable for women's safety.

Restructuring of Kolkata would not only require making it safer for women but also ensuring that men get the same amount of exposure to problems faced by women. Changes might occur if gender sensitization programs were arranged in schools and colleges to increase exposure of both the genders. Even the initiative of "Why Loiter" campaign in Mumbai, named after the book by Shilpa Phadke (2011) with the same title, was started as a response to the brutal exploitative cases faced by women in Delhi. It is an excellent form of movement to make women reclaim the public space and to do away with "Stranger Danger" from men. It could help in not only make women feel safe in the public domain, but also generate awareness among men to be less hostile towards women and to familiarize them at equal footing with themselves. This would also ensure the un-gendering of public spaces by reinstating the balance of power and agency (Chandran, 2016). Taking up these activities and campaigns by local administrative bodies and civil society organizations in Kolkata along with other cities might help in redesigning the whole idea of "New Kolkata".

Constructing a new Kolkata infrastructurally enhanced for women would require a lot of effort which would also require enough willingness to bring about change. The middle class usually benefitted because of their previous influence over the ideological domain of Kolkata and the privileged classes were less bothered about issues unless it concerns them. But the community development and planning could only improve for Kolkata with the involvement of every socio-economic class.

CONCLUSION

In case of India the type of discriminations faced by women might be different from that of the developed countries. It certainly depends on the type of policies made and implemented at each level of the government. If better policies were not made and if these policies were not arbitrated by both men and women, it calls for gendering rather than un-gendering of the process Planning is always not about rational calculations and competitive developments, it is also about creating sustainable environments and safe, equitable spaces for every single individual to enjoy the city in an egalitarian sense. The distinction between men and women has been generalized by the society to such an extent that seeing them at par does not feel very much natural. Instead, it is always shown to be a competitive or comparative analysis. This biased analysis might not be the right approach for constructing a new Kolkata. The present developments of women in important administrative, political, and entrepreneurial roles have opened opportunities for further empowerment and a balanced scope of gender upliftment. Efforts do have to be made in order to bring in changes and the base of it is in education, economy and mindset development through awareness generation.

This planning mechanism might become an uneasy path to dwell in for the Global South but if these policies are propagated and properly implemented from the very local levels, things might take a different turn soon for Kolkata. Building a new Kolkata would include having safer and healthier access to public infrastructure like public toilets, streetlights, and spaces which could be accessed by all types of socio-economic classes without any forms of discrimination practiced against them. Listing the necessary requirements from the life narratives and experiences of women who experience the city becomes crucial and non-negotiable. With the help of the research conducted by the writers, it justified how women respondents have readily contributed their will to bring in necessary shifts in re-imagining the particular field under study. An effective way of imaging the "Right to the City" could involve addition of these narratives of experiences so that it truly becomes a level playing ground to enjoy the city, by all. An avid example to this would be involving participatory practices for urban planning and design, which has been demonstrated in the construction of Nirmaya Place, which involved the using of voices and narratives of sex workers to build their living space (Stone, 2020). The main focus of bringing forward the policy of ungendered city of Kolkata involved the understanding that not one single gendered lens must be used for constructing or imagining the city. Feminist urban planning is not just about uplifting women, but it is also about making others conscious as to why an un-gendered perspective is really a necessity while planning out a whole city.

Disregarding any kind of socio-economic differences or social prejudices could bring about necessary changes which are required in a newer version of Kolkata. Caste discriminatory practices and many other hidden prejudices still continue to thrive in the minds of people and are practiced by all the other generations from younger to older ones. Having a fresh outlook and perspective, having better access to education, giving gender sensitivity and gender awareness programs might bring about possible changes not only for the privileged but also communities who live in the margins of society.

A different and innovative urban experience could only be thought about once the types of problems faced by women are seen with a different lens. The change of lens can only happen once categorization of the types of problems faced by women is carried out through a study conducted throughout Kolkata, which was not possible for this particular study conducted by the researchers. Research with a wider scope could shine a light on more shortcomings and demands from the side of women. Gender sensitive issues and surveys could be taken more in number and considering them while making policies might bring in desired changes. Effective changes in local administration and improvement in transportation, sanitation, streets and employing more women as prescribed by the respondents might become a good steppingstone for New Kolkata.

The New Kolkata would be imagined as a city where women do not have to feel unsafe and restrained by the drawbacks of the government. Here women's roles and expectations would be renegotiated with an improved viewpoint where their voice would matter and be acknowledged. New Kolkata would emerge with the possibility of allowing women to navigate in newer roles and allowing favorable circumstances for their growth in all fields which have been till now dominated by men. Empowerment comes from practical changes which were demanded by the respondents of the study conducted. Without the development of a new perspective of looking at an "equal" world, a New Kolkata cannot be imagined. Un-gendering is the process of breaking down the loopholes of this typical prejudiced society. Restructuring involves imagining newer ways of creating better employment and further empowerment of those marginalized communities who were stuck in these loopholes of gender stereotypes. Better spaces could be constructed where women could make their presence felt without having to face the unnecessary glances.

REFERENCES

Bagchi, I. (2020). *These incidents depict why public washrooms in Kolkata are a nightmare.* https://www.youthkiawaaz.com/2020/12/public-washrooms-in-kolkata-a-nightmare

Basu, P. (2020). *Kolkata one of the safest cities for women, says NCRB data*. https://www.millenniumpost.in/kolkata/kolkata-one-of-the-safest-city-for-women-says-ncrb-data-420181

Basu, S. (2017). *Where are the women in Kolkata*. FirstPost.com.

Beebeejaun, Y. (2017). Gender, urban space, and the right to everyday life. *Journal of Urban Affairs*, *3*(39), 323–334. doi:10.1080/07352166.2016.1255526

Bhandari, A. (2021). Feminist perspectives on space, safety and surveillance: Improving a woman's right to the city. *The Wire*. https://thewire.in/women/feminist-perspectives-on-space-safety-and-surveillance-improving-a-womans-right-to-the-city

Biswas, R. (2019). *Reclaiming the urban: An intersectional analysis of women's and men's experiences of public spaces in Kolkata*. Temple University Graduate Board.

Chandran, R. (2016). *Indian women reclaim public spaces, defying male critics*. Reuters.com.

Day, K. (2011). *Feminist approaches to urban design*. Routledge.

Escalante, S. O., & Valdivia, B. G. (2015). Planning from below: Using feminist participatory methods to increase women's participation in urban planning. *Gender and Development*, *23*(1), 113–126. doi:10.1080/13552074.2015.1014206

Fenster, T. (2006). The right to the gendered city: Different formations of belonging in everyday life. *Journal of Gender Studies*, *14*(3), 217–231. doi:10.1080/09589230500264109

George, H. (2020). *10 reasons explaining the importance of urban planning*. Planningtank.com.

Ghosh, S. (2010). Expressing the self in Bengali women's autobiographies in the twentieth century. *South Asia Research*, *30*(2), 105–123. doi:10.1177/026272801003000201 PMID:20684082

Goel, R. (2018). *Indian cities are just not designed for women*. Quartz India. https://qz.com/india/1375405/indian-cities-are-just-not-designed-for-women

Greed, C. H. (1994). *Women and planning*. Routledge.

Haque, I., Mehta, S., & Kumar, A. (2019). Towards sustainable and inclusive cities: The case of Kolkata. *Observer Research Foundation, 83.* https://www.orfonline.org/research/towards-sustainable-and-inclusive-cities-the-case-of-kolkata-48992/

Joshi, M., & Singh, D. (2021, November 25). It's 2021 — Why Are Public Spaces & Roads Still Unsafe for Women? *The Quint.* https://www.thequint.com/voices/opinion/gender-based-violence-crimes-against-women-ncrb-data-india-public-spaces-roads-safety-concerns#:~:text=Fast%20and%20rashly%20driven%20vehicles,of%20women%20and%20secluded%20neighbourhoods

Kerketta, S., & Maiti, A. (2021). Dimensions of women's safety in urban public places: A cross sectional study of Kolkata metropolitan area. *International Journal of Humanities and Social Science Research, 7*(1), 122–129.

Kitchi, F., Maci, G., & Janssen, A. (2022). *Gender-sensitive infrastructure planning means better cities for everyone.* UrbaNet.info.

Kumari, H. (2022). *Is public commute gender inclusive? Access, safety, and utility of our transport infrastructure.* https://feminisminindia.com/2022/06/06/is-public-commute-gender-inclusive-transport-infrastructure/

Lathia, S., & Mahadevia, D. (2019). Women's safety and public spaces: Lessons from the Sabarmati. *Urban Planning, 4*(2), 154–168. doi:10.17645/up.v4i2.2049

Loreck, J. (2016, January 5). Explainer: What does the 'male gaze' mean, and what about a female gaze? *The Conversation.* https://theconversation.com/explainer-what-does-the-male-gaze-mean-and-what-about-a-female-gaze-52486

Navya, P. K. (2021, March 17). Women's representation in apartment managing committee poor: Survey. *Women's Representation in Apartment Mc, Citizen Matters.* https://bengaluru.citizenmatters.in/womens-representation-apartment-committees-no-better-57109

Patel, M. (2021, November 8) Unequal access to toilets remains a worry and is central to global feminist movement. *The Indian Express.* https://indianexpress.com/article/research/why-unequal-access-to-toilets-is-central-to-the-global-feminist-movement-7613682/

Pathak, P. (2021). *Kolkata: How women walk the city.* OutlookIndia.com.

Pourya Asl, M. (Ed.). (2022). *Gender, place, and identity of South Asian women*. IGI Global. doi:10.4018/978-1-6684-3626-4

Purcell, M. (2002). Excavating Lefebvre: The right to the city and its urban politics of the inhabitant. *GeoJournal*, *58*(2/3), 99–108. doi:10.1023/B:GEJO.0000010829.62237.8f

Ray, B. (1991). Women of Bengal: Transformation in ideas and ideals, 1900-1947. *Social Scientist*, *19*(5/6), 3–23. doi:10.2307/3517870

Roy, S., & Bailey, A. (2021). Safe in the city? Negotiating safety, public space and the male gaze in Kolkata, India. *Cities (London, England)*, *117*, 103321. doi:10.1016/j.cities.2021.103321

Sharma, G. (2016). Impact on society by Indian women English writer. *Notions*, *7*(2), 1–7.

Singh, G. (2019). *Eight months after launch, Kolkata's 'pink taxis' hardly in the pink of health*. CitizenMatters.

Stone, D. (2020). *Niramay – An Unconditional Home. Curry Stone Design Collaborative*. CommunityDesignAgency.com.

Visakha, S. (2021). *A feminist approach to urban planning is vital for the future of cities*. https://asia.fes.de/news/feminist-cities

Weisman, L. K. (1992). *Discrimination by design*. University of Illinois Press.

UN Women. (2013). *Better lighting, wider pavements: Steps towards preventing sexual violence in New Delhi*. UNWomen.org.

Wyckoff, A. & Pilat, D. (2018). *Bridging the digital gender divide: Include, upskill, innovate*. OECD Report.

Zimmerman, J. (2017). *Urban planning has a sexism problem*. NextCity.org.

APPENDIX

Figure 1. Ward 91 Street

Re-Making the City for Women

Figure 2. Ward 91 Public Toilet Interior

Chapter 12
A Conceptual Study of Urban Spaces in Bangladesh:
Exploring Patriarchy From a Feminist Perspective

Nasrin Pervin
Universiti Teknologi Malaysia, Malaysia

Mahani Mokhtar
Universiti Teknologi Malaysia, Malaysia

Nishat Zarin Haque
Pabna University of Science and Technology, Bangladesh

ABSTRACT

Patriarchy has been commonly referred to as autocratic rule by the male mastery both in public and private spheres. It has become a social framework in which men hold essentials to control and prevail in parts of political administration, ethical specialists, social benefit, and control of property. In Bangladesh, men have historically dominated, oppressed, and exploited women. When women grow up, the tradition in which they are raised emphasizes the need for modesty and virginity, particularly for women. This is unassumingly visible not only in the countryside but also in urban spaces. This research examines the notion of patriarchy and its precise relationship to contemporary urban culture in the country. In addition, it investigates patriarchy as a concept from the perspective of feminists to address the fundamental feminist concerns about women's work and lives in the context of the urban spaces in Bangladesh.

DOI: 10.4018/978-1-6684-6650-6.ch012

INTRODUCTION

The term 'patriarchy' is used most often in feminist philosophy to refer to systems of male dominance. Patriarchy derives from the Greek word 'patriarkhēs', which implies "father or chief of a race" (Bhasin, 2006, p.3). In patriarchal societies, women's exploitation, mistreatment, and oppression have always been the main topics of discussion. The structure of our social system always creates barriers and challenges for women even when they have significant impact in society (Matheson et al., 2021). In Bangladesh, the term "patriarchy" refers to a system in which men keep power and control resources while women remain helpless and reliant on men. Although Article 19 and Article 28 of Bangladesh's constitution state that the state shall work to ensure that women and men have equal opportunities and participation in all spheres of national life, respectively, women's roles are still recognized as being equal to those of men in Bangladeshi society. Men still dominate and oppress in the private and public spaces of urban lives in Bangladesh (Chowdhury, 2009). Though females' participation in sustainable economic projects especially in public spaces in urban lives is given importance for economic prosperity (Karim et al., 2018), the patriarchal system in some way limits the rights of women. "Despite change, shift", and migration in societies, the underlying force of patriarchal dominance persists (Bennett, 2007, p. 63). For example, in addition to giving males unlimited precedence, patriarchal culture also restricts women's human rights. In both the public and private arenas, patriarchy refers to male dominance and through patriarchy, women are also barred from economic and political power. However, instead of strong patriarchal control over reproduction, many distinct communities including "coworkers, family, and government", controlled it in their hands (Hardwick, 2020, pp. 43–77). In line with the argument, it is also suggested that by changing norms and practices across generations in families, communities, and broader societies, patriarchy can be eliminated (Shohel et al., 2021). However, traditional society still instils some beliefs and views about what to do and what to avoid, work division, social rules & regulations, dress code, rights, and authority from childhood (Aktar, 2020). Even if it is not explicitly stated in their constitutions or laws, many contemporary societies are patriarchal. Men have more power over ideology, resources, and authority in modern Bangladeshi culture than women do. Words are one aspect of language that is very patriarchal; in Bangladesh, for instance, husbands are addressed as Swami, which means owner. Even the idea of marriage is based on the custom known as Kanyadaan, in which the father of the bride transfers all of his daughter's rights and obligations to her future spouse (Wani, 2019; Mia, 2020). All of these suggest that a woman is owned first by her father, then by her spouse, and finally by her son. However, patriarchy is brought into becoming, maintained, or allowed to wither away in common, rather than being provided in the order of things for "sociomaterial practices" (Mol, 2002, p. 6).

Moreover, like many societies, women are perceived as lesser human beings in the urban spaces in Bangladesh. When people grow up in the city, the socio-cultural tradition in which they are raised emphasizes the need for modesty and virginity, particularly for women. The patriarchal power determines who lives and dies which may be influenced by the intersections of gender and class, and other elements of lived experiences of women living in urban areas (Pierik, 2022). Incorporating women into decision-making process is a perverse way to keep them under control and preserve the existing hierarchical gender structure in exchange for their servitude and support to men's views (Sikweyiya et al., 2020). In addition to that, the religious and social tradition in which they are raised emphasizes the need for modesty and virginity, particularly for women. This is unassumingly visible in the countryside and urban spaces. For example, sharing a personal narrative, Tanha (2021) stated that the effects of patriarchy are a prevalent reality for young women in Bangladesh. In the same line, in another narrative, Bahar (2022) mentioned that the traditional version of hegemonic masculinity is the real cause of the issue because it places men in a dominant position such that women are not coerced into being the inferior gender but rather voluntarily consent to being ruled by their male counterparts. Women still struggle in their everyday life with their own spheres of life in the Bangladeshi cities (Mawa, 2020). Young battle with the constant reminders that they are responsible for how others view them and interact with them and need to keep all elements of their sexuality under control. They must go through many years of suffering and exploitation in a variety of professions and life stages.

In the patriarchal culture of the urban spaces in Bangladesh, women are seen as just sexual objects with no emotions rather than as individuals with feelings. The essence of society has long been recognized in women, but prejudice and oppression have restricted or limited their proficiencies and aptitudes. To fight for the systematic development of women, it is vital to comprehend the system that maintains women's subservience and dominance and deconstruct its inner workings. In the modern world, where women move up based on their skills, patriarchy makes it hard for women to get ahead because patriarchal structures and social interactions are to blame for women's lower or subordinate status in cities. For example, the studies by Wronksa (2018) state that though various governments and international organizations had tackled the issue of street sexual harassment occurring in urban spaces in Bangladesh, the problem still exists and has an impact on people's daily lives, particularly on women and girls and gender inequality and patriarchal norms in Bangladeshi society contribute to the street harassment of women. As women's regular commute habits are impacted, as are their choices regarding whether or not to be in public places, a potential obstacle to ending sexual harassment on the streets is the minimal participation of women in the planning and decision-making processes that are impacted by the patriarchal structures of Bangladeshi urban society. In the same line of argument Shamma (2021) states how Dhaka city has been spatialized and gendered, revealing how women's spatial practices interact with the city's new public space. Though women are able to work in the cities various malls, fashion businesses, and beauty salons, Dhaka's new urban landscape is still gendered and spatialized (Shamma, 2021). Dhaka's new urban area is created by rising consumerism and the expansion of the private service industries, where a great number of women are employed today but conventional patriarchy is being released from its confinement to home spheres as a result of women's advancement and men's unemployment because still men are intimidating women in public spaces as a way to demonstrate their symbolic masculinity which resulted in women's freedom of movement in public places which is constrained by their perception and experience of harassment by some of the city's male residents as well as by women's protective negotiating of the space (Shamma, 2021).

With all these backdrops in mind, this chapter per the authors is written to contribute to developing the framework of feminists' explorations of patriarchy, focusing on feminist humanism and feminist emancipatory theories in more depth to discuss how city and urban spaces are experienced and navigated by individuals and communities in Bangladesh. This work also investigates how the notion of patriarchy still exists in urban spaces of Bangladesh and creates challenges for women in the urban spaces of Bangladesh. Finally, this chapter concludes with suggestions for liberating women from patriarchy and its consequences in the spatialized notions.

Background of the Context: Paradigm of City, Gender, and Space

The largest and most developed region in Bangladesh is the metropolis of Dhaka. It now serves as the nation's financial, cultural, and commercial hub because the nation's liberation, including females in economic growth efforts, has been the primary consideration. Fortunately, a worldwide financial upheaval has been transforming the position of females since the 1980s. Thousands of females have migrated to Dhaka in recent years in search of work (ActionAid, 2014).

Tonkiss (2005) attempts to conceptualize sexuality and location in the town. She looked at how gender issues derived from patriarchal society impact how towns are perceived and used. She explained how city patterns reinforce mechanisms of both gender and sexual disparity. Consequently, gender and sexuality are not determined by physical limitations; instead, they are created by the environment. According to Tonkiss (2005), the connection between independence and risk is related to females' involvement in city areas. Towns are providing young females with fresh employment opportunities and a more liberated lifestyle, and females are moving there in massive quantities. These females receive the benefits of obscurity, governmental prominence, and emotional and spatial freedoms. The prevailing ordering of communal hubs has thus been overthrown by single females, who have also created places for their activities. The town has consequently evolved into a place where females may live freely. According to her theory, anxiety is biased in that it is primarily experienced by females and is primarily brought on by sexual aggression, making females feel more susceptible to male aggression.

Therefore, the dread of sexual abuse and rape is a significant catalyst for females' widespread concern about being abused through aggression. Once more, the spatialization of female security perceptions and hazards is based on unreliable topography. As geographical stability refers to the ways in which different populations use territory in cities and how such uses differ periodically, threat and protection are spatialized, indicating that some areas in the cities are unsafe for females. The misdistribution of toxic masculinity throughout geographical distances also implies that specific periods and locations threaten females. Under men's disorderly behavior at specific moments, Tonkiss (2005) showed that females see the area as unsafe. According to Phadke (2013), Females feel frightened in city open spaces primarily due to the undesirable behavior of uneducated males who are frequently jobless and migrants and discourage them from leaving the area. As a result of their view and practice of assault in urban open spaces, females' liberty and mobility have been greatly limited. Tonkiss (2005) says:

The charged nature of space for many women, and the fraught nature of the female body in space are evident in the advice commonly offered to women if they should find themselves on a deserted street after dark: the notion that you should walk in the middle of the road and not on the pavement literally puts women out of place in ordinary public spaces. It might be good advice, but it underlines the way that having a female body can be a spatial liability, and how certain spaces in the city are experienced as a kind of conflict zone (p. 104).

Valentine (1989) stated that females' utilization of territory is influenced by their social stigma in certain situations and at specified periods. According to a new study by Walsh (2015), females' behavior, mobility, and authority are restricted because of the heightened fear of being targeted in their regular lifestyle beyond the house. Rahbari and Sharepour (2015) reaffirmed that male predominance impedes females' public behaviors in the open metropolitan realm in particular locations at unsafe periods. Females also employ self-defense techniques to shield them from unfavorable events. Hence, Soenen (2007) explained that open places are dynamically generated depending on a person's sexuality, social traits, and background. Cities have been primarily determined and constituted in this way (Tonkiss, 2005). According to Reichenbach (2015), the biased character of specific locations is determined by circumstance and chronology. The region of gender, which limits females' use of cities or geographical behaviors due to their anxiety of and familiarity with abuse as well as the implementation of safety precautions in the urban, is known as the partitioning of territory based on gender in the cities.

Tradition of Spatial Studies and Feminists' Geography in Bangladeshi Context

In Bangladesh, women's organizations and movements created throughout the 1970s and 1990s had a variety of ideological stands in terms of spatial studies. Karmojibi Nari (Working Women), Bangladesh Mohila Parishad (BMP), and others were driven by Marxist theory and philosophy, and they maintained ties to the left-leaning political parties (Banu, n.d.; Banu, 2015). Other women's rights organizations considered groups like Naripokkho as radical because they emphasized women's autonomy and were unafraid to express strong issues concerning female sexuality and dignity (Azim, 2016). The feminist analysis by Rokeya and other writers used by all of these organizations as proof that women's rights concepts had their roots in the ancient Bangladeshi culture (Nazneen et al., 2011). The 1990s and the subsequent decade saw women's movement players rally against fundamental problems: violence against women and the Islamification of the state (Nazneen, 2017). The middle-class biases that exist within the women's movement was organized by women's movement actors, primarily Women for Women, throughout the late 1980s and early 1990s.

As previously said, the majority of women's rights and feminist groups in Bangladesh were founded by urban-based professional, elite, and middle-class women. They were able to provide their time and work for women concerning the condition of women from economic and political angle and their daily experiences of city life. Moreover, being able to give time for an organization and establishing a movement is closely related to the social class (Roy, 2012). This socioeconomic class component of voluntarism has created questions within the women's movement, especially among young feminists, and feminist geographer's concerning the normative ideal that voluntarism occupies within the Bangladeshi feminist movement (Nazneen & Sultana, 2012).

The Bangladeshi background is a dynamic urban environment with the voracious growth of property and infrastructure has resulted in an inherently unstable cityscape for many women in their daily lives. This milieu and its underlying sociopolitical relations have contributed to the creation of the conditions in which women are victims of patriarchal society; they get raped and harassed; they get lost and disappear, resulting in highly gendered forms of displacement of spaces. Deformation entails being chronologically and physically lost, disconnected from one's life, and experiencing an existential feeling of being out of the place geographically. These displacement of women in city has complicated root reasons. The neo-capitalist development's violent exclusions and dispossessions help set the stage, but other elements are equally crucial (Marouzi, 2021). The physicality of gendered bodies, which are rooted in the society is crucial, as is gender difference. In terms of how it is gendered and how it is navigated, space is essential in the urban areas. Physical and gendered vulnerabilities lead dangers related to location, emplacement, and an individual's aptitude for navigating both social and physical space (Gardner, 2022). The gendered and class-based characteristics of spatial precocity in Dhaka resulted in women's oppression that is seen everywhere in the spaces in cities; low-income women and girls get lost in time and space as a consequence of their spatial precocity, suspended in a liminal condition where neither they nor the persons they have lost can be located (Gardner, 2022). The linear progress narratives of development in spatial studies and global feminism are connected to and formed by policy players, state authorities, and women's concerns in modern Bangladesh. Different tales and narratives of women portray how integrating women's lives in spatial studies into global capitalist development researchers and projects like the apparel industry or NGOs might liberate them from the oppression caused by local patriarchal religious and cultural practices (Chowdhury, 2010).

As was mentioned above, Bangladesh has a long history of female activism and their roles reading how women live and work in connection with the patriarchal structural space in the urban spaces in Bangladesh. Very few research has been done regarding the women and their lives in the urban spaces in Bangladesh. The essential feminist themes of choice, autonomy, and opportunity have always been valued by women throughout history. Although by no means comprehensive, this paper aims to put the organizations and people involved in the larger feminist movement in Bangladesh into the perspective of how feminist solidarity, the development of new womanhood, and women's activism against patriarchal society in relation to the urban spaces in modern Bangladesh.

The Concept and Creation of Patriarchy

Patriarchy derives from the Greek word 'patriarkhēs', which implies "father or chief of a race" (Bhasin, 2006, p. 3). Patriarchy has been commonly referred to as autocratic rule by male mastery both in public and private provinces. It has become a social framework in which men hold essential to control and prevail in parts of political administration, ethical specialist, social benefit, and control of property. Patriarchy has been prevalent in the social, civil, political, theological, and economic organizations of many cultures since the late twentieth century. Many modern societies are patriarchal, although their constitutions and rules do not expressly establish them. Feminists use the word patriarchy to define the power dynamic between men and women and identify the underlying reason for women's subjugation. Women are viewed as passive dependents and husbands' property in the family. Since the late twentieth century, patriarchy has been prevalent in many cultures' social, civil, political, theological, and economic organizations.

In the twentieth century, feminist ideologies revised and extended our view of patriarchy. The word 'patriarchy' is often used by feminists to describe the dominant structure between men and women. Feminism, as a philosophy, attempts to call attention to patriarchy's negative impacts on women's lives. They argue that women are abused and subjugated in both the private and public spheres (Millett, 1977; Walby 1990; Bhasin 2006). Most aspects of feminism describe patriarchy as a current unequal social structure that oppresses, discriminates, or subordinates women. Mitchell, a feminist psychologist, uses patriarchy "to refer to kinship systems in which men exchange women" (Mitchell, 1971, p.24). Walby (1990) refers to "patriarchy as a system of social structures and practices in which men dominate, oppress and exploit women" (p. 20). Walby (1990) outlines contemporary political controversies, including Marxism, Radical and Liberal feminism, Post-structuralism, and Dual systems theory. She uses the latest up-to-date scientific research to demonstrate how each can be generalized to various substantive subjects ranging from paid work, housework, and the state to culture, sexuality, and violence. She suggests a synthesis of class analysis with radical feminist theory to understand gender dynamics in terms of patriarchal and neoliberal structure, arguing that sexism has been remarkably adaptable to shifts in women's status and that some of the women's hard-won social advances have been turned into new traps.

Liberal feminism continues to be a dominant standpoint in the feminist thought which synthesizes values of democracy and equality with the concept of women's personal and political freedom. It is about freedom to live one's life as one chooses as well as the freedom to participate in the chosen political conduit. Liberal feminist ideas have overwhelmed radical, Marxist, and socialist feminism ideas (Jaggar, 1983; Jaggar, 1987). Radical feminism over values the structures of dominance whereas liberals see potential in freedom (MacKinnon, 1982; Hirschmann, 2008). Marxist ideas of reproduction's social and historical existence were revised over the 20th century, and many other political theories were developed using their texts (MacKinnon, 1982; Hirschmann, 2008). Marxist feminism focuses on gender roles in the shaping of capitalism, arguing that social norms are determined by the use-value of reproductive labor, the exchange value of income, and the surplus value of the benefit. Socialist feminists viewed childbirth as women's labor in which in the early 1900s ended monogamous marriage and family objectification (Bebel & Lilienthal, 1910). Many feminist theorists, as can be viewed in their recent critical theory work, value socialist and Marxist feminists' observation on material conditions of life and indulge in the hermeneutics of skepticism (Fraser, 2009; Allen, 2007; McAfee, 2008; Young, 2000).

Patriarchy has its historical roots in the family, whose legal and substantive leadership is practiced by the father and is projected to the whole social system, sustained and strengthened by numerous mechanisms/institutions, including the Tradition of Male Unity (McKeon, 1995; Sultana, 2012). The roots of the patriarchal system and its structure of society suggest that the roles of genders are related deeply to the socio-cultural and behavioral norms and values in society as who is desirable to whom in different sectors depends largely on the specific gender (Fernea, 2003; Sultana, 2012). Traditionalists claim that men are born to rule, and women are born to be inferior when it comes to life and origins of patriarchy (Bahlieda, 2015; McAfee, 2018). Some of them deny it, arguing that patriarchy is man-made, not normal, and therefore unchangeable; sexism is not universal, but rather man-made and can be reversed (Sultana, 2012; Mikkola, 2008; Mikkola, 2009). While there are biological distinctions between men and women, these differences should not be used to explain a male-dominated sexual hierarchy; therefore, gender stereotypes have long been the focus of a conventional quest for biological theories.

Before the nineteenth century, this debate regarding the notion of patriarchy was predominantly religious, with patriarchy being regarded as the natural order; however, Darwin's (1859) evolutionary theories explained evolution from a biological order (cited in Than et al., 2022). To be sure, Darwin (1859) never advocated for Social Darwinism or the application of evolutionary principles to human creation and social behaviors. Sociobiology is the modern term for using biological theories to describe social phenomena. Nonetheless, sociobiologists use biology to understand social behaviors, such as gender stereotypes, sexuality, and male domination as Patriarchy, according to them, is more a product of innate biology than of social conditioning (Little, 2016). Females nearly often spend more resources in producing offspring than males, and as a result, females are an advantage for which males contend, according to one evolutionary sociobiological explanation for the root of patriarchy (Little, 2016). According to social constructionist hypotheses, people generate gender norms within a society that want to imbue a specific structure with significance to challenge gender stereotypes and are actively toying with and negotiating gender roles (Holmes, 2007). One factor that females consider when choosing a partner is which males have more money to support them and their children and this makes men ambitious and manages to gain wealth in order to contend with other men.

Monagan (2010) expands on the concept of patriarchy which is rooted in a social structure where the father bears primary responsibility for and authority over his family, however, patriarchy's true reach extends far beyond the confines of the familial realm (cited in Bahlieda, 2015). According to Johnson (2005), patriarchy has three distinguishing characteristics: societal patriarchy exists to the extent that it promotes how males are privileged through dominance, their credentials; how the world is centered through their male orientations; and the passion for power and control to make the men oppress the oppressor as a fundamental component. When Hartmann (1981) defines the term, he highlights the paradoxical complexity that accompanies the presence of patriarchy concerning women: Patriarchy is a loosely organized gender-based system where men keep the faith and have solidarity with other men, irrespective of their distinct class, and race or ethnicity, with a shared value about their superiority over women and a desire to keep women subordinate. As the patriarchal structure is hierarchical, men coming from different backgrounds, and classes are connected with each other when it comes to dominating women because they share the same bond; moreover, they rely on one another to maintain that dominance as hierarchies function partly by creating vested interests in the status of social positions (Hartman, 1981, p.197).

HISTORY OF FEMINISM

In the 15th century, Pizan (1364-1430) was the first woman to 'take up her pen in defense of her sex,' according to Simone De Beauvoir (1908-1986) (cited in Watt, 2022, n. p.). Incorporating women's theoretical contributions requires vast historical geography (Bressey, 2010). The first wave in the US occurred in the late 19th and early 20th centuries and the results of the feminist movement (Butler, 1994) were the ability to own property, the equal wage for men and women, the right to start divorce proceedings (including contraception and abortion) and the right to vote are all (Messer-Davidow, 2002). In 1931, different organizations developed a feminist framework to break the unequal distribution of power, resources, and opportunities that exist in societies (John, 1998). It has become a social framework in which the notion of men holding the power in different sectors be it political, economic or professional, or social needs to be redistributed for women's freedom and development. Feminism has moved from the equal rights and women's autonomy movement of the last century to being multifaceted tagging as revolutionaries, radicals, Marxists, socialists, and liberals. Socialist feminism focuses on the gender elements of the welfare state, while liberal feminism emphasizes institutional change. Black feminism grew in popularity as a reaction to the feminist and civil rights movements' misogyny. They fought for racial and caste equality. For example, "Body positivity" is a social movement that combines feminist ideas of equality, social justice, and cultural analysis based on a woman's weight (Boling, 2011, pp.110-123). 1920s feminism is concerned with inequities, collective social and political interests, and women's autonomy. This century's reformers and revolutionaries grew and divided into major categories: Revolutionaries, Radicals, Marxists, and Aocialists.

Female emancipation and equality were the main goals of the first wave of feminism, whereas female oppression was the main focus of the second. The first wave-feminism questioned why women were oppressed and what role they should play in society to protect them. Capitalism and patriarchy are essential to comprehending women's oppression, according to materialist feminism (the late 1970s) and feminism's social construct view of gender imposes gender responsibilities on women, such as childbearing. Female equality is materialist feminism's ideal society and this idea emphasizes social change rather than economic system reform (Jackson, 2001). Women's rights activism returned in the late 1960s, after a 40-year break. It was released in 1967 and is generally credited with launching second-wave feminism in the Netherlands (Stewart et al., 1998). Mecha sprang out of the 1969 Chicago Youth Liberation Conference as female voices started to be heard in the male-dominated conference debate by exploring the Chicana Feminist Movement which started when women went home as activists. France's feminist thinkers in the 1970s addressed feminism via feminine literature, which influenced literary works greatly (Wright, 2000). All these authors' works reflected strongly on women's rights and struggles. The third wave concentrated on eradicating gender stereotypes and extending feminism to encompass women of all races, classes, and cultures (Tong, 2009) which proposed three stages to women's concerns: female empowerment as individual change, simple solutions to the difficulties women face regarding financial matters, the decision-making process for their professional roles and giving importance to their in-built powers for their self-improvements (Rockler, 2006). However, the rights and equality of women regarding financial matters and the dominance of men in professional fields are already discussed and addressed by many feminists (Narayan, 1998). As a result of fourth-wave feminism, though feminism has reduced domestic violence against males in six-fold ways (Pynchon, 2011), male violence and femicides against women have increased significantly (Holson, 2019).

The major feminists' thoughts and discussions are based on sex and gender inequality, discrimination based on race and socio-cultural-economic structure, male dominance, and women subordination. The systems and mechanisms in the urban spaces of Bangladeshi society are largely dependent on these notions which influence how equality and justice prevail in the lives of women in society. Therefore, it is perceived that through the explorations of the existing conditions in the current socio-cultural patriarchal systems, the study would be able to reveal in which conditions the reality happens and what might work best for social justice for women working at urban spaces in Bangladesh. In addition to that, this research is challenging traditional society with an aspiration to create awareness and professional opportunities for the oppressive characters while at the same time providing spaces for unheard female voices to speak for themselves as Egbert and Sanden (2019) suggest.

The Role of Patriarchy in Women's Subordination in the Urban Spaces in Bangladesh

Patriarchy is the most fundamental aspect of society that has existed from the dawn of time and almost definitely since the beginning of recorded history more than 5000 years ago (Lerner, 1986). According to Lerner's (1986) fundamental work on patriarchy and the distinction between oppression and subordination, subordination is a state of being compelled to remain under the authority of others. Subordination is sometimes a kind of what is referred to as silent aggression; additionally, it reflects both women's and men's unconscious and conscious socialized acceptance of patriarchy (Lerner, 1986). Thus, the subordination of women refers to the societal condition in which women are compelled to remain under men's authority. Patriarchy uses socialization to enforce certain social norms, traditions, and social duties to maintain men's dominance over women. Socialization occurs mainly during childhood when boys and girls learn to behave appropriately for their gender. All socialization agents, including the family, church, legal system, economic and political system, educational institutions, and media, are cornerstones of a patriarchal system and structure. The word "social structure" is critical here since it indicates a rejection of both biological determinism and the idea that each male is in a dominating position and each woman is in a subservient one. "In this system, women's labor power, reproduction, sexuality, movement, and property — as well as other economic resources - are all subject to patriarchal control" (Walby, 1990, p. 20).

The creation of private and public worlds of the urban spaces for women and males has been used by patriarchal ideology to keep women out of power structures. Walby's (1990) patriarchal theories demonstrate "two different kinds of patriarchy: private and public patriarchy" (p.24) which are vigilant in the public and private domains of Bangladeshi women's lives in cities. Household production is the primary location of women's subjugation under private patriarchy and public patriarchy is mostly found in public spaces such as the workplace and the state.

Moreover, patrilineal descent and patrilocal residency are two terms used to describe patriarchal systems (Sultana, 2012) that exist in the urban spheres in Bangladesh. Discrimination of all kinds creates social, political, economic, religious, and cultural divides between men and women, resulting in a male-dominated society. It also abolishes women's equality with males, establishes women's subordination, and creates a social structure that fosters compliance in that space. As the "bottom rung of poverty, illiteracy, and landlessness" is populated by women (Mahtab, 2007, pp. 20-21), women suffer the most severe consequences of birth discrimination, which denies them access to all possibilities and advantages in family and social spheres of urban life, such as education and health. As a result, they are in the most precarious situation and become victims of the most heinous kinds of violence. Women's rights are often violated under Islamic law. There is ample evidence that the rights enshrined in religious laws are often ignored in a patriarchal culture controlled by men. As a result, the patriarchal claim that religion subordinates women is not entirely accurate; rather, patriarchal supporters in society use religion as a weapon to maintain their control over the private and public spaces of women.

The human race has long prided itself on having a moral consciousness that guides human behavior. The internal psychological battle that all people go through in choosing their actions. Patriarchy is a system that keeps women in inferior positions. Discrimination, disrespect, insult, control, exploitation, oppression, and violence are manifestations of everyday subordination, regardless of class. For example, a few instances reflect a specific type of discrimination and a particular element of patriarchy. Men's control over women and girls, sexual harassment in the workplace, lack of inheritance or property rights for women, lack of male control over women's bodies and sexuality are just a few examples that affect the spaces of women.

As a result, attitudes and behaviors that devalue women and oppress them are found in our homes, social relationships, religious institutions, and institutions of all kinds. Patriarchy is the sum of all the male dominance we witness around women. Most of the women in our society suffer from depression which are possibly caused by what Johnson (2005) stated are mostly patriarchal aggression, dominance, and control. The torch of patriarchy has been passed down from generation to generation, father to son, dynasty to dynasty, as an acknowledged and unalterable male societal dominance and authority. Again, religion was the first servant of patriarchy since men developed methodical ideas that glorified their exploits and supremacy (Johnson, 2005; Lerner, 1997). Most significantly, patriarchy has institutionalized male dominance, aggression, and control in human interactions, preventing the creation of more effective social systems from governing human behavior (Bahlieda, 2015; Lerner, 1986) which certainly affects the perspectives of urban spaces of Bangladeshi women.

Explorations of Patriarchy in Urban Spaces in Bangladesh

Just like in other countries, patriarchy exists and is enrooted in a society like Bangladesh where women are perceived as in subordinate positions which are also part of society and cultures. The studies of Sultana (2012) in the Bangladeshi context posit that even the working mothers living in urban area, when it comes to their children's education in a circumstance of rationed educational opportunity, prefer sons' education to daughters' which allows society to see women as subordinate to the very beginning at their life. This is also a side effect of society's dominant patriarchal ideology, which places women in conflicting positions in the private and public spaces of their lives, therefore, patriarchy dominates both the public and private lives of women where their relationships with men are dictated by misinterpreting (or selectively referring from) the religious book according to Chowdhury (2009). Moreover, education and paid jobs are yet to overcome the deeply rooted effect of patriarchy (Chowdhury, 2009). In Bangladeshi urban society, men control, exploit and dominate women in every sphere of their lives to varying degrees; even the women do not choose when, and how many children they should have (Hossen, 2020). The three features of men's position and roles in women-centered development initiatives are: men fear the loss of authority, recognize women's role in family welfare, and women's independence of men's engagement in women-focused development initiatives are suggested by Karim et el. (2018). Married men's view of marriage in urban society is patriarchal oriented as they think women should be ready for every beck and call, and if they are not obliging sexually, they can be punished (Islam & Karim, 2012). Another reason could be the unequal gender disparity that exists in urban society and the discrimination that is present in the laws and policies which are derived from patriarchal notions that discourage women to seek recourse or expect fairness (Monsoor, 1999). Coming to terms with or making sense of changing reality in a gender-biased society could lead to confusion in the urban spaces of Bangladesh (Monsoor, 1999). A case study of Intimate partner violence IPV in the Bangladeshi context suggests that it is not always men to resolve interpersonal conflict; rather it could be gender-based hierarchy status resolving which makes even women tacitly justify Intimate Partner Violence (Sayem et al., 2012).

The Challenges Professional Women face in the Bangladeshi Urban Spaces

In the social urban context of Bangladesh, there is a great imbalance between the rights of men and women in every sphere of life, where it is considered that women deserve fewer advantages than men. While the birth of a male child is counted as a blessing, a female infant is granted as a burden, because of social taboos, norms, religious points of view etc. (Ahmed, 2019). Moreover, women are regarded as the tool of reproduction in society (Ghose et al., 2017). The tradition of the typical patriarchal kinship thoughts does not let women get equal rights and opportunities, rather let them depend on male figures (Ali, 2012). Thus, they do not get proper education facilities, medical or health treatment, job opportunities, and possessions (Hussein, 2017; Nazneen, 2017; Raihan & Bidisha, 2018) even if they are living in Modern Dhaka, capital of Bangladesh.

In cities, patriarchy works as the stumbling block against the development and empowerment of women (Haque & Druce, 2019). Women are generally considered as the reproducers, besides playing the role of doing all sorts of domestic work including - cooking, cleaning, and most importantly, nurturing children (Sultana, 2021). Women do not have the power of making resolutions, not even about their own life, whether it is the matter of education, employment, or even choosing their life partners; all of such responsibilities and decisions are taken by the male persons of their family (Mahmud, 2003; Rahman & Islam, 2013). The main target of patriarchy is to confirm women's inferiority and reliance on men in every aspect of life, where men rule over the entire family and society (Azim, 2010; Raihan et al., 2018). Similarly, in rural areas, the patriarchal family system is much influenced by the ideals of patriarchal gender terms (Raihan et al., 2018). According to researchers, the patriarchal gender norms obstruct women's development in Bangladesh (Karim et al., 2012; Karim et al., 2016). Therefore, patriarchy causes the supreme obstacle against the development and setting up of equivalent rights for women in urban and rural spaces in Bangladesh.

In poor families either in rural or urban areas, girls are most often pressured to focus much on domestic work, rather than getting institutional education (Mahmud & Bidisha, 2018). Thus, the efforts of the female children in maintaining the household responsibilities, such as raising their younger siblings, and doing the chores, put a greater impact on the family's economy, while the mothers engage themselves in earning outside the home (Sultana, 2012).

The inferiority of women, including the infraction against their basic human rights, injustice, and obstruction against their establishment in society, are caused by discrimination against women, which has become one of the most troubled burning issues for the last twenty years (Ganguly, 2020). In the patriarchal system, women are considered subordinates to men in all the sectors of social, economic, political, cultural, and religious issues (Wiegand, 2012; Sultana, 2012). The male-constructed society wants to abolish the equality between males and females, considering women as less intelligent, weak, and inferior (Sultana, 2012, pp. 11-13). The traditional family and kinship practices cause women's lower position and reliance upon men, which is the root of the patriarchal establishment in urban development of Bangladesh, where women are supposed to be subordinate to men in all spheres of life. Patriarchy rules over the cities in different ways, which include (Sultana, 2012):

- Male children are given much more priority in society rather than female ones, who are being neglected and threatened like their mothers, but the oppression done by their fathers and their parental families.

- Men are free from all sorts of domestic work with the excuse of earning outside, while women and female children remain confined to the household chores, the works which bring no admiration, appreciation, or identification.
- Girls are deprived of educational facilities, where it is considered that education is more important for boys. Therefore, women do not get equivalent opportunities to nourish their talents from childhood.
- Girls do not have independence or permission to go outside the home to meet with their friends or to earn money in the patriarchal society. If they go out, they must come back home before sunset.
- Threatening and beating up wives is a regular thing in society, where the patriarchal standards cause the worst domestic violence, which has been deeply rooted in the strictness of the patriarchal culture.
- Sexual exploitation at the worksite is a significant point that Bangladeshi professional women face, most often. Even sometimes they have to lose their job if they do not respond to the needs of their employer.
- Although in Muslim families, sisters get half of their brother's share of the property, Hindu women actually get nothing; whereas, Christian women get an equivalent portion of the property as their brothers. However, because of the patriarchal nature of the urban society, women often face discrimination and are completely denied their legal property rights.
- Men exploiting women, or ruling over their bodies is a usual matter.
- Women are devoid of their reproductive rights, where their male partners decide about family planning.
- Generally, women are not allowed to choose their life partners, and they have to agree with the decisions about marriage taken by the male members of their family. Even they cannot support their own relatives, once they are married.
- According to the Holy Quran, both men and women have to keep modesty, which is considered as 'purdah', where women have to cover themselves properly with clothes. However, the patriarchal biased system of society uses this concept of 'purdah' to control women's voice and mobility, rather than focusing on the purdah of men as well. Therefore, purdah has become a perplexing system in society, putting much more than limitations on the dress code and physical movement of women (Sultana, 2012, pp. 11-13).

Radical Feminism and Eradication of Patriarchy in the Urban Societies of Bangladesh

Human interactions and connections alter cultural and social institutions through time, having a significant effect on society, is referred to as social reformation or social transformation. Radical social change, defined as a profound transformation of a community, neighborhood, region, or the whole globe toward greater economic equality, and political involvement, and achieved via the activities of a powerful and varied popular movement, is obviously in the air we now breathe. Radical feminism has played a significant role in developing a feminist understanding of women's oppression that has influenced other feminist currents (for example, revolutionary feminism and Marxist feminism).

The view of radical feminism's main aim is liberating women from male-imposed norms and establishing a society based on female values (Willis, 1984). Most women who identify as radical feminists really support a cultural feminist agenda that grew out of radical feminism's ideals to eliminating male dominance in all aspects of social and economic life of different spaces of women's lives. Women, children, and weak males are routinely abused by men under patriarchy, according to radical feminism (Willis, 1984). Radical feminism compels us to consider male and female bodies and male sexual abuse and exploitation.

Radical feminism affirms sexual dimorphism, devalues masculinity, and demonstrates female moral superiority. A superior female essence opposes the tendency towards androgyny and the minimization of gender distinctions (Alcoff, 1988). Moreover, "the ultimate aim of feminist revolution must be, unlike the first feminist movement, not just the eradication of male privilege but also the sex differentiation itself" (Firestone, 1970, p.11). In line with that argument, by citing Fahs (2011), radical feminist Atkinson (2000) wrote in her foundational piece "Radical Feminism":

The first dichotomous division of this mass [mankind] is said to have been on the grounds of sex: male and female ... it was because half the human race bears the burden of the reproductive process and because man, the 'rational' animal, had the wit to take advantage of that, that the child bearers, or the 'beasts of burden,' were corralled into a political class: equivocating the biologically contingent burden into a political (or necessary) penalty, thereby modifying these individuals' definition from the human to the functional, or animal (p.85).

Women living in the urban spaces of Bangladesh seem to be granted gender equality under the country's constitution and general law. However, the patriarchal interpretation of the law perpetuates patriarchal views. That being said, the legal status of Bangladeshi women is much better than their reality status. The patriarchal ideology determines our femininity and masculinity, assigning women and men distinct roles, rights, and obligations. Gender-based culture should be altered, and the time has arrived to bring about a fundamental transformation of patriarchy's dominating ideology; therefore, initiating the philosophy of radical feminism (Willis, 1984) by abolishing male dominance in all social and economic urban settings while acknowledging that women's experiences are influenced by other social divides such as race, class, and sexual orientation should be given importance.

Discrimination against women places women in an inferior position which violates their fundamental human rights and obstructs inequality goals, peace, and progress. The radical feminist perspective encompasses a range of views on women's oppression. The approach often focuses on sisterhood, substantial distinctions between men and women, and a shared experience of suffering and oppression as the primary basis of feminist political action. Male power, according to radical feminist analysis, is not confined to the public spheres of politics and paid employment but also extends into private life; this means- traditional concepts of power and politics are challenged and stretched to such 'personal' spheres of life as the family and sexuality, both of which are viewed as instruments of patriarchal domination.

By building equality, radical feminists are trying to give women a chance to fulfill their potential. Radical Feminists see the family as predominantly patriarchal and argue for its destruction in favor of alternative family arrangements and sexual interactions. Radical Feminists have proposed various alternatives, including separatist — women-only communes – and matrifocal (female-centered) homes. Additionally, some adhere to political Lesbianism and political celibacy, seeing heterosexual partnerships as sleeping with the enemy. Radical feminists have often been instrumental in establishing and operating refuges for women victims of male violence. According to radical feminist theory, the biological distinctions between men and women underpin women's subordination, a relationship that existed prior to the economic or racial oppression of women's bodies. Radical feminists make explicit connections between knowledge and experience, challenge the foundations of Western science and reason, and engage critically with the concept of objectivity and the idea of an unbiased observer (King, 1994). Radical feminists advocate for family members to practice democracy, equality, and mutual respect. True peace in society can only be achieved via personal peace. And if civilizations ensure that all citizens have fundamental capacities, including physical integrity and allegiance, choices may be recognized within an oppression-free framework in the spaces of both cities and villages.

Eradication of the Concept of Men's Domination and Women's Subordination

The term male dominance evolved in the twentieth century as a conceptual label to characterize the unequal power relations between men as a group and women as a group. Male dominance is one of the earliest known and most widespread forms of inequality in human history.

Power is normally never given; power normally needs to be taken. We live in a male-dominated world with a male-dominated culture. Centuries of patriarchy and discrimination have left a damaging legacy. Sexist attitudes and stereotypes are widespread in Governments, the private sector, academia, the arts, science and technology, and even in civil society and international organizations. The key to changing our civilization lies in understanding patriarchy and its overwhelming control over who we are, how we act, and how we think as a human civilization. Still, half of the total population doesn't see patriarchy as a problem (Johnson, 2005). Everything we see currently has patriarchy as its foundation. The birth of patriarchy in each new generation is in the family either in city or rural areas. Thus, the family is a critical area of change if patriarchy is ever to be reformed. The work of Charles Darwin (1859) in the 19th century exacerbated the mythical view of societal violence as normalized through his work *The Origin of Species*. In his research on natural selection, Darwin (1859) noted that animals compete for resources to survive, which resulted in the survival of the fittest, the most intelligent, and the strongest (Schaefer, 2022) and increased the quality of the surviving breeding line. Violence is the constant that defines all human and animal experiences, with one significant exception animals kill only to survive, and humans do not kill to survive. Yet, they continue to do so despite this. The physically strongest and best breeding line no longer stays as humankind has evolved.

In order for women's rights to be respected, men have to fulfill their duties to respect their wives, daughters, mothers, and other women in their lives. Women have to learn self-respect and seize more than the few, meager opportunities that patriarchal society has availed them. Once women and men together exercise their duties for respect of self and others, they will be psychologically and socially capable of respecting and recognizing one another's rights in law and culture. It begins with a change in self-understanding, for both men and women. A psychological change of such depth requires reform of education on the deepest level too, and only comprehensive education and religion can accomplish this kind of change in different domains of urban society.

Progress for women and girls means changing the unequal power dynamics that underpin discrimination and violence. Discrimination against women damages communities, organizations, companies, economies, and societies- all spaces of urban lives. That is why all men should support women's rights and gender equality. In our modern patriarchal world, we accept male dominance and subordination and encourage, condone, and celebrate it. Eradicating all these requires changing all the social changes at the source, not the presentation of the problems. As we are working toward cultural change, we also need to work on changing ourselves-the only element we have complete control over. As Lerner (1997) pointed out, "The system of patriarchy is a historic construct; it has a beginning; it will have an end.

Its time seems to have nearly run its course—it no longer serves the needs of men or women and in its inextricable linkage to militarism, hierarchy, and racism it threatens the very existence of life on earth" (p. 229).

CONCLUSION

The social transformation has been mirrored and controlled by feminist movements. Changes in society's basic institutional structures—the economy, the state, and the family—have weakened the foundation for inequality that exist in the urban atmospheres in Bangladeshi society and radical feminism advocates for a radical reorganization of that problems in that society. Male supremacy is abolished in all social and economic urban contexts while acknowledging that other social divisions, such as race, class, and sexual orientation, impact women's experiences. As the radical feminist recognizes larger systems of dominance than any one person, seeing women as objects of men's desire (Welch, 2015) -the patriarchal control of women in urban spaces should be taken into consideration to understanding the cause of power differentials. However, ambitious women may attempt to develop themselves via solo efforts or by collaborating with other women in an environment that improves their chances in their spaces. Whenever and whenever circumstances arose, some women took advantage of them to better their lives. Women who attained legal status, education, and some freedom from domestic duties in the nineteenth century started to push for the same voting rights as men. Educated long-term workers and young women in college were especially dissatisfied in the second half of the twentieth century. They began to demand the same employment prospects and treatment from employers as men in comparable situations which shows women have started raising their voice to break the shackles in the urban spatial context. Women should be motivated to organize when they realize their aspirations are unattainable on their own. Collective action could also be a sensible approach that women can take as their aspirations are the realistic objectives that are being unfairly and unreasonably thwarted. More women with severely unfulfilled aspirations, personal independence, and the ability to organize arise from these societal developments. Therefore, feminist movements aid in the advancement of greater equality that is brought about by structural urban improvements, as well as the direction of changes in women's social identities in the urban spaces of Bangladesh. The gradual disentanglement of patriarchal disparity developed from socio-economic structure weakens the inequality that is deeply rooted in the urban area of Bangladesh. However, institutional growth will lead men to accept and understand and relearn what they have learned from the patriarchal society.

Overall, Bangladeshi women working in urban spaces need to improve themselves which will contribute more to reduce inequity than the much more well-documented initiatives. Countless women have taken chances, suffered adversity, and defied conventions to improve their lives during the last 150 years. These women, sometimes working alone and relying only on their determination, exerted constant pressure on gender disparity, causing it to decrease in urban and rural areas of Bangladesh. A double standard of highly valuing physical, sexually appealing looks cannot exist in the urban spaces of a society where women work the same way men do. There is no longer any space for women to remain reliant on males in a society where they are expected to think, act, and provide for themselves. When women take action all that is required for us is to listen to their experiences and their perceptions because they all collectively make up their spatial practices in the city. Inspiring future generations to join the struggle, we hope, will be the bold work of the women who came before us.

REFERENCES

ActionAid. (2014). *Safe Cities for Women: From reality to rights.* https://actionaid,ie/wp-content/uploads/2016/10/Safe-Cities-for-Women-from-Realities-toRights-1.pdf

Ahmed, M. (2019). *Breaking harmful taboos in society, Sex education is a must to prevent gender-based violence.* https://www.thedailystar.net/opinion/society/news/breaking-harmful-taboos-society-1772890

Aktar, T. (2020). Patriarchal society is a curse for Bangladeshi women, It's time to raise our voice against injustice. *Economics and Politics.* https://www.meer.com/en/64001-patriarchal-society-is-a-curse-for-bangladeshi-women

Alcoff, L. (1988). Cultural feminism versus post-structuralism: The identity crisis in feminist theory. *Signs (Chicago, Ill.), 13*(3), 405–436. doi:10.1086/494426

Ali, R. (2012). Changing expectations of gender roles in Bangladesh. *Research Monograph Series, 52.* https://bigd.bracu.ac.bd/wp-content/uploads/2020/03/Changing-Expectations-of-Gender-Roles-in-Bangladesh-The-Case-of-Female-Field-Staff-of-BRAC_Monograph_52.pdf

Allen, A. (2007). *The politics of our selves: Power, autonomy, and gender in contemporary critical theory.* Columbia University Press. doi:10.7312/alle13622

Azim, F. (2010). The new 21st century woman. In F. Azim & M. Sultan (Eds.), Mapping women's empowerment: Experience from Bangladesh, India and Pakistan (pp. 261-78). The University Press Limited.

Azim, F. (2016). Secularism and women's movement in Bangladesh. In M. Mukhopadyay (Ed.), *Feminist movement and complicity*. Zubaan Publishers.

Bahar, N. S. (2022). *Nothing is more alarming than when women do patriarchy's work for it*. https://www.thedailystar.net/views/opinion/news/women-can-internalise-patriarchy-too-2986921

Bahlieda, R. (2015). The legacy of patriarchy. *Counterpoints, 488*, 15–67. https://www.jstor.org/stable/45136330

Banu, A. (2015). Global-local interactions: First three decades of women's movement in Bangladesh. *Journal of the Asiatic Society, 60*(2), 203–230.

Banu, A. (n.d.). *Feminism in Bangladesh (1971-2000): Voices from the movement* [PhD thesis]. University of Dhaka, Bangladesh.

Bebel, A., & Lilienthal, M. S. (1910). *Woman and socialism*. Good Press.

Bennett, J. (2007). *History matters: Patriarchy and the challenge of feminism*. University of Pennsylvania Press. doi:10.9783/9780812200553

Bhasin, K. (2006). *What is patriarchy? Women unlimited*. Academic Press.

Boling, P. (2011). On learning to teach fat feminism. *Feminist Teacher, 21*(2), 110–123. doi:10.5406/femteacher.21.2.0110

Bressey, C. (2010). Victorian 'anti-racism' and feminism in Britain. *Women a Cultural Review, 21*(3), 279–291. doi:10.1080/09574042.2010.513491

Butler, J. (1994). Feminism by any other name (Judith Butler interviews Rosi Braidotti). *Differences: A Journal of Feminist Cultural Studies, 6*(2–3), 272–361.

Chowdhury, E. (2010). Feminism and its 'other': Representing the 'new woman' of Bangladesh. *A Journal of Feminist Geography Place and Culture, 3*, 301-318. . doi:10.1080/09663691003737587

Chowdhury, F. (2009). Theorising patriarchy: The Bangladesh context. *Asian Journal of Social Science, 37*(4), 599–622. doi:10.1163/156853109X460200

Darwin, C. (1859). *On the Origin of Species*. John Murray.

Egbert, J., & Sanden, S. (2019). *Foundations of education research understanding theoretical components*. Routledge. doi:10.4324/9780429452963

Fahs, B. (2011). Ti-Grace Atkinson and the legacy of radical feminism. *Feminist Studies, 37*(3), 561–590. doi:10.1353/fem.2011.0047

Fernea, R. (2003). Gender, sexuality and patriarchy in modern Egypt. *Critique*, *12*(2), 141–153. doi:10.1080/1066992032000130602

Firestone, S. (1970). *The dialectic of sex: The case for feminist revolution*. William Morrow and Company.

Fraser, N. (2009). *Scales of justice: Reimagining political space in a globalizing world*. Columbia University Press.

Ganguly, M. (Ed.). (2020). *"I Sleep in My Own Deathbed" Violence against Women and Girls in Bangladesh: Barriers to Legal Recourse and Support*. https://www.hrw.org/report/2020/10/29/i-sleep-my-own-deathbed/violence-against-women-and-girls-bangladesh-barriers

Gardner, K. (2022). Lost and abandoned: Spatial precarity and displacement in Dhaka, Bangladesh. *Ethnos. Journal of Anthropology*, 1–19. Advance online publication. doi:10.1080/00141844.2022.2052925

Ghose, B., Feng, D., Tang, S., Yaya, S., He, Z., Udenigwe, O., Ghosh, S., & Feng, Z. (2017). Women's decision-making autonomy and utilisation of maternal healthcare services: Results from the Bangladesh Demographic and Health Survey. *BMJ Open*, *7*(9), e017142. doi:10.1136/bmjopen-2017-017142 PMID:28882921

Haque, F., & Druce, S. C. (2019). *Gender disparity in Bangladesh: The study of women's vulnerable situations in patriarchal society and the rise of gender equality*. Academy of Brunei Studies.

Hardwick, J. (2020). *Sex in an old regime city: Young workers and intimacy in France, 1660-1789*. Oxford University Press. doi:10.1093/oso/9780190945183.001.0001

Hartmann, H. I. (1981). The family as the locus of gender, class, and political struggle: The example of housework. *Signs (Chicago, Ill.)*, *6*(3), 366–394. doi:10.1086/493813

Hirschmann, N. J. (2008). *Gender, class, and freedom in modern political theory*. Princeton University Press.

Holmes, J. (2007). Social constructionism, postmodernism and feminist sociolinguistics. *Gender and Language*, *1*(1), 51–65. Advance online publication. doi:10.1558/genl.2007.1.1.51

Holson, L. M. (2019). *Murders by intimate partners are on the rise, study finds*. https://www.nytimes.com/2019/04/12/us/domestic-violence-victims.html

Hossen, M. S. (2020). Patriarchy practice and women's subordination in the society of Bangladesh: An analytical review. *Electronic Research Journal of Social Sciences and Humanities*, *2*(3), 51–60.

Hussein, N. (2017). *Negotiating middle-class respectable femininity: Bangladeshi women and their families*. South Asia Multidisciplinary Academic Journal. doi:10.4000amaj.4397

Islam, M., & Karim, K. M. R. (2012). Men's views on gender and sexuality in a Bangladesh village. *International Quarterly of Community Health Education*, *32*(4), 339–354. doi:10.2190/IQ.32.4.f PMID:23376759

Jackson, S. (2001). Why a materialist feminism is (still) possible—And necessary. *Women's Studies International Forum*, *24*(3–4), 283–293. doi:10.1016/S0277-5395(01)00187-X

Jaggar, A. (1987). Love & Knowledge: Emotion in Feminist Epistemology. In S. Kemp & J. Squires (Eds.), Feminisms. Oxford UP.

Jaggar, A. M. (1983). *Feminist politics and human nature, philosophy and society*. Rowman & Allanheld.

John, M. (1998). Feminism, internationalism and the West: Question from the Indian context. *Centre for Women's Development Studies*, *27*, 1–24.

Johnson, A. (2005). *The gender knot: Unraveling our patriarchal legacy*. Temple University Press.

Karim, K. M. R., Emmelin, M., Lindberg, L., & Wamala, S. (2016). Gender and women development initiatives in Bangladesh: A study of rural mother center. *Social Work in Public Health*, *31*(5), 369–386. doi:10.1080/19371918.2015.1137517 PMID:27149647

Karim, K. M. R., Emmelin, M., Resurreccion, B., & Wamala, S. (2012). Water development projects and marital violence: Experiences from rural Bangladesh. *Health Care for Women International*, *33*(3), 200–216. doi:10.1080/07399332.2011.603861 PMID:22325022

Karim, R., Lindberg, L., Wamala, S., & Emmelinn, M. (2018). Men's perceptions of women's participation in development initiatives in rural Bangladesh. *American Journal of Men's Health*, *12*(2), 398–410. doi:10.1177/1557988317735394 PMID:29025358

King, K. (1994). *Theory in its feminist travels: Conversations in U.S. Women's movements*. Indiana University Press.

Lerner, G. (1986). *The creation of patriarchy*. Oxford University Press.

Lerner, G. (1997). *Why history matters: Life and thought*. Oxford University Press.

Little, W. (2016). *Gender, sex, and sexuality*. BC Open Textbooks.

MacKinnon, C. A. (1982). Feminism, Marxism, method, and the State: An agenda for theory. *Signs (Chicago, Ill.)*, *7*(3), 515–544. doi:10.1086/493898

Mahmud, S. (2003). Is Bangladesh experiencing a feminization of the labour force? *Bangladesh Development Studies*, *29*(1), 1–37.

Mahmud, S., & Bidisha, S. (2018). Female labor market participation in Bangladesh: Structural changes and determinants of labor supply. In S. Raihan (Ed.), *Structural change and dynamics of labor markets in Bangladesh* (pp. 51–63). Springer. doi:10.1007/978-981-13-2071-2_4

Mahtab N. (2007). *Women in Bangladesh from inequality to empowerment*. A H Development Publishing House.

Marouzi, S. (2021). *Frank Plumpton Ramsey: A feminist economist?* Center for the History of Political Economy at Duke University Working Paper Series. doi:10.2139/ssrn.3854782

Matheson, A., Kidd, J., & Came, H. (2021). Women, patriarchy and health inequalities: The urgent need to reorient our systems. *International Journal of Environmental Research and Public Health*, *18*(9), 4472. doi:10.3390/ijerph18094472 PMID:33922437

Mawa, B. (2020). Challenging patriarchy: The changing definition of women's empowerment. *Social Science Review*, *37*(2), 239–265. doi:10.3329sr.v37i2.56510

McAfee, N. (2008). *Democracy and the political unconscious*. Columbia University Press. doi:10.7312/mcaf13880

McAfee, N. (2018). Feminist Philosophy, *Stanford Encyclopedia of Philosophy*. https://plato.stanford.edu/entries/feminism-political/#Bib

McKeon, M. (1995). Historicizing patriarchy: The emergence of gender difference in England, 1660-1760. *Eighteenth-Century Studies*, *28*(3), 295–322. https://www.jstor.org/stable/2739451

Messer-Davidow, E. (2002). *Disciplining feminism: From social activism to academic discourse*. Duke University Press.

Mia, B. (2020). Custodial torture: Laws and practice in Bangladesh. *Electronic Research Journal of Social Sciences and Humanities*, *2*(2), 232–246.

Mikkola, M. (2008). Feminist perspectives on sex and gender. *Stanford Encyclopedia of Philosophy*. https://plato.stanford.edu/entries/feminism-political/#Bib

Mikkola, M. (2009). Gender Concepts and Intuitions. *Canadian Journal of Philosophy*, *39*(4), 559–583. doi:10.1353/cjp.0.0060

Millett, K. (1977). *Sexual politics*. Virago.

Mitchell, J. (1971). *Women's estate*. Penguin.

Mol, A. (2002). *The body multiple: Ontology in medical practice*. Duke University Press. doi:10.1215/9780822384151

Monagan, S. (2010). Patriarchy: Perpetuating the practice of female genital mutilation. *International Research Journal of Arts & Humanities*, *37*, 83–101.

Monsoor, T. (1999). *From patriarchy to gender equity: Family law and its impact on women in Bangladesh*. The University Press Limited.

Narayan, U. (1998). Essence of culture and a sense of history: A feminist critique of cultural essentialism. *Hypatia*, *13*(2), 86–106. doi:10.1111/j.1527-2001.1998.tb01227.x

Nazneen, S. (2017). The women's movement in Bangladesh: A short history and current debates. Friedrich-Ebert-Stiftung Bangladesh Office, 3.

Nazneen, S., Hossain, N., & Sultan, M. (2011). *National discourses on women's empowerment in Bangladesh: Continuities and change*. IDS Working Papers, 2011: 1-41. doi:10.1111/j.2040-0209.2011.00368_2.x

Nazneen, S., & Sultan, M. (2012). Contemporary feminist politics in Bangladesh. In S. Roy (Ed.), *New South Asian feminism: Paradoxes and possibilities*. Zed Books. doi:10.5040/9781350221505.ch-004

Phadke, S. (2013). Unfriendly bodies, hostile cities: Reflections on loitering and gendered public space. *Economic and Political Weekly*, *48*(39), 50–59.

Pierik, B. (2022). Patriarchal power as a conceptual tool for gender history. *The Journal of Theory and Practice.*, *26*(1), 71–92. doi:10.1080/13642529.2022.2037864

Pynchon, V. (2011). Women's economic power decreases domestic violence against both genders. *Forbes*.

Rahbari, L., & Sharepour, M. (2015). Gender and realization of women's right to the city in Tehran. *Asian Journal of Social Science, 43*(3), 227–248. doi:10.1163/15685314-04303002

Rahman, I. R., & Islam, R. (2013). *Female labour force participation in Bangladesh: trends, drivers and barriers.* International Labour Organization. https://www.ilo.org/newdelhi/whatwedo/publications/WCMS_2501 12/lang--en/index.htm

Raihan, S., Bidisha, S., & Jahan, I. (2018). Unpacking unpaid labor in Bangladesh. *Indian Journal of Labour Economic.* doi:10.1007/s41027-018-0115-6

Raihan, S., & Bidisha, S. H. (2018). *Bangladesh economic dialogue on inclusive growth policy brief: Addressing female employment stagnation in Bangladesh.* A research paper on Economic Dialogue on Inclusive Growth in Bangladesh. Retrieved from https://asiafoundation.org/wp- content/uploads/2018/12/EDIG-Policy-Brief-Female-employment-stagnation-in-Bangladesh.pdf

Reichenbach, A. (2015). Gazes that matter: Young Emirati women's spatial practices in Dubai. *Urban Anthropology and Studies of Cultural Systems and World Economic Development, 44*(1/2), 113–195.

Rockler, N. R. (2006). "Be your own windkeeper": Friends, feminism, and rhetorical strategies of depoliticization. *Women's Studies in Communication, 29*(2), 244–264. doi:10.1080/07491409.2006.10162500

Roy, S. (2012). Politics, passion and professionalization in contemporary feminist politics in India. *Sociology, 45*(4), 587–601. doi:10.1177/0038038511406584

Sayem, A. M., Begum, H. A., & Moneesha, S. S. (2012). Attitudes towards justifying intimate partner violence among married women in Bangladesh. *Journal of Biosocial Science, 44*(6), 641–660. doi:10.1017/S0021932012000223 PMID:22687269

Schaefer, D. O. (2022). *Wild experiment: Feeling science and secularism after darwin.* Duke University Press.

Shamma, W. T. (2021). Gendering and spatializing the new urban space: A study on working women in the city of Dhaka, Bangladesh. *Social Science Review, 37*(2), 125–144. doi:10.3329sr.v37i2.56508

Shohel, T. A., Niner, S., & Gunawardana, S. (2021). How the persistence of patriarchy undermines the financial empowerment of women microfinance borrowers? Evidence from a southern sub-district of Bangladesh. *PLoS One, 16*(4), e0250000. doi:10.1371/journal.pone.0250000 PMID:33909670

Sikweyiya, Y., Addo-Lartey, A. A., Alangea, D. O., Dako-Gyeke, P., Chirwa, E. D., Coker-Appiah, D., Adanu, R. M. K., & Jewkes, R. (2020). Patriarchy and gender-inequitable attitudes as drivers of intimate partner violence against women in the central region of Ghana. *BMC Public Health*, *20*(1), 682. doi:10.118612889-020-08825-z PMID:32404153

Soenen, R. (2007). Everyday urban public space: Turkish immigrant women's perspective. *Journal of Housing and the Built Environment*, *22*(4), 411–413. doi:10.100710901-007-9094-5

Stewart, A. J., Settles, I. H., & Winter, N. J. G. (1998). Women and the social movements of the 1960s: Activists, engaged observers, and nonparticipants. *Political Psychology*, *19*(1), 63–94. doi:10.1111/0162-895X.00093

Sultana, A. (2012). Patriarchy and women's subordination: A theoretical analysis. *Arts Faculty Journal*, *4*, 1–18. doi:10.3329/afj.v4i0.12929

Sultana, R. (2021). Household responsibilities: Roles of women and their family members during coronavirus lockdown period. *IQAC Project of Jagannath University*, *6*, 1-17.

Tanha, K. (2021). *Patriarchy, give me my country back. A personal account of a survivor of sexual violence and oppression.* https://www.thedailystar.net/views/opinion/news/patriarchy-g ive-me-my-country-back-2209466

Than, K., Garner, T., & Taylor, A. P. (2022). What is Darwin's theory of evolution? *Live Science.* https://www.livescience.com/474-controversy-evolution-works.html

Tong, R. (2009). *Feminist thought: A more comprehensive introduction.* Westview Press.

Tonkiss, F. (2005). Space, the city and social theory: Social relations and urban forms. *Polity*.

Valentine, G. (1989). The geography of women's fear. *Area*, *21*(4), 385–390.

Walby, S. (1990). *Theorizing patriarchy.* Blackwell Publishers Ltd.

Walsh, S. M. (2015). Safety spheres: Danger mapping and spatial justice. *Race, Gender, & Class*, *22*(1&2), 122–142.

Wani, A. R. (2019). Role and status of women in sikh religion through Sri Guru Nanak perspectives. *Electronic Research Journal of Literature*, *1*, 13–19.

Watt, D. (2022). *In defense of her sex: Travelling through time with Christine de Pizan (Review)*. https://www.historytoday.com/archive/review/defence-hersex#:~:text=In%20The%20Second%20Sex%2C%20Simone,of%20Charles%20V%20in%20Paris

Welch, S. (2015). *Existential eroticism: A feminist approach to understanding women's oppression-perpetuating choices.* Lexington Books.

Wiegand, C. (2012). *Violence against women in Bangladesh.* https://www.e-ir.info/2012/04/30/violence-against-women-in-bangladesh/

Willis, E. (1984). Radical feminism and feminist radicalism. *Social Text, 9*(10), 91–118. doi:10.2307/466537

Wright, E. (2000). *Lacan and postfeminism (postmodern encounters).* Totem Books or Icon Books.

Wronska, A. (2018). *The place of women in public space: A case study of street harassment in Bangladesh* [MA Dissertation]. Lund University. https://lup.lub.lu.se/luur/download?func=downloadFile&recordOId=8945534&fileOId=8945536

Young, I. M. (2000). *Inclusion and Democracy, Oxford Political Theory.* Oxford University Press.

Chapter 13
Engendering the City:
A Participatory Approach to Gender-Responsive Planning and Urban Design in Cairo

Jiayi Jin
https://orcid.org/0000-0002-8009-4814
Northumbria University, UK

Kexin Huang
Northumbria University, UK

Mingyu Zhu
Newcastle University, UK

ABSTRACT

The city of Cairo has witnessed a considerable increase in crimes against women, compelling women to avoid or minimise their use of public spaces in recent years. The absence of consideration for women in city planning has made Egyptian women feel further excluded and threatened by the public space, in addition to the patriarchal social relations and religious conservatism. As part of the 'gender-inclusive cities' research project, this study adopts a participatory approach as a tool for women's empowerment with the goal of promoting bottom-up models of planning, dissolving gendered norms, and improving women's status in a patriarchal society. The chapter provides an example of localised gender-inclusive design addressing women's spatial sensibilities and connecting them to the broader objectives of participation and emancipation. The findings of this study can help planners and policy makers co-create safer public spaces for local women, reduce spatial inequality, and facilitate their right to the city.

DOI: 10.4018/978-1-6684-6650-6.ch013

INTRODUCTION

The 20th century marks the start of normalising women's involvement in the city and growing inclusion in the public domain and marking the massive shift of daily gender patterns in the city (Meece et al., 2006), defined by people's lifestyle, composed of the shifting societal views and expectations, and individual ambitions, thereby working as an invisible demographic shift in cities. This development has led to the increase of women's involvement in the public sphere of the city, no longer being confined to the private sphere of the household. The form and structure of the contemporary city is, however, threatening this advancement by perpetuating the "traditional" gender roles within society through the use of a city structure that makes it difficult for women to balance the time between societal gender expectations and their personal aspirational opportunities spatially, especially with places socialised by patriarchal religious structures. The city was therefore used to divide and control the 'natural' division between the sexes (Roberts, 1998) through its structure that rigidly defined public and private spaces; men's and women's spaces respectively (Kuhlmann, 2013), therefore bringing threats to women with their increased patronage, who were not considered in the design of public spaces as direct participants.

The relationship between the different genders and the city is a topic that has been thoroughly researched from a sociological perspective, thereby paying greater attention to the relationships between people, including gender roles and power relations in cities (Bier, 2011; Casanova, 2009; Casanovas et al., 2015). How these societal relationships then reflect into space during the development and growth of the city form and structure is, however, not as thoroughly and extensively explored in a way that results in concrete conclusions and design interventions about gender equality in the networks of the city.

The study is based on a series of public co-creation workshops on 'Gender-inclusive Cities' based in Cairo, Egypt, where is known to be one of the least gender-equal regions globally (Haines, 2017; Kato, 2017). Women and girls in Egypt face violence on a disturbing scale both at home and in public. A 2017 Reuters Survey of 19 megacities worldwide ranked Cairo as the most dangerous megacity for women (Thomson Reuters Foundation, 2017). While parts of the city retain a form of pre-industrial structure that allows some people to combine production and reproduction activities in one space, it has yet to establish a spatial framework within which women are free to roam public spaces alone and access services to increase their quality of life. This means it is easier for people who only need to engage in paid work to navigate the city, while those with unpaid responsibilities are increasingly disadvantaged by the same structure. Due to societal gender relations in Egypt, those systematically disadvantaged are predominantly women. Whether intentionally made that way or not, the result of contemporary urban planning and design paradigms is women being unable to access the same opportunities and participate in the local economy the way men are enabled to. The pervasiveness and frequency of sexual harassment also make them feel unsafe or uncomfortable when accessing public spaces in the city. Attacks against women and girls in the public domain have long plagued Egyptian society, and women and girls of all ages face sexual harassment at every step of their daily life: in the streets and on public transport, in schools and universities, and at their workplaces.

The authors hope to increase awareness of gender-based inequalities at a local level and involve local citizens to highlight how public spaces can take action to tackle the issues raised. The research team has worked closely with local community-based organisations and design agencies in implementing and perpetuating a strategic framework for urban planning to enable local women to have a wider range of access to their needs and opportunities in the public space, thereby enhancing their quality of life and potential for social mobility. The end of this research outlines design strategies and recommendations that can be served as a guideline for gender-inclusive planning and design processes toward meaningful, effective outcomes and long-term improvements. This planning paradigm is centred around gender equality and planned co-creation sessions help to emphasise the significance of providing an evolutionary, adaptable, and thereby appropriable and participative approach to spatial planning and design, as a core factor in reducing spatial inequalities in the city.

BACKGROUND

The Gendered Body in a Contemporary City

Cities are spaces of opportunity, where there is a higher range of prospects and aspirations for individuals to pursue than in semi-urban and rural areas (Tacoli & Satterthwaite, 2013). Women are therefore allowed to be more independent and are given more possibilities through the city, where they can experience "some relaxation of the rigid social values and norms that define women as subordinated to [...] men generally" (Pepera, 2019; Tacoli & Satterthwaite, 2013). Not only can women participate in a wider range of educational and employment opportunities, particularly with higher demands for varying skillsets in various fields (Goldin & Katz, 1996), but there are also more opportunities for engagement with society outside the household in the different varieties of public and semi-public spaces present in the city. Even more so with increasing globalisation, cities have become spaces with endless amounts of things to do, see and experience, in both the positive and negative sense.

However, when it comes to the essence of the form and structure of the city, particularly relating to the networks and how these different spaces are linked with each other, authors believe current urban design practices have not gone far enough with accommodating women and adapting to the 'invisible' demographic shift mentioned earlier. Spatial design is still regarded with the same lens as before this change in people's patterns, and large problems that come with this lack of consideration are dealt with retroactively through measures of social isolation and induced fear of public space, which make the city increasingly less hospitable for women. Regarding social isolation, this is not necessarily a gendered problem of the city; individuals who live alone will also face the struggles of balancing housework with paid work, as the unpaid work for the household is necessary for the household to function, whether or not the women are the ones to be tasked with them. Some families have contributions done equally by both men and women, however, when it comes to the average household and larger families, where the individuals in question have to work to support those living with them, while taking care of others within the household in the meantime if they are children or elderly, and/or disabled, this task more often than not falls onto the "wife" in the family (Silbaugh, 2007; Tacoli & Satterthwaite, 2013). These women are consequently unable to manage enough time in the day to do housework, care for the household, travel, and pursue their ambitions, while also taking care of their physical and mental health. As the "tradition" was, the city is built by men, around the idea that a man goes to work during regular working hours, while his wife is at home taking care of the house and those living inside it; it is therefore built around stereotypical assumptions about masculinity and femininity in the city which induces women's fear in public space (Roberts, 1998).

Women's fear for their personal safety is a strong factor in their decisions to participate in urban life (Tacoli & Satterthwaite, 2013). Due to the higher risks of violence, while women have a higher degree of autonomy in cities, it is again cut short by perceived fear of certain urban spaces, which can hinder them from pursuing the opportunities they aspire for; they are "vulnerable to the fear of harassment and attack and [...] this considerably limits their use and enjoyment of public spaces in the city" (Roberts, 1998). A lot of the fear perceived by women in cities is a result of certain land-use and accessibility patterns laid across cities, such as a lack of visibility in public spaces, inconsiderable transport systems and poor infrastructure designs (Kuhlmann, 2013). Kuhlmann (2013) makes a point to note that women are not afraid of the places with bad lighting, lines of sight and psychical or social visibility themselves, but are afraid of "becoming victims of crime while unobserved by social control measures" (p. 192). Therefore, an understanding of the systems at work in space results in these kinds of inconsiderate spaces with heightened vulnerability for women.

Looking back at the quote from Sassen's work – Globalisation and its Discontents (Sassen, 1998, p. 82), it becomes apparent that not only does the male-led culture and power dynamics in the global economy exclude the workers and sectors from the image of globalisation, but because of the covering of these majority-women economic sectors, the problems and inconveniences they encounter in their patterns through the city are also, in effect, hidden from the mainstream planning and design considerations. This results in the emergence of retroactive plans when the problems grow out of hand that push women further into the private sphere of the city despite them putting in the effort to enter the public sphere. Kirsten Day (2006) extends this discussion by reviewing feminist approaches to urban design and public space, she argues that focusing on crime and safety displaces the fact that women have historically employed public space as a medium for struggle against oppression. Day suggests that designers and planners should move beyond "universal design" (Day, 2006) criteria as their normative goal and think about networks of public spaces that can accommodate needs and aspirations characteristic of specific social groups. In that respect, physical features of such public networks and individual spaces become crucial to enabling women to become leaders in their cities and communities. Even though women's fear of/in public space will not be removed by better lighting design, landscape of urban furniture alone, feminist designers and planners have offered successful examples for how increasing women's safety leads to a fundamental rethinking of women's roles and place in the city.

Gender Inequalities Reflected in Social Contexts and Urban Settings in Egypt

Gender inequality exists in all societies around the world. The trending hashtag #metoo, ordinally introduced by activist Tarana Burke, collected several million stories about sexual harassment and assault against women every year (Khomami, 2017; Tuerkheimer, 2019), with a wide range of territories. However, based on social indicators and gender statistics, "women in the Arab region are on average more disadvantaged economically, politically, and socially than women in other regions" (as cited in Khalil, 2017, p. 1). Egypt is one example of those Arabic countries where sexism and inequality have continued to thrive, leaving women and girls vulnerable and excluded from decision making regarding their own quality of life (Sweeting, 2020). United Nations Development Programme (UNDP), which is looking at indicators like the pay gap and number of women in parliaments, ranked 150 countries on gender equality in 2019, Egypt has a Gender Inequality Index (GII) of 0.449, ranking it at 108 out of 162 countries (UNDP, 2020). Only 18% of the working-age women are now participating in the economy, compared to 65% of men (El-Kot et al., 2021), gender inequality in Egypt was also severely exacerbated after the pandemic (Samari, 2021).

Women in Egypt face inequalities across policy and community sectors as well as in the household, especially after the rise of Islamic conservatism in the 1980s (Braker, 2018; El-Safty, 2004). In this country, married males typically function as household heads and make choices for the whole family (Bier, 2011). On the contrary, women take on traditional roles in the household and seldom enter the workforce (Assaad et al., 2018). The difficulties with overcoming gender inequalities are rooted in the social construction of genders: In 'women working' Casanovas et al. (2015) define gender as [a] societal and cultural construct based on the biological differences between the sexes that assign different capacities, behaviour, emotional and intellectual characteristics to girls, women, boys, men, and trans* people. These attributes vary according to society's relationship between sexes. The definition makes clear that these attributes are changeable due to their socially contracted nature (Casanova, 2009). Currently, in Egypt, the majority of women are still doing the larger share of unpaid (and often unappreciated) labour. Leave the numbers about job opportunities alone, a person's gender influences almost all activities and experiences. The struggle of men and women of course is connected: While men are not socially allowed to take certain roles, like the homemaker or having a job in care, these responsibilities mostly have to be done by women.

The dichotomy of gender roles created a gendered perception of space, as men perceive public space as their own territory while women perceive it as a daily ambush (Braker, 2018). Consequently, women in Cairo face significant spatial barriers to access employment opportunities, manifested in increased safety risks in space, which heavily reduces their mobility capacity. This is perceived as the natural state of the city despite it not always having been the case (Ilahi, 2009). From the 1920s to the 1970s, feminist movements in Egypt made significant progress in freeing themselves from the long-standing patriarchal chains, obtaining equal education, expanding professional opportunities and making changes in the status law, which made them successfully acquire their share of public space (Braker, 2018). However, the rise of neoliberalism and the religious dogmas under patriarchal interpretations since the 1970s marks a distinctive regression in women's status in Egyptian society(De Koning, 2009). In a sprawling wave of economic frustration and despair, men become more violent towards governments, the built environment and women (Braker, 2018). Since the patriarchal social expectations assert that men should be the head of the household and be prioritised in economic and political matters, the fact that more and more women had education and permanent jobs while some men were lagging behind was seen as unacceptable and abnormal (Braker, 2018; El-Kot et al., 2021). This was when women were forced back into the domestic space by a juxtaposition of patriarchy and conservative religious and cultural doctrines. Today, despite equal degrees of higher education between women and men, women make up the majority of the unemployed workforce. Because of the increasing absence of women in the public sphere of the city, women in Cairo have visibly less freedom than men to perform their tasks. Increased safety risks in the city, particularly related to sexual harassment and assault, drive women away from public spaces. This further makes them avoid facilities and structures that allow them to access opportunities but require them to use public spaces, including public transportation (Ilahi, 2009).

As the capital city, Cairo is recognised as one of the top 10 most populated metropolitan regions globally, host to a fifth of Egypt's 100 million inhabitants in the Greater Cairo Metropolitan Region and just over 9.5 million inhabitants within the city bounds of Cairo (UNFPA, 2018). The increasingly popularised development of new towns and gated communities, which end up not having access to public transportation, is another factor that contributes to the hindrance of many women's mobility because they rarely own cars themselves or are not allowed to drive because of religious/cultural reasons. This makes them reliant on other members of the household to drive them to the nearest public transportation stop, particularly when they cannot drive themselves to their destination immediately, thereby interlinking schedules further in a way that leaves these people tired before reaching their work or classrooms, and after arriving home as well (idem). Still having tasks to complete within these times of energy depletion discourages those whose schedule functions this way from engaging in education or employment, and pursuing their aspirations, when the time wasted to strive for it leaves them with a lower quality of life. Derived from statistics by the Central Agency for Public Mobilisation and Statistics (CAPMAS). The percentage of employed women per neighbourhood with a temporary jobs map (TADAMUN, 2019) shows that participation in the formal or informal labour force is linked to the availability of either proximally (idem). These temporary jobs also tend to be less secure, with lower wages, thereby keeping the wealth distribution fixed to the local conditions. As such, it can be concluded that a lack of distribution and connectivity to employment opportunities is one of the causes of women's lower access to opportunities in the city. This is not considering the safety and comfort issues that come with busy public transport or informal modes of transport, such as minibuses and taxis, which are becoming increasingly unsafe for women travelling alone due to the prevalence of stories of harassment and kidnapping, that incrementally deter women from using them out of fear (ITDP, 2019). This lack of a sense of safety in the public sphere and in public transport therefore keeps Egyptian women from liberating themselves through income-based independence.

Additionally, in the last years since the 2011 uprising, repeated attacks on women protesters around Cairo's iconic Tahrir Square have drawn attention to the endemic sexual harassment and violence faced by women in Egypt in the public sphere.

Successive authorities have used the violence as a way to smear their political opponents and, under Mohamed Morsi's rule, even blamed the women themselves. The problem is compounded by an inadequate legal framework, as well as the long-term failure of the security forces and judicial authorities to take complaints of sexual harassment or other forms of gender-based violence seriously.

A Dialectical Discussion of Gender-responsive Planning and Design

The issue of women and gender in city planning and design became prominent in the 1970s when feminist activist-professionals seeped their ideas into practice, particularly in the United States and several European countries. Academics started following up on the issue in the 1980s and made significant progress in the city planning literature during this time with work produced by Clara Greed, Marion Roberts, Jos Boys, Dory Reeves, Teresa Boccia, Sasa Lada, Liisa Horelli, Inés Sánchez de Madariaga, and others (De Madariaga & Neuman, 2020). Today, progressive urban planners, designers architects and policymakers developed a series of approaches and methods to address women's needs for agency, safety, access and comfortability in cities. For instance, 'Gender mainstreaming' is a process that involves the integration of a gender perspective into the planning and design of policies, programmes and projects to promote equality between women and men and combat discrimination. They use tools such as Gender stakeholder consultation to promote evidence-based and participatory policy-making (The European Institute for Gender Equality, 2022).

The dual approach of combining gender mainstreaming and specific measures for the advancement of women, to ensure better policy making and better use of resources is implemented in the United Nation's 2030 Agenda for Sustainable Development, which includes a stand-alone goal on gender equality and the empowerment of women and girls as well as other gender-sensitive goals. 'Gender-inclusive urban planning and design' incorporate cross-sector departments, strategies, typologies and fields of expertise to integrate participatory engagement with community and government project partners in developing a built environment that is more inclusive, for men and women, for those with disabilities and for those who are marginalised and excluded (World Bank Group, 2020). The group designed and used tools to collect data, such as Walk Audit to document and examine the physical aspects and social uses of the studied area, as well as public space checklists to understand if a public space is well-designed and gender-inclusive.

Although the European approach was overall practically-oriented, some theoretical frameworks were also being developed. For example, feminist urban scholars adopted and developed Henri Lefebvre's 'the right to the city' and incorporated feminist agendas, which termed the 'neo-Lefebvrian right to the city', as they identified that there was a lack of perspectives on gender inequalities in his work because of the philosopher's predominate concern with the work-class in cities due to his Marxist tradition.

The right to the city is not simply the right to access education or work. Rather, it is the right to belong everywhere, to inhabit cities through independent exploration, to influence institutions as well as attain a livelihood. It is also the right to encounter difference: not only different people, but different experiences – not only a limited 'leisure' experience, but meaningful encounters across social classes in daily life (Whitzman, 2013, pp. 32-52).

In this way, the right to the city is inextricably linked to the active participation of women in building safer and more inclusive cities. The right to the gendered and feminist city serves as an alternative to solve the conflicts over urban planning and design against patriarchal cities and prevent the violation of women's right to participate not only in public affairs and decision-making but also in a variety of urban activities because of gendered power relations (Fenster, 2005). Intersectionality serves as a critical lens to understanding any gender issues because women are not a homogenous group, so different women experience different degrees of problems and risks based on factors such as their age, educational level, class, ethnicity and nationality. Hanson (2010, p.17) argues that the social, cultural and geographic context is 'absolutely central' in understanding the relationships between gender and mobility. Loukaitou-Sideris (2020) identifies that there is significantly less research on gendered urban planning and design in the Global South than in the Global North, despite the fact that gender inequalities are often more pronounced in the latter. She found that women in the Global South face more acute problems in terms of mobility in cities. For example, they have less access to motorised transportation, own fewer cars or have driver's licences, and some women's mobility is even more constrained than others because of religious/cultural norms preventing them from driving, cycling or using transit (Loukaitou-Sideris, 2020). This situation in research calls for more voices from women and other underrepresented social groups in the Global South, especially from the Middle East, most of Africa, South Asia and Latin America.

In Egypt, the centrality of women's corporeality in public debate became clearer during and after the Egyptian uprising in 2011, a revolution that sought democracy and social justice but excluded women from reconstructing the Egyptian constitutional referendum, barred them from committees chosen to negotiate with the military forces (Hafez, 2016). Moreover, they were repeatedly harassed and threatened with gang rape in Tahrir Square. Hafez (2016) contends that gender becomes the principal instrument that defines the urban space envisioned by the Egyptian state. The authors argue that despite the gender-related issues that are pressing in urban Egypt, it does not get enough attention it needs from academics and practitioners. Situating in the aforementioned practices and literature, this research aims to develop a framework of gender-responsive design for the local context, which goes beyond "universal design" (Day, 2006) by addressing the imperative issue of gender inequalities in the city's public space and contributing to a transnational understanding of gendered experiences in cities.

ENGENDERING THE CITY: A PARTICIPATORY APPROACH

Our research activities in Cairo were supported by different researchers, urban experts and activists from two organizations CLUSTER and UN Women (Egypt), with the aim to make the city more inclusive for all genders and sexualities, regardless of age, abilities, class, religion or economic background. The majority of research activities has been conducted in the summer of 2022, as an extension of our current research project 'Gender-inclusive Cities' which got funded in October 2021, the authors conducted a series of webinars and on-site participatory workshops with the local residents and students, women's groups and local NGOs in this context. It attracted more than 300 participants between June and September, 80% of them were women from both urban and rural locations around the Greater Cairo Region. The participatory approach serves as an empowerment tactic that promotes feminist urban planning techniques. It is a method of challenging planning that views the city as a neutral environment and exclusively employs statistics, plans, and models, in contrast, it respects local expertise, particularly that of women. The experiences, needs, and individual and collective knowledge of local women and girls have been carefully accessed in this process to develop gender criteria. Moreover, this overall participatory approach makes an important contribution to bring gender issues to the center in the formulation of future urban development, provide a much stronger emphasis on gender equality as a development objective, and on the mainstreaming of gender issues as integral to locally owned development strategies.

Framing and Insight Gathering through the Online Seminar

Research activities with this participatory approach were divided into two phases: during phase 1, the research team develops an online seminar with the Department of Architecture, Cairo University on creating a safe city for all. It starts with online mapping and questions students from Egypt and the UK to map how they navigate their way around the city, with 10 questions based on their daily experiences like 'What do you think about when you step out at night?' and 'what prevents you from accessing public streets or using public transport? These were simple questions

Engendering the City

Figure 1. A collective respond on 'What do you think about when you step out at night?' by Egyptian and UK students during the online mapping workshop. (Gender-inclusive Cities, 2022)

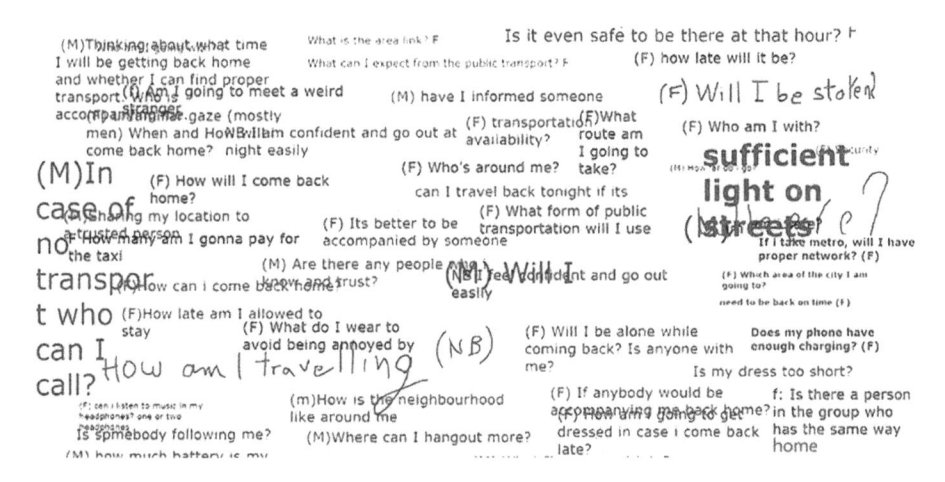

posed but the complexity of gendered experiences and multiplicities of identities filled up the group brainstorm board within a few minutes It is a successful cross-cultural exchange between Egyptian and UK students which seeks out ways to break out of rigid assumptions about gender inequality. While the difference in the student's personal experiences based on gender were evident as shown in Figure 1, the similarities between the Egyptian and UK students were remarkable to see.

We began with very concrete qualitative analyses of daily life in contemporary cities, then zoomed in to carefully untangling how each of these 'local' problems on gender differences is connected or influenced by and reconstituting the daily experience in the city. Intersectionality became an important point of discussion. Following this online mapping, the student pairs also discussed the meaning of urban planning from a gender perspective and the importance of considering women's everyday life as a source of knowledge, then shared their collaborative reflections on their relationship with their city.

Both the UK and Egyptian students raised their concerns about the increasing sexual harassment and gender-based violence in both countries. The consequences of the relentless sexual and gender-based violence against women and girls in the public sphere are dire for women's freedom of movement and enjoyment of other rights, ranging from political participation to access to education and health. Multiple female students expressed that they tend to make arrangements in relation to their travel routes and daily plans with a view to mitigating exposure to the risks of sexual harassment and assaults in public spaces. And sometimes daily activities become a struggle due to the problem of 'street harassment', "*this profoundly impacts on women's consciousness, physical well-being, liberty and fundamental rights*" said by one Egyptian student in the webinar panel discussion.

Neighbourhood-Level Interactions and Co-Planning Sessions

From this point on, phase 2's on-the-ground interaction began in collaboration with the Cairo Safe City and Safe Public Spaces Programme. Utilizing the "evaluation of everyday networks" technique, the study team walks across three Cairo neighbourhoods, including Zamalek, Al Manial, and As Sabityyah, and investigates women's everyday life via mapping with the local residents. On a map, every woman has to locate her home and the public spaces, facilities, and services she uses in her neighbourhood, town, or city. Once they have located these elements, participants mark on the map the paths and routes they use, how they move between places – walking, by bus, by car, whether they move alone or with someone, and which activities they develop. The individual exercise ends by identifying elements that favour, or make difficult, the development of their everyday life.

Every map also included a ballot chart to ask people to vote for what is important to them in a public space - greenery, safety, seating, street food, shopping, sense of freedom, scenic beauty, entertainment, toilets, accessibility, etc. Through these neighbourhood-level discussions, what started emerging were city-level patterns of how people from diverse backgrounds navigate in their city and what are the most inclusive spaces that work for all. People began sharing their gendered experiences and barriers in mobility physical, social and economic. In As Sabtiyyah, most women shared that, religious spaces or coffee shops were their favoured public space since that's one place they feel they are "allowed". While female residents of Zamalek felt that their neighbourhood was safer than most other neighbourhoods in the city, but it's still prone to late night crime due to the absence of "eyes on street" in its design. Female participants from the local neighbourhoods have all shared their recognised gender divisions in access to different spaces within the city "...*many things here (Cairo) are difficult for women, I don't feel safe in public transportation, unless using women-only carriages, I hope to see buses cover all of Cairo and not only the popular spots...*". "*We see women struggling in all aspects. Even a simple walk on the street, and they are easily subjected to harassment, whether verbal or even physical.*" Unsurprisingly, sexual harassment and violence were the biggest fear for all women due to the gendered power relations reflected in space design in Cairo. The research team heard the same story in each of the three neighborhoods surveyed (Zamalek, Al Manial, and As Sabityyah): young women are frightened for their physical safety, and angry that this harassment and bullying is not taken seriously. "*Harassment should not be seen as part of a "normal" life for anyone*" said *by a young participant in Zamalek. "...and it is not harmless fun. It is frightening, disempowering and completely unacceptable."*

The mapping and selected conversations between participants and researchers have been shared in the public exhibition at a central and opento-all public venue, as shown in Figure 2. The public discussion and co-creation activities were continued, and all visitors to the exhibition were invited to share their comments and contribute ideas on what they would do to make their respective neighbourhood more gender-inclusive with powerful as well as playful ideas. Each participant group was encouraged to share their findings with the other groups in order to create a collective list of favourable and unfavourable elements that affect daily life within a specific urban built environment. This makes people more conscious of how they may shape the community's priorities and the factors that must be taken into account when planning by reaching a consensus as women move from the personal to the collective experience. Many participants in these sessions regonised that the city of Cairo has significant problems in terms of its layout and infrastructure, which has hindered communications and mobility to adjacent neighbourhoods, especially for women and the girls.

In addition, the fact that many local neighbourhood like As Sabityyah had been settled without much planning or public spending on infrastructure had led to a lack of public spaces, and poor-quality facilities. By co-planning and placemaking, everyday public spaces such as an underpass, a pavement, the space under a metro line or around the Bus Rapid Transit (BRT) stations, and selected courtyards of cultural spaces were transformed into vibrant public places where people from all walks of life came together to participate in the discourse generated. There were several interactive public activities designed to include people's voices and experiences through their daily life experiences, which entails situational performances of superiority and deference, and senses of belonging and nonbelonging in the urban public space. Particular gender and class performances determine in which parts of the city one can feel at home, and how one is seen and treated in different spaces on Cairo's segmented map. Another activity crowd-sourced different genders' mobility across the city by asking them what kind of public space they frequent the most, when and through which mode of transport. By tying their responses through different coloured threads/points, the visitors created a city-level pattern of their relationship with the city. An integral approach of the project was not just on-street neighbourhood discussions and public interactions but also connecting to policy and governance to mainstream the discourse on gender and sexuality. The results were sent to the planning department of each municipality at the end of phase 2, which in some cases have been included in the local neighbourhood plan.

Figure 2. Participatory co-planning sessions and public exhibition of 'Gender-inclusive Cities: How to design the city for ALL?' which invites the public to share their experiences in their local neighbourhoods. (Gender-inclusive Cities, 2022)

Design Strategies and Recommendations

Based on the diverse information gathered from workshops and the exhibition, the research team carefully examined how participants perceive relationships between socio-cultural, spatial and functional phenomena in the city of Cairo, and converted their perceptions of the streets, parks, squares and other public spaces into achievable goals for improvement. It outlines broad commitments that will serve as a guideline for gender-inclusive planning and design processes toward meaningful, effective outcomes and long-term improvements in the status of women and girls, which can be summarised in 5 design strategies: 1) Safe: In both public and semi-public settings, everyone is free from real and perceived danger, and all spaces are considered safe and respectable for women's socialising; 2) Freedom: all genders have freedom of movement in the public space, women can be 'bi-rahithum' (at ease), dress and socialise as they like, without being annoyed or being seen as disreputable; 3) Accessible: Everyone can access the public realm easily and comfortably and use every inch of the public spaces and all services on offer, without suspicious and restrictions; 4) Connected - To get connected with different opportunities and services provided, everyone can move around the city easily and economically to accumulate wealth and achieve economic or social independence; and 5) Healthy - Everyone has the opportunity to lead an active lifestyle, free from environmental health risks, women and girl can access to a variety of leisure spaces with the mixed-gender public in their neighbourhoods. And new urban development or regeneration projects in the city should allow easy access for all. Although these objectives seem rather radical to the current gendered cityscape in Cairo, they are presented as urbanist imaginations that have the potential to galvanise social and spatial changes.

Figure 3. Spatial translation of the gender-inclusive design strategies with one local street in Al Manial, Cairo. (Gender-inclusive Cities, 2022)

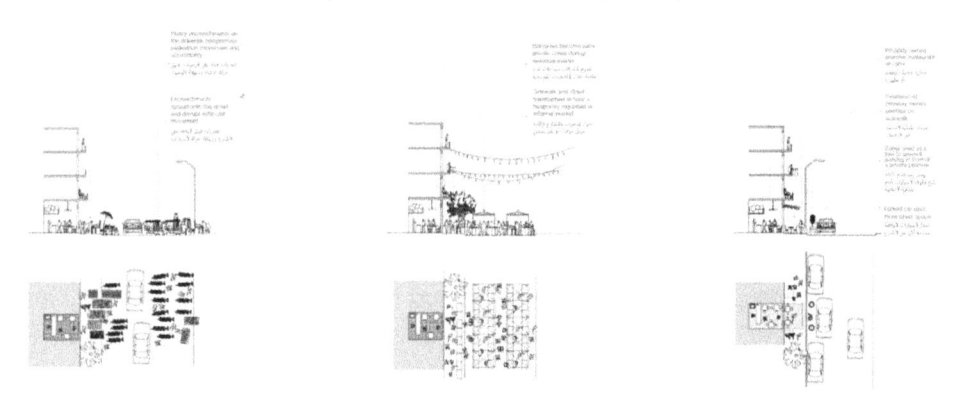

The public sphere, as Habermas et al. (1974) denotes, is "the entire realm of our social life in which something approaching public opinion can be formed" (p.49), and material space is included. Therefore, the negotiation and appropriation of the public space in Cairo should be viewed as a form of political contestation against gender inequality. When women, girls, and sexual and gender minorities of all ages and abilities have access to mobility, safety and freedom, health and hygiene, and security of tenure, they have the same right to the city as straight, physically fit men. Through incorporating these gender-inclusive design strategies on the street for different events and activities (Figure 3), these interventions enable local women to share the same freedoms, opportunities, and levels of participation in their neighbourhoods, access a full range of public services, workplaces and other key amenities whenever they need or want. Eventually, adaptable street interventions contribute to the urban development process of combining productive and reproductive roles efficiently and unlocking new economic opportunities for all citizens. As a result of their comfort and sense of community in the city, local women and girls will be able to maintain their mental, physical, and emotional well-being, and create social networks to help them deal with the demands of daily urban life. They can build wealth and other assets to maintain security and agency for long-term prosperity and have an equal voice in public decisions that affect them.

A key recommendation for future planning is carefully designing the pedestrian network to connect public services and appropriable spaces between transport stops and market areas, to form an even distribution of services across clusters, so there's no lack or overabundance in one area. Secondly, minimising women's barriers to accessing economic and leisure opportunities through the development of principles that establish gender-inclusive spatial networks that coincide with the local socio-cultural conditions, so women's economic empowerment including women's ability to participate equally in existing street markets will be increased. Thirdly, incorporating different social activities can appropriate urban spaces and generate a responsive urban design that embraces diversity and promote inclusion. For instance, some underused spaces can be transformed into temporary art spaces and pop-up shops where different social groups can enjoy the spaces equally. Last but not the least, this "Gender-inclusive urban planning" should incorporate cross-sectoral initiatives to address gender requirements holistically since gender inequality is a cross-cutting a cross-cutting issue that can only be solved by collaborating across different sectors, practices, and fields of knowledge. In addition to this horizontal, cross-sectoral integration, gender inclusion must be vertically integrated — linking "on-the-ground" community expertise with government-level policy and action — to ensure sustainable impact as well as promote vertical communication and collaboration on future projects. Local community and government partners should be brought together to co-define project goals and methodologies; carry out project activities; and evaluate project success.

FUTURE RESEARCH DIRECTIONS

Further elaboration of this research may be possible with direct involvement between urban designers, policy-makers and local women to capture the ingrained intangible elements of culture that can be used to further ground the strategic framework in the local fabric. Given the local sensitivities of place, the more this research can be embedded within the specific local research, the more it can facilitate the revealing of these intangible aspects that may have been overlooked in this research; this may include a longer period of ethnographic approach to investigate local conditions, issues and identify needs and solutions. To progress the research further, an improvement in the way of facilitating the evaluation of the critical spaces and informing their design conditions should be made, to better prepare for the implementation process. In the meanwhile, a future direction of this research could also be conducted to mitigate the specific local constraints and implement an evolutionary system to achieve spatial gender equality. For example, by defining where to locate functions, it becomes possible to introduce specific actions, in a way that allows the project to grow into a city-transformative movement for gender inclusion. This includes more design-based, co-creative activities between self-organised local actors and urban experts, developing this new paradigm for urban planning and design, and more specific programmes of requirements based on prior research. Finally, this research can then also be explored in the dimension of the participation of other marginalised groups or communities, to identify possible differences in implementation if the needs and patterns considered are not that of women, but of other minority groups.

CONCLUSION

Due to the changing economic climate induced through processes of globalisation, urbanisation and capitalism, the global economy has shifted to an increased demand for feminisation to increase the available workforce and accessibility to the city. Because of this, women's role within cities is changing, from being limited to the private domain, to expanding into the public, however, urban spaces are not being transformed accordingly in support of this socio-economic transformation. The recent discussions over the revival of neo-Lefebvrian discourses based on the right to the city are symptomatic of the gender neglect in most urban thought. And this neglection is especially obvious in the city of Cairo, where women continue to endure an unequal position when accessing the city, and they are still facing multiple social, religious, and legal discourses that support and legitimise gender inequalities. In this context, the transformation of gendered cityscape is also a form of political contestation against gender inequality prevalent in the society, in order to ensure "Access is guaranteed to all citizens" (Habermas et al., 1974).

As a group of urban planners, the authors argue that transferring the socio-economic change into spatial form is necessary to improve gender equality, increase social resilience and allow spaces to adapt to changing demographic contexts. Through our online and physical workshops with local students and residents in Cairo, the authors successfully identified a range of gender-related problems that are influenced by and reconstituting the daily experience in the city. This investigation helps us to establish more nuanced understandings and, consequently, develop strategies and recommendations to support gendered and grounded notions of everyday rights. By changing the physical dynamics in the city, it is possible the cultural and power relations within society could also see a shift towards an equal and inclusive world for women with increased safety and comfort in public space. People shape the city, but the city also shapes its people. Destroying the spatial systems that stemmed from the division of gendered tasks and the assigning of gender norms may therefore be key to gradually dissolving these norms in society itself and increasing the quality of life for women in the city.

The authors also acknowledge that engendering the city will be a lengthy process in the setting of many socio-cultural obstacles, particularly in non-western nations and Islamic contexts. It is vital to keep in mind that classic feminist methods may require to be reevaluated and closely tied to the local and current needs and context while (re)designing and (re)developing public spaces. The focus on women's rights in the city might be most effective when it is embedded in the sine qua non for both social and economic advancement (Kato, 2017). More and more local-based co-creation and co-planning activities between urban designers and local women could be planned, not only to change structural and unconscious biases that limit the potential of women, but also to emphasise their contributions to creating a safer place against gender-based bias and violence. Hence, changing perceptions about women's role in the city is an indispensable requirement for shaping urban space for inclusion and equity that Egypt so desperately needs.

And finally, the authors believe this "Gender-inclusive urban planning" ought to include cross-sectoral activities to meet gender requirements holistically because this is a cross-cutting problem that can only be remedied by working across many sectors, practices, and fields of knowledge. Partners from the local government and communities should be mobilised to co-define project objectives, co-plan all the procedures, carry out project activities and assess project performance collectively. The authors are encouraged to continue the 'Gender-inclusive Cities' project with identified future research directions, aiming to tackle gender discriminations and their spatial manifestations in order to create well-connected, safe public spaces with local communities and design organisations, using transportation planning, cohesive urban policies, and well-thought spatial designs for engaging the city, and through using participative processes to thoroughly understand women's needs. There could be more efficient and comprehensive approaches to include diverse perspectives in planning strategies if multiple rights to the city are considered, and their spatial tactics are identified. A renewed commitment to the multiple uses of space that is attentive to different users within the urban design framework has the potential to maintain a more complete sense of gendered rights in everyday life.

ACKNOWLEDGMENT

This research was supported by Northumbria Seed Fund 2022 and Northumbria University. We thank our colleagues from CLUSTER and UN Women who provided insight and expertise that greatly assisted all the research activities in Cairo, and we would like to express our gratitude to all staff from CUFE Architecture Department for the enthusiasm they brought to this research and the exhibition and workshop spaces they provided at their department. We would also like to show our gratitude to all the participants in the mapping sessions and the following exhibition for sharing their insights and experiences with us.

REFERENCES

Assaad, R., Hendy, R., Lassassi, M., & Yassin, S. (2018). Explaining the MENA paradox: Rising educational attainment, yet stagnant female labor force participation. *IZA Discussion Paper Series, 11385.* https://www.iza.org/publications/dp/11385/explaining-the-mena-paradoxrising-educational-attainment-yet-stagnant-female-labor-force-participation

Bandura, A. (1977). Self-efficacy: Toward a unifying theory of behavioral change. *Psychological Review, 84*(2), 191–215. doi:10.1037/0033-295X.84.2.191 PMID:847061

Bier, L. (2011). *Revolutionary womanhood: Feminisms, modernity, and the state in Nasser's Egypt.* Stanford University Press. https://www.sup.org/books/title/?id=18176

Braker, B. (2018, August). Women in Egypt: The myth of a safe public space. *Jane Jacobs Is Still Here: Report of the Conference Jane Jacobs 100.* https://www.researchgate.net/publication/327285947_Women_in_Egypt_The_myth_of_a_safe_public_space

Casanova, J. (2009). Religion, politics and gender equality: Public religions revisited. In S. Razavi (Ed.), *A debate on the public role of religion and its social and gender implications* (pp. 5–33). UN Research Institute for Social Development.

Casanovas, R., Ciocoletto, A., Salinas, M. F., Valdivia, B. G., Martinez, Z. M., & Escalante, S. O. (2015). *Women working: Urban assessment guide from a gender perspective.* Col.lectiu Punt 6.

Day, K. (2006). Being feared: Masculinity and race in public space. *Environment & Planning A, 38*(3), 569–586. doi:10.1068/a37221

De Koning, A. (2009). Gender, public space and social segregation in Cairo: Of taxi drivers, prostitutes and professional women. *Antipode, 41*(3), 533–556. doi:10.1111/j.1467-8330.2009.00686.x

De Madariaga, I. S., & Neuman, M. (2020). Planning the gendered city. In I. S. De Madariaga & M. Neuman (Eds.), *Engendering cities: Designing sustainable urban spaces for all* (1st ed., pp. 1–15). Routledge. doi:10.4324/9781351200912-1

El-Kot, G., Leat, M., & Fahmy, S. (2021). The nexus between work-life balance and gender role in Egypt. In T. A. Adisa & G. Gbadamosi (Eds.), *Work-Life Interface* (pp. 185–213). doi:10.1007/978-3-030-66648-4_7

El-Safty, M. (2004). Women in Egypt: Islamic rights versus cultural practice. *Sex Roles, 51*(5), 273–281. doi:10.1023/B:SERS.0000046611.31760.04

Fenster, T. (2005). The right to the gendered city: Different formations of belonging in everyday life. *Journal of Gender Studies, 14*(3), 217–231. doi:10.1080/09589230500264109

Goldin, C., & Katz, L. (1996). Technology, skill, and the wage structure: Insights from the past. *The American Economic Review, 86*(2), 252–257. https://www.jstor.org/stable/2118132

Habermas, J., Lennox, S., & Lennox, F. (1974). The public sphere: An encyclopedia article. *New German Critique, NGC, 3*(3), 55. doi:10.2307/487737

Hafez, S. (2016). *Egypt, uprising and gender politics: Gendering bodies/gendering space.* https://pomeps.org/egypt-uprising-and-gender-politics-gendering-bodiesgendering-space

Haines, G. (2017). *Mapped: The best (and worst) countries for gender equality.* http://www.telegraph.co.uk/travel/mapsand- graphics/mapped-the-best-and-worst-countries-for-gender-equality/

Hanson, S. (2010). Gender and mobility: New approaches for informing sustainability. *Gender, Place and Culture, 17*(1), 5–23. doi:10.1080/09663690903498225

Ilahi, N. (2009). *Gendered contestations: An analysis of street harassment in Cairo and its implications for women's access to public spaces.* https://www.ocac.cl/wp-content/uploads/2015/01/Nadia-Ilahi-Gendered-Contestations-An-Analysis-of-Street-Harassment-in-Cairo-....pdf

ITDP. (2019). *In Cairo, ITDP works to improve transport access for women.* https://www.itdp.org/2019/03/14/itdp-improves-transport-women-cairo/

Kato, M. (2017). Women of Egypt. *The Cairo Review of Global Affairs.* https://www.thecairoreview.com/essays/women-of-egypt/

Khalil, R., Moustafa, A. A., Moftah, M. Z., & Karim, A. A. (2017). How knowledge of Ancient Egyptian women can influence today's gender role: Does history matter in gender psychology? *Frontiers in Psychology, 7,* 2053. doi:10.3389/fpsyg.2016.02053 PMID:28105022

Khomami, N. (2017). *#MeToo: How a hashtag became a rallying cry against sexual harassment.* https://www.theguardian.com/world/2017/oct/20/women-worldwide-use-hashtag-metoo-against-sexual-harassment

Kuhlmann, D. (2013). *Gender studies in architecture: Space, power and difference.* Routledge. doi:10.4324/9780203522554

Loukaitou-Sideris, A. (2020). A gendered view of mobility and transport: Next steps and future directions. In I. S. De Madariaga & M. Neuman (Eds.), *Engendering cities: Designing sustainable urban spaces for all* (pp. 19–37). Routledge. doi:10.4324/9781351200912-2

Meece, J. L., Glienke, B. B., & Burg, S. (2006). Gender and motivation. *Journal of School Psychology*, *44*(5), 351–373. doi:10.1016/j.jsp.2006.04.004

Pepera, S. (2019). *Women and the City.* https://womendeliver.org/women-and-the-city/

Roberts, M. (1998). Urban design, gender and the future of cities. *Journal of Urban Design*, *3*(2), 133–135. doi:10.1080/13574809808724421

Samari, G. (2021). Coming back and moving backwards: Return migration and gender norms in Egypt. *Journal of Ethnic and Migration Studies*, *47*(5), 1103–1118. doi:10.1080/1369183X.2019.1669437 PMID:33716548

Sassen, S. (1998). *Globalization and its discontents: Essays on the new mobility of people and money.* New Press.

Silbaugh, K. (2007). Women's place: Urban planning, housing design, and work-family balance. *Fordham Law Review*, *76*(3), 1797–1852. https://ir.lawnet.fordham.edu/cgi/viewcontent.cgi?article=4340&context=flr

Sweeting, L. (2020). Bruised but never broken: The fight for gender equality in Egypt and Bangladesh. *Global Majority*, *11*(2), 102–116.

Tacoli, C., & Satterthwaite, D. (2013). Gender and urban change. *Environment and Urbanization*, *25*(1), 3–8. doi:10.1177/0956247813479086

TADAMUN. (2019). *Women and Precarious Employment: A spatial analysis of economic insecurity in Cairo's neighborhoods.* http://www.tadamun.co/women-and-precarious-employment-a-spatial-analysis-of-economic-insecurity-in-cairos-neighborhoods/?lang=en#.Y1jqK3bMJjE

The European Institute for Gender Equality. (2022). *Gender mainstreaming*. https://eige.europa.eu/gender-mainstreaming

Thomson Reuters Foundation. (2017). *Inform. Connect. Empower.* https://www.trust.org/documents/trf-2020.pdf

Tuerkheimer, D. (2019). Beyond #MeToo. *New York University Law Review*, *94*, 1146. https://papers.ssrn.com/abstract=3366126

UNDP. (2020). *Human Development Report 2020, The Next Frontier: Human Development and the Anthropocene*. https://www.undp.org/egypt/press-releases/human-development-report-2020

UNFPA. (2018). *UNFPA Annual Report 2018*. https://www.unfpa.org/publications/unfpa-annual-report-2018

Whitzman, C. (2013). Women's safety and everyday mobility. In C. Whitzman, C. Legacy, C. Andrew, F. Klodawsky, M. Shaw, & K. Viswanath (Eds.), *Building inclusive cities* (1st ed., pp. 32–52). Routledge. doi:10.4324/9780203100691-12

World Bank Group. (2020). *Handbook for Gender-Inclusive Urban Planning and Design*. https://www.worldbank.org/en/topic/urbandevelopment/publication/handbook-for-gender-inclusive-urban-planning-and-design

Compilation of References

ActionAid. (2014). *Safe Cities for Women: From reality to rights*. https://actionaid,ie/wp-content/uploads/2016/10/Safe-Cities-for-Women-from-Realities-toRights-1.pdf

Agustini, N. W. (2014). Feminism: The cases of Mariam and Laila in A Thousand Splendid Suns. *Humanis*, *9*(1), 1–8.

Ahmed, M. (2019). *Breaking harmful taboos in society, Sex education is a must to prevent gender-based violence*. https://www.thedailystar.net/opinion/society/news/breaking-harmful-taboos-society-1772890

Akbar, P. (2017). *Leila*. Simon & Schuster.

Akhtar, N. (2008). Pakistan, Afghanistan, and the Taliban. *International Journal on World Peace*, *25*(4), 49–73. https://www.jstor.org/stable/20752859

Aktar, T. (2020). Patriarchal society is a curse for Bangladeshi women, It's time to raise our voice against injustice. *Economics and Politics*. https://www.meer.com/en/64001-patriarchal-society-is-a-curse-for-bangladeshi-women

Alcoff, L. (1988). Cultural feminism versus post-structuralism: The identity crisis in feminist theory. *Signs (Chicago, Ill.)*, *13*(3), 405–436. doi:10.1086/494426

Alexander, C., Chatterji, J., & Jalais, A. (2016). *The Bengal Diaspora: Rethinking Muslim Migration*. Routledge.

Ali, R. (2012). Changing expectations of gender roles in Bangladesh. *Research Monograph Series, 52*. https://bigd.bracu.ac.bd/wp-content/uploads/2020/03/Changing-Expectations-of-Gender-Roles-in-Bangladesh-The-Case-of-Female-Field-Staff-of-BRAC_Monograph_52.pdf

Ali, M. (2004). *Brick Lane*. Black Swan.

Alimardani, M., & Elswah, M. (2021). Digital orientalism: #SaveSheikhJarrah and Arabic content moderation. *POMEPS Studies 43. Digital Activism and Authoritarian Adaptation in the Middle East*, *43*, 69–76.

Al-Kassim, D. (2013). Psychoanalysis and the postcolonial genealogy of queer theory. *International Journal of Middle East Studies*, *45*(2), 343–346. doi:10.1017/S0020743813000093

Allen, A. (2007). *The politics of our selves: Power, autonomy, and gender in contemporary critical theory.* Columbia University Press. doi:10.7312/alle13622

Alter, A. (2018). *How feminist dystopian fiction is channeling women's anger and anxiety.* Retrieved October 27, 2022, https://www.nytimes.com/2018/10/08/books/feminist-dystopian-fiction-margaret-atwood-women-metoo.html

Amar, P. (2013). *The security archipelago: Human-security states, sexuality, politics and the end of neoliberalism.* Duke University Press.

Amir-Ebrahimi, M. (2006). Conquering enclosed public spaces. *Cities (London, England)*, *23*(6), 455–461. doi:10.1016/j.cities.2006.08.001

Andretta, M., Piazza, G., & Subirats, A. (2015). Urban dynamics and social movement. In D. D. Porta & M. Diani (Eds.), *The Oxford handbook of social movements* (pp. 200–215). Oxford University Press.

Andrews, A. (2016). *(Re)Defining Afghan women characters as modern archetypes using Khaled Hosseini's A Thousand Splendid Suns and Asne Seierstad's The Bookseller of Kabul* [Master's Thesis, Liberty University]. Scholar's Crossing. https://digitalcommons.liberty.edu/masters/402

Aneja, A. (2019). *Women's and gender studies in India.* Routledge.

Anzaldúa, G. (1987). *Borderlands/La frontera: The new mestiza.* Aunt Lute.

Arjmand, R. (2016). *Public urban space, gender and segregation: Women-only urban parks in Iran.* Routledge. doi:10.4324/9781315603025

Ashcroft, B. (2012). Introduction: Spaces of utopia. *Spaces of Utopia*, *2*(1), 1–17.

Ashcroft, B. (2016). *Utopianism in postcolonial literatures.* Routledge. doi:10.4324/9781315642918

Asl, M. P. (2019). Leisure as a space of political practice in Middle East women life writings. *GEMA Online Journal of Language Studies*, *19*(3), 43–56. doi:10.17576/gema-2019-1903-03

Asl, M. P. (2020). The politics of space: Vietnam as a Communist heterotopia in Viet Thanh Nguyen's The Refugees. *3L: Language, Linguistics, Literature*, *26*(1), 156–170. doi:10.17576/3L-2020-2601-11

Asl, M. P. (2022). Gender, space and counter-conduct: Iranian women's heterotopic imaginations in Ramita Navai's City of Lies: Love, sex, death, and the search for truth in Tehran. *Gender, Place and Culture*, *29*(9), 1296–1316. doi:10.1080/0966369X.2021.1975100

Asl, M. P. (2022). Truth, space, and resistance: Iranian women's practices of freedom in Ramita Navai's City of Lies. *Women's Studies*, *51*(3), 287–306. doi:10.1080/00497878.2022.2030342

Assaad, R., Hendy, R., Lassassi, M., & Yassin, S. (2018). Explaining the MENA paradox: Rising educational attainment, yet stagnant female labor force participation. *IZA Discussion Paper Series, 11385*. https://www.iza.org/publications/dp/11385/explaining-the-mena-paradoxrising-educational-attainment-yet-stagnant-female-labor-force-participation

Azim, F. (2010). The new 21stcentury woman. In F. Azim & M. Sultan (Eds.), Mapping women's empowerment: Experience from Bangladesh, India and Pakistan (pp. 261-78). The University Press Limited.

Azim, F. (2016). Secularism and women's movement in Bangladesh. In M. Mukhopadyay (Ed.), *Feminist movement and complicity*. Zubaan Publishers.

Baccolini, R., & Moylan, T. (2003). *Dark horizons: Science fiction and the dystopian imagination*. Psychology Press.

Bagchi, I. (2020). *These incidents depict why public washrooms in Kolkata are a nightmare*. https://www.youthkiawaaz.com/2020/12/public-washrooms-in-kolkata-a-nightmare

Baghat, R. B., Roy, A. K., & Sahoo, H. (2021). *Migration and urban transition in India*. Routledge.

Bagheri, N. (2014). Mapping women in Tehran's public spaces: A geo-visualization perspective. *Gender, Place and Culture, 21*(10), 1285–1301. doi:10.1080/0966369X.2013.817972

Bahar, N. S. (2022). *Nothing is more alarming than when women do patriarchy's work for it*. https://www.thedailystar.net/views/opinion/news/women-can-internalise-patriarchy-too-2986921

Bahlieda, R. (2015). The legacy of patriarchy. *Counterpoints, 488*, 15–67. https://www.jstor.org/stable/45136330

Bahri, D. (1998). Terms of engagement: Postcolonialism, transnationalism, and composition studies. *JAC, 18*(1), 29–44. PMID:9700526

Bandura, A. (1977). Self-efficacy: Toward a unifying theory of behavioral change. *Psychological Review, 84*(2), 191–215. doi:10.1037/0033-295X.84.2.191 PMID:847061

Banerjee, S. (1997). *Kabuliwalar Bangali Bou*. Bhasha O Sahitya.

Banu, A. (n.d.). *Feminism in Bangladesh (1971-2000): Voices from the movement* [PhD thesis]. University of Dhaka, Bangladesh.

Banu, A. (2015). Global-local interactions: First three decades of women's movement in Bangladesh. *Journal of the Asiatic Society, 60*(2), 203–230.

Banu, S. S. (2016). Discrimination, war and redemption in Khaled Hosseini's The Kite Runner and A Thousand Splendid Suns. *Language in India, 16*(8), 180–193.

Barnett, R. R. (1997). Women and pipelines: Afghanistan's proxy wars. *Asia and the Pacific, 73*(2), 283-296. https://www.jstor.org/stable/2623829

Basu, P. (2020). *Kolkata one of the safest cities for women, says NCRB data*. https://www.millenniumpost.in/kolkata/kolkata-one-of-the-safest-city-for-women-says-ncrb-data-420181

Basu, S. (2017). *Where are the women in Kolkata*. FirstPost.com.

Bebel, A., & Lilienthal, M. S. (1910). *Woman and socialism*. Good Press.

Bedi, K. (1995). *I dare!* Hay House (India) Publishers Pvt. Ltd.

Bedi, K. (2012). *Dare to do: For the new generation*. Hay House (India) Publishers Pvt. Ltd.

Bedi, K. (2008). *Empowering women...As I see....* Sterling Paperbacks.

Beebeejaun, Y. (2017). Gender, Urban Space, and the Right to Everyday Life. *Journal of Urban Affairs, 39*(3), 323–334. doi:10.1080/07352166.2016.1255526

Bennett, J. (2007). *History matters: Patriarchy and the challenge of feminism*. University of Pennsylvania Press. doi:10.9783/9780812200553

Beriss, D. (2018). *Black skins, French voices: Caribbean ethnicity and activism in urban France*. Routledge. doi:10.4324/9780429502040

Berry, J., Moore, T., Kalms, N., & Bawden, G. (Eds.). (2021). *Contentious cities: Design and the gendered production of space*. Routledge.

Bhabha, H. K. (1994). *The Location of culture*. Routledge.

Bhandari, A. (2021). Feminist perspectives on space, safety and surveillance: Improving a woman's right to the city. *The Wire*. https://thewire.in/women/feminist-perspectives-on-space-safety-and-surveillance-improving-a-womans-right-to-the-city

Bharucha, R. (2014). *Terror and performance*. Routledge. doi:10.4324/9781315794488

Bhasin, K. (2006). *What is patriarchy? Women unlimited*. Academic Press.

Bhattacharjee, S., & Karmakar, G. (Eds.). (2022). *The city speaks: Urban spaces in Indian Literature*. Routledge. doi:10.4324/9781003323761

Bhattacharya, M. (2022). The partition: A Heterotopic transcendence in self- identity of the Bengali women migrants. In M. Pourya Asl (Ed.), *Gender, place, and identity of South Asian women* (pp. 44–67). IGI Global. doi:10.4018/978-1-6684-3626-4.ch003

Bier, L. (2011). *Revolutionary womanhood: Feminisms, modernity, and the state in Nasser's Egypt*. Stanford University Press. https://www.sup.org/books/title/?id=18176

Biswas, R. (2019). *Reclaiming the urban: An intersectional analysis of women's and men's experiences of public spaces in Kolkata*. Temple University Graduate Board.

Blumer, H. (2008). Social movements. In V. Ruggiero & N. Montagna (Eds.), *Social movements: A reader* (pp. 64–72). Routledge.

Boehmer, E. (2009). *Stories of women: Gender and narrative in the postcolonial nation.* Manchester University Press.

Boling, P. (2011). On learning to teach fat feminism. *Feminist Teacher, 21*(2), 110–123. doi:10.5406/femteacher.21.2.0110

Bondi, L. (1998). Gender, class, and urban space: Public and private space in contemporary urban landscapes. *Urban Geography, 19*(2), 160–185. doi:10.2747/0272-3638.19.2.160

Booth, W. C. (1961). *The rhetoric of fiction.* University of Chicago Press.

Bork-Hüffer, T. (2016). Migrants' agency and the making of transient urban spaces. *Population Space and Place, 22*(2), 124–127. doi:10.1002/psp.1891

Bose, S., & Jalal, A. (2017). *Modern South Asia: History, culture, political economy.* Routledge. doi:10.4324/9781315106076

Boulaich, K. (2019). The silent revolution of public spaces in Afghanistan. Clean and Green Cities (CGC) Programme-United Nations Human Settlements Programme (UN-Habitat).

BowmaniZ. (2021). Now is the time for Black queer feminist ecology. *Law & Sexuality.* https://ssrn.com/abstract=3795137

Braker, B. (2018, August). Women in Egypt: The myth of a safe public space. *Jane Jacobs Is Still Here: Report of the Conference Jane Jacobs 100.* https://www.researchgate.net/publication/327285947_Women_in_Egypt_The_myth_of_a_safe_public_space

Brassard, C., & Joshi, D. U. (2020). *Urban spaces and gender in Asia.* Springer.

Bressey, C. (2010). Victorian 'anti-racism' and feminism in Britain. *Women a Cultural Review, 21*(3), 279–291. doi:10.1080/09574042.2010.513491

Bridge, G., & Watson, S. (Eds.). (2011). *The new Blackwell companion to the city.* Wiley-Blackwell. doi:10.1002/9781444395105

Brownlee, J. (2013). *Violence against copts in Egypt.* Carnegie Endowment for International Peace.

Bunce, S., Livingstone, N., March, L., Moore, S., & Walks, A. (2020). Conclusion. In S. Bunce, N. Livingstone, L. March, S. Moore & A. Walks (Eds.), Critical dialogues of urban governance, development, and activism: London and Toronto (pp. 297-305). UCL Press.

Bunker, R. J. (2014). The emergence of feral and criminal cities: US Military implications in a time of austerity. *The Land Warfare Papers, 99*(2), 1–14.

Butler, J. (1990). *Gender trouble: Feminism and the subversion of identity.* Routledge.

Butler, J. (1994). Feminism by any other name (Judith Butler interviews Rosi Braidotti). *Differences: A Journal of Feminist Cultural Studies*, *6*(2–3), 272–361.

Butler, J. (2004). An essay in phenomenology and feminist theory. In H. Bial (Ed.), *The Performance Studies Reader* (pp. 154–165). Routledge.

Butler, J. (2016). *Frames of war: When is life grievable?* Verso Books.

Call, C. T. (2008). The fallacy of the "Failed State." *Third World Quarterly*, *29*(8), 1491–1507. doi:10.1080/01436590802544207

Carey, A. C., Block, P., & Scotch, R. K. (2020). *Allies and obstacles: Disability activism and parents of children with disabilities*. Temple University Press.

Caruth, C. (2016). *Unclaimed experience: Trauma, narrative, and history*. Johns Hopkins University Press. doi:10.56021/9781421421650

Casanova, J. (2009). Religion, politics and gender equality: Public religions revisited. In S. Razavi (Ed.), *A debate on the public role of religion and its social and gender implications* (pp. 5–33). UN Research Institute for Social Development.

Casanovas, R., Ciocoletto, A., Salinas, M. F., Valdivia, B. G., Martinez, Z. M., & Escalante, S. O. (2015). *Women working: Urban assessment guide from a gender perspective*. Col.lectiu Punt 6.

Chakrabarty, D. (2000). *Provincializing Europe: Political thought and historical difference*. Princeton University Press.

Chakravarti, U. (2018). Gendering caste: Through a feminist lens. *Sage (Atlanta, Ga.)*.

Chandran, R. (2016). *Indian women reclaim public spaces, defying male critics*. Reuters.com.

Channa, S. M. (2013). *Gender in South Asia: Social imagination and constructed realities*. Cambridge University Press. doi:10.1017/CBO9781107338807

Chatterjee, P. (2008). Women and the nation: The trouble with their voices. In M. E. John (Ed.), *Women's studies in India: A reader* (pp. 309–316). Penguin Books.

Chattopadhyay, S. K. (2018). *Gender socialization and the making of gender in the Indian context*. Sage Publications. doi:10.4135/9789353280628

Chaudhary, P. (2020). Women resistance and power relation in Khaled Hosseini's A Thousand Splendid Suns. *Journal of Xi'an University of Architecture & Technology*, *12*(4), 5493–5502.

Chiesa, L. (2016). *Space as Storyteller: Spatial Jumps in Architecture, Critical Theory, and Literature*. Northwestern University Press. doi:10.2307/j.ctv47w5px

Chowdhury, E. (2010). Feminism and its 'other': Representing the 'new woman' of Bangladesh. *A Journal of Feminist Geography Place and Culture*, *3*, 301-318. . doi:10.1080/09663691003737587

Chowdhury, S. (2019). *Understanding heterotopia: Foucault's spatial context to society*. . doi:10.13140/RG.2.2.11385.11367

Chowdhury, F. (2009). Theorising patriarchy: The Bangladesh context. *Asian Journal of Social Science*, *37*(4), 599–622. doi:10.1163/156853109X460200

Christophers, B., Lave, R., Peck, J., & Werner, M. (2018). *The Doreen Massey reader*. Agenda Publishing.

Cixous, H., & Clement, C. (1986). *The newly born woman*. University of Minnesota Press.

Crang, P., Dwyer, C., & Jackson, P. (2003). Transnationalism and the spaces of commodity culture. *Progress in Human Geography*, *27*(4), 438–456. doi:10.1191/0309132503ph443oa

Curran, W. (2018). *Gender and gentrification*. Routledge.

Darke, D. (2014). *My House in Damascus*. HAUS Publishing. doi:10.2307/j.ctt1zxsm5n

Darwin, C. (1859). *On the Origin of Species*. John Murray.

Das, S. R. (2020). *Dystopia and Indianness in Post-Millennial Indian Fiction*. https://www.pwcenglish.com/2020/04/06/dystopia-and-indiannes s-in-post-millennial-indian-fiction/

Dashgupta, P. (2020, February). *'Real' to the 'Hyperreal': A Study of the Postmodern and Dystopian Cityscape in Ruchir Joshi's The Last Jet-Engine Laugh and Prayaag Akbar's Leila*. Melow.

Datta, A. (2021). *Gender, space and agency in India: Exploring regional genderscapes*. Routledge.

Davies, D., & Boehmer, E. (2018). *Planned violence: Post/Colonial urban infrastructure, literature and culture*. Springer.

Day, K. (2006). Being feared: Masculinity and race in public space. *Environment & Planning A*, *38*(3), 569–586. doi:10.1068/a37221

Day, K. (2011). *Feminist approaches to urban design*. Routledge.

De Koning, A. (2009). Gender, public space and social segregation in Cairo: Of taxi drivers, prostitutes and professional women. *Antipode*, *41*(3), 533–556. doi:10.1111/j.1467-8330.2009.00686.x

De Madariaga, I. S., & Neuman, M. (2020). Planning the gendered city. In I. S. De Madariaga & M. Neuman (Eds.), *Engendering cities: Designing sustainable urban spaces for all* (1st ed., pp. 1–15). Routledge. doi:10.4324/9781351200912-1

Dhagamwar, V. (1992). Law, power and justice. *Sage (Atlanta, Ga.)*.

Dhakal, S. (2020). Endurance of women in Afghan society in Khaled Hosseini's A Thousand Splendid Suns (Book review). *Molung Educational Frontier*, *10*(1), 229–233. doi:10.3126/mef.v10i0.34088

Dharmani, D., & Singh, R. (2018). Women as nation in Khaled Hosseini's A Thousand Splendid Suns. *Language in India.*, *18*(1), 209–217.

Di Biase, M. A., Zhang, F., Lyall, A., Kubicki, M., Mandl, R. C., Sommer, I. E., & Pasternak, O. (2019). Neuroimaging auditory verbal hallucinations in schizophrenia patient and healthy populations. *Psychological Medicine*, *50*(3), 403–412. doi:10.1017/S0033291719000205

Diani, M. (2003). Introduction. In M. Diani & D. McAdam (Eds.), *Social movements and networks: Relational approaches to collective action* (pp. 1–18). Oxford University Press. doi:10.1093/0199251789.003.0001

Diani, M. (2008). The concept of social movement. In V. Ruggiero & N. Montagna (Eds.), *Social movements: A reader* (pp. 266–271). Routledge.

Diani, M., & Porta, D. D. (2006). *Social movements: An introduction*. Blackwell Publishing.

Domaradzka, A. (2018). Urban social movements and right to the city: An introduction to the special issue on urban mobilization. *Voluntas*, *29*(4), 607–620. Advance online publication. doi:10.100711266-018-0030-y

Dorman, W. (2011). Of demolitions and donors: The problematics of state interventions in informal Cairo. In D. Singerman (Ed.), *Cairo contested: Governance, urban space, and global modernity* (pp. 262–290). American University of Cairo Press.

Duff, K. (2014). *Contemporary British Literature and urban space: After Thatcher*. Palgrave. doi:10.1057/9781137429353

Eder, K. (2015). Social movements in social theory. In D. D. Porta & M. Diani (Eds.), *The Oxford handbook of social movements* (pp. 31–49). Oxford University Press.

Egbert, J., & Sanden, S. (2019). *Foundations of education research understanding theoretical components*. Routledge. doi:10.4324/9780429452963

El-Kot, G., Leat, M., & Fahmy, S. (2021). The nexus between work-life balance and gender role in Egypt. In T. A. Adisa & G. Gbadamosi (Eds.), *Work-Life Interface* (pp. 185–213). doi:10.1007/978-3-030-66648-4_7

El-Safty, M. (2004). Women in Egypt: Islamic rights versus cultural practice. *Sex Roles*, *51*(5), 273–281. doi:10.1023/B:SERS.0000046611.31760.04

Elyachar, J. (2003). Mappings of power: The State, NGOs, and international organizations in the informal economy of Cairo. *Comparative Studies in Society and History*, *45*(3), 571–605. doi:10.1017/S0010417503000264

Escalante, S. O., & Valdivia, B. G. (2015). Planning from below: Using feminist participatory methods to increase women's participation in urban planning. *Gender and Development*, *23*(1), 113–126. doi:10.1080/13552074.2015.1014206

Essa, L. (2021). Of other spaces and others' memories: Reading graveyards in Arundhati Roy's *The Ministry of Utmost Happiness* and Regina Scheer's *Machandel*. *Comparative Literature Studies*, *58*(4), 744–779. doi:10.5325/complitstudies.58.4.0744

Fahs, B. (2011). Ti-Grace Atkinson and the legacy of radical feminism. *Feminist Studies*, *37*(3), 561–590. doi:10.1353/fem.2011.0047

Fariman, M. A. (2022). Closedness and openness in Tehran: A feminist critique of Sennett. *Gender, Place and Culture*, 1–22. doi:10.1080/0966369X.2022.2092074

Feminist Majority and Avia. (1997, October). Afghanistan. *Off Our Backs*, *27*(9), 4.

Fenster, T. (2006). The right to the gendered city: Different formations of belonging in everyday life. *Journal of Gender Studies*, *14*(3), 217–231. doi:10.1080/09589230500264109

Fernandes, L. (Ed.). (2014). *Routledge handbook of gender in South Asia*. Routledge. doi:10.4324/9781315848501

Fernea, R. (2003). Gender, sexuality and patriarchy in modern Egypt. *Critique*, *12*(2), 141–153. doi:10.1080/1066992032000130602

Firestone, S. (1970). *The dialectic of sex: The case for feminist revolution*. William Morrow and Company.

Fischer-Tiné, H., & Framke, M. (Eds.). (2022). *Routledge handbook of the history of colonialism in South Asia*. Routledge.

Fitzpatrick, C. (2009). New orientalism in popular fiction and memoir: An illustration of type. *Journal of Multicultural Discourses*, *4*(3), 243–256. doi:10.1080/17447140902972305

Formes, M. (2005). Post-colonial domesticity amid diaspora: Home and family in the lives of two English sisters from India. *Journal of Social History: Kith and Kin: Interpersonal Relationships and Cultural Practices*, *39*(2), 467–482. doi:10.1353/jsh.2005.0134

Foucault, M. (1994). Des espaces autres [1967/1984]. In Dits et Øcrits. 1954–1988 (Vol. 4, pp. 752–762). Gallimard.

Foucault, M., & Miskowiec, J. (1986). Of other spaces. *Diacritics*, *16*(1), 22–27. doi:10.2307/464648

Francisco, V., & Rodriguez, R. M. (2014). Countertopographies of migrant women: Transnational families, space, and labor as solidarity. *Working USA*, *17*(3), 357–372. doi:10.1111/wusa.12119

Fraser, N. (2009). *Scales of justice: Reimagining political space in a globalizing world*. Columbia University Press.

Friedman, S. S. (1998). *Mappings: Feminism and the cultural geographies of encounter*. Princeton University Press.

Friesen, W., Murphy, L., & Kearns, R. (2005). Spiced-up Sandringham: Indian transnationalism and new suburban spaces in Auckland, New Zealand. *Journal of Ethnic and Migration Studies*, *31*(2), 385–401. doi:10.1080/1369183042000339981

Gaard, G. (1993). *Ecofeminism: Women, animals, nature*. Temple University Press.

Gaard, G. (1997). Toward a queer ecofeminism. *Hypatia*, *12*(1), 114–137. doi:10.1111/j.1527-2001.1997.tb00174.x

Gajjala, R. (2019). *Digital diasporas: Labor and affect in gendered Indian digital publics*. Rowman & Littlefield.

Ganguly, M. (Ed.). (2020). *"I Sleep in My Own Deathbed" Violence against Women and Girls in Bangladesh: Barriers to Legal Recourse and Support*. https://www.hrw.org/report/2020/10/29/i-sleep-my-own-deathbed/violence-against-women-and-girls-bangladesh-barriers

Gardner, K. (2022). Lost and abandoned: Spatial precarity and displacement in Dhaka, Bangladesh. *Ethnos. Journal of Anthropology*, 1–19. Advance online publication. doi:10.1080/00141844.2022.2052925

Gender and International Migration. (n.d.). Retrieved from United Nations: https://sitreport.unescapsdd.org/gender-and-international-migration

George, H. (2020). *10 reasons explaining the importance of urban planning*. Planningtank.com.

Ghose, B., Feng, D., Tang, S., Yaya, S., He, Z., Udenigwe, O., Ghosh, S., & Feng, Z. (2017). Women's decision-making autonomy and utilisation of maternal healthcare services: Results from the Bangladesh Demographic and Health Survey. *BMJ Open*, *7*(9), e017142. doi:10.1136/bmjopen-2017-017142 PMID:28882921

Ghosh, S. (2010). Expressing the self in Bengali women's autobiographies in the twentieth century. *South Asia Research*, *30*(2), 105–123. doi:10.1177/026272801003000201 PMID:20684082

Gikandi, S. (1996). *Maps of Englishness: Writing identity in the culture of colonialism*. Columbia University Press.

Gillis, M. J., & Jacobs, A. T. (2019). *Introduction to women's and gender studies*. Oxford University Press.

Gilman, C. P. (1981). *The Yellow Wallpaper*. Virago Press.

Goel, R. (2018). *Indian cities are just not designed for women*. Quartz India. https://qz.com/india/1375405/indian-cities-are-just-not-designed-for-women

Golabi, M. (2022). Aesthetics of invisibility in Iranian women's identity and their domestic space during the 1980s. *Gender, Place and Culture*, *29*(11), 1616–1638. doi:10.1080/0966369X.2022.2056146

Goldin, C., & Katz, L. (1996). Technology, skill, and the wage structure: Insights from the past. *The American Economic Review*, *86*(2), 252–257. https://www.jstor.org/stable/2118132

Compilation of References

Gonsalves, T. (2022). *Women in the civil services: Gender and workplace identities in India.* Taylor and Francis. doi:10.4324/9781003193630

Gordan, M., & Almutairi, A. S. (2013). Resistance, a facet of post-colonialism in women characters of Khaled Hosseini's A Thousand Splendid Suns. *International Journal of Applied Linguistics and English Literature, 2*(3), 240–247. doi:10.7575/aiac.ijalel.v.2n.3p.240

Gottdiener, M., & Budd, L. (2005). Key concepts in urban studies. *Sage (Atlanta, Ga.).*

Greed, C. H. (1994). *Women and planning.* Routledge.

Group, I. C. (2014). *Policing urban violence in Pakistan.* Asia Report.

Guha, K. (2021, December 5). *Prayaag Akbar on the experiences and influences that Shaped Leila.* Retrieved August 28, 2022. https://www.thehindu.com/lit-for-life/love-and-other-jihads-prayaag-akbar-talks-about-his-novel-leila/article61450463.ece

Gupta, S. (2022). (Dis) Locating homeland: Border (home) land in Taslima Nasreen's French Lover and Monica Ali's Brick Lane. In M. Pourya Asl (Ed.), *Gender, Place, and Identity of South Asian Women* (pp. 1–22). IGI Global. doi:10.4018/978-1-6684-3626-4.ch001

Haan, A. (2000). Migrants, Livelihoods and Rights. The relevance of Migration in Development Policies, Social Development, Working Paper No.-4.

Habermas, J., Lennox, S., & Lennox, F. (1974). The public sphere: An encyclopedia article. *New German Critique, NGC, 3*(3), 55. doi:10.2307/487737

Hadi, N. H. A., & Asl, M. P. (2022). The real, the imaginary, and the symbolic: A Lacanian reading of Ramita Navai's City of Lies. *GEMA Online Journal of Language Studies, 22*(1), 145–158. doi:10.17576/gema-2022-2201-08

Hafez, S. (2016). *Egypt, uprising and gender politics: Gendering bodies/gendering space.* https://pomeps.org/egypt-uprising-and-gender-politics-gendering-bodiesgendering-space

Haines, G. (2017). *Mapped: The best (and worst) countries for gender equality.* http://www.telegraph.co.uk/travel/mapsand-graphics/mapped-the-best-and-worst-countries-for-gender-equality/

Hannah, M. G. (2021). *Direction and Socio-spatial Theory: A political economy of oriented practice.* Routledge.

Hanson, S. (1992). Geography and feminism: Worlds in collision? *Annals of the Association of American Geographers, 82*(4), 569–586. doi:10.1111/j.1467-8306.1992.tb01718.x

Hanson, S. (2010). Gender and mobility: New approaches for informing sustainability. *Gender, Place and Culture, 17*(1), 5–23. doi:10.1080/09663690903498225

Haque, I., Mehta, S., & Kumar, A. (2019). Towards sustainable and inclusive cities: The case of Kolkata. *Observer Research Foundation, 83*. https://www.orfonline.org/research/towards-sustainable-and-inclusive-cities-the-case-of-kolkata-48992/

Haque, F., & Druce, S. C. (2019). *Gender disparity in Bangladesh: The study of women's vulnerable situations in patriarchal society and the rise of gender equality*. Academy of Brunei Studies.

Hardwick, J. (2020). *Sex in an old regime city: Young workers and intimacy in France, 1660-1789*. Oxford University Press. doi:10.1093/oso/9780190945183.001.0001

Harraswatch. (2022). *It has nothing to do with your coverage*. https://harasswatch.com/news/1908/

Hartmann, H. I. (1981). The family as the locus of gender, class, and political struggle: The example of housework. *Signs (Chicago, Ill.), 6*(3), 366–394. doi:10.1086/493813

Harvey, D. (2003). *The new imperialism*. Oxford University Press. doi:10.1093/oso/9780199264315.001.0001

Harvey, D. (2012). *Rebel cities: From the right to the city to the urban revolution*. Verso.

Hashemi, K. C. (2018). The girls of Enghelab Street: Women and revolution in Modern Iran. *IMEIS Annual Conference*.

Herbert, C. (2014). Postcolonial cities. In K. McNamara (Ed.), *The Cambridge companion to the city in literature* (pp. 200–215). Cambridge University Press. doi:10.1017/CCO9781139235617.017

Hillier, B. (2001). A Theory of the City as Object or, How Spatial Laws Mediate the Social Construction of Urban Space. Proceedings: *3rd International Space Syntax Symposium*, (p. 2). Atlanta.

Hirschmann, N. J. (2008). *Gender, class, and freedom in modern political theory*. Princeton University Press.

Holmes, J. (2007). Social constructionism, postmodernism and feminist sociolinguistics. *Gender and Language, 1*(1), 51–65. Advance online publication. doi:10.1558/genl.2007.1.1.51

Holson, L. M. (2019). *Murders by intimate partners are on the rise, study finds*. https://www.nytimes.com/2019/04/12/us/domestic-violence-victims.html

Hooks, B. (1986). Sisterhood: Political solidarity between women. *Feminist Review, 23*(1), 125–138. doi:10.1057/fr.1986.25

Hosseini, K. (2007). *A Thousand Splendid Suns*. Bloomsbury Publishing.

Hossen, M. S. (2020). Patriarchy practice and women's subordination in the society of Bangladesh: An analytical review. *Electronic Research Journal of Social Sciences and Humanities, 2*(3), 51–60.

Hussein, N. (2017). *Negotiating middle-class respectable femininity: Bangladeshi women and their families*. South Asia Multidisciplinary Academic Journal. doi:10.4000amaj.4397

Hyndman, J. (2004). Mind the gap: Bridging feminist and political geography through geopolitics. *Political Geography*, *23*(3), 307–322. doi:10.1016/j.polgeo.2003.12.014

Ilahi, N. (2009). *Gendered contestations: An analysis of street harassment in Cairo and its implications for women's access to public spaces.* https://www.ocac.cl/wp-content/uploads/2015/01/Nadia-Ilahi-Gendered-Contestations-An-Analysis-of-Street-Harassment-in-Cairo-....pdf

Iran Human Rights. (2018). *"Girls of the Revolution Street" Challenging 39 Years of Repression.* Iran Human Rights. https://iranhr.net/en/articles/3215/

Islam, M., & Karim, K. M. R. (2012). Men's views on gender and sexuality in a Bangladesh village. *International Quarterly of Community Health Education*, *32*(4), 339–354. doi:10.2190/IQ.32.4.f PMID:23376759

ITDP. (2019). *In Cairo, ITDP works to improve transport access for women.* https://www.itdp.org/2019/03/14/itdp-improves-transport-women-cairo/

Ivanchikova, A. (2017). Imagining Afghanistan in the aftermath of 9/11: Conflicting literary chronographies of one invasion. *Textual Practice*, *31*(1), 197–216. doi:10.1080/0950236X.2016.1237987

Jackson, S. (2001). Why a materialist feminism is (still) possible—And necessary. *Women's Studies International Forum*, *24*(3–4), 283–293. doi:10.1016/S0277-5395(01)00187-X

Jacobsen, K. A. (Ed.). (2016). *Routledge handbook of contemporary India*. Routledge.

Jaggar, A. (1987). Love & Knowledge: Emotion in Feminist Epistemology. In S. Kemp & J. Squires (Eds.), Feminisms. Oxford UP.

Jaggar, A. M. (1983). *Feminist politics and human nature, philosophy and society*. Rowman & Allanheld.

Jakobsen, P., Jonsson, E., & Larsen, H. G. (2022). *Socio-Spatial Theory in Nordic geography: Intellectual histories and critical interventions*. Springer. doi:10.1007/978-3-031-04234-8

Jameela, N. (2005). *The Autobiography of a Sex Worker*. Westland Ltd.

John, M. (1998). Feminism, internationalism and the West: Question from the Indian context. *Centre for Women's Development Studies*, *27*, 1–24.

Johnson, P. (2016). *Brief history of the concept of heterotopia (revised)*. http://www.heterotopiastudies.com

Johnson, A. (2005). *The gender knot: Unraveling our patriarchal legacy*. Temple University Press.

Jordan, D. (2008). *Apocalypse: Living dangerously, population and the looming disasters of the 21st century*. Chipmunka Publishing.

Joshi, M., & Singh, D. (2021, November 25). It's 2021 — Why Are Public Spaces & Roads Still Unsafe for Women? *The Quint.* https://www.thequint.com/voices/opinion/gender-based-violence-crimes-against-women-ncrb-data-india-public-spaces-roads-safety-concerns#:~:text=Fast%20and%20rashly%20driven%20vehicles,of%20women%20and%20secluded%20neighbourhoods

Joyia, M. I., Farooq, U., Ghafoor, S., & Gull, A. (2017). Courageous women: A study of resilience of women in Khaled Hosseini's novel A Thousand Splendid Suns. *Language in India, 17*(1), 98–108.

Kabeer, H., & Chaudhary, P. (2020). Afghan minorities and ethnic tension in The Kite Runner and A Thousand Splendid Suns. *European Journal of Molecular and Clinical Medicine, 7*(3), 1415–1425.

Karim, K. M. R., Emmelin, M., Lindberg, L., & Wamala, S. (2016). Gender and women development initiatives in Bangladesh: A study of rural mother center. *Social Work in Public Health, 31*(5), 369–386. doi:10.1080/19371918.2015.1137517 PMID:27149647

Karim, K. M. R., Emmelin, M., Resurreccion, B., & Wamala, S. (2012). Water development projects and marital violence: Experiences from rural Bangladesh. *Health Care for Women International, 33*(3), 200–216. doi:10.1080/07399332.2011.603861 PMID:22325022

Karim, R., Lindberg, L., Wamala, S., & Emmelinn, M. (2018). Men's perceptions of women's participation in development initiatives in rural Bangladesh. *American Journal of Men's Health, 12*(2), 398–410. doi:10.1177/1557988317735394 PMID:29025358

Kateja, A., & Jain, R. (Eds.). (2021). *Urban growth and environmental issues in India.* Springer Nature.

Kato, M. (2017). Women of Egypt. *The Cairo Review of Global Affairs.* https://www.thecairoreview.com/essays/women-of-egypt/

Katrak, K. (2006). *The Politics of the female Body: Postcolonial women writers.* Rutgers University Press.

Kelman, I., & Clark-Ginsberg, A. (2022). An urban governance framework for including environmental migrants in sustainable cities. *Climate (Basel), 10*(8), 121. doi:10.3390/cli10080121

Kenny, K. (2013). *Diaspora: A very short introduction.* Oxford University Press. doi:10.1093/actrade/9780199858583.001.0001

Kerketta, S., & Maiti, A. (2021). Dimensions of women's safety in urban public places: A cross sectional study of Kolkata metropolitan area. *International Journal of Humanities and Social Science Research, 7*(1), 122–129.

Kettaf, F., & Moscarelli, F. (2010). Understanding public space concepts as key elements of sustainable urban design. *Sustainable Architecture and Urban Development, 3*, 229–244.

Khader, J. (2013). *Cartographies of transnationalism in postcolonial feminisms: Geography, culture, identity, politics.* Lexington Books.

Compilation of References

Khair, T. (2001). *Babu fictions: Alienation in contemporary Indian English novels.* Oxford University Press.

Khair, T., & Doubinsky, S. (2011). Reading literature today: Two complementary essays and a conversation. *Sage (Atlanta, Ga.).* Advance online publication. doi:10.4135/9788132107750

Khalil, R., Moustafa, A. A., Moftah, M. Z., & Karim, A. A. (2017). How knowledge of Ancient Egyptian women can influence today's gender role: Does history matter in gender psychology? *Frontiers in Psychology, 7,* 2053. doi:10.3389/fpsyg.2016.02053 PMID:28105022

Khan, R. N. (2017). Representation of the Afghan national identity in Hosseini's A Thousand Splendid Suns. *Dialogue (Pakistan), 12*(1), 75–89.

Khatam, A. (2009). The Islamic Republic's failed quest for the spotless city. *Middle East Report (New York, N.Y.), 250,* 44–49.

Khomami, N. (2017). *#MeToo: How a hashtag became a rallying cry against sexual harassment.* https://www.theguardian.com/world/2017/oct/20/women-worldwide-use-hashtag-metoo-against-sexual-harassment

Kilani, K. (2019). *Fleeing the ring road.* Al-Mahroosa Publisher Ltd.

Kinderman, M., & Rohleder, R. (Eds.). (2020). *Exploring the spatiality of the city across cultural texts.* Springer. doi:10.1007/978-3-030-55269-5

King, K. (1994). *Theory in its feminist travels: Conversations in U.S. Women's movements.* Indiana University Press.

Kitchi, F., Maci, G., & Janssen, A. (2022). *Gender-sensitive infrastructure planning means better cities for everyone.* UrbaNet.info.

Konchan, V. (2012). *Urban Poetics: A Call from (and to) the Wild.* https://sites.lsa.umich.edu/mqr/2012/10/urban-poetics-a-call-from-and-to-the-wild/

Koonings, K., & Kruijt, D. (2007). *Fractured cities: Social exclusion, urban violence & contested spaces in Latin America.* Zed Books Ltd. doi:10.5040/9781350220225

Kovačević, V., & Malenica, K. (2021). Heterotopia and postmodern community in the context of migration and relationship towards migrants. *Italian Sociological Review, 11*(1), 63–86. doi:10.13136/isr.v11i1.415

Kuhlmann, D. (2013). *Gender studies in architecture: Space, power and difference.* Routledge. doi:10.4324/9780203522554

Kumari, H. (2022). *Is public commute gender inclusive? Access, safety, and utility of our transport infrastructure.* https://feminisminindia.com/2022/06/06/is-public-commute-gender-inclusive-transport-infrastructure/

Kumar, R., Korff, M., & Sudhir, K. (2018). *A gender atlas of India: With scorecard.* Sage Publication. doi:10.4135/9789353287832

Lai, J. S. (2022). *Asian American connective action in the age of social media: Civic engagement, contested issues, and emerging identities.* Temple University Press.

Lalitha, K. (2008). Women in revolt: A historical analysis of the progressive organisation of women in Andhra Pradesh. In M. E. John (Ed.), *Women's studies in India: A reader* (pp. 32–41). Penguin Books.

Lam, M. (2009). The politics of fiction: A response to new orientalism in type. *Journal of Multicultural Discourses, 4*(3), 257–262. doi:10.1080/17447140903198496

Lathia, S., & Mahadevia, D. (2019). Women's safety and public spaces: Lessons from the Sabarmati. *Urban Planning, 4*(2), 154–168. doi:10.17645/up.v4i2.2049

Lau, L., & Mendes, A. C. (2019). Romancing the other: Arundhati Roy's *The Ministry of Utmost Happiness. Journal of Commonwealth Literature,* 1–16. doi:10.1177/0021989418820701

Leber, A., & Abrahams, A. (2021). Social media manipulation in the MENA: Inauthenticity, inequality, and insecurity. *Digital Activism and Authoritarian Adaptation in the Middle East, 48.*

Lefebvre, H. (1974). La production de l'espace. *Anthropos.*

Lefebvre, H. (2003). *The urban revolution (R. Bononno, Tran.).* University of Minnesota Press. (Original work published 1970)

Lefebvre, H. (2007). *The production of space* (D. Nicholson-Smith, Trans.). Blackwell Publishing.

Lefteri, C. (2019). *The Beekeeper of Aleppo.* Manilla Press.

Lehane, D. (2003). *Shutter Island.* Morrow.

Lerner, G. (1986). *The creation of patriarchy.* Oxford University Press.

Lerner, G. (1997). *Why history matters: Life and thought.* Oxford University Press.

Leza, C. (2019). *Divided peoples: Policy, activism, and indigenous activities on the U.S.-Mexico border.* The University of Arizona Press. doi:10.2307/j.ctvrf89pr

Linz, J. (2000). *Totalitarian and authoritarian regimes.* Lynne Rienner Publishers. doi:10.1515/9781685850043

Little, W. (2016). *Gender, sex, and sexuality.* BC Open Textbooks.

livemint. (2013, September 5). *Indian writer Sushmita Banerjee shot dead in Afghanistan.* Retrieved from livemint: https://www.livemint.com/Politics/VjV6CNEl5wptQRgdTS9fGP/Indian-writer-Sushmita-Banerjee-shot-dead-in-Afghanistan.html

Lobo, S. (2009). Urban clan mothers: Key households in cities. In S. A. Krouse & H. A. Howard (Eds.), *Keeping the campfires going* (pp. 1–21). University of Nebraska Press. doi:10.2307/j.ctt1dgn4sz.5

Loreck, J. (2016, January 5). Explainer: What does the 'male gaze' mean, and what about a female gaze? *The Conversation.* https://theconversation.com/explainer-what-does-the-male-gaze-mean-and-what-about-a-female-gaze-52486

Loukaitou-Sideris, A. (2020). A gendered view of mobility and transport: Next steps and future directions. In I. S. De Madariaga & M. Neuman (Eds.), *Engendering cities: Designing sustainable urban spaces for all* (pp. 19–37). Routledge. doi:10.4324/9781351200912-2

Luthra, S. (2021). *Gender and education in India: A reader*. Taylor and Francis. doi:10.4324/9781003191612

Macaluso, A., & Briscoe, I. (2015). Trapped in the city: Communities, insecurity and urban life in fragile cities. *Knowledge Platform Security and Rule of Law*, 1-15.

MacKinnon, C. A. (1982). Feminism, Marxism, method, and the State: An agenda for theory. *Signs (Chicago, Ill.)*, *7*(3), 515–544. doi:10.1086/493898

MacKinnon, R. (2010). *Networked authoritarianism in China and beyond: Implications for global internet freedom. In Liberation Technology in Authoritarian Regimes.* Stanford University.

Mahmud, S. (2003). Is Bangladesh experiencing a feminization of the labour force? *Bangladesh Development Studies*, *29*(1), 1–37.

Mahmud, S., & Bidisha, S. (2018). Female labor market participation in Bangladesh: Structural changes and determinants of labor supply. In S. Raihan (Ed.), *Structural change and dynamics of labor markets in Bangladesh* (pp. 51–63). Springer. doi:10.1007/978-981-13-2071-2_4

Mahtab N. (2007). *Women in Bangladesh from inequality to empowerment*. A H Development Publishing House.

Mallapragada, M. (2014). Rethinking desi: Race, class, and online activism of South Asian immigrants in the United States. *Television & New Media*, *15*(7), 664–678. doi:10.1177/1527476413487225

March, L. (2020). Queer and trans* geographies of liminality: A literature review. *Progress in Human Geography*, *45*(3), 455–471. doi:10.1177/0309132520913111

Marouzi, S. (2021). *Frank Plumpton Ramsey: A feminist economist?* Center for the History of Political Economy at Duke University Working Paper Series. doi:10.2139/ssrn.3854782

Marron, O. (2011). Alternative theory of mind for artificial brains: A logical approach to interpreting alien minds. In P. Leverage (Ed.), *Theory of minds and literature* (pp. 187–200). Purdue University Press.

Martos-Hueso, M. E., & García-Ramírez, P. (2010). *An interview with Bharati Mukherjee.* doi:10.25115/riem.v0i1.365

Massey, D. (1994). *Space, place and gender*. University of Minnesota Press.

Massey, D. (2005). *For space*. Sage Publications.

Matheson, A., Kidd, J., & Came, H. (2021). Women, patriarchy and health inequalities: The urgent need to reorient our systems. *International Journal of Environmental Research and Public Health*, *18*(9), 4472. doi:10.3390/ijerph18094472 PMID:33922437

Mawa, B. (2020). Challenging patriarchy: The changing definition of women's empowerment. *Social Science Review*, *37*(2), 239–265. doi:10.3329sr.v37i2.56510

Mayer, T. (2013). Embodied nationalisms. In L. Staeheli, E. Kofman, & L. Peake (Eds.), *Mapping women, making politics* (pp. 154–168). Routledge.

McAfee, N. (2018). Feminist Philosophy, *Stanford Encyclopedia of Philosophy*. https://plato.stanford.edu/entries/feminism-political/#Bib

McAfee, N. (2008). *Democracy and the political unconscious*. Columbia University Press. doi:10.7312/mcaf13880

McDowell, L. (1993). Space, place and gender relations: Part II. Identity, difference, feminist geometries and geographies. *Progress in Human Geography*, *17*(3), 305–318. doi:10.1177/030913259301700301

McDowell, L. (1999). *Gender, identity and place: Understanding feminist geographies*. Polity Press.

McKeon, M. (1995). Historicizing patriarchy: The emergence of gender difference in England, 1660-1760. *Eighteenth-Century Studies*, *28*(3), 295–322. https://www.jstor.org/stable/2739451

McLeod, J. (2011). *Beginning postcolonialism*. Viva Books.

Meece, J. L., Glienke, B. B., & Burg, S. (2006). Gender and motivation. *Journal of School Psychology*, *44*(5), 351–373. doi:10.1016/j.jsp.2006.04.004

Mela, A., & Toldo, A. (2019). *Socio-spatial inequalities in contemporary cities*. Springer. doi:10.1007/978-3-030-17256-5

Merry, S. E. (2001). Spatial governmentality and the new urban social order: Controlling gender violence through law. *American Anthropologist*, *103*(1), 16–29. doi:10.1525/aa.2001.103.1.16

Messer-Davidow, E. (2002). *Disciplining feminism: From social activism to academic discourse*. Duke University Press.

Mia, B. (2020). Custodial torture: Laws and practice in Bangladesh. *Electronic Research Journal of Social Sciences and Humanities*, *2*(2), 232–246.

Mikkola, M. (2008). Feminist perspectives on sex and gender. *Stanford Encyclopedia of Philosophy*. https://plato.stanford.edu/entries/feminism-political/#Bib

Mikkola, M. (2009). Gender Concepts and Intuitions. *Canadian Journal of Philosophy*, *39*(4), 559–583. doi:10.1353/cjp.0.0060

Miles, M. (2019). *Cities and literature: Routledge critical introductions to urbanism and the city*. Routledge.

Millett, K. (1977). *Sexual politics*. Virago.

Mitchell, J. (1971). *Women's estate*. Penguin.

Mokhles, S., & Sunikka-Blank, M. (2022). 'I'm always home': Social infrastructure and women's personal mobility patterns in informal settlements in Iran. *Gender, Place and Culture*, *29*(4), 455–481. doi:10.1080/0966369X.2021.1873743

Mol, A. (2002). *The body multiple: Ontology in medical practice*. Duke University Press. doi:10.1215/9780822384151

Monagan, S. (2010). Patriarchy: Perpetuating the practice of female genital mutilation. *International Research Journal of Arts & Humanities*, *37*, 83–101.

Monsoor, T. (1999). *From patriarchy to gender equity: Family law and its impact on women in Bangladesh*. The University Press Limited.

Monterescu, D., & Rabinowitz, D. (2007). *Mixed towns, trapped communities: Historical narratives, spatial dynamics, gender relations and cultural encounters in Palestinian-Israeli towns*. Ashgate Publishing.

More, K., & Whittle, S. (1999). *Reclaiming genders: Transsexual grammars at the fin de siècle*. Cassell.

Mukherjee, B. (1971). *The Tiger's Daughter*. Ballantine.

Mukherjee, B. (1989). *Jasmine*. Virago.

Mukherjee, B. (2002). *Desirable daughters*. Bentang.

Mukherjee, B., Blaise, C., Connell, M., Grearson, J., & Grimes, T. (1990). An Interview with Bharati Mukherjee. *The Iowa Review*, *20*(3), 7–32. doi:10.17077/0021-065X.3908

Müller, M. G., & Torp, C. (2009). Conceptualising transnational spaces in history. *European Review of History: Revue Europeenne D'histoire*, *16*(5), 609–617. doi:10.1080/13507480903262587

Mustafa, W. (2021). Paradise in hell: Mapping out utopian cartographies in Margaret Atwood's MaddAddam trilogy. *SAGE Open*, *11*(4), 1–9. doi:10.1177/21582440211061571

Mutekwa, A. (2013). "In this wound of life …": Dystopias and dystopian tropes in Chenjerai Hove's *Red Hills of Home*. *Journal of Literary Studies*, *29*(4), 98–115. doi:10.1080/02564718.2013.856662

Nadolny, A. (2015). Henri Lefebvre's concept of urban space in the context of preferences of the creative class in a modern city. *Quaestiones Geographicae*, *34*(2), 29–34. doi:10.1515/quageo-2015-0012

Naghibi, N. (2007). *Rethinking global sisterhood: Western feminism and Iran*. University of Minnesota Press. doi:10.5749/j.cttts4mn

Narayan, U. (1998). Essence of culture and a sense of history: A feminist critique of cultural essentialism. *Hypatia*, *13*(2), 86–106. doi:10.1111/j.1527-2001.1998.tb01227.x

Nasreen, T. (2002). *French lover* (S. Guha, Trans.). Penguin Books.

Navya, P. K. (2021, March 17). Women's representation in apartment managing committee poor: Survey. *Women's Representation in Apartment Mc, Citizen Matters*. https://bengaluru.citizenmatters.in/womens-representation-apartment-committees-no-better-57109

Nazneen, S. (2017). The women's movement in Bangladesh: A short history and current debates. Friedrich-Ebert-Stiftung Bangladesh Office, 3.

Nazneen, S., Hossain, N., & Sultan, M. (2011). *National discourses on women's empowerment in Bangladesh: Continuities and change*. IDS Working Papers, 2011: 1-41. doi:10.1111/j.2040-0209.2011.00368_2.x

Nazneen, S., & Sultan, M. (2012). Contemporary feminist politics in Bangladesh. In S. Roy (Ed.), *New South Asian feminism: Paradoxes and possibilities*. Zed Books. doi:10.5040/9781350221505.ch-004

News Reports from Afghanistan. (2001, November). *Images of sexuality and reproduction: services: Meeting women's needs*. Retrieved January 13, 2020, from https://www.jstor.org/stable/3776142

Nichols, W. J., & Uitermark, J. (2017). Cities and social movements: Immigrant rights and activism in the United States, France and the Netherlands, 1970-2015. John Wiley & Sons, Ltd.

Norton, R. J. (2003). Feral cities. *Naval War College Review*, *56*(4), 98–106.

Nünning, A. (1997). "But why will you say that I am mad?" On the Theory, History, and Signals of Unreliable Narration in British Fiction. *AAA: Arbeiten Aus Anglistik Und Amerikanistik*, *22*(1), 83–105.

Nünning, A. (2008). Reconceptualizing the theory, history and generic scope of unreliable narration: Towards a synthesis of cognitive and rhetorical approaches. In E. D'hoker & G. Martens (Eds.), *Narrative Unreliability in the Twentieth-Century First-Person Novel* (pp. 29–76). De Gruyter. doi:10.1515/9783110209389.29

Oatley, K. (2011). Theory of mind and theory of minds in literature. In P. Leverage (Ed.), *Theory of minds and literature*. Purdue University Press.

Oberhauser, A. M., Fluri, J. L., Whitson, R., & Mollett, S. (2018). *Feminist spaces: Gender and geography in a global context*. Routledge.

Ooryad, S. K. (2020). Conquering, chanting and protesting: Tools of kinship creation in the girls of Enghelab Street (non-)movement in Iran. In G. Bauer, A. Heise-von der Lippe, N. Hirschfelder, & K. Luther (Eds.), Kinship and collective action in literature and culture (pp. 129–149). Academic Press.

Oosterlynck, S., Loopmans, M., Schuermans, N., Vandenabeele, J., & Zemni, S. (2016). Putting flesh to the bone: Looking for solidarity in diversity, here and now. *Ethnic and Racial Studies*, *39*(5), 764–782. doi:10.1080/01419870.2015.1080380

Pain, R. (2001). Gender, race, age and fear in the city. *Urban Studies (Edinburgh, Scotland)*, *38*(5), 899–913. doi:10.1080/00420980120046590

Panigrahi, S. (2019). Shadowy lines and floating spaces: Amitav Ghosh's heterotopic imagination in The Shadow Lines. *South Asian Review*, *40*(1-2), 65–76. doi:10.1080/02759527.2019.1593747

Patel, M. (2021, November 8) Unequal access to toilets remains a worry and is central to global feminist movement. *The Indian Express*. https://indianexpress.com/article/research/why-unequal-access-to-toilets-is-central-to-the-global-feminist-movement-7613682/

Patel, G. (2020). Gender trouble in South Asia. *The Journal of Asian Studies*, *79*(4), 947–967. doi:10.1017/S0021911820002399

Pathak, P. (2021). *Kolkata: How women walk the city*. OutlookIndia.com.

Pepera, S. (2019). *Women and the City*. https://womendeliver.org/women-and-the-city/

Perez, A. (2018). "Tu Reata Es Pi Espada": Elizabeth Sutherland's Chicana formation. In D. Espinoza, M. E. Cotera, & M. Blackwell (Eds.), *Chicana Movidas: New narratives of activism and feminism in the movement era* (pp. 245–260). University of Texas Press. doi:10.7560/315583-015

Phadke, S. (2013). Unfriendly bodies, hostile cities: Reflections on loitering and gendered public space. *Economic and Political Weekly*, *48*(39), 50–59.

Pierik, B. (2022). Patriarchal power as a conceptual tool for gender history. *The Journal of Theory and Practice.*, *26*(1), 71–92. doi:10.1080/13642529.2022.2037864

Pilcher, J., & Whelehan, A. (2004). *50 key concepts in gender studies*. Sage Publication. doi:10.4135/9781446278901

Porta, D. D., & Diani, M. (2015). Introduction: The field of social movement studies. In D. D. Porta & M. Diani (Eds.), *The Oxford handbook of social movements* (pp. 1–30). Oxford University Press. doi:10.1093/oxfordhb/9780199678402.013.61

Portes, A., Guarnizo, L. E., & Landolt, P. (1999). The study of transnationalism: Pitfalls and promise of an emergent research field. *Ethnic and Racial Studies*, *22*(2), 217–237. doi:10.1080/014198799329468

Post, E. A. (2018). Cities and politics in the developing world. *Annual Review of Political Science*, *21*(1), 115–133. doi:10.1146/annurev-polisci-042716-102405

Pourgharib, B., Hamkhiyal, S., & Asl, M. P. (2022). A non-orientalist representation of Pakistan in contemporary western travelogues. *GEMA Online Journal of Language Studies*, *22*(3), 103–118. doi:10.17576/gema-2022-2203-06

Pourya Asl, M. (Ed.). (2022). Gender, place, and identity of South Asian women. IGI Global., https://doi.org/10.4018/978-1-6684-3626-4.

Pourya Asl, M. (Ed.). (2022). *Gender, place, and identity of South Asian women*. IGI Global., doi:10.4018/978-1-6684-3626-4

Pourya Asl, M. P. (2020). Spaces of change: Arab women's reconfigurations of selfhood through heterotopias in Manal al-Sharif's Daring to Drive. *KEMANUSIAAN the Asian Journal of Humanities*, *27*(2), 123–143. doi:10.21315/kajh2020.27.2.7

Prasad, N. (2007). *Women and development*. A P H Publishing Corporation.

Pratt, N. (2020). Embodying geopolitics: Generations of women's activism in Egypt, Jordan, and Lebanon. University of California Press.

Proust, M. (2003). *In search of lost time: Finding time again* (I. Patterson, Trans.). Penguin.

PTI. (2013, September 6). *Indian author Sushmita Banerjee, who wrote about her dramatic escape from Taliban shot dead in Afghanistan*. Retrieved from India Today: https://www.indiatoday.in/world/rest-of-the-world/story/sushmita-banerjee-shot-dead-in-afghanistan-escape-from-taliban-book-210014-2013-09-04

Puar, J. (2013). Rethinking homonationalism. *International Journal of Middle East Studies*, *45*(2), 336–339.

Purcell, M. (2002). Excavating Lefebvre: The right to the city and its urban politics of the inhabitant. *GeoJournal*, *58*(2/3), 99–108. doi:10.1023/B:GEJO.0000010829.62237.8f

Pynchon, V. (2011). Women's economic power decreases domestic violence against both genders. *Forbes*.

Qamar, S., & Shakeel, R. K. (2015). Representation of Afghan institution of marriage in Khaled Hosseini's and The Mountains Echoed and A Thousand Splendid Suns: A cultural study. *International Journal of English and Literature*, *5*(1), 57–64.

Rafiq, A. (2016). Operation Karachi: Pakistan's military retakes the city. *National Interest*.

Compilation of References

Rahbari, L., Dierickx, S., Coene, G., & Longman, C. (2021). Transnational solidarity with which Muslim women? The case of the my stealthy freedom and World Hijab Day campaigns. *Politics & Gender, 17*(1), 112–135. doi:10.1017/S1743923X19000552

Rahbari, L., & Sharepour, M. (2015). Gender and realization of women's right to the city in Tehran. *Asian Journal of Social Science, 43*(3), 227–248. doi:10.1163/15685314-04303002

Rahman, I. R., & Islam, R. (2013). *Female labour force participation in Bangladesh: trends, drivers and barriers.* International Labour Organization. https://www.ilo.org/newdelhi/whatwedo/publications/WCMS_2501 12/lang--en/index.htm

Raihan, S., & Bidisha, S. H. (2018). *Bangladesh economic dialogue on inclusive growth policy brief: Addressing female employment stagnation in Bangladesh.* A research paper on Economic Dialogue on Inclusive Growth in Bangladesh. Retrieved from https://asiafoundation.org/wp- content/uploads/2018/12/EDIG-Policy-Brief-Female-employment-stagnation-in-Bangladesh.pdf

Raihan, S., Bidisha, S., & Jahan, I. (2018). Unpacking unpaid labor in Bangladesh. *Indian Journal of Labour Economic.* doi:10.1007/s41027-018-0115-6

Rajan, G., & Desai, J. (2013). *Transnational feminism and global advocacy in South Asia.* Routledge. doi:10.4324/9780203718469

Rajghatta, C. (2006-2007). Across the black waters. *India International Centre Quarterly, 33*(3/4), 116–127.

Raju, S. (Ed.). (2011). *Gendered geographies: Space and place in the South Asia.* Oxford University Press.

Rani, E. (2020). Feministic perspectives of Afghan women in Khaled Hosseini's A Thousand Splendid Suns. *A Journal of Composition Theory, 13*(3), 665-669.

Rashid, A. (1999). The Taliban: Exporting extremism. *Foreign Affairs, 78*(6), 22–35. doi:10.2307/20049530

Rashidi, Y. E. (2016). *Chronicle of a Last Summer.* Tim Duggan Books.

Ray, B. (1991). Women of Bengal: Transformation in ideas and ideals, 1900-1947. *Social Scientist, 19*(5/6), 3–23. doi:10.2307/3517870

Ray, D. (2022). *Postcolonial Indian city-literature: Policy, politics and evolution (Routledge research in postcolonial literatures).* Routledge. doi:10.4324/9781003166337

Reichenbach, A. (2015). Gazes that matter: Young Emirati women's spatial practices in Dubai. *Urban Anthropology and Studies of Cultural Systems and World Economic Development, 44*(1/2), 113–195.

Riaz, A., & Rahman, M. S. (Eds.). (2016). *Routledge handbook of contemporary Bangladesh*. Routledge. doi:10.4324/9781315651019

Rieker, M., & Ali, K. (Eds.). (2008). *Gendering urban space in the Middle East, South Asia, and Africa*. Springer. doi:10.1057/9780230612471

Roberts, M. (1998). Urban design, gender and the future of cities. *Journal of Urban Design*, *3*(2), 133–135. doi:10.1080/13574809808724421

Rockler, N. R. (2006). "Be your own windkeeper": Friends, feminism, and rhetorical strategies of depoliticization. *Women's Studies in Communication*, *29*(2), 244–264. doi:10.1080/07491409.2006.10162500

Rodriguez, N. M., Martino, W. J., Ingrey, J. C., & Brockenbrough, E. (2016). *Critical concepts in queer studies and education: Queer counterpublic spatialities*. Palgrave Macmillan.

Rose, G. (1993). Women and everyday space. In *Feminism and geography: The limits of geographical knowledge*. University of Minnesota Press.

Roy, A. (1997). *The God of Small Things*. India Ink.

Roy, A. (2005). The loneliness of Noam Chomsky. In A. Roy (Ed.), *An Ordinary Person's Guide to Empire* (pp. 45–74). Penguin.

Roy, A. (2017). *The Ministry of Utmost Happiness*. Penguin Random House.

Roy, A. (2020). *Azadi: Freedom, fascism, fiction*. Penguin Random House.

Roy, S. (2012). Politics, passion and professionalization in contemporary feminist politics in India. *Sociology*, *45*(4), 587–601. doi:10.1177/0038038511406584

Roy, S., & Bailey, A. (2021). Safe in the city? Negotiating safety, public space and the male gaze in Kolkata, India. *Cities (London, England)*, *117*, 103321. doi:10.1016/j.cities.2021.103321

Rubin, & R., B. (1997). Women and pipelines: Afghanistan's proxy wars. *Asia and the Pacific*, *73*(2), 283-296.

Sadiki, L. (Ed.). (2020). *Routledge handbook of Middle East politics*. Routledge. doi:10.4324/9781315170688

Samantroy, E., & Nandi, S. (2022). *Gender, unpaid work and care in India*. Taylor and Francis. doi:10.4324/9781003276739

Samari, G. (2021). Coming back and moving backwards: Return migration and gender norms in Egypt. *Journal of Ethnic and Migration Studies*, *47*(5), 1103–1118. doi:10.1080/1369183X.2019.1669437 PMID:33716548

Sapkota, B. (2020). Ideological essentialization of Afghan women in Hosseini's A Thousand Splendid Suns. *The Batuk*, *6*(1), 55–62. doi:10.3126/batuk.v6i1.32628

Sarrimo, C. (2020). Mapping a postmodern dystopia: Hassan Loo Sattarvandi's construction of a Swedish suburb. In K. Malmio & K. Kurikka (Eds.), *Contemporary Nordic literature and spatiality*. Palgrave Macmillan. doi:10.1007/978-3-030-23353-2_3

Sassen, S. (1998). *Globalization and its discontents: Essays on the new mobility of people and money*. New Press.

Sayem, A. M., Begum, H. A., & Moneesha, S. S. (2012). Attitudes towards justifying intimate partner violence among married women in Bangladesh. *Journal of Biosocial Science*, *44*(6), 641–660. doi:10.1017/S0021932012000223 PMID:22687269

Schaefer, D. O. (2022). *Wild experiment: Feeling science and secularism after darwin*. Duke University Press.

Schiller, N. G., Basch, L., & Blanc, C. S. (1995). From immigrant to transmigrant: Theorizing transnational migration. *Anthropological Quarterly*, *68*(1), 48–63. doi:10.2307/3317464

Shaban, N. (2021). *The Influence of Geopolitics on the Resistance Movement Against Compulsory Hijab in Iran* [Unpublished doctoral dissertation]. University of Colorado at Boulder.

Shabanirad, E., & Seifi, E. (2015). Postcolonial feminist reading of Khaled Hosseini's A Thousand Splendid Suns. *International Journal of Women's Research*, *3*(2), 241–254.

Shahani, N. (2021). *Pink revolutions: Globalization, Hindutva, and queer triangles in contemporary India*. Northwestern University Press.

Shah, N. (2022). *How do we design gender-sensitive cities? Start by listening to women and other genders. Question of Cities: Forum for Nature*. People, and Sustainability.

Shahrokni, N. (2014). The mothers' paradise: Women-only parks and the dynamics of state power in the Islamic Republic of Iran. *Journal of Middle East Women's Studies*, *10*(3), 87–108. doi:10.2979/jmiddeastwomstud.10.3.87

Shahrokni, N. (2019). *Women in place: The politics of gender segregation in Iran*. University of California Press.

Shameem, B. (2014). Living on the edge: Women in Khaled Hosseini's A Thousand Splendid Suns. *Research Journal of English Language and Literature*, *2*(4), 62–66.

Shamma, W. T. (2021). Gendering and spatializing the new urban space: A study on working women in the city of Dhaka, Bangladesh. *Social Science Review*, *37*(2), 125–144. doi:10.3329sr.v37i2.56508

Shapiro, L. B. (2010). *Middle Eastern women's issues: An analysis of a Thousand Splendid Suns and the New York Times* [Doctoral dissertation]. University of Florida.

Sharma, G. (2016). Impact on society by Indian women English writer. *Notions*, *7*(2), 1–7.

Shi, L., & Zhu, Q. (2018). Urban space and representation in literary study. *Open Journal of Social Sciences*, *06*(09), 223–229. doi:10.4236/jss.2018.69015

Shohel, T. A., Niner, S., & Gunawardana, S. (2021). How the persistence of patriarchy undermines the financial empowerment of women microfinance borrowers? Evidence from a southern sub-district of Bangladesh. *PLoS One*, *16*(4), e0250000. doi:10.1371/journal.pone.0250000 PMID:33909670

Siahmansouri, M., & Hoorvash, M. (2020). Heroic west, villainous east: A postcolonial interpretation of narrative structure in Khaled Hosseini's A Thousand Splendid Suns. *Journal of Research in Applied Linguistics*, *11*(2), 95–106.

Sikweyiya, Y., Addo-Lartey, A. A., Alangea, D. O., Dako-Gyeke, P., Chirwa, E. D., Coker-Appiah, D., Adanu, R. M. K., & Jewkes, R. (2020). Patriarchy and gender-inequitable attitudes as drivers of intimate partner violence against women in the central region of Ghana. *BMC Public Health*, *20*(1), 682. doi:10.118612889-020-08825-z PMID:32404153

Silbaugh, K. (2007). Women's place: Urban planning, housing design, and work-family balance. *Fordham Law Review*, *76*(3), 1797–1852. https://ir.lawnet.fordham.edu/cgi/viewcontent.cgi?article=4340&context=flr

Sims, D. (2010). *Understanding Cairo: The logic of a city out of control*. American University of Cairo Press.

Singerman, D. (2002). The Politics of Emergency Rule in Egypt. *Current History (New York, N.Y.)*, *101*(651), 29–35. doi:10.1525/curh.2001.101.651.29

Singh, A. (2022). *Gender, violence and performance in contemporary India*. Routledge.

Singh, G. (2019). *Eight months after launch, Kolkata's 'pink taxis' hardly in the pink of health*. CitizenMatters.

Singh, G. (2022). Afghan women authors' discourses of resistance: Contesting interplay between gender, place, and identity. In M. P. Asl (Ed.), *Gender, Place, and Identity of South Asian Women* (pp. 152–177). IGI Global. doi:10.4018/978-1-6684-3626-4.ch008

Singh, J. (2022). *Feminist literary and cultural criticism: An analytical approach to space*. Springer. doi:10.1007/978-981-19-1426-3

Sinno, N. (2020). Utopian/dystopian Lebanon: Constructing place in Jabbūr al-Duwayhī's Sharīd al-manāzil. *Middle Eastern Literatures*, *23*(3), 177–197. doi:10.1080/1475262X.2021.1917831

Smith, C. E. (2015). State, violence, mobility and everyday life in Cairo, Egypt. *Theses and Dissertations-Geography*, *34*(6), 1–178.

Smith, F. M. (2001). Refiguring the geopolitical landscape: Nation,'transition' and gendered subjects in post-cold war Germany. *Space and Polity*, *5*(3), 213–235. doi:10.1080/13562570120104418

Smith, M. P. (2001). *Transnational urbanism: Locating globalization*. Blackwell.

Smith, S. (2012). Intimate geopolitics: Religion, marriage, and reproductive bodies in Leh, Ladakh. *Annals of the Association of American Geographers*, *102*(6), 1511–1528. doi:10.1080/00045608.2012.660391

Soenen, R. (2007). Everyday urban public space: Turkish immigrant women's perspective. *Journal of Housing and the Built Environment*, *22*(4), 411–413. doi:10.100710901-007-9094-5

Soja, E. W. (1989). *Postmodern geographies: The reassertion of space in critical social theory*. Verso.

Soja, E. W. (1996). *Thirdspace: Journeys to Los Angeles and other real-and-imagined place*. Blackwell Publishers.

Soja, E. W. (2000). *Postmetropolis: Critical studies of cities and regions*. Blackwell Publishers.

Soja, E. W. (2010). *Seeking spatial justice*. University of Minnesota Press. doi:10.5749/minnesota/9780816666676.001.0001

Solomon, E. (2012). *Darkness at noon in the mind of fearful Damascus*. https://www.reuters.com/article/us-syria-damascus-mood-idUSBRE8B30RF20121204

Spain, D. (2014). Gender and urban space. *Annual Review of Sociology*, *40*(1), 581–598. doi:10.1146/annurev-soc-071913-043446

Spivak, G. C. (1988). Can the subaltern speak? In C. Nelson & L. Grossberg (Eds.), *Marxism and the interpretation of culture* (pp. 271–316). University of Illinois Press.

Staeheli, L. A., & Kofman, E. (2013). Mapping gender, making politics: Toward feminist political geographies. In L. Staeheli, E. Kofman, & L. Peake (Eds.), *Mapping women, making politics* (pp. 1–13). Routledge. doi:10.4324/9780203328514-11

Stauv, A. (2018). *The Routledge companion to modernity, space and gender*. Routledge.

Stewart, A. J., Settles, I. H., & Winter, N. J. G. (1998). Women and the social movements of the 1960s: Activists, engaged observers, and nonparticipants. *Political Psychology*, *19*(1), 63–94. doi:10.1111/0162-895X.00093

Stone, D. (2020). *Niramay – An Unconditional Home. Curry Stone Design Collaborative*. CommunityDesignAgency.com.

Stroope, S. (2012). Caste, class, and urbanization: The shaping of religious community in contemporary India. *Social Indicators Research*, *105*(3), 499–518. doi:10.100711205-011-9784-y

Stuhr, R. A. (2011). *A Thousand Splendid Suns: Sanctuary and resistance*. https://repository.upenn.edu/library_papers/79

Sudradjat, I. (2012). Foucault, the other spaces, and human behaviour. *Procedia: Social and Behavioral Sciences*, *36*, 29. doi:10.1016/j.sbspro.2012.03.004

Suleiman, Y., & Muhawi, I. (Eds.). (2006). *Literature and nation in the Middle East*. Edinburgh University Press. doi:10.3366/edinburgh/9780748620739.001.0001

Sultana, R. (2021). Household responsibilities: Roles of women and their family members during coronavirus lockdown period. *IQAC Project of Jagannath University, 6*, 1-17.

Sultana, A. (2012). Patriarchy and women's subordination: A theoretical analysis. *Arts Faculty Journal, 4*, 1–18. doi:10.3329/afj.v4i0.12929

Sundaresan, I. (2008). *In the Convent of Little Flowers*. Washington Square Press.

Sweeting, L. (2020). Bruised but never broken: The fight for gender equality in Egypt and Bangladesh. *Global Majority, 11*(2), 102–116.

Tacoli, C., & Satterthwaite, D. (2013). Gender and urban change. *Environment and Urbanization, 25*(1), 3–8. doi:10.1177/0956247813479086

TADAMUN. (2019). *Women and Precarious Employment: A spatial analysis of economic insecurity in Cairo's neighborhoods*. http://www.tadamun.co/women-and-precarious-employment-a-spatial-analysis-of-economic-insecurity-in-cairos-neighborhoods/?lang=en#.Y1jqK3bMJjE

Tally, R. T. Jr., (Ed.). (2017). *The Routledge handbook of literature and space*. Taylor & Francis. doi:10.4324/9781315745978

Tally, R. Jr. (2013). *Spatiality*. Routledge.

Tanha, K. (2021). *Patriarchy, give me my country back. A personal account of a survivor of sexual violence and oppression*. https://www.thedailystar.net/views/opinion/news/patriarchy-give-me-my-country-back-2209466

Tanweer, B. (2013). *The Scatter Here is Too Great*. Random House India.

Taubenfeld, H. J. (1969). *Outer space: The "territorial" limits of nations-Article 9*. Fordham University Press. https://ir.lawnet.fordham.edu/flr/vol38/iss1/9

Tawfik, K. A. (2008). *Utopia*. Bloomsbury Qatar Foundation publishing.

Than, K., Garner, T., & Taylor, A. P. (2022). What is Darwin's theory of evolution? *Live Science*. https://www.livescience.com/474-controversy-evolution-works.html

The European Institute for Gender Equality. (2022). *Gender mainstreaming*. https://eige.europa.eu/gender-mainstreaming

Thomson Reuters Foundation. (2017). *Inform. Connect. Empower.* https://www.trust.org/documents/trf-2020.pdf

Tickell, A. (Ed.). (2016). *South-Asian fiction in English: Contemporary transformations*. Springer. doi:10.1057/978-1-137-40354-4

Tompkins, K. W., Aizura, A. Z., Bahng, A., Chávez, K. R., Goeman, M., & Musser, A. J. (Eds.). (2021). *Keywords for gender and sexuality studies*. New York University Press.

Tong, R. (2009). *Feminist thought: A more comprehensive introduction*. Westview Press.

Tonkiss, F. (2005). Space, the city and social theory: Social relations and urban forms. *Polity*.

Tuerkheimer, D. (2019). Beyond #MeToo. *New York University Law Review*, *94*, 1146. https://papers.ssrn.com/abstract=3366126

Tyagi, A., & Sen, A. (2019). Love-Jihad (Muslim sexual seduction) and ched-chad (sexual harassment): Hindu nationalist discourses and the ideal/deviant urban citizen in India. *Gender, Place and Culture*, *27*(1), 104–125. doi:10.1080/0966369X.2018.1557602

UN Women. (2013). *Better lighting, wider pavements: Steps towards preventing sexual violence in New Delhi*. UNWomen.org.

UNDP. (2020). *Human Development Report 2020, The Next Frontier: Human Development and the Anthropocene.* https://www.undp.org/egypt/press-releases/human-development-report-2020

UNFPA. (2018). *UNFPA Annual Report 2018*. https://www.unfpa.org/publications/unfpa-annual-report-2018

Valentine, G. (1989). The geography of women's fear. *Area*, *21*(4), 385–390.

Vanhoose, K., & Savini, F. (2017). *The social capital of urban activism: Practices in London and Amsterdam city*. http://rsa.tandfonline.com

Vera-Sanso, P. (2012). Gender, poverty and old-age livelihoods in Urban South India in an era of globalisation. *Oxford Development Studies*, *40*(3), 324–340. doi:10.1080/13600818.2012.710322

Versey, F. (2021, August 18). *Essay: She couldn't escape the Taliban - On Sushmita Banerjee, author of A Kabuliwala's Bengali Wife*. Retrieved from Hindustan Times: https://www.hindustantimes.com/books/essayshe-couldn-t-escape-the-taliban-on-sushmita-banerjee-author-of-a-kabuliwala-s-bengali-wife-101629314082282.html

Villanueva, G. (2022). *Promoting urban social justice through engaged communication scholarship: Reimagining place*. Routledge.

Visakha, S. (2021). *A feminist approach to urban planning is vital for the future of cities*. https://asia.fes.de/news/feminist-cities

Viswanathan, G. (1998). *Outside the fold: Conversion, modernity, and belief*. Princeton University Press. doi:10.1515/9781400843480

Walby, S. (1990). *Theorizing patriarchy*. Blackwell Publishers Ltd.

Walsh, S. M. (2015). Safety spheres: Danger mapping and spatial justice. *Race, Gender, & Class*, *22*(1&2), 122–142.

Wani, A. R. (2019). Role and status of women in sikh religion through Sri Guru Nanak perspectives. *Electronic Research Journal of Literature*, *1*, 13–19.

Ward, B. M. (2022). *Living Detroit: Environmental Activism in an age of urban crisis*. Routledge.

Watt, D. (2022). *In defense of her sex: Travelling through time with Christine de Pizan (Review)*. https://www.historytoday.com/archive/review/defence-hersex#:~:text=In%20The%20Second%20Sex%2C%20Simone,of%20Charles%20V%20in%20Paris

Weisman, L. K. (1992). *Discrimination by design*. University of Illinois Press.

Welch, S. (2015). *Existential eroticism: A feminist approach to understanding women's oppression-perpetuating choices*. Lexington Books.

Whitzman, C. (2013). Women's safety and everyday mobility. In C. Whitzman, C. Legacy, C. Andrew, F. Klodawsky, M. Shaw, & K. Viswanath (Eds.), *Building inclusive cities* (1st ed., pp. 32–52). Routledge. doi:10.4324/9780203100691-12

Whorf, B. L. (1956). *Language, thought and reality* (J. B. Corroll, Ed.). MIT Press.

Wiegand, C. (2012). *Violence against women in Bangladesh*. https://www.e-ir.info/2012/04/30/violence-against-women-in-bangladesh/

Willis, E. (1984). Radical feminism and feminist radicalism. *Social Text*, *9*(10), 91–118. doi:10.2307/466537

Wolff, J. (2010). Urban spaces keynote: Unmapped spaces — gender, generation and the city. *Feminist Review*, *96*(1), 6–19. doi:10.1057/fr.2010.12

Wolfreys, J. (2002). *Introducing criticism at the 21st Century*. Edinburgh University Press.

World Bank Group. (2020). *Handbook for Gender-Inclusive Urban Planning and Design*. https://www.worldbank.org/en/topic/urbandevelopment/publication/handbook-for-gender-inclusive-urban-planning-and-design

Wrede, T. (2015, Spring). Introduction to special issue--Theorizing space and gender in the 21st century. *Rocky Mountain Review,* *69*(1), 10-17. https://www.jstor.org/stable/24372860

Wright, E. (2000). *Lacan and postfeminism (postmodern encounters)*. Totem Books or Icon Books.

Wronska, A. (2018). *The place of women in public space: A case study of street harassment in Bangladesh* [MA Dissertation]. Lund University. https://lup.lub.lu.se/luur/download?func=downloadFile&recordOId=8945534&fileOId=8945536

Wulandari, S. (2012). The oppression against women in Afghanistan portrayed in Khaled Hosseini's A Thousand Splendid Suns. *Diglossia: Jurnal Kajian Ilmiah Kebahasaan dan Kesusastraan, 4*(1), 1-11.

Wyckoff, A. & Pilat, D. (2018). *Bridging the digital gender divide: Include, upskill, innovate.* OECD Report.

Xiao-yan, L. (2014). Theory of mind and the unreliable narrator. *US-China Foreign Language, 12*(5), 422–428. doi:10.17265/1539-8080/2014.05.010

Yawari, A. W. (2011). *The inner strength of women in Khalid Hosseini's A Thousand Splendid Suns and Alice Walker's The Color Purple* [Master's thesis, Selcuk University]. Selcuk University Digital Archive Systems.

Yeasmin, F. (2020). Khaled Hosseini's A Thousand Splendid Suns: A saga of Afghanistan. *Research Journal of English Language and Literature., 8*(3), 381–390.

Yengde, S. (2019). *Caste matters*. Penguin Random House India Publication.

Yip, N. M., Martinez López, M. A., & Sun, X. (2019). Introductory remarks and overview. In N. M. Yip, M. A. Martinez López, & X. Sun (Eds.), *Contested cities and urban activism* (pp. 3–24). Palgrave Macmillan. doi:10.1007/978-981-13-1730-9_1

Young, I. M. (2000). *Inclusion and Democracy, Oxford Political Theory*. Oxford University Press.

Yousufzai, M. (2019). *We are displaced: My journey and stories from refugee girls around the world*. Little, Brown, and Company.

Yuval-Davis, N. (2016). Power, intersectionality and the politics of belonging. In W. Harcourt (Ed.), *The Palgrave handbook of gender and development* (pp. 367–381). Palgrave Macmillan. doi:10.1007/978-1-137-38273-3_25

Zimmerman, J. (2017). *Urban planning has a sexism problem*. NextCity.org.

Zine, J. (2006). Between orientalism and fundamentalism: The politics of Muslim women's feminist engagement. *Muslim World Journal of Human Rights, 3*(1), 1-24. doi:10.2202/1554-4419.1080

Zunshine, L. (2011). Theory of mind and fiction of embodied transparency. In P. Leverage (Ed.), *Theory of minds and literature* (pp. 56–92). Purdue University Press.

About the Contributors

Moussa Pourya Asl is a Senior Lecturer in literary studies at Universiti Sains Malaysia, where he also obtained his PhD (English Literature) from School of Humanities. His primary research area is in diasporic literature and gender and cultural studies, and he has published several articles in the above-mentioned areas in Women's Studies, Gender, Place & Culture, Asian Ethnicity, American Studies in Scandinavia, Cogent: Arts & Humanities, Gema Online, and 3L.

* * *

Kawthar Yasser Al Othman has completed her PhD in English Literature at the University of Glasgow. Her thesis studies spatiality in Arab American migrant fiction from a geocritical perspective. Her primary research interests are postcolonial literature, Anglophone Arab literature and geocriticism.

Moulina Bhattacharya is a doctoral researcher in English at Christ University, India. Her field of study includes nonfictional life-writing, Postcolonial literature, and sociolinguistics. She has presented papers on the Neo-historic aspect of Indian political literature and dystopic web series at the universities of India and the United States. Her previous publications are on heterotopic transcendence and transdisciplinary modes of language and communication. WordPress site: . ORCID: 0000-0001-9389-846X.

Monali Chatterjee has been teaching English Literature, Language and Communication Studies in several colleges and universities in India and abroad for about two decades. She has also taught English Language in the UK. An ardent lover of music, dance, poetry and drama, she is professionally trained in Indian classical music, dance and art. She has presented papers in many international conferences and has published widely on higher education, diaspora studies, South Asian Literature and Film Studies apart from poetry in popular dailies.

About the Contributors

Srestha Chatterjee graduated with a postgraduate degree in Sociology from St.Xavier's College (Autonomous), Kolkata. Her research interest mainly includes gender, feminist urban planning and visual sociology. She has published articles in online blogs including Doing Sociology.

Shilpi Gupta is an Assistant Professor at the Department of Languages at Vellore Institute of Technology, Vellore, India. She graduated in Women and Gender Studies at the University of Granada, Spain. Her primary research area is in diasporic literature and gender and cultural studies, and she has published several articles in the above-mentioned areas in Indi@log, Rupkatha, Instituto Universitario de Estudios de Género, Universidad Carlos III de Madrid, and IGI Global.

Nishat Zarin Haque holds a BA in English from Pabna University of Science and Technology (PUST), Bangladesh. She is currently pursuing a Master's in Business Administration at North South University, Bangladesh. Her primary research interest area is in gender and feminism.

Kexin Huang is the Research Assistant for 'Gender-inclusive Cities'. Her research of interest includes gender, urban space, aesthetics, migration, neoliberalism and body politics. More specifically, she looks at women and gender minorities' embodiment in urban and public spaces, especially in neoliberal societies, with close attention to intersectionality. In her research, she focuses on the discursive power structures and resistance as an approach to investigating gender-based inequalities.

Jiayi Jin is an Assistant Professor in Architecture at Northumbria University. Her current research projects look at the persisting inequality in current societies and grassroots approaches to sustainable development. She is the PI of 'Gender-inclusive Cities' research project, which investigates spatial structure of public spaces, including the mobility networks, functional distribution and presence of appropriable spaces. The project also adopts co-creative processes as critical dimensions to achieve a state of social resilience in these systems, promoting both spatial and social mobility across the city.

Kiron Susan Joseph Sebastine is a Doctoral Research Scholar in the Department of English Language and Literature at Amrita Vishwa Vidyapeetham, Kochi Campus, India. Her primary research area is in Travel Literature, Gender, and Cultural Studies. She has published articles in Rupkatha Journal on Interdisciplinary Studies in Humanities and International Journal of Psychosocial Rehabilitation. She has also contributed a book chapter in the edited volume Gender, Place and Identity of South Asian Women published by IGI Global.

About the Contributors

Maryam Lashkari is a Ph.D. candidate in human geography at York University, Canada. Her primary research area is in feminist geopolitics and urban geography.

Anjum Khan M. is working as Assistant Professor of English in Avinashilingam Institute for Home Science and Higher Education for Women, Coimbatore. She has 10 years of teaching experience and 10 years of research experience. Her research experience includes guiding M. Phil and Ph.D. candidates and working on research projects. Her areas of research have been British Literature, Immigrant Canadian Literature, Disability Studies, and Cultural Studies. However, she is interested in teaching subjects like history, literature, disability studies, and literary theories. She is the author of 2 books - Ethnic Silhouettes, M.G. Vassanji in the Light of New Historicism and Narrating Bodies, Reading Anosh Irani. She has also coedited a volume of essays published by Lexington Press America. She has published several research articles in reputed national and international journals, chapters in books and presented papers in national and international conferences and has conducted workshops on journalism and assistive technology. She has also delivered academic and motivational lectures in colleges and corporate institutes.

Mahani Mokhtar holds a PhD in Education from the School of Education, University of Bristol. She is currently working as an Associate Professor in education and development at University Technology Malaysia, Malaysia. Her primary research area is in education and development, and she has published several articles in the above-mentioned areas in Man in India, American Scientific Publishers, International Education Studies, Qualitative Report, Mediterranean Journal Of Social Sciences, Review Of European Studies, and International Journal For Innovation Education And Research.

Anushyama Mukherjee is currently an Assistant Professor, Department of Sociology, St. Xavier's College (Autonomous), Kolkata. She completed her doctoral research from the University of Hyderabad, Department of Sociology in 2015 on the topic of the Indian diaspora in the Arab Gulf countries. Dr Mukherjee has published her research widely, in Economic and Political Weekly, Contemporary South Asia, Routledge International, Sociological Bulletin and other outlets. Dr Mukherjee is also working as the Project Director, Global Siblings & Inequality in India along with Prof Nazli Kibria, Professor, Boston University.

Sandhya Devi N. K. is a PhD scholar in English Literature at Presidency University, Bangalore. Her primary research areas are Queer Studies, Gender Studies, Cultural Studies, Partition Literature and World Literature, and she has published

About the Contributors

several articles and chapters in the above-mentioned areas in IGI Global, Pertanika and several other reputed journals.

Kirankumar Nittali is an Assistant Professor - Senior Scale at the Department of English, Presidency University, Bangalore. He has obtained Ph.D. degree in English from Centre for English Studies, Central University of Jharkhand, Ranchi and an MA from Karnataka University Dharwad. He has taught English language, Communicative Skills Business English and English literature for various courses and is having experience of over 10 years of academics in various reputed institutes. He has presented several papers at national/international conferences and several articles of research by him are published in international journals such as Rupkatha Journal of Social Science and Humanities, IGI Global, USA and UGC approved journals.

Nasrin Pervin holds an MA in English Language Teaching from the Nottingham Trent University, UK. She is currently working as a senior lecturer in English language teaching at North South University, Bangladesh. She is also a Phd student at the University of Technology, Malaysia. Her primary research area is in education and development, and she has published several articles in the above-mentioned areas in Journal of Education, Journal of Professional Development in Education, Journal of Faculty of Humanities and Law, International Journal of Social Sciences and Education, International Journal of English Language, Literature in Humanities, International Journal of English Language and Literature Studies, and Panini.

Meghna Prabir, Associate Professor of English and Cultural Studies at Christ University, India, earned a PhD from Stella Maris College, India (2008-2011) that focused on contrapuntal readings of queer Muslim identity in Agha Shahid Ali's poetry and transnationalism in Michael Ondaatje's works. Prabir's postdoctoral research at Christ University (2015-the present) focuses on intersectional queer ecologies and has included a funded research project (2017-20) on intersections between gender studies and ecological discourses. The author's publications include a chapter on queer ecologies and science fiction in Ecofeminist Science Fiction: International Perspectives on Gender, Ecology, and Literature (Routledge Studies in World Literatures and the Environment, 2021) and a contribution on BIPOC trans literature in the upcoming Routledge Handbook of Trans Literature. Prabir is currently editing a collection of critical essays titled Queer Ecologies: Intersectional Perspectives from South Asia.

Jason Tan Jian Wei is working as a part-time research assistant in the School of Humanities, Universiti Sains Malaysia. His primary research area is in diasporic literature in English and gender and cultural studies.

Abida Younas holds a Ph.D. in English Literature from the School of Critical Studies, University of Glasgow, UK. She is currently working as a Postgraduate teaching assistant at the University of Glasgow. Her major interest lies in researching newer possibilities and she likes to explore new areas related to the current situation of Postcolonial countries (South Asian and Middle Eastern Countries) and its effect on contemporary literature. Along with publication in different journals, she has also delivered twelve papers at different International and National conferences held in Pakistan, the UK, and the USA.

Mingyu Zhu is a Research Assistant for 'Gender-inclusive Cities'. His research mainly covers the digitalisation of the urban environment and interactions between data-driven models and human behaviour.

Index

A

Afghanistan 3, 18-22, 26-32, 34, 36, 176-196
Aleppo 1-3, 5-7, 11-16
Arundhati Roy 82-83, 99, 217

B

Bharati Mukherjee 37, 45, 54, 57

C

Cairo 2-3, 5-10, 15-17, 269-270, 274-275, 278, 280-283, 285-289
Caste 37-46, 48-56, 58, 72, 87-88, 102-105, 109, 112, 117-118, 121, 123, 127, 171, 229, 234, 249
Casteism 109, 112, 121, 186
City 1-3, 5-18, 26-27, 34, 40, 43, 46-48, 59-64, 73-74, 79, 83, 103-104, 106-109, 111-116, 121-124, 126-132, 135, 139-142, 144-146, 153-156, 160-161, 165-168, 170-172, 176, 180, 182, 185, 187, 189, 191, 193-196, 200, 203, 205-207, 209, 212-213, 216-231, 233-237, 242-246, 258, 260, 262, 266-267, 269-283, 285-289
City-Space 59-60, 79
Class 3, 6, 37-47, 49-50, 52-57, 84-85, 87, 102-104, 108-109, 111, 114, 116-119, 122-123, 127, 139-140, 172, 196, 226, 229, 232, 242, 245, 247, 249, 252, 256-257, 259, 262, 267, 277-278, 281

D

Damascus 1-3, 5-7, 11-12, 15-17
Dystopia 18-23, 25-28, 32, 59, 61, 63-64, 73, 75, 80, 196

E

Empowerment 2, 54, 103, 132-134, 149, 152, 154, 160, 164, 166-167, 170, 173, 202, 233-234, 250, 254, 260, 264-266, 269, 276, 278, 283

F

Feminism 32, 40, 42, 56, 59, 64, 74, 146, 150, 162, 173-174, 194, 200-202, 214, 222, 228, 240, 246-247, 249-250, 255-256, 259-261, 263-266, 268
Feminist 21, 35, 40, 54, 56, 59, 61, 64, 80, 84, 86-87, 90, 99, 103, 123-124, 130, 133, 148-152, 154-155, 157, 169-170, 172-173, 179, 192, 195, 199-206, 208-209, 211-220, 222, 225-227, 233, 235-237, 240-241, 243, 245-247, 249-250, 256-257, 259-268, 273-274, 276-278, 285
Feminist Dystopia 59, 61, 64
Feminist Geography 103, 148-152, 154-155, 216, 261
Feral Cities 1-7, 12, 15, 17
Futuristic Urbanism 59

G

Gaze 69, 106-107, 110-111, 161, 220, 236-237
Gender 2, 10, 17, 21, 35, 37-47, 49-57, 61, 80-81, 83, 85, 87, 89, 93-94, 96, 99-109, 112, 114-124, 133-134, 146, 148-158, 160, 162-174, 178-179, 181, 186, 188, 194-197, 202-203, 212-216, 218, 228-230, 232-237, 240, 242-243, 245-251, 253-254, 256, 258, 260, 262-267, 269-271, 273-274, 276-281, 283-290
Gender and Space 240
Gender Discrimination 102, 158, 174, 269
Gender Planning 216
Gender Segregation 96, 148, 153, 157, 203, 214
Geopolitics 176-177, 203-204, 209, 213-214
Global landscape 1-2

H

Heterotopia 20, 22-24, 27-31, 33, 93, 176-177, 183, 195

I

Identity 2-3, 17, 34-35, 38, 42-44, 49, 53, 55-57, 72, 80-83, 85-86, 88-90, 93, 97-100, 102-103, 106, 120, 123, 127, 130-131, 141-144, 146, 151-153, 156, 164-165, 171, 173-174, 179, 184, 191, 194, 196, 201, 213-214, 230, 237, 260
Inclusivity 90, 143, 155, 222
India 2, 17, 33-34, 37, 42-48, 52, 55, 58-59, 61, 63, 73, 77, 82, 84, 88, 90-92, 98, 100-106, 108, 112, 116-117, 121-124, 126, 128, 131, 133, 135-137, 145-146, 148, 153, 169, 176-178, 180-182, 184, 190-192, 194-196, 216-218, 224, 233, 235, 237, 260, 266
India Vision Foundation 128
Intersectionality 53, 55, 72, 82, 84, 203, 215, 277, 279

J

Jwalamukhi 139, 141-142

K

Karachi 2-3, 5-10, 15, 17, 152-153, 168, 170
Khaled Hosseini 18-19, 21, 23, 31, 33-36
Kiran Bedi 126, 128, 131-133, 135-136, 138, 140

M

Marital Migration 176, 179, 181, 183
Megacities 1-4, 6-7, 92, 270

N

Nalini Jameela 126, 128, 131, 134, 138-142
Narrative Reliability 59, 61, 64
Navjyoti India Foundation 128
New Geography of Identity 38, 42-43

O

Oppression 19-21, 24, 27, 30-31, 36, 40, 42, 51, 83, 85-87, 89, 94, 98, 149-155, 164, 188, 190, 201, 206, 241-242, 246, 250-252, 254, 256-257, 267, 273

P

Participation 104, 131, 135, 144, 150, 218, 222, 231, 235, 241, 243, 263-264, 266, 269, 275, 277, 279, 283-284, 287
Patriarchal Culture 54, 149, 240-242, 252, 255
Patriarchy 29-30, 32, 45-46, 52, 101, 103, 105, 108-109, 117, 121, 148-149, 155, 157, 160, 163, 171, 186, 188, 202, 217, 240-243, 246-256, 258, 261-267, 274
Performativity 88-89, 92
Postcolonial Spatialities 84, 87
Prison Reforms 128, 136-137
Private Space 105-107, 122, 148, 150, 152-158, 160-164, 166, 182, 186
Public Space 30, 106, 148, 150, 154-156,

Index

158, 160, 162-163, 173-174, 176-177, 182, 195, 200, 206, 217-219, 221, 232, 237, 243, 265, 267-269, 271-274, 276, 278, 280-283, 285, 287

Q

Queer 73, 82, 84-86, 88-90, 92-94, 97-100, 103, 148-150, 152, 154, 156-157, 164-167, 170-172, 174, 179
Queer Ecology 84
Queer Geography 84, 148, 150, 152, 156, 170
Queer Studies 82, 85, 89, 92, 100

R

Radical Feminism 247, 255-256, 259, 261, 268
Representation 26, 28, 34-35, 41, 44, 55, 60, 63, 75, 77, 81, 103-104, 110, 141-142, 166, 218, 222, 226-230, 236
Right to the City 10, 15-16, 126, 129, 142, 144-145, 216-218, 223, 233, 235, 237, 266, 269, 276-277, 283, 285

S

Sati 48, 115-116, 118, 121
Scale 44, 78, 143, 181, 200, 203-205, 210, 212, 270
Sex Worker 126, 128, 140-141, 145
Social Movements 42, 126-132, 135, 139, 141, 143-146, 267
Social Sustainability 269
Socio-Spatial 97, 101-102, 105-106, 121-123, 126, 152
Solidarity 40, 56, 142, 181, 199-210, 212-214, 246, 249
South Asian Diaspora 37-38, 40-41, 43, 54-55, 169
Space 3, 8, 10, 15-16, 18-20, 22-29, 31-33, 38-43, 50, 54, 56, 59-61, 64, 72-73, 78-79, 81-82, 84, 87, 93-94, 96, 98, 103, 106-107, 111-113, 116, 121-123, 127, 132, 135, 140, 143-144, 149-158, 160-168, 171, 173-174, 176-179, 182-187, 189-190, 193-197, 200-201, 203-207, 209-214, 216-219, 221-222, 231-233, 235, 237, 240, 243-244, 246, 251, 260, 262, 265-274, 276-278, 280-283, 285-289
Spatial 1-2, 4, 18-19, 21-23, 28, 31, 33, 39, 43, 59-61, 87, 93, 100, 103-104, 116, 126-127, 133, 143-144, 149-154, 157-160, 162-168, 170, 172-173, 178, 185, 187-188, 192, 194-196, 200, 203, 205, 209, 243-246, 259-260, 262, 266-267, 269-272, 274, 282-286, 289

T

Taliban 26-27, 153, 175, 177-178, 180, 182, 184, 186-187, 189, 192-194, 196-197
Territory 2-4, 180, 184, 193-194, 244-245, 274
Theory of Mind 61-62, 76, 81
Tihar Jail 128, 135-137, 140
Tradition 51, 73, 101, 115-117, 130, 164, 240, 242, 245, 248, 253, 272, 277
Transnational 8, 37-43, 48, 54-58, 96, 127, 130, 184, 199-205, 207-208, 211, 214, 278
Transnational Urban Spaces 37-38, 40-41, 54-55
Trauma 8, 14, 50, 63, 66, 68-69, 75-76, 80, 96, 159, 163, 165-166, 194

U

Urban 2-7, 10, 13, 15-17, 27, 37-41, 43, 45, 54-55, 59-64, 72-73, 80-81, 84, 87-90, 93-94, 98, 101-107, 109-116, 118-119, 121-124, 126-131, 133-134, 138-140, 142-157, 159-160, 162-173, 176-179, 183-187, 189-191, 193-196, 199-201, 203-207, 209, 211-212, 217-220, 222-223, 226, 229, 233-237, 240-246, 250-256, 258-260, 266-267, 269-273, 276-279, 281-287, 289-290
Urban Design 195, 235, 269, 272-273, 284, 286, 289
Urban Space 15-16, 38, 54, 60, 64, 81, 87, 103, 105, 112, 116, 122-123, 140,

143-144, 153-155, 157, 162-166, 168, 173, 176-179, 183-187, 190, 194-196, 201, 203, 205, 211-212, 217, 235, 266, 277, 286

V

Virtual 199-201, 203-204, 209, 211-212

W

War 4, 12, 14, 17, 19-20, 31, 33, 91, 152, 173, 177, 180, 185, 188, 190-192, 200, 204, 211, 213-214

Recommended Reference Books

IGI Global's reference books can now be purchased from three unique pricing formats:
Print Only, E-Book Only, or Print + E-Book.
Shipping fees may apply.
www.igi-global.com

Global Politics, Political Participation, and the Rise of Nationalism

ISBN: 9781799873433
EISBN: 9781799873457
© 2021; 213 pp.
List Price: US$ 175

Information Technology Trends for a Global and Interdisciplinary Research Community

ISBN: 9781799841562
EISBN: 9781799841579
© 2021; 374 pp.
List Price: US$ 195

Critical Perspectives on Social Justice in Speech-Language Pathology

ISBN: 9781799871347
EISBN: 9781799871361
© 2021; 355 pp.
List Price: US$ 195

Indigenous Research of Land, Self, and Spirit

ISBN: 9781799837299
EISBN: 9781799837312
© 2021; 301 pp.
List Price: US$ 185

Transforming Urban Nightlife and the Development of Smart Public Spaces

ISBN: 9781799870043
EISBN: 9781799870067
© 2021; 290 pp.
List Price: US$ 195

Natural Healing as Conflict Resolution

ISBN: 9781799836650
EISBN: 9781799836674
© 2021; 301 pp.
List Price: US$ 195

Do you want to stay current on the latest research trends, product announcements, news, and special offers?
Join IGI Global's mailing list to receive customized recommendations, exclusive discounts, and more.
Sign up at: **www.igi-global.com/newsletters**.

Publisher of Timely, Peer-Reviewed Inclusive Research Since 1988

IGI Global
PUBLISHER of TIMELY KNOWLEDGE

www.igi-global.com   Sign up at www.igi-global.com/newsletters   facebook.com/igiglobal   twitter.com/igiglobal

Ensure Quality Research is Introduced to the Academic Community

Become an Evaluator for IGI Global Authored Book Projects

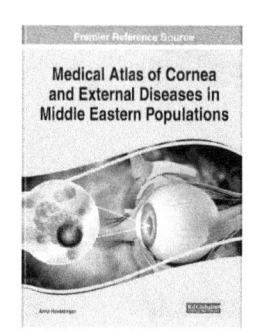

The overall success of an authored book project is dependent on quality and timely manuscript evaluations.

Applications and Inquiries may be sent to:
development@igi-global.com

Applicants must have a doctorate (or equivalent degree) as well as publishing, research, and reviewing experience. Authored Book Evaluators are appointed for one-year terms and are expected to complete at least three evaluations per term. Upon successful completion of this term, evaluators can be considered for an additional term.

If you have a colleague that may be interested in this opportunity, we encourage you to share this information with them.

Easily Identify, Acquire, and Utilize Published Peer-Reviewed Findings in Support of Your Current Research

IGI Global OnDemand

Purchase Individual IGI Global OnDemand Book Chapters and Journal Articles

For More Information:
www.igi-global.com/e-resources/ondemand/

Browse through 150,000+ Articles and Chapters!

Find specific research related to your current studies and projects that have been contributed by international researchers from prestigious institutions, including:

- Massachusetts Institute of Technology
- HARVARD UNIVERSITY
- COLUMBIA UNIVERSITY IN THE CITY OF NEW YORK
- Australian National University

- Accurate and Advanced Search
- Affordably Acquire Research
- Instantly Access Your Content
- Benefit from the InfoSci Platform Features

> *It really provides* an excellent entry into the research literature of the field. *It presents a manageable number of* highly relevant sources *on topics of interest to a wide range of researchers. The sources are* scholarly, but also accessible *to 'practitioners'.*
>
> - Ms. Lisa Stimatz, MLS, University of North Carolina at Chapel Hill, USA

Interested in Additional Savings?

Subscribe to

IGI Global OnDemand *Plus*

Learn More

Acquire content from over 128,000+ research-focused book chapters and 33,000+ scholarly journal articles for as low as US$ 5 per article/chapter (original retail price for an article/chapter: US$ 37.50).

6,600+ E-BOOKS.
ADVANCED RESEARCH.
INCLUSIVE & ACCESSIBLE.

IGI Global e-Book Collection

- **Flexible Purchasing Options** (Perpetual, Subscription, EBA, etc.)
- Multi-Year Agreements with **No Price Increases** Guaranteed
- **No Additional Charge** for Multi-User Licensing
- No Maintenance, Hosting, or Archiving Fees
- Transformative **Open Access Options** Available

Request More Information, or Recommend the IGI Global e-Book Collection to Your Institution's Librarian

Among Titles Included in the IGI Global e-Book Collection

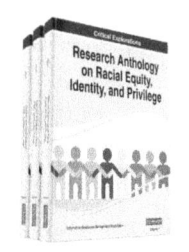

Research Anthology on Racial Equity, Identity, and Privilege (3 Vols.)
EISBN: 9781668445082
Price: US$ 895

Handbook of Research on Remote Work and Worker Well-Being in the Post-COVID-19 Era
EISBN: 9781799867562
Price: US$ 265

Research Anthology on Big Data Analytics, Architectures, and Applications (4 Vols.)
EISBN: 9781668436639
Price: US$ 1,950

Handbook of Research on Challenging Deficit Thinking for Exceptional Education Improvement
EISBN: 9781799888628
Price: US$ 265

Acquire & Open

When your library acquires an IGI Global e-Book and/or e-Journal Collection, your faculty's published work will be considered for immediate conversion to Open Access *(CC BY License)*, at no additional cost to the library or its faculty *(cost only applies to the e-Collection content being acquired)*, through our popular **Transformative Open Access (Read & Publish) Initiative**.

For More Information or to Request a Free Trial, Contact IGI Global's e-Collections Team: eresources@igi-global.com | 1-866-342-6657 ext. 100 | 717-533-8845 ext. 100

Have Your Work Published and Freely Accessible
Open Access Publishing

With the industry shifting from the more traditional publication models to an open access (OA) publication model, publishers are finding that OA publishing has many benefits that are awarded to authors and editors of published work.

- Freely Share Your Research
- Higher Discoverability & Citation Impact
- Rigorous & Expedited Publishing Process
- Increased Advancement & Collaboration

Acquire & Open

When your library acquires an IGI Global e-Book and/or e-Journal Collection, your faculty's published work will be considered for immediate conversion to Open Access *(CC BY License)*, at no additional cost to the library or its faculty *(cost only applies to the e-Collection content being acquired)*, through our popular **Transformative Open Access (Read & Publish) Initiative**.

- Provide Up To **100%** OA APC or CPC Funding
- Funding to Convert or Start a Journal to **Platinum OA**
- Support for Funding an **OA Reference Book**

IGI Global publications are found in a number of prestigious indices, including Web of Science™, Scopus®, Compendex, and PsycINFO®. The selection criteria is very strict and to ensure that journals and books are accepted into the major indexes, IGI Global closely monitors publications against the criteria that the indexes provide to publishers.

WEB OF SCIENCE™ **Compendex** **Scopus®** **PsycINFO®** **IET Inspec**

Learn More Here:

For Questions, Contact IGI Global's Open Access Team at openaccessadmin@igi-global.com

IGI Global
PUBLISHER of TIMELY KNOWLEDGE
www.igi-global.com